ORGANIZATIONAL COMMUNICATION AND CHANGE

edited by

Philip Salem
Southwest Texas State University

HAMPTON PRESS, INC.
CRESSKILL, NEW JERSEY

100407993
658.45
ORG

Copyright © 1999 by Hampton Press, Inc.

All rights reserved. No part of this publication may be reproduced, stored in a retrieval system, or transmitted in any form or by any means, electronic, mechanical, photocopying, microfilming, recording or otherwise, without permission of the publisher.

Printed in the United States of America

Library of Congress Cataloging-in-Publication Data

Organizational communication and change / edited by Philip J. Salem.
     p. cm. -- (Hampton Press communication series)
    Includes bibliographic references and index.
    ISBN 1-57273-116-8 -- ISBN 1-57273-117-6
    1. Communication in organizations. I. Salem, Philip J.
II. Series.
HD30.3.0722 1999
658.4'5--dc21   99-36048
                                                      CIP

Hampton Press, Inc.
23 Broadway
Cresskill, NJ 07626

ORGANIZATIONAL COMMUNICATION AND CHANGE

WITHDRAWN
FROM THE LIBRARY OF
UNIVERSITY OF ULSTER

100407993

Communication and Social Organization
Gary L. Kreps, series editor

CONTENTS

PREFACE

In February 1976, I was fortunate enough to host a postdoctoral conference on organizational communication. Speakers and presenters at that conference included Belle Bernstein, Larry Browning, Richard Cheatham, Frank Dance, Cal Downs, Gerald Goldhaber, Claudia Hale, Len Hawes, Fred Hilpert, Robert Hopper, Bonnie Johnson, James Kitchens, M. L. McLaughlin, John Mikelson, Darrell Piersol, Ernest Stech, and Jack Whitehead. It was the first conference sponsored by the Speech Communication Association research board, and the first organizational communication conference sponsored by any national communication association.

I hosted a similar event running from February 8 to 13, 1996. The theme of the old conference was about reviewing and explicating the boundaries of organizational communication as a discipline, but the theme this time was about organizational communication and change. The older conference was only a research conference of 2-1/2 days. The recent event began with 2-1/2 days of training and workshops for executives, and then an additional 2-1/2 days of scholarship.

There were five panels of scholarship in both conferences: (a) domain, (b) theory, (c) research methods, (d) application, and (e) criticism. Elwood Murray suggested these five categories as being central to defining a discipline, and I used them again in 1996 to cast a wide net to attract a variety of scholarship. In 1996, I organized the last panel around the term *social responsibility*, an expression suggested by Stan Deetz and consistent with Murray's use of the term *criticism*. Because both conferences were organized in a similar fashion, it is possible to compare and contrast the scholarship and to describe ways in which organizational communication and organizational communication scholarship have changed over the last 20 years. This book contains papers from both conferences.

The first chapter of this book contains my own opening remarks at the 1996 conference. The chapter begins by describing the nature of change, including different orders of change and the oscillating, multilevel nature of change. The majority of the chapter contains a review of the published literature referenced in four bibliographical databases. The review is organized around the five areas of a discipline, and each subsection concludes with a summary description of the changes in the literature over 20 years. The chapter concludes with a series of challenges facing the discipline as it approaches the next century.

The next two chapters, part of the Domain section, reflect some of the changes in the study of organizational communication. Gerald Golhaber's chapter, which is *20 years old*, is one part textbook and one part research report. He describes what he believes to be the most important constructs for both research and application, and then provides the preliminary results of the ICA Organizational Communication Audit. He presents "what we now know" from his perspective in 1976, and his description of "military type" organizations seems very contemporary. How much more do we know?

Whereas Goldhaber reviews organizational communication, Linda Putnam's piece is a review of the research about organizational communication, yet it is much more than a review. She identifies four dominant traditional perspectives, and then describes three emergent discourse perspectives. She argues that these newer approaches devalue the instrumental aspects of organizational communication in favor of the more constitutive features.

Frank Dance's chapter begins the Theory section. He presents a theory of organizational communication as an extension of his own more general theory of human communication. He is careful to situate his theory among other theories, and he is precise in the scope and range of his ideas. Although only a "Prolegomena to a Primitive Theory," the piece is exemplary in its precision, and as evidence that organizational communication theories are, first and foremost, communication theories.

Carolyn Baldwin Leveque and Scott Poole examine systems theory in the fifth chapter. First, they present a revisionist history of organizational communication studies focusing on the ideas that attracted many of us to systems theory, and several interpretive assumptions that seem to challenge the utility of those systems ideas in contemporary research. They argue that concerns for the complexity, dynamism, and emergence of systems are part of vibrant, contemporary systems thinking, and they conclude by presenting exemplars of systems thinking employed in some current research.

Bonnie Johnson's chapter is the last essay from the 1976 conference in this volume. She employs a diverse literature from Carroll

Arnold, Jay Hall, Alfred Shutz, and Karl Weick to develop a model of communication technology she calls "coordination formats." The chapter deals with fundamental questions about communication. What are the differences between oral and written communication? What are the differences between reflective communication and communication without reflection? What is the nature of planning? How does communication function as collective decision building? The paper simultaneously reflects the focus on fundamental questions and the tendency to cull ideas from diverse fields so common 20 years ago, and it anticipates several contemporary research interests.

Eric Eisenberg, Linda Andrews, Alexandra Murphy, and Linda Laine-Timmerman explore an old issue—leadership—but in a contemporary way. First, they review the contemporary literature on organizational change, and then they describe three approaches for accomplishing that change. Although this literature suggests different types of leadership, the authors argue that each approach holds differing assumptions about the nature of change and the nature of communication. The chapter exemplifies the movement from focusing on more instrumental features of communication to viewing communication as constitutive, and its examination of dialogue seems to be a natural extension of some of the ideas with which Johnson wrestled in 1976.

The Methods section reflects much of the diversity of contemporary research. Ofer Meilich took on the task of describing a complex statistical procedure that could prove useful for both quantitative and qualitative researchers. His description of neural network analysis includes fundamental models of neural network procedures, and a description of both advantages and disadvantages of the analytical approach. He then demonstrates the process with a case study.

The ninth chapter is about historical data an aspect of research completely different than that of the previous chapter. Katherine Miller reminds us of the importance of locating our research within an historical context. She identifies several ways to develop theory using historical data, but also describes the challenges faced by researcher of historical data. She concludes by identifying instances of organizational communication research employing historical data, including her own ongoing research about identification and communication.

The Methods section concludes with an essay by Patricia Riley. Research methods of all types are under scrutiny, and Riley describes not only the philosophical issues, but also the pragmatic issues related to time, money, and politics. She identifies "problems," but she also identifies ways of dealing with the problems. I'm not sure one piece could adequately cover all the issues about research methods, but this one certainly comes close to sounding like the conversations I've had and heard in the last 20 years.

Lisette van Gemert and Egbert Woudstra begin the Applications section with a study of the relationships between oral and written communication. They begin by reviewing the business communication literature noting that, until recently, researchers and textbook writers failed to connect the two types of communication. They employ a document design model to examining the development of written documents by an engineering firm for a government agency. They employed qualitative methods to describe the cyclical interaction between the various forms of communication.

Cal Downs concludes the section with an analysis of how organizational communication has been applied by academicians. First, he comments on the importance of organizational communication applications and then he launches into a contrast between universities and other organizations. He concludes by identifying eight challenges for contemporary professionals.

The Social Responsibility section begins with an essay about the modern health care system. Gary Kreps suggests that health care delivery systems alienate and marginalize their customers, especially women. He does not present customers as helpless victims, and he advocates a more proactive approach consistent with contemporary consumerism and team approaches to quality. Gary's review of this literature and his arguments point to mutual responsibilities, and he describes ways both individuals and health organizations could respond.

Catherine Becker and Steven Levitt began their research as a qualitative investigation about women in organizations. Their interview data led them to perform several types of content analysis, and their results reveal how the subjects, contemporary women in the workforce, think about power, technology, and the relationships between the two. It has been argued that technology has the ability to change the dynamics of power. Their results highlight the fact that the use of technology occurs as part of an already established social structure, and, in some cases, the use of technology may simply reinforce existing disparities.

Stan Deetz describes the workplace as a site for responsibility influenced by a variety of private, public, and marketplace systems. He argues that old systems have failed, making it difficult for individuals to exercise choice, and he uses critical theory and his own criticisms of ideology to develop a dialogic stakeholder model. In the end he describes ways of increasing voice for marginalized stakeholders.

I want to end this preface by recasting three of my concerns. The contrasts between 1976 and 1996 are as stark as the comparison of the second chapter to the last chapter, and I have noted several of these differences in my own contribution. However, both Gerry Goldhaber's piece and Stan Deetz's piece allude to very traditional bureaucratic organizations. My first concern is that the nature of organizations is changing very rapidly and these old structures may be less important than the newer forms of human organization and the problems they bring.

On a recent flight home from Seattle, I met a woman who was traveling to Austin to spend a week with her boyfriend. She and he are from Ohio, she graduated from a college in Ohio and worked for a health company in Chicago, and she was now living in Tucson as part of her work for her company. She is a physical therapist, and she was heavily recruited. Her company in Chicago manages several health care facilities, and it manages a select labor force. She was sent to work at one of their facilities, but after 6 months she had requested a transfer to a different facility to be closer to her boyfriend. Part of her trip was to decide on the best locations and the future of their relationship together. Even if the week ended with the end of their relationship, she had already decided to move to one of several different facilities on a regular basis.

She works in a brokered organizational environment that is quite different from a bureaucratic one. Although I summarized some of the advantages and disadvantages to such an organization in the first table of my own chapter, it would be easy to view such a list as applicable only to very small organizations or to organizations with high R&D budgets. One does not think of health care this way.

These systems have their own practical problems. "Organizational Alzheimer's" refers to the loss of corporate memory, and a bureaucratic organization could suffer from this if it "downsized" too rapidly or to too great an extent. In such a case, the organization risks making old mistakes—mistakes known by the managers and workers now employed elsewhere. In a brokered environment, the loss happens within a project or on site, in the case of my new acquaintance, at the health facilities she leaves every 6 months. Today, some of this lost information can be retrieved on-line, but much will still be lost. Add to this concerns about commitment and loyalty, and things appear to be very different than 20 years ago.

The most intriguing thing for me about the changes in organizations is that it challenges some long-held notions about "an organization." If the physical therapist I noted earlier has some sense of organizational commitment, where is the organization that gains from this commitment? To be sure, she is committed to her clients and her own sense of responsibilities and duties, but that is a personal commitment. Most, if not all, the authors in this volume would agree that organizations are constituted locally in the interactions of and especially the communication of individuals. How do these interactions constitute "an organization," which features of the interactions are discretely "organizational," and how is this process similar to or different from the constituting of the immediate interpersonal relationship? These are not new questions, and I am not the first to ask them, but the changes in contemporary organizing stimulate noting them again. How such questions are answered is central to defining the domain of organizational communication.

A second concern is the lack of attention to international cultural differences. The 1996 conference was a truly international meeting, and I am pleased that several papers from outside the United States were part of the conference and are part of this volume. However, it is still too easy to assume the conditions in one's own national culture are the norm. The Internet made it possible to send the call for papers for the conference to other countries. The new information technologies also make it possible to develop cooperative research projects exploring different cultures.

This cultural nearsightedness may be part of a broader intellectual myopia that is my last concern. Ironically, the new information technology simultaneously discourages and encourages this malady. More and varied communication is possible, but there is also overload. There are choices to be made. The infection works its way into the system when we reject an idea not because of its merit but because we prejudged the idea due to its age (too new or too old), its disciplinary identity (from Communication, Sociology, Linguistics, Management, etc.), its research methods or paradigmatic biases, its practicality (too theoretical or too applied), its academic rigor (too scholarly or too popular), or a host of other similar factors. The infection works like a virus when individuals restrict their interactions to those with similar predispositions, when interactions serve to reinforce the predispositions. The disease can reach epidemic proportions when "factions" develop. In any event, there develops a blind acceptance of some ideas and a resistance to change—a "hardening of the categories," an expression Elwood Murray liked.

It may take a dramatic event to improve vision. While attending an International Communication Association conference in Berlin, I enrolled for a full-day workshop on systems theory. When I arrived at the room for the morning session, I was happy to see Elwood there, and I looked forward to some lively workshop discussions. The workshop director, Dr. Smith (not his real name), began the session with some introductory interviews and activities designed to make us more comfortable with each other. By chance, he paired himself with Elwood, and he appeared to have a pleasant conversation with this older, unassuming man. When we ended the activity with introductions, Dr. Smith seemed pleased to announce that his partner was one of the founders of the association and that he was honored to have him in the workshop.

We were all seated at one large table, and Dr. Smith then distributed some material and topic outlines of the morning session. He opened a three-ring binder and proceeded to read to us from it. He was reading something he hoped to publish, one of his own works on systems theory. At first, we all listened attentively, but after 15 minutes we were a bit restless. Elwood seemed distracted, occasionally gazing out the window. "Excuse me, Dr. Smith," Elwood said slowly, "how does any of this help people communicate better?" "That question is irrelevant," said Dr. Smith in a polite but somewhat irritated tone. "On the contrary," said someone else at the table, "that is the most relevant thing I've heard all morning." Dr. Smith became a bit defensive, but he was rescued by the mid morning coffee break. Only half the participants returned after the break. Elwood left after 5 more minutes. I didn't come back for the afternoon sessions. Someone who attended all day told me there were less than five people there at the end.

A few days later, I attended the "Top Papers" program of the Interpersonal Communication Division. The audience responded well to the presentation of the papers and the response, all of which were typical of the time. When the floor was opened for questions, I was startled to see Dr. Smith standing at a microphone to ask a question. "How do these papers help people communicate better?" he asked.

No undertaking of this sort can be done alone. I am grateful for the support of my university, Southwest Texas State University, and my colleagues in the Department of Speech Communication. I am especially grateful for the support and encouragement of the department's chair, Steven Beebe.

The 1996 Conference on Organizational Communication and Change would not have occurred without the support of several sponsoring organizations. The International Communication Association and the Speech Communication Association lent their names to my effort, and the SCA Research Board once again endorsed an organizational communication conference hosted by this department. Organizations that lent financial support included Century Communications, Coca-Cola, Colorado Springs Utilities, Electronic Data Systems Corporation, and First USA. A special thanks goes to Robert Heiling, Shari Bracy, and Barbara Hatch, alumni who made some of these contributions possible. I am very grateful for the continuing support of Darrell Piersol.

The first 3 days of the conference consisted of workshops and presentations, and the consultants and trainers involved in this effort donated their services. My thanks to Barry Spiker, Phil Clampitt and Laurey Berk, Rob Epstein, Larry Browning, and Christopher Avery. I was honored to have Carl Larson participate, and I am grateful to Kitty Sweeney for her contributions and encouragement.

The last 3 days of the conference consisted of scholarship. My thanks to the nearly 30 scholars that submitted their work, and especially to the authors of the 16 papers that were presented. I was fortunate to have Stan Deetz, Cal Downs, Eric Eisenberg, Patricia Riley, and Linda Putnam review papers for the conference. They were instrumental in helping create interesting and exciting panels.

Randa Nelson of the Austin Marriott at the Capitol insured that our accommodations were first-class. David Hess, Vicki Locke, C. J. Mills, Patricia Phillips, and Eric Timmerman helped insure that the conference ran smoothly. A special thanks to Heather Harward and Todd Leach, my chief assistants and firefighters during the conference.

Thanks to Rhonda Brooks, our department's manuscript typist, for her help with the manuscripts for the conference and this volume. Sue Hall, the department's office manager and control center, helped manage the accounts and the coordination of other personnel. She was the university's Employee of the Year for 1996, but she is our Employee of the Year every year.

Finally, thanks to Gary Kreps, the series editor, and to Barbara Bernstein, the president of Hampton Press. Gary, thanks for recommending this effort, and for your advice and counsel. Barbara, thanks for your encouragement when I brought this idea to you nearly a year before I submitted the proposal, and thanks for the efficient processing of this manuscript.

part one

ORGANIZATIONAL COMMUNICATION AND CHANGE

one

THE CHANGES AND CHALLENGES FOR ORGANIZATIONAL COMMUNICATION IN THE NEXT CENTURY

Philip Salem

Southwest Texas State University

The Organizational Communication and Change conference of 1996 was the second organizational communication research conference sponsored by the Speech Communication Department at Southwest Texas State University. The first conference occurred in 1976, and it was the first such event approved by the Research Board of the Speech Communication Association. The themes of the old conference were about reviewing and explicating the boundaries of organizational communication as a discipline. The papers presented at the second conference describe changes in the ways people enact and make sense of organizational communication including some behaviors that stimulate and constitute change.

The first purpose of this chapter is to identify characteristics of change. The analysis of change describes dimensions that are, in part, common to all living systems. Alternately, the analysis gives special attention to human sense making. The present conference, like the last, features five panels organized around the notion of a *discipline*. Murray (1972) defined a discipline as a unified body of knowledge possessing a specified domain, a theoretical foundation, various methods of research,

3

a system of application, and a method of criticism or evaluation. Goldberg and Larson (1975) employed this notion of a discipline to orient students to group communication. Murray's distinctions provide a convenient way to frame questions and to organize research.

The second purpose of this chapter is to describe the changes in organizational communication scholarship since the last conference. This review employs the notion of discipline to direct the reflective process at answering five specific questions: (1) What has been the domain of organizational communication? (2) How have theories been developed in this body of knowledge? (3) What research methods have been employed? (4) How has knowledge, gained by research, been applied? (5) What criteria have been used to evaluate research and application? The first part of this chapter presents a review of research published in journals over the last 20 years.

Finally, this chapter identifies the challenges that are ahead as the new century approaches. The last section combines features of the first two to pose questions about the domain, theory, research methods, application, and criticism of organizational communication. The challenges are the natural outgrowth of an evolving discipline and an evolving society.

THE NATURE OF CHANGE

• *Change involves differences over time.* Difference is necessary for sensation and perception, and difference is the foundation of information. A singular property of change is that the differences are evident by comparing two or more points in time. Change shares some characteristics such as frequency, variety, and magnitude with other constructs that suggest difference. Duration and rate are more about change than about difference. An expression such as "changes over time" is redundant.

• *Change is normative.* Both difference and time are relative to the organism's information processing. Living systems recognize change as a disruption of equilibrium. The organism seeks outcomes and pursues those outcomes within a range of behaviors and outcomes specified in the organism's genetic code and in the calibrations that are part of its decider mechanism(s) (Miller, 1978). Human higher mental processes include abilities to displace and decenter (Dance & Larson, 1976). Humans can anticipate and experience change as a violation of perceptual expectations or as inconsistent behavior. In organizations, the perception of a performance gap may lead to innovation, another change (Rogers & Agarwala-Rogers, 1976).

- *There are different orders of change.* Humans are purposeful and can choose both behaviors and goals (Ackoff & Emery, 1972). First-order change involves evaluating the outcomes of behaviors and adjusting behaviors to maximize goals (Argyris, 1993). In organizations, second-order change, metanoia, occurs when there is a change of goals and in the ways of making sense of behavior and outcomes (Argyris, 1993; Senge, 1990). In family systems, second-order change is often accomplished through therapy (Fisch, Weakland, & Segal, 1982). In organizational systems, the change is part of double feedback learning—learning that challenges the organizational culture (Argyris, 1993). Learning of this sort consists of activities designed to question tacit assumptions and values. Organizational members, similar to family members, examine the rules that define their role behavior, the deep structure of the system.

- *The enablers of change may be internal or external.* Predictors of organizational change include external characteristics such as environmental competitiveness, complexity, and turbulence, and also internal factors such as personality variables and the structure and culture of the organization (Huber, Sutcliffe, Miller, & Glick, 1995; Slocum & Lei, 1995). The internal factors influence directly the system's behavior and its ability to evaluate outcomes. The organization's behavior in turn influences the external factors and the system's perception of those factors.

  Humans connect with their environment through mutually causal links. The behaviors of the system alter the system's perceptions of the environment. Humans enact their environments (Weick, 1979). When the organism behaves, it alters its environment, and when the organism evaluates the outcomes, the organism learns about the responses and reactions of other systems. Any adjustment in behavior of the organism is, in part, a product of the organism's goals and capabilities and, in part, a response to the outcomes mutually produced by the interaction of the organism with its environment.

- *Change alters the structure of the system.* When first-order change—simple learning—involves changes in the degree or manner of performing previously performed behaviors, change reinforces existing structures. For example, when routines are refined to improve efficiency, these changes support the existing set of rules that called for those routines. All systems tend toward maximization (Katz & Kahn, 1978). When there is little environmental equivocality or pressure, the system tends to acquire more and more resources, and each cycle of behavior becomes more structured and more efficient at using those resources. The system centralizes as it reduces the equivocality in its processes.

When first-order change produces innovation, the level of uncertainty increases inside the system. The adoption of innovations inside organizations is a process that moves from novelty to routinization (Rogers, 1986; Rogers & Agarwala-Rogers, 1976). However, the process also means that the system stretches horizontally. Adoption means that the organization has added an additional behavior to its repertoire, and the new behavior poses a challenge to the old methods of control. When institutionalization has been accomplished, incorporation is complete, and there have been few changes in the methods of control.

The continued processing of novel inputs will challenge the rules for processing equivocality (Weick, 1979). The continued acquisition of behaviors into a system's repertoire will push the system to capacity and challenge methods of control. In either event, the system will overload. The overload may result in the segmentation of the system into smaller systems or in the increased complexity of the system with new processing rules.

In the most turbulent environments, there must be fewer processing rules to allow for greater innovation of behavior. Behavior cycles, rather than rules, become the dominant method of reducing uncertainty (Weick, 1979). *Vivisystems* is one name for such systems, and swarms are a common metaphor for them. Table 1.1 displays the advantages and disadvantages of such systems.

Research and development efforts often proceed in such a manner. Skunk works and service brokers are parts of such systems. The movements from bureaucracies to project designs, matrix structures and dynamic networks are efforts at dealing with turbulent environments (Banner & Gagne, 1995). All these forms flatten hierarchies.

• *Change happens in oscillating cycles.* There is the natural tendency of living systems to map features of their environments and to acquire new behaviors (Buckley, 1967). This tendency toward novelty runs counter to the system tendencies toward stability and efficiency. Change proceeds through alternating cycles of behavior as it evolves. Table 1.2 displays the general pattern.

An important feature of the stages displayed in the table is that systems move through a stage of increased variety followed by a stage moving toward stability and vice versa. The system oscillates between the two trajectories.

• *Change is multilevel.* The model in Table 1.2 displays stages as a system evolves into more complex systems (see Salem, 1997). In such a case, what emerges is a system whose levels may be moving in opposite

Table 1.1. The Advantages and Disadvantages of Vivisystems.

Advantages	Disadvantages
Adaptable. Because there is so little specialization but great flexibility, the system can adjust to a greater range of changes.	*Nonoptimal.* Because of the redundancy of parallel processes and the tolerance of error, the system is inefficient.
Evolvable. The locus of adaptation moves from one part of the system to another as needed.	*Noncontrollable.* There can be no centralized control, but the system can be guided at leverage points.
Resilient. Because there is a multitude of parallel processes and individuals with similar abilities, failures remain small.	*Nonpredictable.* Novelty is emergent and nonlinear.
Boundless. Positive feedback leads to more order as one structure serves as the beginning-point for the next one.	*Nonunderstandable.* Events are not "caused" in any linear manner but through the interdependencies and intersecting logics dispersed horizontally throughout the system.
Novelty. They are sensitive to initial conditions, contain exponential combinations of behavior through many inter-linked individuals, and allow for individual variation and imperfection.	*Nonimmediate.* It takes time for the system to coordinate the parts, and there is often a lag between behaviors and outcomes.

From Kelly (1994). © 1994 by *Wired*. Adapted with permission.

trajectories. As one level of the system moves toward novelty, the levels immediately above it and below it are moving toward stability. As one level of the system is moving toward stability, the levels immediately above and below it are moving toward novelty. In a vivisystem, parallel systems may link while moving in differing directions.

What follows is a description in the differences over time in the scholarship of organizational communication. The description includes comments about the normative nature and the order of these changes. The structural impacts, the oscillating cycles, and the multilevel nature of change are part of the final section of this chapter.

Table 1.2. A Four Stage Model of Morphogenesis.

Stage	Description
Emergence	The system acquires new behaviors to map the environment. The number of categories in the field increases, pushing the system toward entropy, but this is slowed by the movement toward nonrandom probabilities for each category reflecting the environment.
Divergence	The organism overloads and adjusts. That is, the system seeks to maximize, and so it enacts behavior producing input that exceeds it capacity. Paradox appears in the system rules. Probabilities move to randomness. The system attempts various nonsocial adjustments.
Transformation	The system chooses a multichannel adjustment. It couples with another system. The coupling creates a suprasystem whose behavior is defined by the transitional behaviors of the now subsystems. The number of potential behaviors available to the suprasystem is equal to the product of the number of categories from the systems that created it. The number of behaviors that can be controlled by the suprasystem is equal to the number of behaviors that may be matched in the transitional field. For the suprasystem, this is emergence.
Convergence	The system adjusts probabilities with other systems to match behaviors in the transitional field. For a given system, entropy moves to the minimum. For the suprasystem defined by the transitional field, as systems move to minimum entropy, the suprasystem controls more and more categories of behavior. For the suprasystem, this is a divergence stage.

From Salem (1997). © 1997 by Ablex. Reprinted by permission.

THE CHANGES IN ORGANIZATIONAL COMMUNICATION

The 1976 conference began with a review of 10 years of journal literature (Salem, 1976). That paper included a thorough review of all national and regional speech communication journals and 20 selected social science journals published over the previous 10 years. Additionally, researchers randomly selected articles from organization and management journals in an effort to "spot check" the same 10 years.

The following review began with the collection of material from four bibliographical databases. The Educational Resources Information Center (ERIC) database combines material from *Resources in Education* and the *Current Index to Journals in Education* since 1966. ABI/INFORM contains selective coverage of over 1,400 business related journals and periodicals since 1971. PsychLIT is the computer equivalent to *Psychological Abstracts* and reports material since 1974. *Sociofile* is the equivalent of *Sociological Abstracts* and covers material since 1974. All databases produced bibliographical information and abstracts for published material that included "organizational communication" in its title, abstract, or text (when available) or as a descriptor from 1975–1994. Table 1.3 displays the frequency of organizational communication material from each source.

The databases are similar in some ways, but different in others. All the databases include material from national communication journals, and all databases appear to have gaps in their records, especially in the late 1970s and early 1980s. This is due, in part, to the failure of editors or scholars to label their material consistently or to submit their material for review or inclusion. There also appears to be problems with the ways in which databases catalog and identify material. Asking for a search of material designated as "journal article" will produce a different list than asking for "research articles." ERIC is the most inclusive source, containing citations and material from convention papers, curriculum material, and a variety of unpublished reports. ABI/INFORM includes book reviews and some calls for papers. PsychLIT and Sociofile include only published research material, but they are likely to exclude some theory pieces and some types of research included in the other two. Of course, the databases vary in the journals reviewed.

In order to clarify the pattern of research over the period, Table 1.3 also displays the frequency of organizational communication research published in *Communication Monographs* (CM) and in *Human Communication Research* (HCR). These journals average the publication of one or two pieces per year, but the publication rate is uneven over the 20 years. By contrast, the *Quarterly Journal of Speech* published four organizational communication pieces over the 20-year period, and the *Journal of Communication* published six.

In recent years, only a few journals account for the majority of organizational communication published research or systematic reports of application cited in ERIC. *Management Communication Quarterly*, the *Public Relations Review*, the *Journal of Technical and Business Communication*, and the journals affiliated with the American Business Communication Association consistently produce more organizational communication material than the journals affiliated with the Speech Communication Association or the

Table 1.3. A Comparison of the Frequency of Organizational Communication Material Identified in Four Electronic Databases and Two Communication Journals.

	Databases				Journals	
Year	ERIC	ABI/INFORM	PsychLIT	Sociofile	CM	HCR
1975	68	3	3	1	0	0
1976	123	5	2	0	0	1
1977	140	9	5	3	2	1
1978	191	3	6	4	8	3
1979	140	3	2	4	1	1
1980	138	5	2	2	2	2
1981	136	8	2	0	0	0
1982	132	6	3	1	1	2
1983	133	6	5	1	0	0
1984	138	9	6	1	1	1
1985	176	7	4	3	0	1
1986	151	4	4	4	1	2
1987	148	8	7	1	3	0
1988	102	9	7	5	1	0
1989	107	7	4	4	2	2
1990	91	10	3	7	0	1
1991	108	5	4	9	1	0
1992	105	6	5	10	1	1
1993	153	10	4	8	4	1
1994	137	7	2	8	2	2
Totals	2617	130	80	76	30	21

International Communication Association. The emergence of these journals accounts for some increases in the number of articles reported, but this emergence also suggests a change in the distribution of articles. A greater percentage of articles finds its way into journals more focused on organizational communication, and a lower percentage of articles is in journals of national and international communication associations. Finally, the following review does not account for the journals affiliated with many professions. For example, the review does not account for the many journals in public administration or health administration. There are many publications related to organizational communication in these sources, but they were not included as part of the 1976 review, and there was not enough time to include them in this review.

Summarily, the following descriptions are based on a review of material published in journals from 1975–1994 and cited in one or more of four databases as being about organizational communication. This includes the journals covered in the 1976 review and journals that originated during the period. The content of this material includes opinion pieces, theoretical efforts, research of varying methodologies, and reports of organizational communication applications. Published reports, textbooks, books, curriculum materials, convention papers, and unpublished material were not a part of the surveyed material.

Domain

Domain refers to the phenomena under investigation. Domain is not theory. A theory is a set of relational statements (Dance & Larson, 1976; Dubin, 1978); what the statements relate indicates the domain. For example, to state that the clarity of internal communication is related to organizational culture suggests a domain consisting of the following: communication clarity, internal communication, and organizational culture.

The 1976 review organized communication constructs into categories suggested by textbooks. For this review, the reviewer employed current textbooks by Daniels and Spiker (1994), Eisenberg and Goodall (1993), Goldhaber (1993), Kreps (1990), Miller (1995), and Pepper (1995). All these books contain the same general categories of organizational communication, but each brings a nuance to the understanding of each category. These texts also reflect the elaboration of some categories, suggesting an increase in the complexity of the domain.

Kast and Rosenzweig (1970) list five attributes of an organization: goals, technology, structure, psycho-social system, and management. These attributes are defined in such a way that nearly all of organizational research may be classified as falling within the definitional boundaries of one of these attributes. Adding elements of culture improves the psychosocial category, but there is little need to alter these terms to classify literature. These are the same categories used in 1976.

Communication Dimensions

Internal/External. Internal communication involves only members within an organization. External communication involves at least one communicator who is not a member of the organization. Some articles do not directly clarify this distinction, but the articles focus concern on one but not the other. Grunig (1978) investigated the relationships between customers and employees with the communication among employees, but studies combining internal and external communication are rare.

There has been an increase in the number of articles dealing with external communication. Botan and Frey (1983) explored the communication between workers and unions, Sankowsky (1989) discussed the ways in which professional norms are communicated to therapists, and Grunig (1982) tested the external communication aspects of a situational theory (Grunig, 1975). There is also some recent research related to boundary spanning (Finet, 1993). There are reports on the constraints faced by public relations practitioners (Sweep, 1994), and reports of the extent to which a college library was able to provide information to its customers (Lowry, 1994).

Descriptive or evaluative reports of external communication practices in education was a common feature of the early part of the period (Gratz & Salem, 1981), and continues to be a strong part of the literature reported in ERIC. Across all databases, there are proportionality more articles about external communication than in 1976. However, the vast majority of the literature is about internal communication. Unless specifically noted, all the remaining citations in this review are about internal communication.

Formal/Informal. An organization is a contrived system of roles (Katz & Kahn, 1978). When an individual communicates as part of an organizational role, the communication is considered to be formal. Any other communication is considered to be informal.

As was the case in 1976, there were few articles about informal communication. Wilson (1992) looked at diagonal communication patterns, and Campbell and Campbell (1988) studied the communication occurring in faculty lounges. Bailey (1991) was one of the few researchers to identify his focus as in a formal organization. Most articles focus on relationships that authors present as formal (e.g., superior-subordinate), but the level of formality is seldom the focus of investigation. Unless specifically noted, all the remaining citations in this review are about formal communication.

Verbal/Nonverbal. Verbal communication is language-like, for example, memos, conversations, speeches, and so forth (Goldhaber, 1993). Nonverbal communication is non linguistic and generally refers to such behaviors as touching, voice inflection, kinesics, proxemics, and so on. This is an old distinction.

Allen and Fustfeld (1975) explored the influences of architectural arrangements on communication, but there are few studies focusing on nonverbal communication. Some research focuses on types of communication style, a combination of verbal and nonverbal communication. For example, Chua and Gudykunst (1987) performed a cross-cultural comparison of conflict styles. However, even approaches like this are rare. Most articles are explicitly or implicitly about verbal communication, either directly focusing on some communication technology saturated with language (e.g., memos, superior-subordinate interaction, computers, etc.) or asking questions about content normally communicated verbally. This is similar to the situation in 1976.

Communication Technology. Technology refers to knowledge or the employment of knowledge to perform certain tasks (Kast & Rosenzweig, 1970). In this case, communication technology refers to the employment of knowledge to communicate. Alternative expressions include media and diffusion methods (Goldhaber, 1993). It is one of the uses of the term *channel* (Berlo, 1960). This is a new category, one not employed as a separate category in the 1976 review.

There is research on older forms of written technology such as memos and proposals (Yates & Orlikowski, 1992). The most articles related to the newer technologies are about media choice (e.g., Rice, 1993). Some employ a media gratifications model (Dobos, 1992), whereas others use media richness ideas (Daft & Lengel, 1986).

Most of articles describe aspects of face-to-face interaction (e.g., superior-subordinate interaction, small-group behavior), and newer research methods focused on narratives reinforce the focus on face-to-face communication. However, there has been an increase in the number of articles about written messages due mostly to the emergence of journals focused on writing (e.g., *Journal of Technical Writing, Written Communication*) and the material produced by the American Business Communication Association. Although still dominated by articles about face-to-face interaction, the journal literature has been changing into a richer mix of material about a wider range of communication technology.

Level of Relationship. This refers to the type of relationship under investigation. The choices for this category include (a) individual to organization, (b) dyadic relationships, (c) small groups and teams, (d) intergroup and interunit relations, (e) interorganizational relations, and (f) social networks. In 1976, most of the journal literature was about small groups, and articles about the superior-subordinate dyad were a close second. There were also several pieces about networks as that area of investigation was beginning to emerge. There are still articles about groups and teams (e.g., Keyton, 1993), and some articles focus on the superior-subordinate dyad (Morrow, 1981). However, more articles investigate several dyadic or group relationships at once. The most common combination is to investigate superior-subordinate communication along with coworker communication (e.g., Blackeney, 1985; McGee, Goodson, & Cashman, 1987; Putti, Ayree, & Phua, 1990). There are also still articles about networks (e.g., Johnson, 1992a, 1992b).

The biggest change has been the emergence of research about the individual's relationship with the organization. Some research focuses on a specific problem such as preparations for retirement (Avery & Jablin, 1988), but the biggest growth has been in critical studies and cultural studies related to power and politics. These articles describe broad social processes and their impact on individuals.

A review of 289 organizational communication articles published in the 1980s organized the research into three topics: (a) climate and culture, (b) superior subordinate relations and communication; and (c) power, conflict, and politics (Wert-Gray, Center, Brashers, & Meyers, 1991). Most of the articles in the first and third categories focus on the individual-organization interface. As noted earlier, most recent research tends to include superior-subordinate communication with other dyadic concerns.

The articles over the last 20 years are mostly about the individual-organization level of relationship, followed by concerns for a variety of dyadic relationships. This is a significant change from 1976. The most articles in the period from 1964 to 1975 were about groups and then the superior-subordinate relationship.

Organizational Dimensions

Goals. The desired outcomes of an organization are the organizational goals. The relationship of communication to goal formation or descriptions of communication given different goals are not popular areas of investigation. The majority of articles related to goals are about organizational communication effectiveness (OCE), Greenbaum's expression in the *Organizational Communication Abstracts.* These articles explore how well communication might assist in accomplishing organizational goals.

There is a dynamic tension between the desire for (a) efficiency and (b) production and the desire for (c) innovation, (d) quality, and (e) morale. Organizations typically define effectiveness by efforts at some combination of these goals. However, behavior that enhances the chances for the first two goals diminishes the likelihood of the other three, and resources devoted to the last three reduce the chances for the first two (Hage, 1980). Organizational members are often in the paradoxical situation of attempting to satisfy two or more mutually exclusive goals (Quinn, 1988).

Snyder and Morris (1984) did assess the performance of workers, and Morrow (1981) looked at unit performance, but there is very little research about communication and efficiency, production, innovation, or quality. By far the greatest amount of articles is about the relationship between communication and some variation of morale. This includes articles about communication and commitment (Putti et al., 1990), job involvement (Courtright, Fairhurst, & Rogers, 1989), job satisfaction (Koike, Gudykunst, Stewart, & Ting-Toomey, 1988), motivation (Cussella, 1982), and trust (Blackeney, 1985). This conclusion is similar to the one made in 1976.

Organizational Technology. *Technology* refers to knowledge or the employment of knowledge to perform certain tasks (Kast & Rosenzweig, 1970). In this instance, technology refers to the way organizations accomplish their goals. Articles about organizational technologies might be concerned with comparing different ways of performing the task or assessing an innovation. A communication technology may be the technology being explored, communication may be part of the specific goal of the technology, communication may be an intervening factor, or changes in communication may be an incidental result of the technology.

As noted earlier, the ERIC database includes many reports of organizational technologies in organizations. These may be descriptive or evaluative reports, and the journals that publish these reports include the *Journal of the Association for Communication Administration, Business Officer, Research Management Review, Cause–effect, College and University, Canadian Journal of Information and Library Science, Journal of Dental Education, Educational Record*, and so on. Some of these reports could be case studies, but most are short (under 10 pages), and they provide a description, analysis, or evaluation of some technology, including the part related to communication. In most instances, these reports do not reflect an awareness of contemporary theory or research, but a concern for "effective communication." They seem more influenced by the trade press then the academic press. This is similar to the situation that existed in 1976, except there is a greater volume of such reports.

Structure. The established pattern of relationships among organizational components is the organizational structure (Kast & Rosenzweig, 1970). Structural factors include level of formality, differentiation, centralization, and configuration (see Blau, 1975). Koike et al. (1988) did include the direction of information flow across a structure in their research, and Courtright et al. (1989) compared communication in two different structures, but such studies are rare. Communication interests have focused on networks (e.g., Johnson, 1992a, 1992b) and structuration (e.g., McPhee, 1989; Riley, 1983), but organizational communication researchers do not generally investigate structure (Jablin, 1987).

Psychosocial System. Studies of the individual in social relationships are psychosocial research (Kast & Rosenzweig, 1970). The psychosocial system includes such things as status, roles, worker satisfaction, conflict, culture, and so on. The psychosocial system is the most popular area of investigation.

As noted earlier, most of the articles about organizational goals focused on morale and a host of psychosocial outcomes. Morley and Shockley-Zalabak (1985) included future employment expectations in their comparison of gender communication. Both gender concerns and future employment expectations are psychosocial areas not normally associated with organizational effectiveness studies.

Of course, the biggest growth in this area has been in articles about culture. Chua and Gudykunst (1987) explored differences in conflict styles in organizations in high and low context cultures, and their approach represents a traditional way of viewing culture. Honikman (1987) and Mumby (1987) both investigated political activities in organizational cultures, and they represent the more contemporary concerns.

Management. The principle concern of management is decision making (Kast & Rosenzweig, 1970; Katz & Kahn, 1966). From 1965 to 1974, communication research focused on two areas: (a) methods of decision making and (b) leadership. The 1976 review described this area as the organizational dimension with the greatest research. O'Reilly (1980) focused on managers in his study of load, but there were few articles exploring management or mangers from 1975 to 1994. The only exceptions might be some of the organizational technology reports noted earlier. This is a significant change over the 20-year period.

Theory

A theory is a set of relational statements (Dubin, 1978). It is identifiable because a particular unit of domain is common to all the relational statements in the set. At a minimum, theories of any sort seek to explain phenomena.

Theories may emerge deductively as a researcher may employ a variety of previously built theories to create a new one. The new theory usually emerges about the interface of the old ones. A rigorous strategy directed at creating testable hypotheses may then be employed (Dubin, 1978). Theories may also emerge inductively. Theory may emerge grounded in qualitative data. The data may suggest categories, and a model of the relationships between categories is one form of theory (Strauss & Corbin, 1990). Furthermore, the interface of a variety of previously demonstrated ideas or hypotheses may suggest a proposition. The interface of propositions may suggest laws of interaction (Dubin's term), and a set of such laws is a theory.

In 1976, journals were not likely to publish models or theories; rather, books presented the explanation of a theory. However, the extent of theory development could be analyzed by describing the complexity of the research designs. The notion of the efficiency of a law of interaction suggested criteria for evaluating theory from the propositions or hypotheses in the study (Dubin, 1978). The 1976 review concluded that most organizational communication research is at a low level of efficiency. That is, the ideas tested sought to demonstrate that the presence or absence of some factor was associated with the presence or absence of another factor, or that there was a correlation between factors. There were few efforts at more sophisticated multiple factor procedures, and there were few efforts at modeling, either statistically or symbolically. For the most part, research was generated by the efforts to solve problems, rather than to build theory. The review concluded that organizational communication was atheoretical.

Things have changed. First of all, traditional empirical research has become more sophisticated and multivariate studies are the norm, suggesting greater theoretical complexity as well. However, an even bigger change has been the publication of a host of theories in journals. Some follow a more traditional pattern of reviewing the literature and generating ideas (e.g., Keyton, 1993), and many develop theory grounded in data (e.g., Browning, 1978; Howard & Geist, 1995). Scholars have used rhetorical theories (e.g., Yates & Orlikowski, 1992), and speech act theory (Sullivan, 1988). There have been theories of narrative (Weick & Browning, 1986), and cultural theories (Pacanowsky & O'Donnell-Trujillo, 1983). There are also metatheoretical concerns that transcend any one approach (e.g., Monge, Farace, Eisenberg, Miller, & White, 1984). Reviews of organizational communication theories (e.g., Fulk & Boyd, 1991) occur more frequently. There has been considerable theory development from 1975 to 1994.

Research Methods

In 1969, a scholar expressed his concerns about organizational scholarship in the following way:

Even though case studies have a richness of detail, they have at least four drawbacks: they are (a) situation specific, (b) ahistorical, (c) tacitly prescriptive, and (d) one-sided. (p. 18)

It is difficult to tell what the group being described has done in the past that is being *repeated* in the present, and it is even harder to discover what it is about the environment that produces this repetition. Precisely this information is needed if lawful relationships are to be stated. (p. 19)

The experimental method, whether applied in field experiments . . . controlled naturalistic observation . . . contrived laboratory experiments . . . or simulated environments . . . is the principal tactic by which more durable data and useful data can be obtained. (p. 21)

In 1979, the same author presented a series of anecdotes and wrote the following:

There is not an underlying "reality" waiting to be discovered. Rather, organizations are viewed as the inventions superimposed on flows of experience and momentarily imposing some order on those streams. (pp. 11-12)

The activity of appreciating was implicit in the approach taken to each incident. Brief attempts were made to embellish each example, to examine it from a variety of angles, and to add to its richness . . . In the process of embellishing, reworking and contemplating each prior example, we begin to identify some elements associated with organizing. In each example, some portions of the stream of experience was bracketed, and efforts were made to turn the stream into information and then to do something about the information that had been constructed. (p. 12)

These are striking differences between Karl Weick's comments about research methods in the first edition (1969) of *The Social Psychology of Organizing* and his comments in the second edition (1979). Weick had turned to qualitative and interpretive methods.

Communication scholars had been employing qualitative methods in the 1970s (e.g., Browning, 1978), but there is little doubt that the special issue of the *Western Journal of Speech Communication* in spring, 1982 (volume 46, no. 2) stimulated the greater use of such methods. Clair's (1994) use of discourse analysis reflects the strengths of such methods by generating explanations that would be difficult to demonstrate with other methods. There have been advances in other methods (e.g., Corman & Scott, 1994), and much research still approaches data critically or quantitatively. However, research in organizational communication employs more varied methods today than it did 20 years ago.

Application

Organizational communication research and theory have had two principle areas of application: (a) application to education and (b) application to the organization. There have been two methods of organizational application: (a) short-term practical (training sessions, sensitivity groups, etc.) and (b) long-term analytical (development work and strategic planning).

Some articles share teaching units (e.g., Infante, 1995) whereas others describe experiential activities for teaching organizational communication (e.g., Lederman & Stewart, 1987, 1991). There have been surveys of doctoral communication programs, including those in organizational communication (Edwards, Watson, & Barker, 1988). However, a recent survey about the teaching of the undergraduate organizational communication course suggests that pedagogy is changing very slowly (Treadwell & Applebaum, 1995). The top four texts used in the course (Goldhaber, 1993, used by 21.1%; Frank & Brownwell, 1989, used by 21.4%; Shockley-Zalabak, 1991, by 21.1%; and Daniels & Spiker, 1994, by 17.9%) present predominantly traditional approaches to the area.

Glauser and Axley (1983) discovered that the vast majority of faculty are more involved in training activity than development activity. Trainers have been interested in various models of communication training (e.g., Christian & Nykodym, 1986), and in the use of technology in training (Hillelsohn, 1984). However, there have been few efforts to assess the effectiveness of such training, and some have suggested that there are little long-term effects (Goodale, 1987).

There are very few articles about development efforts. Alderfer (1977) described a lengthy intergroup intervention, and Stone and Allen (1990) provided a way for HRD specialists to consider introducing newer technologies. Most organizational communication development reports still remain proprietary.

Social Responsibility

Critical research and the development of critical standards have long been a major part of the speech communication tradition. Criticism may take the form of an explicit statement of criteria and direct evaluation. Critical standards emerge from an analysis or purposeful review of literature (e.g., this chapter), or from descriptive surveys.

At the 1996 conference, social responsibility was the term for concerns about critical standards and ethics. There has been a substantial increase in the development of social responsibility literature in the journals over the last 20 years, as well as a general concern for ethics (e.g., Nicotera & Cushman, 1992) and a concern for ethics in a particular type of communication such as public relations (Pratt, 1994). In other instances, the focus may have been on feminist issues (e.g., Buznell, 1994; D. Cameron, 1994) and issues of diversity (Limaye, 1994). There was no literature like this 20 years ago.

Summary

Currently, the domain of organizational communication is about internal, formal, verbal, face-to-face communication concerned with how the individual relates to the organization and its culture. The domain includes an emphasis on psychosocial and cultural concerns, both in terms of the effectiveness of organizations, and the development of organizational cultures and the place of the individual in those cultures. This domain has evolved over the last 20 years and has a limited concern for management and organizational structure.

There has been considerable development of organizational communication theory, a diversity of research methods and the development of literature on the social responsibilities of organizations. In addition, there has been little published on the application of this knowledge, either to enhance education or the organization.

THE CHALLENGES OF THE NEXT CENTURY

Sven Birkerts is the author of *The Guttenberg Eliges* (1995) and was part of a forum about technology in *Harpers* ("What are we doing on-line?" 1995). At one point, the discussion turned to problems related to the anonymity of users on-line. His response was, "I want my hierarchy." He was having difficulty recognizing the credible source from the adolescent prankster and having trouble separating '"fact" from "fantasy." He wanted some social stratification, and he wanted some sense of a depth of thought.

Patti is the name of the character in the 1987 Paul Schrader film *Light of Day*. She is in her early twenties, an unmarried mother who has given her child to her mother, and the member of a rock and roll band. Her brother Joe, a one-time member of an earlier band, has come to see his sister backstage before a scheduled show to inform her that her mother is ill and may die. Before he can tell Patti the news, they squabble over Patti's responsibilities to her child and her family. Patti interrupts her brother and says:

I've been trying to live my life by an idea. See that machine [points to a video game], that's an idea. Rock'n roll, that's an idea. All those video monsters . . . bip, bip, bip. All those bip-bips are separate, and no idea is any more important than another. Nothing comes together. No heaven, No hell. Just moments. If moments connect, you accept Mom's world . . . Look, you see those idiots over here [points to two napping band members]. They think they are going to be stars. They said there's going to be deals, limos, demos. Did you ever here me talk like that? Nah! I go out there every night just to hear the beat . . . That's all there is man.

Patti has a very broad view of time. There is no history, and nothing connects. She lives in a simulacum where everything is real and nothing is real.

The current rate of change in society in general and in organizational communication in particular is altering conceptual and social structures. As a field of study it is less centralized and specialized, and more inventive and flexible. However, change oscillates, and some levels experience stability while others experience variety. Birkerts wants things to move toward stability, but Patti would rather not even discuss the idea of a pattern over time.

What follows is a set of concerns about the rate of change in organizational communication. The over-arching challenge is to find the most productive mix of novelty and stability, of breadth and depth, and of creativity and efficiency. Each of the following sections identifies the specific challenges confronting the various aspects of organizational communication.

Domain

It has become trite to suggest that organizational communication is a fragmented field of study. Smith (1996) argued that this is all illusory, and that the various approaches to organizational communication have more commonalties than differences. Shelby (1993) reviewed teaching material for organizational communication, business communication, management communication and corporate communication and found few differences.

Twenty years ago, there were organizational communication interest groups in the International Communication Association, and in the Academy of Management, but there was no such group in the Speech Communication Association. Since that time, SCA has acquired its own interest group, added an applied communication interest group, approved the formation of training and development group, and found members ready to propose a business communication group. The conceptual and theoretical commonalties are not apparent to many people.

The challenge is for integration. Does the expression "organizational communication" still coherently describe the domain?

What is the jurisdiction of the expression "organizational communication"? Others have raised these conceptual questions about communication studies in general (Cray & Hazen, 1995). A more practical concern is for the division of the house, a separation of scholars and practitioners among and between themselves. Consider what would happen if SCA went on to approve a business communication group and a new group in organizational communication theory. Then, what would go on in the old organizational communication group?

Theory

Theory development has proceeded energetically, regardless of methodology or paradigm. Part of this growth is due to yet another interdisciplinary interface. Communication studies have alternately been aligned with literature, history, political science, psychology, and sociology and anthropology. In some cultures, the interface is with linguistics, and business schools have discovered organizational communication as their enrollments have tapered. Each interface began as an attempt at analoguing, efforts at grafting constructs and relationships used in one discipline on to the study of communication There are new metaphors. "Communication works as if it were X (insert your favorite metaphor)."All of this is fine as long as the interfaces improve our understanding of communication. This requires theories with depth, theories that push beyond taxonomic issues to the *relationships* between the constructs. The challenge is to continue to develop theories with depth.

Research Methods

Research methods provide some evidence to support claims. In most cases, support comes from some combination of logic and various types of data, depending on the nature of the methodology. John Brockman, author of *The Third Culture* (1996), a book about technology and society has a decided preference for data.

> The literary culture was an establishment that dictated fashionable discourse. It favored opinions and ideology over empirical testing of ideas—commentary spiraling upon commentary. As a cultural force, it is a dead end. (cited in Leggiere, 1995, p. 172)

On the other hand, George Englebretsen is a member of a philosophy department, and he is bothered by a lack of logic:

> Freed from the confines of logic, discourse can now become open, honest, sincere, politically sensitive, historically conditioned. Premoderns and moderns based their willingness to accept or reject a speaker's claim on

their judgement of how well it seemed to fit the facts of the case and to what extent it was logically consistent with the speaker's other claims or assumptions. By contrast, postmoderns "play the believing game," accepting the speaker's claim according to the sincerity the speaker exhibits. Truth and coherence are no longer allowed to bully us in our communicative efforts. Expertise and authority are no longer the possession of only a few. We all share expertise and authority equally. Communication is finally democratic. The premodern and modern informed and rational despots have been overthrown. We are *all* informed; we are *all* rational. (Englebretsen, 1995, p. 52)

The problem is how to deal with Patti, Schrader's (1987) postmodern character who cannot distinguish fact from fantasy and who does not recognize any rational order. Patti is not alone. A recent poll indicated that 40% of the public uses a radio talk show as its primary source for news. There is trouble distinguishing the event from the reporter from the editorial writer from the entertainer.The challenge is, again, one of depth. The challenge is for researchers to discover criteria for rejection. That is, when is the evidence to a claim sound, and when should it be rejected? This challenge is one of depth because it assumes researchers can distinguish claims from evidence; it also assumes that researchers can distinguish research from other forms of human expression.

A recent special issue of the *Western Journal of Communication* addressed concerns about the soundness of evidence. Liska and Chronkite (1994) noted that the authors who preceded them in the issue—authors from a variety of methodologies—had strikingly similar notions of when evidence was good. Evidence is good when it is linked to a paradigm, linked to theory, systematically gathered, linked directly to claims, comparable, representative, consistent, verifiable, compelling, and consequential. Although some of the authors used different labels for these ideas, and although there might not be complete agreement on one or two of these qualities, the fact that there appears to be so much agreement suggests that it would be possible to describe criteria even in this pluralistic methodological environment.

What about Patti? Patti isn't interested in making a record. She doesn't see a need or a reason to connect anything or preserve a performance. She is only interested in the personal gratification of being part of the beat. She would not be likely to be an educator because she would have no sense of truth, or right, or have need to connect generations or to teach others how to connect ideas. Should a discipline provide her with an avenue of self-expression?

This is a hard question to answer in the abstract. It is easier to answer in the practical decisions an editor must make about what to publish. For most journals, the primary function is to disseminate material to a community of scholars or practitioners, and the editor could easily reject a submission because she or he believed it did not benefit the community that supported and funded the journal. Such a rejection could occur even if the evidence were good. These decisions are part of being an editor.

Perhaps there should be a journal for Patti, but the notion of submitting something that could be rejected runs counter to Patti's view of life. What she wants is the opportunity to be part of the flow, to express for the sheer pleasure of expression. She will be difficult to deal with in the future because one has the feeling that there is more to it than her just making a home page and sending it into cyberspace.

Application

There has always been a problem with not having much published literature on organizational communication application. The pure academics may think the consultants are charlatans just selling snake oil because what they do seem so secretive. One has the feeling that the consultants are hiding something. The end result is the academics who might be able to help others don't.

Many trainers know only the material they need to deliver the workshop. The rest is just packaging. The successful ones charge a handsome fee for the show, but it is all show. There is a technology to training, one that could help academicians teach. There is also a craft to consulting, one that could help academicians research. Of course, the formal theory and research that is part of academic life would and is of benefit to the trainers and consultants that routinely participate in academic activities. The problem is that the two groups seldom make an effort to share resources. The challenge is, once again, integration.

Social Responsibility

The assumption behind most social responsibility research is that there is an oppressive bureaucracy or at least power elites within a relatively large organization. Furthermore, these circumstances put certain minority stakeholders at a disadvantage. To be sure, these are the circumstances in many organizations and those situations demand redress.

The organizational landscape is changing, however. This is an age in which information technology has enormous promise to circumvent hierarchies, to leave social collectives "out of control" (Kelly, 1994). Furthermore, there is a growing recognition that quality cannot be achieved through large bureaucracies, and so the size of organizations and organizational work units is shrinking. Technology allows for demassifying production and for decentralized structures. Change, however, is oscillating and multilevel. In Austin, TX, there are large companies (Motorola, IBM, etc.), but the city includes small software companies—skunkworks—that thrive. In such an environment, who is responsible, and for what? In fluid or smaller structures, responsibilities rest with individuals . . . for everything.

Some social stratification is inevitable, and the larger social structures will not disappear. They do serve several useful functions including providing a way to deal with overload (Galbraith, 1977). When someone is appointed or elected as a manager, the person in that role relieves those below of the privilege and the responsibility of certain decisions. The worker gives up some autonomy for a simpler existence. Some social information is processed by someone else. What is more, demassification will be fine for those that want to bear the responsibility of caring for and making decisions about a custom product or service. Others will be quite content to let the company keep the warranty. These individuals will have forfeited their responsibilities.

Ridley Scott's (1996) *White Squall* is a film about responsibilities. Christopher Sheldon owned and directed the Albatross, a square-rigged brigantine sailboat that served as a one-year precollege boarding school. In 1960-1961, the Albatross encountered a storm on its return home, and 4 of the 13 teenage boys died along with two crew members, including Sheldon's wife. When the survivors returned to port in St. Petersburg, the Coast Guard conducted a hearing to determine the cause of the deaths, and, there was the possibility that Sheldon would lose his seaman's license. Prior to the hearing, Scott depicts the surviving boys quarreling and pointing fingers at each other for their actions during the crisis. At the hearing, the first two boys to testify deny that Sheldon was responsible for the deaths. The second boy, the helmsman during the mishap, tries to shoulder the blame for the boat's capsizing. Sheldon rises and tells the boys to stop trying to protect him. He will shoulder any blame alone, he says. One of the boys confronts Sheldon with his own on board teaching. The ship's motto, engraved on the ship's bell, is "Where one goes, so go all." The boys are willing to share responsibilities.

The larger social structures, like the smaller ones, are the constructions of the social actions of individuals. To what extent are individuals responsible for those structures?

> We create and maintain organizational forms consistent with our level of collective maturity and our shared identity. If we see ourselves as separate, fearful, shame-ridden people whose best hope for happiness is to manipulate our external circumstances so that they please us, we get the bureaucratic form. If we are willing to accept personal responsibility for expressing transcendent values, for living in true, spiritual identity,

we will create flexible, nonhierarchical politics-free organizations. *We create our own reality.* We produce what is consistent with our inner structures of consciousness. (Banner & Gagne, 1995, p. 97)

What we see and experience as the world out there is nothing more or less than a reflection of what is contained (and agreed on) in consciousness. If we see a scary world, this is an indication that we are scared inside. If we see a turbulent world, we have turbulent thoughts and feelings inside. (p. 319)

The challenge ahead is to develop literature on personal responsibility.

CONCLUSION

This chapter began with a consideration of some of the features of change. Change is about differences over time. Change is normative, and there are different orders of change. There may be multiple causes of change, but change of any sort generally alters the structure of a system. Change oscillates between movement toward stability and movement toward variety, and some parts of a system are likely to be moving in one direction while other parts move in the opposite direction.

The anchor or norm for describing change in organizational communication journal literature is the state of that literature in 1975-1976. Since then there have been several changes. First, the domain of organizational communication is more complex. It now includes a greater interest in communication technologies than 20 years ago, although the vast majority of the literature is still about face-to-face communication. The domain includes an increase in material about the relationship of the individual to the organization and less material about small group communication. As it was 20 years ago, the majority of material is still about internal, formal, verbal, dyadic communication, especially between co-workers and between supervisors and subordinates. There has been an increase in the amount of material related to psychosocial factors, especially material dealing with organizational culture. There has also been a meaningful decrease in the number of articles dealing with management concerns and decision making. The domain of organizational communication is similar to 20 years ago in the many scholarly articles about organizational communication effectiveness and the many practitioner reports of organizational practices that might have communication implications. There are still only a few articles about communication and organizational structure. Second, the journals published more and more purely theoretical pieces, from a variety of paradigms, over the period. There were few articles about organizational communication theories prior to 1976. Third, the articles include a noticeable increase in the variety of research methods. Prior to 1976, researchers employed quantitative approaches to the exclusion of other methods, and today there has been an increase in the number of articles containing a variety of qualitative methods or a variety critical methods. Fourth, there has been little growth in the number of articles about organizational communication education, training, or consultant development activities. Fifth, there is growing and developing body of literature about the social responsibilities of organizations and their members.

The increased complexity and growth have influenced the structure of the field. The challenges for the domain are to more clearly identify the boundary and to employ constructs and ideas that integrate the efforts of diverse approaches to the field. The challenge for theory is to develop explanations of greater depth and richness. The challenge for methods is to delineate and clarify criteria for the acceptance or rejection of research from an increasingly wider range of methods. A challenge for application is to find opportunities to bring academic and nonacademic professionals together to share in their ideas. Finally, there is a need to develop literature on the responsibilities individuals have to each other in their communication and the responsibilities they share for the organizations they construct.

part two

ORGANIZATIONAL COMMUNICATION DOMAIN

two

ORGANIZATIONAL COMMUNICATION IN 1976: PRESENT DOMAIN AND FUTURE DIRECTIONS

Gerald M. Goldhaber

State University of New York-Buffalo

The age of "future shock" is upon us. We are all subjected to instant travel, instant change and instant communication. Today, in 1976, we can send a man to the moon in less time than it takes for a parcel-post package to travel from Boston to San Francisco. Within 5 minutes we can talk on the telephone to almost any part of the world. Satellite networks enable us to be eyewitness observers at the funeral of a world leader, the landing of a spaceship on the moon, or even a full-scale war—without ever leaving our living rooms.

Despite many space-age communication victories, however, we still witness the moral decay of our government and political institutions, the disintegration of our families, and the bankruptcy of our businesses. It appears that advances in technological communications are not positively related to successful interpersonal communication. In fact, the relationship between the two may be inverse.

In 1956 William Whyte labeled most of us "organization men" because of the large amount of time we spend within organizations. In 1973, Harry Levinson claimed that this is still true, that "90 percent of those who work do so in organizations" (p. 75). When we add the time we spend in civic and social clubs, religious and educational institutions, hospitals, banks, and so forth, it is relatively simple to conclude that today all of us are organization men and women.

Because we spend most of our waking time in organizations, it is obvious that the problems of our cities, universities, and businesses are problems of organizations. One might hypothesize that given the technology to conquer outer space, we should be able to master the daily "people problems" we face in our complex organizations. One might hypothesize that given our current social psychological and clinical-medical models of handling people, we would be able to minimize intra- and intergroup conflict and the morale and motivation problems associated with managing complex organizations.

Yet despite the research reported by our nation's leading organizational experts advocating new approaches to structuring organizations and managing people, most organizations today rigidly adhere to the military model with control directed from the top of the hierarchy. Despite the findings of our behavioral scientists, most organizations maintain detailed job descriptions and specific goal-oriented objectives with an absolute minimum of flexibility. To compound the problem, many managers, fresh from a "sensitivity training session" or a "group dynamics workshop" or an "organization development seminar," claim to be "new people with a changed outlook on life and their job." It only takes a few weeks (or days) for them to return to their old ways of management based on "carrot-and-stick" philosophies of dealing with people. Levinson called this the "jackass fallacy" and predicted that organizational crises will continue as long as managers, superiors, and leaders maintain this basic attitudinal structure of "the powerful treating the powerless as objects as they maintain anachronistic organizational structures that destroy the individual's sense of worth and accomplishment". The evidence ("increased inefficiency, lowered productivity, heightened absenteeism, theft, and sometimes outright sabotage") would seem to support Levinson's conclusion that our organizations are still in a state of crisis which will ultimately result in both their destruction and the alienation of our youth.

Since 1938, when Chester Barnard defined the main task of an executive as that of communication, it has been demonstrated continuously that organization man and woman is a communicating person. To illustrate this, I'd like to quote from a *Newsday* story:

> Edward Carlson, chairman and chief executive officer of United Airlines, travels an estimated 200,000 miles a year, using much of that time to communicate with approximately 50,000 employees. Carlson, who stops frequently to hold formal meetings, informal chats or just

shake hands, has called the program "visible management." He has encouraged company managers to also make themselves as "visible" as possible, and the company feels that the program has helped considerably in United's major financial turnaround of recent years. ("In Industry," 1975, p. 29)

Various national surveys have shown that United's "visible management" policy is a rarity in business. Communications within private companies generally are poor and neglected and sometimes a severe problem, despite the fact that managers spend an estimated 75% of their time in some form of communication.

Before Carlson took charge people were poorly informed; they didn't understand why certain policies were necessary. A poorly informed workforce is not a very productive one. United lost $41 million in 1970 and Carlson joined the company that December. After edging back slowly at first, United last year, in the height of the energy crisis, had a record $86.3 million in profits. "We work pretty hard at communications—all of us," Carlson said. "In my visits I constantly encourage employees to raise problems and suggestions. In turn, we are careful to respond to their ideas, because we really do care about what our employees are thinking."

Many organizations, however, frequently are not even conscious of communications problems. During the last 15 years many speech and speech communication departments have begun offering courses to study this phenomenon of people communicating in organizations. In 1970 Wright and Sherman conducted a survey of speech communication graduate programs offering courses in organizational communication. Among the conclusions of the survey were:

1. 54% of the sample indicated that they either offer or planned to soon offer at least one course in organizational communication.
2. Classes in organizational communication typically enroll full-time students in speech communication, as well as students from a variety of departments and colleges (usually business).
3. The areas of emphasis for organizational communication courses were relatively equally dispersed among theory, research, and application.
4. The most frequently studied organization setting was business and industrial organizations.
5. A majority of the completed questionnaires indicated that more courses should be offered in the area of organizational communication.

In 1974, Downs and Larimer conducted a similar survey and reported:

1. 61% of their sample offer courses in organizational communication (mostly one or two courses/department).
2. 40% of their sample offer a major or a minor concentration in this area.
3. 60% of the course offerings have been originated in the last 5 years.
4. 35% of their sample report mostly nonspeech majors as enrollees in the organizational communication courses.

It is apparent from the results of these surveys that the field of organizational communication has shown remarkable growth in just a few years. All indications are that this growth will continue in the coming decade. Students who enter the field of communication are demanding an education that will lead directly to a future occupation or profession (other than more education). Organizational communication as a field would appear to answer these student demands. However, what is organizational communication? What does it include and exclude?

DEFINING ORGANIZATIONAL COMMUNICATION

I recently surveyed the literature and found over 50 "organizational communication" experts, each with their own perception of the domain of the field. Redding and Sanborn (1964) defined organizational communication as the sending and receiving of information within a complex organization. Their perception of the field (as evidenced by their sourcebook reader) included internal communication, human relations, management-union relations, downward, upward, and horizontal communication, communication skills (speaking, listening, writing) and communication program evaluation. Katz and Kahn (1966) perceived organizational communication as the flow of information (the exchange of information and the transmission of meaning) within an organization. Using the general systems model developed for the physical sciences by von Bertalanffy (1956, 1962) and others, Katz and Kahn defined organizations as open systems and discuss such properties as the importing of energy from the environment, the transformation of this energy into some product or service into the environment, and the reenergizing of the system from energy sources found once again in the environment. Zelko and Dance (1965) primarily discussed the "skills" of communicating in businesses and professions (speech making, listening, interviewing, counseling, conferences, selling, persuading, etc.). They perceive organizational communication as interdependently including both internal (upward, downward, horizontal) and external (public relations, sales, advertising) communication. Lesikar (1972) shares Zelko and Dance's perceptions of internal/external communication and adds a third dimension—personal communication (the informal exchange of information and feelings among organizational members).

Thayer (1968), also using the general systems approach to communication, referred to organizational communication as "those data flows that subserve the organization's communication and intercommunication processes in some way" (p. 103). He identified three communication systems within the organization: operational (task- or operations-related data); regulatory (orders, rules, instructions); and maintenance/development (public and employee relations, advertising, training). Bormann, Howell, Nichols, and Shapiro (1969) limited their study or organizational communication to "speech communications" (as opposed to written communication) within a system of overlapping and interdependent groups. They emphasized the communication skills of listening, meeting in small groups, and speaking to persuade. Huseman, Logue, and Freshley (1969) edited a reader that limited the field of organizational communication to organizational structure, motivation, and such communicative skills as listening, speaking, writing, interviewing, and discussing. Several writers (e.g., Lesikar, 1972; Schutte & Steinberg, 1960; Vardaman & Vardaman, 1973) emphasized in their studies the written media of communication (reports, letters, memos, bulletins, proposals, etc.).

More recently, Greenbaum (1971, 1972) perceived the field of organizational communication as including the formal and informal communication flow within the organization. He preferred to separate internal from external organizational communication and views the role of communication primarily as one of coordination (of the personal and organizational objectives and problem-solving activities). Witkin and Stephens (1972) defined an organizational communication system as the interdependencies and interactions that serve the purposes of the organization. Haney (1973), using a general semantics approach to communication, defined organizational communication as the coordination (by communication) of a number of people who are interdependently related.

This conceptual disparity is further illustrated by Downs and Larimer's (1974) finding that the following 21 areas of subject matter are currently being taught in organizational communication courses: Downward Communication, Upward Communication, Organizational

Theory, Horizontal Communication, Decision Making, Small Group Communication, Leadership, Research Techniques, Motivation, Interviewing, Change and Innovation, Conflict Management, Organizational Development, Conference Techniques, Management Theory, Consultation Training, Listening, Job Satisfaction, Public Speaking, Writing, and Sensitivity Training.

What does all of this mean? It is apparent that definitions, approaches to and perceptions of organizational communication are legion. It is apparent that organizational communication can mean and refer to whatever the author wants. Despite this wide variety of viewpoints, a few common strands can be detected in many of the 50 perceptions:

1. Organizational communication occurs within a complex open system that is influenced by and influences its environment.
2. Organizational communication involves messages—their flow, purpose, direction and media.
3. Organizational communication involves people, their attitudes, feelings, relationships, and skills.

These propositions lead to my definition of organizational communication: the flow of messages within a network of interdependent relationships. This perception of the field of organizational communication includes four key concepts, each of which I now define and illustrate briefly: messages, networks, interdependent, and relationship.

Messages

The following messages were taken from letters on file at the San Antonio Veterans Administration written by wives, husbands, mothers, and fathers:

> "Both sides of my parents are poor and I can't expect nothing from them, as my mother has been in bed for one year with the same doctor, and won't change."
> Please send me a letter and tell me if my husband has made application for a wife and baby."
> "I can't get any pay. I has 6 children, can you tell me why this is?"
> "I am forwarding you my marriage certificate and my 2 children, one is a mistake as you can plainly see."

"I am annoyed to find out that you branded my child as
illiterate, it is a dirty lie as I married his father a week
before he was born."

"You changed my little boy to a girl, does this make a
difference?"

"In accordance with your instructions, I have given birth
to twins in the enclosed envelope."

"My husband had his project cut off 2 weeks ago and I
haven't had any relief since."

Undoubtedly, the senders of these letters may not have had the
same meanings in their minds as may be interpreted by some readers. In
fact, many of the senders probably would deny any other possible
interpretation of their messages except the one they intended. How
often do we assign a meaning to a message and assume that because we
know what it means, so shouldn't everyone else?

In a popularly used teaching film on communication (More than
Words, 1959), a manager is upset with his employee for not following
his explicit instructions for completing a "model job." When the worker
joyfully displayed his electrical-mechanical simulation "model," his boss
angrily shouted, "I didn't ask you for this!" The employee, now
frightened by his employer's loud, shrill voice and fast-moving gestures,
proclaimed, "But boss, you asked me to produce a model job, and that's
what I did!" The now almost violent boss screamed, "But I didn't mean
that you should build a model. I meant that you should do a model job,
a good job, an excellent job!" The employee interrupted, "But boss, that's
not what you said!" In a final shout of despair, the boss yelled, "Don't
listen to what I say, listen to what I mean!"

In organizational communication we study the flow of messages
throughout organizations. Organizational message behavior can be
examined according to several taxonomies: language modality; intended
receivers; method of diffusion; purpose of flow. Language modality
differentiates verbal from nonverbal messages. Examples of verbal
messages in organizations are letters, speeches, and conversations. With
verbal messages we are most interested in studying the exact word
choice used in the speech, letter, or conversation. Nonverbal messages
are primarily unspoken or unwritten. Examples of nonverbal messages
are body language (eye movement, gesturing, etc.), physical
characteristics (height, weight, hair length), touching behavior (hand
shaking, stroking, hitting), vocal cues (tone, pitch, rhythm), personal
space (spatial arrangements, territoriality), objects (glasses, wigs,
clothing), and the environment (room size, furniture, music).

Intended receivers include those people either within or outside the organization. The former examines messages intended for internal use, the latter for external. Examples of internal message systems include memos, bulletins, and meetings. External message behavior is illustrated by advertising campaigns, public relations efforts, sales efforts, civic duties, and so forth. Internal messages are intended for consumption by the employees of the organization.

Method of diffusion identifies the particular communication activity employed during the sending of the messages to other people. Diffusion implies that messages are spread throughout the organization (either widely or narrowly). Here we are interested in how messages are spread. Most organizational communication diffusion methods can be divided into two general categories: those using "software," and those using "hardware" for dissemination. The latter depend on electrical or mechanical power to make them function; the former depend on our individual abilities and skills (particularly thinking, writing, speaking, and listening). Included in the software methods are such oral (face-to-face) communication activities as conversations, meetings, interviews, and discussions, as well as such written activities as memos, letters, bulletins, reports, proposals, policies, manuals, and so forth. Examples of hardware are telephone, teletype, microfilm, radio, walkie-talkie, videotape, and computer.

Purpose of flow refers to why messages are sent and received in organizations and what specific function they serve. Redding (1967) suggested three general reasons for message flow within an organization: task, maintenance, and human. Task messages relate to those products, services, or activities of specific concern to the organization—for example, messages about improving sales, markets, quality or service, quality of products, and so on. Maintenance messages, such as those pertaining to policy or regulation, help the organization to remain alive and perpetuate itself. Human messages are directed at people within the organizations their attitudes, morale, satisfaction, and fulfillment.

Thus, in any organization we recognize the different modalities, audiences, diffusion methods, and purposes of messages. Because we are primarily concerned with *speech communication* phenomena within organizations, usually limit our discussion of *message* behavior to include: *verbal/nonverbal* messages *orally diffused* to *internal audiences* for *task, maintenance, and human purposes.*

Networks

The following message[1] was communicated from a Colonel to a Major: "At nine o'clock tomorrow there will be an eclipse of the sun, something which does not occur every day. Get the men to fall out in the company street in their fatigues so that they will see this rare phenomenon, and I will then explain it to them. Now, in case of rain, we will not be able to see anything, of course, so then take the men to the gym." The Major passed on the message to the Captain: "By order of the Colonel tomorrow at nine o'clock there will be an eclipse of the sun. If it rains, you will not be able to see it from the company street, so, then, in fatigues, the eclipse of the sun will take place in the gym, something which does not occur every day." The Captain then said to the Lieutenant: "By order of the Colonel in fatigues tomorrow, at nine o'clock in the morning the inauguration of the eclipse of the sun will take place in the gym. The Colonel will give the order if it should rain, something which does occur every day." The Lieutenant then told the Sergeant: "Tomorrow at nine, the Colonel in fatigues will eclipse the sun in the gym, as it occurs every day if it's a nice day. If it rains, then this occurs in the company street." The Sergeant then assured the Corporal: "Tomorrow at nine, the eclipse of the colonel in fatigues will take place because of the sun. If it rains in the gym, something which does not take place every day, you will fall out in the company street."

Finally, one Private said to another Private: "Tomorrow, if it rains, it looks as if the sun will eclipse the Colonel in the gym. It's a shame that this does not occur every day." This example illustrates the most commonly written about pattern of communication within an organization—that which exists downward from superior to subordinate and so on until the message is diffused throughout the organization. By no means, however, is this pattern the only one used in most organizations. Organizations are composed of a series of people who occupy certain positions or roles. The flow of messages between and among these people exists over pathways called communication networks. It is entirely possible for a communication network to exist which includes only two people, a few people, or the entire organization. Many factors influence the nature and scope of the network:

- *Role relationship*—is the employee communicating according to a formally prescribed role or via an informal

---

[1]I first heard this story in a speech delivered by W.C. Redding at the University of New Mexico, March 6, 1973. The original source is believed to be the U.S. Army at West Point Academy, NY.

- *Direction of the message flow*—is the message flowing up, down, across, or diagonally throughout the organization?
- *Serial nature of message flow*—are details of the message being omitted, added, highlighted, or modified?
- *Content of the message*—is the message verbal or nonverbal, task, maintenance or human in purpose, hard or soft in diffusion method?

Interdependence

Earlier I defined an organization as an open system whose parts all related to its whole and its environment. I say that the nature of this relationship is interdependent or interlocking because all parts within the system affect and are affected by each other. This means that a change in any one part of the system will affect all other parts of the system. This means also that, in a sense, communication networks within an organization can be seen as *overlapping* one another.

Implications for the concept of interdependence center on the relationships between the people who occupy the various organizational roles. For example, when a manager makes a decision, he or she would be wise to account for the implications of his decision on the entire organization. Of course, one way to account for the interdependent relationships affected by and affecting a decision is to communicate all possible messages to all possible people within the organization. Naturally, this would cause the organization to collapse from information overload. On the other hand, too little information communicated may affect other variables such as morale, attitude, production, and turnover. Somewhere there exists an appropriate amount of messages that prove effective at maintaining the organization's existence without succumbing to overload in the system. To further illustrate the concept of interdependence I describe an incident here that occurred at the University of New Mexico.

A graduate teaching assistant once read a poem containing profane language to his English class. Word of this act reached one member of the New Mexico Legislature who loudly denounced the instructor, his deeds, and the entire university for apparently condoning this act. The legislator ultimately introduced a resolution into the legislature calling for a reduction of the university's budget to one dollar. Although the motion failed, public attitudes toward the university were negatively affected for several years. Even today, 7 years after the incident, some members of the public reported in an attitude survey that they still "hold it against the university for allowing swearing in class."

Relationships

The last of the four key concepts inherent in my definition of organizational communication is "relationship." Exactly what relationships are important for study in an organization? Because an organization is an open, living social system, its connecting parts function at the hands of people. In other words, the networks through which messages travel in organizations are connected by people. Thus, we are interested—by studying roles, positions, and nets—in studying the relationships among people. Human relationships within the organization are studied by focusing on the communication behavior of the people involved in the relationship. We study the effects of these behaviors on specific relationships within the organization's subparts as they interact with each other. We study employee attitudes, skills, and overall morale as they affect and are affected by their organizational relationships. When we focus on the major ways people relate to one another in an organization, we usually identify three: the dyad (two people interacting); the small group (3 to approximately 12 people interacting); and public relationships (interaction with large groups).

ORGANIZATIONAL COMMUNICATION RESEARCH

If we agree that organizational communication is the flow of messages within a network of interdependent relationships, what is the current state of our knowledge about organizational communication? After three decades of research, what have we learned about the way people send and receive messages in complex organizations? One scholar, attempting to answer that question (Redding, 1972), has concluded:

> through scientific and empirical study lies the only safe road to a valid and a practical understanding of human communication . . . in organizations. However, that road, at this point in time, is barely more than a tow-path for most of its length, full of holes and interrupted by numerous unfinished sections as well as washed-out bridges! (p. 6)

Redding went on to add, "The total output of reasonably scientific, empirically data-based-research efforts is very small indeed!" (p. 8). If Redding is correct, and I suspect he is, then we haven't learned very much in 30 years!

Possible reasons for this lack of generalizable conclusions related to organizational communication theory building may be found in the methodologies employed by the researchers themselves. Careful reviews of the organizational communication literature reveal that most studies have used survey or interview techniques, have been done in organizations with relatively small (but available) samples, have ignored the multivariate approach crucial to the complete understanding of an organization and its multiplicity of interdependent variables, have not carefully adhered to basic psychometric methods when using or designing measuring instruments, and have not replicated their procedures in a variety of different organizations.

Recognizing this lack of generalizability of conclusions about organizational communication, a group of researchers within the International Communication Association began the Communication Audit Project in 1972. For the past 4 years and led by myself, Gary Richetto of the Williams Companies of Tulsa, OK, and Harry Dennis of the Executive Committee of Milwaukee, WI, over 100 researchers from six countries have contributed to this project. The goals are to:

1. Establish a normed databank to enable comparisons to be made between organizations on their communication systems
2. Establish, through these comparative studies, a general external validation of many organizational communication theories and propositions
3. Provide research outlets for faculty and professionals and graduate students
4. Establish the International Communication Association as a visible center for organizational communication measurement.

The "communication audit" methodology of the ICA has several advantages not found in most research reported in the literature:

1. It uses a variety of measurement techniques (five) to converge on a core of communication behavior
2. It relies on cooperation from several large organizations providing a large sample for the database
3. It allows several multivariate comparisons among key organizational variables, especially by interfacing the findings of the five measurement techniques
4. It has been carefully and rigorously developed after 4 years of library research and five pilot tests in a wide variety of organizations
5. Its standardized measurement procedures allow for research replication and generalizability of findings.

During the past year, the "communication audit" has been successfully pilot tested in five organizations (a utility company, a hospital, a manufacturing company, a school system, and a U.S. Senator's office) with total samples exceeding 2,000 employees. As a result of our pilot tests, we have now been able to improve the validity and reliability of our instruments as well as maximize the efficiency of our entire audit procedure. We are currently making plans to do additional audits in the United States, Finland, England, Canada, and Mexico.

Although we have been involved in pilot tests of our audit procedure, we have begun to notice some commonalties among our conclusions about organizational communication in our clients' organizations. Some caution should be used in citing these findings; however, they do represent conclusions drawn from five different organizations, the data of which was all collected using standardized procedures and common instruments. I would like to conclude by mentioning some of our more commonly reported and repeated findings:

Concl

1. Most employees seem to like their immediate work environment and the people with whom they work closest—their work groups and immediate supervisors— but aren't that satisfied with their organization at large, its reward system, and their contributions to the organization as a whole.

2. Most employees are receiving the information they need to do their daily jobs, but are not receiving all the information they want, particularly related to organization-wide concerns, problems, goals, decisions, and mistakes; the exception is the manufacturing company, where downward communication was very effective on almost all subjects.

3. Opportunities exist for employees to voice their opinions upward, particularly about work activity and staff progress, but the existence of adequate and appropriate follow-up is definitely lacking at the top of most organizations; especially missing is the opportunity for adequate upward flow related to evaluating supervisors' performance.

4. Horizontal communication, particularly information sharing between work groups, is weak or nonexistent, creating some problems of mistrust and unnecessary conflict and/or competition.

5. Face-to-face and written channels of communication appear to operate more effectively than such hardware as bulletin boards, videotape presentations, telephones, and computer printouts.
6. Employees are least satisfied with information sources most removed from their immediate work environment (top management, their boss' superiors) and most satisfied with sources closest to their daily work performance (their boss, coworkers).
7. Of the four traits related to the quality of information (clarity, appropriateness, timeliness, believability), only timeliness—getting messages on time—appears to be a problem, particularly related to messages originating from top management.
8. The overall communication climate was more negative than positive for most of the organizations.
9. The most important communication problems experienced by employees related to the inadequacy or absence of information needed and/or wanted to do a good job, the misuse of authority or incorrectly following procedures to do a job, and ineffective interpersonal relationships due to personality clashes or poor cooperation.
10. In the larger organizations (over 500 employees) many employees are relatively isolated from both the necessary and incidental information flow.

We realize that these findings are only the beginning. Our ultimate goal is to build a databank large enough to allow most organizations to compare themselves on key communication behaviors. We live in an age of organizations and we are all affected by them every day. Organizations as communication systems are in a state of crisis mainly due to archaic structures and faulty communication. If we are to move beyond the "tow-path" of our current research status, if we are to improve the daily flow of information in organizations, if we are to build our databank of valid and reliable findings, then we must embark on an international cooperative research endeavor, heretofore unseen among communication professionals. Researchers must sacrifice individual designs and personal glories so that a commonly employed methodology, resulting in externally valid findings, will allow our theories of organizational communication to be built on a foundation of hard data. This, I submit to you, is the state of our art today and our challenge for the coming decades of tomorrow.

three

SHIFTING METAPHORS OF ORGANIZATIONAL COMMUNICATION: THE RISE OF DISCOURSE PERSPECTIVES

Linda L. Putnam

Texas A&M University

Organizational communication scholarship grew out of concerns for the ways that communication can contribute to organizational effectiveness. This instrumental view of communication dominated the field for several decades. Communication was a skill that made individuals more effective communicators on the job or a factor that contributed to system-wide effectiveness or ineffectiveness (Redding & Tompkins, 1988). Even when scholars entered the arenas of organizational culture, symbols, and meaning, the dominant thrust of this work centers on the instrumental use of communication. That is, to talk about how communication enables network development, facilitates organizational identification, promotes assimilation, or controls the worker is to center on the instrumental or "tool" nature of communication. In this chapter, I contend that traditional research domains in organizational communication are governed by instrumentality and that the emergent domains, ones grounded in discourse perspectives, have the potential to focus on expressive rather than instrumental concerns. This chapter also contends that organization communication scholars both inside and outside the field are shifting toward discourse perspectives rather than relying on conduit conceptions of communication. This discourse perspective, I contend, is consistent with the changes that are occurring in organizations and with the challenges that organizational communication scholars are likely to face in the next century.

SHIFTING GROUND IN ORGANIZATIONAL COMMUNICATION

The early 1980s marked a radical shift in organizational communication scholarship, although not necessarily a complete break with the past. Concomitant with similar critiques in organizational studies, scholars challenged the absence of theoretical frameworks and the nature of organizational reality embedded in traditional research (Putnam & Cheney, 1983; Redding & Tompkins, 1988). Nested within these critiques were challenges to the treatment of communication as a variable or a linear transmission (Putnam, 1983). Organizational communication became defined as "the study of messages, information, meaning, and symbolic activity" that constitutes organizations (Putnam & Cheney, 1985, p. 131). New research domains began to focus on the meanings of organizational events (Donnellon, Gray, & Bougon, 1986; Gray, Bougon, & Donnellon, 1985); strategic ambiguity (Eisenberg, 1984); language, symbols, and organizational culture (Frost, Moore, Louis, Lundberg, & Martin, 1985; Pacanowsky & O'Donnell-Trujillo, 1983; Pondy, Frost, Morgan, & Dandridge, 1983; Rosen, 1985; Smircich, 1983); organizational identification and unobtrusive control (Tompkins & Cheney, 1983, 1985); communication rules and scripts (Harris & Cronen, 1979; Schall, 1983); corporate public discourse (Cheney, 1983; Cheney & Vibbert, 1987; Grunig, 1984); and the exercise of power and control through distorted communication (Conrad, 1983; Deetz & Kersten, 1983; Edwards, 1979; Riley, 1983).

As R. C. Smith (1993, 1996), Taylor (1995), and Taylor, Cooren, Girous, & Robichand (1996) pointed out, organizational communication is also struggling at the metatheoretical level with the relationship between communication and organization. R. C. Smith's (1993, 1994) relational metaphors provide a foundation for understanding alternative perspectives of organizational communication. Her insights about the way domains within the field cast this relationship as possession, containment, production, comparison, and equivalence are provocative ways of assessing the consistency/inconsistency of representation in the field. In like manner, Taylor's (1993, 1995) work on conversation and text as metaphors of equivalency in the organizational communication relationship challenge our conceptualizations of research domains. My position parallels many of their ideas, but differs from their approaches in the level in which I address domains in the field. However, I will refer back to their work in my discussion of the evolution and shifts in organizational communication research domains.

DOMINANT PERSPECTIVES IN RESEARCH DOMAINS

Four dominant perspectives in organizational communication have governed research and thinking in the past. These perspectives function as metaphors of communication or as ways of understanding domains and orientations to research. The four perspectives include: conduit, lens, linkage, and symbol (see Table 3.1). By selecting these labels, I am privileging communication as figure and placing organization as ground. I argue in another work (Putnam, Phillips, & Chapman, in press) that metaphors of both processes are embodied in any form of representation, but for the purposes of this chapter, I am centering on the way communication is conceived in these relationships. Even though these perspectives differ in ontological and epistemological roots of organizations, they embrace a common orientation to communication in the literature. Moreover, the challenges that emerging perspectives—namely, performance, voice, and discourse—face is to move out of an instrumental orientation into a new role for communication in a postmodern era.

The evolution and development of organizational communication studies parallel research in other areas of our field. The *conduit* perspectives (Axley, 1984; Reddy, 1979) of communication that cast organizations as containers permeates the field's functionalist literature, as R. C. Smith (1996) pointed out. However, it is not simply that organizations are containers for communication or that internal and external are clearly demarcated, it is the notion that communication within this perspective aims to accomplish the instrumental goals, such as convey information accurately, achieve task objectives, and serve organizational functions. A vast majority of the current research that centers on adoption and use of communication technologies, improving performance feedback, and fostering organizational change is driven by not only, conduit assumptions of message flow, but also conceptualizations of communication as a tool.

The *lens* perspective of organizational communication treats communication as a filter that centers on the searching, retrieving, and routing of information. Research on information flow and decision

Table 3.1. Dominant Perspectives of Organizational Communication.

Perspective	Definition	Research Areas
Conduit	Transmission of information between senders and receiver Organizations as containers	Adoption of communication technology Information overload Task coordination
Lens	Filter that protects, shields, searches, retrieves, and routes information Organization as information-processing system	Information flow and decision making Media richness Information distortion Perceived environmental uncertainty Performance feedback
Linkage	Connector that ties people together Organizations as networks of relationships	Network roles and configurations Density of links Informal networks Weak and strong ties
Symbol	The creation, maintenance, and transformation of meaning Sensemaking Organizations as symbolic milieu	Organizational narratives Rites and rituals Organizational cultures Cultural change

making, superior- subordinate communication, perceived environmental uncertainty, performance feedback, media richness, and communication technology adopt a lens perspective by treating organizations as sensors, brains, and information-processing organisms. The instrumental nature of communication is evident in concerns for performance monitoring (Huber, 1991), defining stakeholder relationships (Grunig & Grunig, 1992), and enhancing effectiveness through matching media with the organizational task (Daft, Lengel, & Trevino, 1987). Although this perspective adopts many assumptions of a containment view of the communication and organization relationship, it also treats organizations as communication through the information-processing modality that governs much of this work. Organizations, then, are not simply containers for communication; rather they are information-processing systems. At the comparison level, organizations are understood as communication.

Another perspective of communication that surfaces in the literature is *linkage* or *connector*. In this view, communication produces organizations as networks of interconnected relationships. The literature on network roles and structures, however, tends to adopt a stance that organizations produce linkages, whereas work on emergent networks places communication as the producer of organizations. Linkage, however, as Taylor (1993) pointed out, is often a variation of linear models of communication. Specifically, the degree of participation or inclusion in networks stems from the presence or absence of a link, the amount of communication exchanged, the directionality of messages, and the type of content discussed. Although network studies have a descriptive cast, they also wrestle with instrumental questions to show that dense networks aid in adopting new ideas and facilitating positive attitudes toward new technologies (Albrecht & Hall, 1991; Fulk, 1993). Even comparisons among strong and weak ties center on the role of tight couplings in adapting to environmental changes, enhancing legitimacy, meeting regulatory requirements, and forming opportunities for transcending organizational boundaries (Granovetter, 1973; Papa, 1990; Stohl, 1995). Thus, network research is also driven by ways that linkages serve instrumental ends.

Finally, the *symbol* perspective shifts the foci to communication as the creation, maintenance, and transformation of meaning. Communication is sensemaking through the production of symbols that make the world meaningful. Rooted in the links between symbols and culture, the relationship between communication and organization varies in this literature. Some studies, as R. C. Smith (1996) noted, illustrate how communication produces culture, whereas other literature presumes the existence of culture and examines the role of meaning as contained within organizations or as the way that organizations produce sensemaking.

Even though researchers emphasize the complex meanings that characterize organizational life, they conceive of narratives, rites and rituals, and metaphors as instruments that socialize newcomers (M. H. Brown, 1985), legitimate power relationships (Mumby, 1987), enhance identification (Kreps, 1989), perform managerial roles (Trujillo, 1985), and act as implicit mechanisms of control (Kunda, 1992). Rites and rituals make public the private values of an organization's culture. They serve instrumental functions by conferring status, evaluating performance, anointing membership, and recognizing commitment (Rosen, 1985; Trice & Beyer, 1984). Practitioners often employ symbols to diagnose problems, to change cultures, and to enhance organizational effectiveness (Coffman & Eblen, 1987).

In these traditional perspectives, the conceptualization of communication is guided by instrumental goals and needs. This situation is not in itself detrimental; however, I contend that the relationship of communication and organization is defined fundamentally through communication serving organizational ends. The changes that I see in more recent approaches to organizational communication is the potential, if not the practice, of altering the dependency of communication on organizational instrumentality. The issue is not simply eliminating rationality as a guiding principle of organizing, but the way in which researchers and scholars conceive of the communication and organization relationship has been fundamentally rooted in instrumentality.

EMERGENT PERSPECTIVES IN RESEARCH DOMAINS

Three emergent perspectives offer the potential to ground communication and organization in a relationship that redefines or changes the bond between instrumentality, communication, and organization. These emergent perspectives are performance, voice, and discourse (see Table 3.2). In the *performance* perspective, *social interaction* becomes the focal point for organizational communication research. Performance refers to process and activity, rather than to an organization's productivity or output. Performance combines Turner's (1980) view of "accomplishment" with Goffman's (1959) notion of "presentation." In this metaphor, "organizational reality is brought to life in communicative performances" (Pacanowsky & O'Donnell-Trujillo, 1983, p. 131). Communication consists of interconnected exchanges, for example, message–feedback–response, action–reaction–adjustment, symbolic action–interpretation– reflection, and action–sense–making. Social interaction is rooted in the sequences, patterns, and meanings that stem from exchanging verbal and nonverbal messages.

Table 3.2. Emerging Perspectives of Organizational Communication.

Perspective	Definition	Research Areas
Performance	Organizations as coordinated actions Social interactions Process and activity as patterns of meaning	Dynamic processes Interlocked behavior Sequences of events Streams of experience Reflexivity
Voice	Expressions and suppression of organizational members Equality of voice Effort to be heard Occasions to speak	Power and control Suppressed conflict Empowerment Participation Marginality
Discourse	The way organizational understanding is produced and reproduced through language Languages, grammars, and discursive acts that form conversation Organizations as texts	Discursive practices Discourse as knowledge Dialogue

University
of Ulster
LIBRARY

The key features of this perspective are dynamic processes, interlocking behaviors, reflexivity, sensemaking, and collaboration (Fisher, 1978). Performances, then, are interactional, contextual, episodic, and improvisational (Pacanowsky & O'Donnell-Trujillo, 1983). Communication becomes part of an ongoing series of cues, without a clear beginning and ending. Individuals bracket or punctuate streams of experience to make sense of their interactions (Watzlawick, Beavin, & Jackson, 1967; Weick, 1979). Communicative acts form patterns of contiguous acts, interlocked behaviors, episodes, and incidents. Rather than centering on task activities, organizational communication functions as passion developed through organizational storytelling, sociality through performing small talk, and politics through displaying personal strength (Pacanowsky & O'Donnell-Trujillo, 1983). Communication centers on coproduction as it surfaces in research on structuration, but also on the structure–action relationship that redefines the nature of instrumentality. Communication as a constitutive process no longer services organizational ends. Rather through a reciprocal relationship, instrumentality becomes the codevelopment of organizing.

In the performance perspective, organizations emerge as *coordinated actions*. That is, both communicating and organizing are the enacting of rules, structures, and environments through social interaction. Performance, however, serves as an umbrella for perspectives that stem from such diverse roots as cybernetic theory, self-referential systems, dramaturgy, symbolic interaction, phenomenology, and hermeneutics. These schools cluster into the categories of enactment (Weick, 1979); coproduction (Boje, 1991; Eisenberg, 1990); and storytelling (Boje, 1991, 1995; Jones, Moore, & Snyder, 1988). Social interaction is both behavioral and symbolic, with a simultaneous emphasis on action and sensemaking (see Table 3.3). Storytelling in this metaphor is not monologic but interactionally achieved through discourse (Boje, 1991). Storytellers and listeners serve as coauthors to simultaneous construct and make sense of their interactions. Researchers act as organizational detectives who engage in storytelling through constructing plots based on organizational talk (Goodall, 1989) and through writing and staging organizations as theatrical productions (Mangham & Overington, 1987).

Enactment serves as a heuristic in which organizational scholars theorize about the role of communication in organizational culture (Bantz, 1989, 1993); strategic management (Gioia, 1986; Smircich & Stubbart, 1985); negotiation and conflict management (Putnam, 1989); and public relations (Sproule, 1989). Enactment liberates organizational environments from being objective events assessed through measures of turbulence, complexity, and load. In the enactment perspective,

Table 3.3. Performance Perspectives of Organizational Communication.

Perspective	Definition	Research Areas
Enactment	Bracketing or punctuating streams of ongoing experience Action–reaction–adjustment	Message equivocality Environmental uncertainty Organizational change Self-referential systems
Co-production	Collaborative performance Coproducing meaning Coconstructing social activities	Jazz performances Improvisations Jamming Coorientation
Storytelling	Coproduction of stories How members introduce stories in conversations How listeners prompt storytellers How stories change and unravel	Story chaining Symbolic convergence theory Organizational images and identities

organizational environments are constructions. Organizations enact their environments, which they, in turn, rediscover and use to constrain or to enable future actions.

Organizations surface as charades, improvisational theater, orchestras, and soliloquies. Soliloquy serves as the forerunner of self-organizing systems (Lotman, 1977; Luhmann, 1990). Organizations talk to themselves to clarify their surroundings and they act to discover what they are doing. The application of self-referential or autocommunication systems to organizations provides new insights into the ways that organizations develop identities and markets through interactions with stakeholders and publics (Cheney & Christensen, in press; Steier & Smith, 1996). Both the enactment and the soliloquy approaches treat communication as producing organizations.

Coproductions are collaborative performances that stem from the way participants producing social practices and coordinating local agreements. For example, improvisations or jazz performances are not simply in the minds of musicians who create their environments; they are worked out through mutual responsiveness, complex verbal and nonverbal cues, shared focus and attention, and altercasting (Bastien & Hostager, 1988, 1992). The dynamic and simultaneous flow of performance and the joint cueing of meanings of the event leads to coconstructing improvisations.

In like manner, *jamming* is a coproduction in which participants experience a transcendence through suspending self-consciousness, co-orienting to each other, and surrendering to the experience (Eisenberg, 1990). Jamming reflects those moments in which organizing magically comes together as in the "flow and zone" of street basketball or a serendipitous encounter of guitarists. As the metaphor of performance suggests, jamming and improvisation treat communication and organizations as coconstructing each other. Communication produces organizations whereas organizations produce communication.

Another way in which organizational members coconstruct performances is through *storytelling*. Storytelling is how members dramatize organizational life and transform mundane events into passions and zeal (Pacanowsky & O'Donnell-Trujillo, 1983). This approach focuses on the way organizational members introduce stories in conversations; how listeners coproduce them through prompting the teller; how stories unravel through subsequent performances of sharing them (Boje, 1991). Stories, then, are not simply cultural artifacts or monologues, rather they emerge as performances that are never complete. Storytelling is often challenged by the listener who interrupts and adds elements to the narrative. Individuals often tell bits and pieces of stories with elaboration developed through pattern fitting. The chaining out of a story is adapted to different audiences through highlighting, eliminating, or modifying the narrative. Communication serves organizations as the process of organizing; thus, it remains instrumental, but shifts the definition of instrumentality away from means–end to process–action. Therefore, the performance perspective redefines instrumentality and casts the communication-organization relationship in a new light.

At the macro level of analysis, organizations are also storytellers. Their images and identities emerge, in part, from the narratives that they construct with different publics (Alvesson, 1990). In a postmodern world in which the presence of grand narratives is problematic (Lyotard, 1984), images become hyperreal; that is, many competing narratives surface, become disassociated from their signifiers, and vie for representational space (Baudrillard, 1983). Images represent a world of flickering visions that play on other images, making it difficult to distinguish between the real and the pseudoevents (Boorstin, 1961). Storytelling about organizations entails a plurality of narratives with multiple voices and interpretations (Boje, 1995). An organization such as Disney Studios aims to write its own historical narrative, but in trying to tell its story, it conflicts with and marginalizes some discourses while privileging others. Enactment, coconstructing, and storytelling represent three diverse but related threads of the performance perspective. This approach treats communication as an outgrowth of a collaborative process in which social and symbolic interaction is dynamic, interconnected, reflexive, and simultaneous. Instrumentality is defined as the process that produces the action of organizing.

An alternative perspective for studying organizational communication is the notion of *voice* that centers on who can speak, when, and in what way. To have a voice is to be able to speak in the context of the organization; organizations, then, exist as a chorus of member voices. The idea of communication as voice clusters into categories of distorted voices, voices of domination, different voices, and access to voice (see Table 3.4). In *distorted voices*, members are able to speak, but not in ways that represent their interests (Alvesson, 1993b; Deetz, 1992a; Haslett, 1990; Thompson, 1984, 1990). Such ideological aspects (Eagleton, 1991; Therborn, 1980; Thompson, 1984) of communication draw attention to the role that meaning plays in the service of power (Fairclough, 1992; Thompson, 1990). Thus, the study of ideology generally focuses on the ways that powerful groups use communication for organizational control (Tompkins & Cheney, 1985; also see Alvesson, 1993b; Barker, 1993; N. Phillips & Brown, 1993). Distorted voices shapes members' ways of speaking, their understandings, and the structures and practices that constitute the organization (Mumby, 1988). Power and meaning join together to distort

Table 3.4. Voice Perspectives of Organizational Communication.

Perspective	Definition	Research Areas
Distorted Voices	Suppression of communication Speaking in organizations to represent employee interests	Ideology Power and meaning Resistance
Voice of Domination	Habitual communication conceals the interests of dominant group	Hegemony Dominant coalitions Emancipation Cooperative control Unobtrusive controls
In a Different Voice	Voices that are ignored, silenced, or misunderstood Biases in patriarchal organizations	Gender Race and Ethnicity Women's experience Marginalized groups
Access to Voice	Speaking that influences decisions, changes organizations, and increases participation Communication as expression	Participation Involvement Workplace democracy Alternative organizational forms Empowerment

voices so that even though voices may be heard, they echo the sentiments of the elite (Clair, 1993a, 1993b).

In the *voice of domination,* speaking becomes hegemonic in that patterns of activity and institutional arrangements culminate in common sense, thus concealing the choices and interests of the dominant group (Deetz, 1992a, 1992b; Deetz & Mumby, 1990; Fairclough, 1992; Mumby, forthcoming). Hegemony exists in everyday activities and influences the way dominant coalitions control organizations through political, cultural, and economic actions (Deetz, 1992b). Deetz's (1992a) study of the role of the corporation in modern society illustrates how the political ideology of managerialism has become hegemonic in that no other solution to organizational problems seems conceivable. As a result, the corporation as the primary institution in society continues to encroach on activities traditionally organized in other ways. Corporations control everything from personal identity to the use of natural resources to definitions of value and distribution of goods and services. Although the study of distorted and dominant voices appears to treat communication as a means of organizational control, I view the relationship as more complex. Communication remains instrumental in this perspective, but it functions not in an overt means–end orientation. Rather, it is the outgrowth of expression and suppression. Thus, the voice perspective of critical theorists alters the view of instrumentality by treating communication as voice that enables expression or suppression. The tautological nature of this relationship suggests that this perspective supports a relationship of being between communication and organization.

The voice perspective finds its most direct and common usage in feminist organizational studies (e.g., Bullis, 1993; Buzzanell, 1994; Fine, 1993; Marshall, 1993b). This work highlights the fact that some people need to speak *in a different voice.* Because their voices are unique, they are often ignored, silenced, or misunderstood. The idea of speaking in a different voice appears in two guises. First, researchers must speak differently (Mumby, 1993b) to uncover the bias inherent in the way we talk about gender and organizations. Feminist scholars are developing ways of speaking that challenge the unexamined assumptions about patriarchal organizations and that represent women's experiences in organizations. Because the voice that expresses women's experience is often silenced (Clair, 1993b, Marshall, 1993b), researchers must work against the backdrop of patriarchy in trying to communicate authentically about women's organizational experiences. Dominant academic forms that shape writing styles and research methods limits efforts to undo the gendered pattern of theorizing (Marshall, 1993b). Feminist literature, then, addresses issues of gaining a voice for academic writers and "unlearning to not speak" (Piercy, 1973).

A second way in which a different voice guides organizational scholarship is concern about the patriarchal bias in organizations. Researchers center on the way this bias limits opportunities for women to participate as women in organizational activities (Bullis, 1993; Marshall, 1993b; Rakow, 1986). Organizational communication practices that range from conversational turn taking to storytelling enact gendered organizations and recreate gender inequality (Bullis, 1993). These studies question the role of communication in constructing gendered organizations and the need for research to move away from treating gender as a variable to conceiving of it as a fundamental organizing principle (Marshall, 1993b).

This notion of a different voice extends to issues of race and ethnicity in organizations. Work in this area examines the communication practices through which race and ethnicity are accomplished (Frankenberg, 1993; Y. Kim, 1994; Nakayama & Kriziek, 1995) and the role of race and ethnicity in organizations (Nkomo, 1992). In each case, a central concern is that minority groups are marginalized because they speak in a different voice. In a different voice, the instrumental relationship between communication and organization draw from suppression/expression but becomes rooted not in dominant coalitions or elites, but in patriarchal practices and ways of knowing. Organizations, therefore, service voice through constituting patriarchal structures and ways of knowing; voice services organizing through reconstituting these ways of knowing.

Another metaphor in the cluster of voice is *access to voice*. In traditional, hierarchical organizations, voice typically refers to participatory processes of organizing. Although most research that studies access to voice targets traditional bureaucratic organizations, other work focuses on alternative organizational forms such as democratic institutions (Cheney, 1995; Deetz, 1992a; Harrison, 1994; Rothschild-Whitt, 1986). These organizations take specific steps to provide members with access to voice. Alternative organizational forms demonstrate how communication develops interdependence and provides a balanced understanding of institutions (Harrison, 1994). Democratic organizations also provide a basis on which to critique traditional bureaucratic forms.

In any movement toward democratization, employees face the assymetry of power based on managerial possession of capital (W. I. Gordon, 1994, p. 286). Consequently, workers find it difficult to develop ways of "making a difference through voice". For example, Barker (1993) provided an ethnographic account of "self-regulated work teams" designed to free employees from bureaucratic control. But rather than freeing workers, the system of concertive control that was developed was more powerful, more invisible, and more difficult to resist than the former managerial control. In this orientation, voice is expression that promotes democracy and new organizational forms; hence, access to voice returns to some of the traditional ways in which we conceive of the instrumental relationship of communication and organization. However, throughout the voice perspectives, communication becomes more than a means to an end. Expression and suppression are more than products, even though they are outgrowths of organizing. Rather, communication becomes expression, and communication and organization exist in a relationship of being (R. C. Smith, 1996).

Voice as a perspective on organizational communication brings together different orientations to the issues of speaking, hearing, and making a difference in organizations. Communication functions simultaneously to express and suppress voice; that is, voices may be heard but they are distorted or dominated; new voices may be added to change existing assymetries, but they result in merely echo them. The organization constitutes a chorus of diverse and often muted voices; the tune they sing is not always clear. The relationship between organization and communication remains instrumental, but instrumentality is reconstituted as expression rather than rational goal attainment or enactment of actions and structures.

The *discourse* perspective offers another alternative to the role of instrumentality—one that decenters means–ends function of communication and privileges the role of conversation in developing community. Discourse refers to language, grammars, and discursive acts that form the foundation of both performance and voice. In the discourse metaphors, communication is a *conversation* in that it focuses on both process and structure, on collective action as joint accomplishment, on dialogue among partners, on features of the context, and on micro–and macroprocesses (Taylor, 1993). Conversation is a simile for organizations. In fact, Bergquist (1993) contended that conversations are both the essence and the product of organizations in that conversations lay the groundwork for community.

Conversation is immediate in its claim on attention, instantaneous in its moment to moment occurrence, and fleeting or ephemeral in its form, yet it relies on patterns that become culturally sanctioned, frames that presuppose prior knowledge, and macroprocesses in which individuals speak as representatives for others (Taylor, 1993). Discourse foregrounds language as the nexus for untangling relationships among meaning, context, and praxis. In the discourse perspective, communication casts organizations as *texts* (Barthes, 1981; Geertz, 1983; Ricoeur, 1979). Texts are sets of structured events or ritualized patterns of interaction that transcend immediate conversations (Taylor, 1993). However, scholars differ in the various senses in which they use texts (a) as the discursive acts inscribed in institutions, (b) as the interpretations of organizational life, and (c) as the ways that organizations are written or authored (Cheney & Tompkins, 1988).

Traditional studies of language and organizational communication center on discourse either as an artifact of organizational culture or as speech acts that serve instrumental needs of organizing (see Putnam & Fairhurst, forthcoming). Either language serves to classify and reflect organizational structures or it performs relational and organizational functions through speech acts. This traditional approach to the study of discourse is evident in studies of ethnography of speaking (Gregory, 1983; Van Maanen, 1973), conversational analysis of performance appraisals or job interview (Morris, 1988; Ragan, 1983); studies of leadership (Fairhurst, 1993; Gronn, 1983), and interactional analysis of group decision making and negotiation (DeSanctis & Poole, 1994; Putnam & Roloff, 1992).

The study of organizational communication as *discursive practices*, however, has broadened the scope of discourse analysis and altered the instrumental relationship between communication and organization. This perspective subsumes research on language as emotional expressions, as genres, as paradox, and as dialogue (see Table 3.5). Discourse, in this orientation, is the way that organizational understanding is produced and reproduced. Labels such as "ideal patient" and "healthcare provider" are not simply terms that classify occupational groups; rather they define expectations, forms of knowledge, and task activities for organizational groups. Adjustments to new organizational experiences may stem from the way that discourse reconstitutes these institutional labels (Loseke, 1989; Sigman, 1986).

Emotion expressions as discursive acts center on the way that members produce organizational knowledge through regulation and control (Conrad & Witte, 1994; Fineman, 1993; Waldron, 1994). Regulation occurs through display rules that translate discourse and emotions into acceptable organizational forms (Hochschild, 1983; Rafaeli & Sutton, 1987; Waldron & Krone, 1991). Emotional expression is intertwined with dichotomies that privilege a rational view of work and marginalize the private, feminine, and informal side of organizational life (Mumby & Putnam, 1992; Putnam & Mumby, 1993). Both the display and the interpretation of emotion hinge on the way that feelings are legitimated and the social costs for displaying emotions (Conrad & Witte, 1994).

Table 3.5. Discourse Perspectives of Organizational Communication.

Perspective	Definition	Research Areas
Emotional expression	The way organizations regulate and interpret expressions of feelings	Emotional labor Display rules Emotional control
Communication genres	Recurring patterns of communicative practices that form interaction routines Institutional templates for social interaction	Communication technologies like memos, meetings, and reports Types of institutional discourse like interviews, legal discourse, and consultations
Paradoxes and irony	Statements and actions that contradict intended meanings	Organizational learning Organizational change Double-bind messages Fragmentation and ambiguity
Dialogue	Authentic deliberations among organizational members Share and learn from experiences Foster deeper understanding	Organizational learning Representing diverse voices Organizational and individual identities Fragmented self

Emotional expression functions as a discursive practice when it is treated as knowledge; that is, language is the depository of reconstructed discourses that legitimate particular practices (Deetz, 1992a). Discourse in this orientation overlaps with the treatment of communication as voice and centers on historically situated thoughts, expressions, and actions (Foucault, 1980). Through embedding discursive practices in history, language functions as an institutional text. Genres or technologies such as interviews, therapeutic discourse, and legal discourse embody social and institutional conventions. Hence, the selection interview is not simply a language game of questions and answers, it is a genre that incorporates bureaucratic placement, market demands, and employee relationships into its discursive practice (Fairclough, 1989).

The study of *communication genres* as discursive practices centers on the form, audience, and sociohistorical situation (Yates & Orlikowski, 1992). Developed from structuration theory, genres are recurring patterns of communicative practices that form types of interaction, for example, reports, memos, meetings, and email. Organizational members enact genres for particular purposes; hence, they become institutional templates for social interaction (Orlikowski & Yates, 1994). However, member actions can deviate from genre templates and change an organization's discourse (Yates, 1993); thus, as people interact, they draw on rules developed through tradition to produce, reproduce, and change genres. Orlikowski and Yates (1994) showed how the presence and the absence of genres such as memos, reference manuals, and dialogue establish an organization's identity as temporary, accountable to a professional community, and flexible in work processes.

Paradoxes and ironies as discursive practices focus on relationships among discourse, meaning, and praxis. *Paradoxes* are statements and actions that are self-contradictory, but seemingly true (Putnam, 1986), whereas irony arises when intended meanings contradict customary meanings (R. H. Brown, 1977). Paradoxical goals can lead to enacting reward structures and operating procedures that violate the overall mission of the organization. For instance, orphanages that develop stringent rules to limit adoptions work against their goals of getting children placed in homes; seniority systems that reward longevity contradict the goals of meritorious performance (Kerr, 1975).

Paradoxes are evident in double-loop learning and organizational changes (Argyris, 1988; Ford & Backoff, 1988; O'Connor, 1995); incongruities between individual and group goals (K. K. Smith & Berg, 1987); dialectical tensions rooted in the "deep structures" of organization life (Benson, 1977; Putnam, 1986); and double-bind messages in superior-subordinate communication (Putnam, 1986;

Tompkins & Cheney, 1985). They appear in the interwoven but oppositional forces that evoke organizational change, namely through struggles between action and structure, internal and external, and stability and instability (Van de Ven & Poole, 1988). Ironic remarks and ironic humor acknowledge the contradictory and paradoxical nature of organizing by disrupting historical frames through reversals in meanings (Filby & Willmott, 1988; Hatch & Ehrlich, 1993; Kunda, 1992). Irony transforms organizational experiences by providing members with an opportunity to confront new versions of social reality and grasp unthinkable propositions (Hatch & Sanford, 1993). In a postmodern world characterized by rapid changes and fragmentation, the management of ironies and paradoxes becomes particularly vital. Understanding and accepting paradoxes as discursive practices becomes a way of navigating in a world defined by ironies and junctures (Smith & Berg, 1987).

Another discursive practice, *dialogue*, also stems from assumptions about postmodern organizations. Participants who engage in dialogue suspend defensive exchange, share and learn from experiences, foster deeper inquiry, and resist synthesis or compromise (Eisenberg & Goodall, 1993). Drawn from Bakhtin (1981) and Buber (1985), dialogue strives for a balance between individual autonomy and organizational constraint through incorporating diverse voices. Dialogue can transform action and promote organizational learning through developing synergy, empathy, and authentic deliberation among individuals (Evered & Tannebaum, 1992; Isaacs, 1993b). Dialogue legitimates each person's experience from connecting with others to determine what counts as knowledge and how it is valued. Self-recognition and transformation arise from the additive nature in which each person's experience contributes to the whole (Eisenberg, 1994).

Although dialogue places humanism at the forefront of organizing, it often misses the politics of experience by grounding discourse in individual identity. When dialogue incorporates postmodernism, it emphasizes how discourse decenters subjects and fragments identities, situates meanings, and locates power in systems that normalize discursive practices (Deetz, forthcoming). By rejecting the notion of autonomous, self-determined individuals, theorists treat discourse as producing identity and as spoken by different selves; thus, the individual is fragmented. Fragmentation provides an opportunity for dialogue, as Townley (1993) illustrated in his essay on discourses of human resource management.

In this poststructuralist treatment of dialogue, meaning is fragmented and localized rather than being universal or fixed. Even words like "the bottom line," "profit and loss," and particular accounting practices have meaning only within the localized, situated discourses that create them (P. Miller & O'Leary, 1987). A deconstruction of management theories demonstrates how organizational texts are localized meanings that often marginalize the voices of those who are absent in these works (Mumby & Putnam, 1992). Finally, consistent with notions of distorted voices, power resides in discourse, not through dominant coalitions, but through the way discursive practices like discipline and surveillance become normalized in social interactions (Foucault, 1977; Knights, 1992).

Treating organizational communication as a discursive practice clarifies the relationship between discourse and texts. A text is the structured sets of events that comprise the organization. These events, created and reconstituted through discourse, have symbolic meaning to participants. A text as symbolic meaning substitutes for treating organizations as objects or entities. Texts are the gestalt meanings aligned with the underlying frames of discursive practices (Strine, 1988; Taylor, 1993). The organizational text, however, should not be treated as a social fact or as a "fixed" meaning. Rather, texts are symbolic forms, open to multiple and unlimited readings, frequently ruptured displays, reflexivity between authors and texts, and concerns for transcendence and transformation (Strine, 1988). Researchers serve as authors who produce both the texts and the readings of the texts as they engage in organizational studies (Cheney & Tompkins, 1988). In the discourse perspective, instrumentality is decentered. Discursive acts as constituted through discourse, normative actions, and localized meanings are not simply expressions they are organizations. Organization and communication become equivalent through the discourse that forms texts.

DISCUSSION AND CONCLUSIONS

This chapter notes changes in research domains through reviewing different perspectives that appear in our literature over the past 15 years. These perspectives represent different orientations to the way instrumentality functions in the communication–organization relationship. I contend that the instrumental aspect of communication and organization is critical to understanding the nature of both constructs.

In general, recent perspectives in organizational communication are moving toward "the linguistic turn in social sciences." The changes in research domains are responding to Pondy and Mitroff's (1979) appeal to embrace language-based conceptions of organizations. Boje (1995) echoed this appeal by claiming that "it is time to . . . move [organizational theory] to discursive metaphors, such as Lyotard's (1984) 'conversation,' Bakhtin's (1981) 'novel,' and Thachankary's (1992) 'text' (p. 1000). The growth of research domains that embrace emotional expression, knowledge, communication genres, paradox, and dialogue attest to this movement in the field. Performance and voice, as precursors to discourse perspectives, also embody assumptions about communication that differ from the tool perspectives evident in conceiving of communication as a conduit, lens, or network.

The instrumental relationship between communication and organization is fundamental to understanding emerging perspectives in the field. Basically, traditional research domains, including the more recent studies of symbols and culture, espouse a view of communication as a means to organizational ends or organizing as a means to communication ends. Research on uses of communication technology, the functions of communication in conflict management, the development of bridges and networks, and information processing in the socialization of newcomers exemplifies this instrumental view. The tool conception of the communication–organization relationship is not simply casting communication as a skill or a system within organizations; rather it represents an ontological stance about organizational communication.

More recent approaches to the study of organizational communication challenge both the definition and centrality of instrumentality. In the performance perspective, communication remains in an instrumental relationship with organization, but the relationship is process–action rather than means–end. In the voice metaphor, instrumentality becomes redefined as expression or suppression rather than being rooted in the rational models of goals, structures, and functions. Finally, in the discourse perspectives, communication is equated with discursive acts that not only constitute organizations but also become the organizing process. Dialogue is community, paradox is fragmentation and ambiguity, and conversations and genres are texts. Thus, new domains of organizational communication reconceptualize instrumentality or decenter it as the essential element in the communication– organization relationship.

part three

ORGANIZATIONAL COMMUNICATION THEORY

four

PROLEGOMENA TO A PRIMITIVE THEORY OF HUMAN COMMUNICATION IN HUMAN ORGANIZATIONS

Frank E. X. Dance
University of Denver

Human communication refers specifically to those communicative abilities and practices peculiar to, and seemingly unique to, human beings. Whereas the repertoire used by humans when communicating may include behaviors drawn from nonhuman animal communicative skills and behaviors, "human communication" as used here, although acknowledging the possible nonhuman animal components, focuses on those aspects of the communicative repertoire of humans that seem to be unique to humans. Although the human communication scholar may be interested in nonhuman animal communication (or what is truly "nonverbal" communication) the human communication scholar is interested in animal communication solely insofar as the animal communication studies enhance the scholar's understanding of human communication. That which is uniquely human in human communication is spoken symbolism and spoken symbolic interaction or speech communication (Dance, 1975).

In this chapter I shall try to accomplish two objectives. First, I explain my use of the term theory and compare and contrast theories of human communication with theories of organizations. Second, I set forth the beginnings of a primitive theory of human communication in human organizations.

THEORY

Theory is a way of organizing reality, happenings, occurrences (Kaplan, 1964). A theory has as its goals to explain, to predict and at times to control. Explanation in theory construction precedes organization, prediction, or control, and explanation and prediction may lead to a sense of understanding. In the end, theory should produce a "sense of understanding" (Reynolds, 1971).

Theories vary in the range of their descriptions and the elegance of their explanations. Hjelmslev's (1961) "empirical principle" states that a theory's:

> description shall be free from contradiction (self-consistent), exhaustive, and as simple as possible. The requirement of freedom from contradiction takes precedence over the requirement of exhaustive description; the requirement of exhaustive description takes precedence over the requirement of simplicity. (p. 11)

In other words, a theory should have internal consistency as it balances the tensions between range and elegance.

A theory may be eclectic or primitive (see Reynolds, 1971; Zetterberg, 1965). An *eclectic* theory is a theory that is derived from sources or research outside of the discipline in which the theory is proposed. For example, the field (or discipline) of medicine is heavily dependent on the disciplines of biology, chemistry, and so forth for its content. There are some who would say that the field of human communication is almost totally derived from bits and pieces of other disciplines such as psychology, sociology, history, and so on.

A *primitive* theory is a theory that is fundamentally derived from within the conceptual structure of the discipline within which it is presented. For example, "set theory" within mathematics would be a primitive theory. There are currently efforts to set forth a primitive theory of human communication. It is important to note that a primitive theory, although substantively derived from the terms and concepts primitive to the discipline within which it is set forth, may be justifiably and appropriately supported by facts and interpretations from outside of the discipline. In other words, a primitive theory may derive its support both primitively and eclectically.

Human communication theory, therefore, consists of statements about human communication *beyond* a specific communicative event, which statements may serve to:

1. Explain (thus enabling organization, and facilitating our ability to)
2. Predict (thus, in combination with explanation, facilitating our ability to)
3. Understand (and at times to)
4. Control

A theory of human communication may be either primitive or eclectic. From my point of view almost all current efforts to build a theory of human communication are fundamentally eclectic (see Figure 4.1).

Organizations utilize a number of theories. Organizations, in their quest after successful operation, utilize theories derived from economics, psychology, anthropology, sociology, and others. As far as I

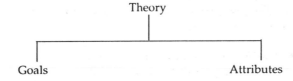

Theory

Goals

1. *To Explain* how the phenomenon works or happens. How well the theory explains is a measure of its power.

2. *To Predict* when the phenomenon will occur, work, or happen. How accurately the theory predicts is a measure of its precision.

3. *To Control* its working or happening.
   a. To make it work or happen,
   b. To prevent it from working or happening
   c. To abort its working or happening,
   d. To interfere with its working or happening.

Attributes

1. *Range*: The number of the instances of the phenomenon covered by the theory.

2. *Elegance*: The succinctness of expression of the theory.

Figure 4.1. The goals and attributes of a theory

can see, organizations do not utilize communication theory except insofar as that term is confused with statistical information theory. Organizations, rather than using human communication theory, use human communication and impose theories of organization on human communication. Organizational theoreticians such as Taylor, Weber, Barnard, McGregor, and Blake and Mouton certainly give their attention to human communication but only insofar as human communication is an epiphenomenon of the organization and the organizational structure. In every instance I can recall when someone speaks of organizational communication, that person is speaking of how organizations affect the flow of human communication rather than how human communication affects the coming into being, the sustaining, and the expiration of organizations. Thus organizational communication is in theory and practice totally eclectic and almost as totally wrong-headed.

Individual human communication precedes complex human organizations. As has been adequately evidenced even from outside the field of human communication, by scholars in social psychology and sociology among others, human society is conceived and maintained in human communication (e.g., Duncan, 1968; Hjelmslev, 1961; Kaplan, 1964; Lieberman, 1967, 1972; Mead, 1934). Human communication rather than being epiphenomenological, rather than arising from society, is the main tent, is the phenomenon itself and itself gives rise to and sustains human society. When we place the organization before human communication, we are then so altering the nature of things that we often find ourselves skewing our priorities so as to place the organization before the humanity which, through its communication, brings the organization into being and maintains it in operation. I do not intend to castigate organizational theorists for this state of affairs. It seems to me it must be terribly difficult for an organizational theorist to utilize human communication theory when such theory is so difficult to find and when found seems to be so eclectically derived as to cause the organizational theorist to rely on the primitive sources rather than on the eclectic theory.

A PRIMITIVE THEORY OF HUMAN COMMUNICATION IN HUMAN ORGANIZATIONS

There are a number of human communication scholars who are trying to build a theory of human communication by deriving their postulates, hypotheses, attributes, and facts, as much as possible from the human communication act itself. In this manner I would suggest these scholars are trying their best to construct a primitive theory of human communication. In addition to such human communication scholars, there are scholars in ancillary disciplines such as linguistics, psycholinguistics and neurolinguistics who are embarked on the same path. With a predisposition I am confident you will understand I have chosen to center my efforts to build a primitive theory of human communication that may be referred to as a functional theory of human communication. Essentially the functional theory of human communication suggests that by virtue of the presence of speech communication in the human being certain functions take place. Note that we are discussing the functions of human communication rather than any purposes of human communication. The difference is that functions happen involuntarily (although theory can be volitionally enhanced) whereas purposes are the results of the conscious intent of the individual. Thus a hammer may have as its function some kind of pounding, but an individual may use the hammer for a wide variety of purposes, such as carpentry, breaking bottles, hurting someone, and on and on. It should be noted that the purposes to which the hammer may be put when being used as a hammer are all derived from the function of the hammer.

The available research, derived primitively and eclectically, seems at this time to support three functions of human communication:

1. The Linking Function through which the individual is linked with human society;
2. The Mentation Function through which the individual develops his higher mental processes; and
3. The Regulatory Function through which the individual regulates his own behavior and the behavior of others (Chomsky, 1966; Dance & Larson, 1972, 1976).

Functions 1 and 3 may have analogues in the non-human species; Function 2 seems completely dependent on speech communication and unique to it. In other words we are certainly aware that animals other than humans both link socially and regulate their own behavior and the behavior of other animals through animal communication. There is inadequate evidence at this time to indicate that animals other than humans are capable of the second function, the development of higher mental processes and the evidence additionally suggests that the second function is related in a determining and dependent manner to the individual's capacity to utilize spoken language. It is my suggestion that human communication augments the functions of animal communication (the analogues of Functions 1 and 3) in such a manner as to inform them with symbolic usage, thus enabling them to acquire their peculiarly human aspects. Whatever the developmental sequence, spoken language uniquely enables humans to link with other humans in human social enterprises, to develop higher mental processes, and to regulate their behavior in peculiarly human ways.

In addition to the functions, this primitive theory of human communication includes other attributes such as the levels on which human communication takes place; the modes through which human communication is expressed and the roles played by human communicators. It should be mentioned here that the theory does not consider all modes (spoken, written, gestured, etc.) as equipotential but insists on the preeminence of the spoken modality developmentally, and in many instances at later times (Dance & Larson, 1972). Obviously the fact that language is spoken is central to this attempt to construct a primitive theory of human communication (Kavanaugh & Cuttings, 1975; Lieberman, 1967, 1972).

Manifestly I have not here presented the arguments supporting the assertions made earlier. Those materials are both too specialized and too lengthy to find a place in this chapter. However, I must continue with the application of this primitive theory of human organizations supposing that you are all convinced and accepting of the primitive theory.

Earlier it was stated that human communication precedes complex human organizations. Next we argued that human communication carries with it three functions and a multiplicity of purposes grounded in these three functions. These three functions of human communication are situated in the individual human being.

The next step in the argument is that all social groups—beginning with the family—are composed of individuals and that the functions of speech communication found in and composing the individual are projected on the social organization composed of these individuals and that in addition the functions are also affected or colored by the social group or organization. The internalized individual functions of speech communication are projected on the externalized social structures and organizations participated in by the individual human being. Just as social problems often have counterparts in familial and interpersonal breakdowns (rejection of parental authority, sex-role stereotyping, maternal overdependency, peer rivalry, etc.), so too international and intersocietal conflicts may be justly viewed as magnifications of the tensions that all too often permeate intrapersonal relations and interpersonal relationships between child and parent, husband and wife, student and teacher, employer and employee, those in authority and those under authority. Interpersonal stresses can often be traced to intrapersonal disruptions in the individual's capacity to relate to his environment (Function 1), or to govern his human behavior by thought rather than solely by emotion (Functions 2 and 3).

Speech communication functions are originally projected in the familial primary group. The family, in turn, is the organizational prototype that prepares (or fails to prepare) the individual for organizational roles in the larger society, so that eventually we see reflected in society as a whole the functions (whether adaptive or maladaptive) of human communication in the individual. The family is ordinarily the primary group that shapes its members' approaches to all other organizations.

The human being enters organizational life with the three functions in operation and the individual's utilization of the functions has been shaped and reinforced by the prototypical organization, the family. However, an individual, as we are well aware, expresses himself through roles. Thus the individuals' projected functions found in organizations, are expressed in organizational and individual roles or in the role in which the interface between individual and organization is most commonly expressed.

The functions of human communication, when developed, are expressed by individuals in roles—both within and without organizations. In addition, purposes are rooted in functions, both functions and purposes are expressed by the individual most frequently in organizational roles.

What comes of all this is that human social organizations will always contain the functions of human communication in different mixtures and different strengths. In a family we will see one member taking primary responsibility for establishing the emotional climate (although not totally neglecting the other functions); another member concerned with planning (Function 2); yet another with getting things organized and accomplished (Functions 2 and 3). So too in a school; or in a team; or in a government agency; or in a small business or in a large multinational corporate enterprise. Organizational roles derive from and are rooted in human communication functions, and an understanding of the fulfillment of organizational roles depends to a great extent upon an adequate understanding of the functions of human communication theory. In such an understanding and the applications that may flow from it, we may indeed find a primitive theory of human communication in human organizations.

A human communication audit was constructed and administered in a small bank. The audit was constructed based on the three functions of human communication. Each audit item was intended to tap the expression of one or some combination of the three functions.

The analysis of the audit and the interviews following the written questionnaire were also intended to develop an audit not of communication messages, or flow, or salience, but of the human communication functions within the organization. Utilizing this theoretical posture the investigators have found ways in which the communicative climate of the organization can be analyzed and hopefully improved so as to meet some of the other organizational goals of the bank. However, the analysis was an analysis of human communication as it affects an organization, not of the organizational impact on the messages of humans.

Examples of the association between roles and functions within this case would be as follows:

role	ascendant function
Receptionist	Function 1—Linking
Auditor	Function 2—Mentation
Operations Officer	Function 3—Regulatory

Other examples of linking functions would include individuals in personnel roles, or public relations roles. Mentation functions would include individuals with primary role responsibility for organizational research and development or for planning. Regulatory function manifestations would be found in individuals fulfilling managerial or supervisory roles.

Of course I am not suggesting a normal functional dominance that excludes the other natural functions of human communication. Quite the contrary, the well-balanced individual, either in or out of a formal organization, tries to maintain a comfortable relationship among all three functions and their expression as purposes through roles.

In fact, within the bank case alluded to earlier, when a role was found to so distort the balance of functions comfortable to the individual so as to almost totally suppress one or more of the functions, the individual often complained of this effect to the interviewer. (At least the interviewer was successful in placing that construction on the remarks made during the interview—e.g., a receptionist who felt that although her job of handling the switchboard was important, she did not know anything else about what was going on in the bank, felt insignificant as a person.)

My argument in this chapter has been for the examination of a primitive theory of human communication in human organizations, as distinguished from an eclectic theory of organizational communication. Some differences between the two types of theoretical approaches have been suggested earlier. Some additional distinctions would be:

Organizational Communication	Primitive Theory
Emphasizes organization in which communication takes place and suggests that the shape or the form of the organization controls or dictates the communication patterns in the organization. The organizational structure is the overriding concern and the communication networks evolve to fit the organizational structure.	Emphasizes an analysis of human communication and the relationship of role to functions of human communication that arise when related to an organization. Suggests that the form ultimately taken by an organization is a reflection of a primitive theory of human communication.

I suggested that there are indeed other elements of the primitive theory besides the functions. Elements such as the difference between spoken and written or gestured messages; the level (intrapersonal, interpersonal, person to persons) or levels on which the communication takes place; and others. A total application of the primitive theory of human communication to human organizations would need to consider these other elements as well as the functions.

My prolegomena, my preliminary discourse and observations, concerning a primitive theory of human communication for human organizations is all but at an end. I have not meant to insinuate that the work hitherto accomplished under the rubric "organizational communication" lacks values. Certainly the publications of Redding (1972), Goldhaber (1974), and the other contributors to this program all testify to the fertile application of insightful minds to perplexing problems. What I mean to do is simply to suggest that there is a further distance for all of us who walk on our way to becoming human communication theoreticians, who can, with our own expertise, help solve the problems of human organizations. Finding the way is difficult to begin with. Walking the path is filled with temptations and tortuous byways. It is, for me, an honor and a challenge just to be invited along on the journey.

In conclusion, I would like to call your attention to some lines of T. S. Eliot that go far toward capturing the spirit in which I prepared this chapter:

V

So here I am, in the middle way, having had twenty years—
Twenty years largely wasted, the years of l'entre deux guerres—
Trying to learn to use words, and every attempt
Is a wholly new start, and a different kind of failure
Because one has only learnt to get the better of words
For the thing one no longer has to say, or the way in which
One is no longer disposed to say it. And so each venture
Is a new beginning, a raid on the inarticulate
With shabby equipment always deteriorating
In the general mess of imprecision of feeling,
Undisciplined squads of emotion. And what there is to conquer
By strength and submission, has already been discovered
Once or twice, or several times, by men whom one cannot hope
To emulate—but there is no competition—
There is only the fight to recover what has been lost
And found and lost again and again: and now, under conditions
That seem unpropitious. But perhaps neither gain nor loss.
For us, there is only the trying. The rest is not our business.
          —T. S. Eliot "East Coker"

five

SYSTEMS THINKING IN ORGANIZATIONAL COMMUNICATION INQUIRY

Carolyn Baldwin Leveque
and Marshall Scott Poole

Texas A&M University

In a revisionist history of organizational communication research, Poole (1997) called for a reexamination and reapplication of systems theory as a guiding principle in organizational communication inquiry. Poole identified a dialectic in recent organizational communication research. He framed the development of interpretive theory in the late 1970s and 1980s as "the cultural antithesis to the systemic thesis" (p. 50) that had dominated the field since its introduction in the 1960s, and points to higher order systems theories as a viable synthesis offering powerful frameworks to give both cultural-interpretive analyses as well as quantitative research broader reach, flexibility, and insight. This chapter extends this argument, suggesting that in order for the field of organizational communication to advance future efforts in theory building and empirical investigation must adopt an analytical stance of systems thinking. Systems thinking rejects old-style system practices of mechanistic reductionism, impoverished operationalization, and limited interpretability, and instead emphasizes the complexity, dynamical processes, and emergent properties inherent in organizational communication. After summarizing Poole's dialectic, foundations for systems thinking are discussed followed by illustrations of systems thinking in practice.

THESIS, ANTITHESIS, AND SYNTHESIS

As *thesis*, systems theory gained a sturdy foothold in the field of organizational communication similar to the social system models popular in the political science and sociology of the time. Largely due to their coincident introduction to the field, systems theory also became inextricably associated with positivistic social science, multivariate statistics, and quantitative measurement. Rather than becoming a powerful instrument of analysis, however, the notion of "system" in organizational communication research was more frequently invoked as a metaphor: vaguely appealing, but also vaguely specified. Many of these early systems models failed to live up to their promise, becoming ceremonial exercises in rigor. Additionally, the quantitative movement in organizational communication also in full force at that time added its own brand of reductionism to the equation, stressing wholesale variablization and the collection of data amenable to a narrow range of statistical analyses. The systems approach rapidly, and quite reasonably, began to lose its patina.

As *antithesis*, the interpretive turn in organizational communication research was in large part a reaction against the constraints imposed both by multivariate analysis and the mechanistic reductionism, impoverished operationalization, and limited interpretability of extant systems models. Organizational scholars turned to organizational culture, symbolism, and critical studies of domination and control in organizations. Similar to the development of systems theory, the interpretive approach brought with it its own preferred methods and data. These included ethnographic, archival, interview and observational methods that generated narratives, accounts, myths, and stories. Although such methodologies gave researchers access to a richer domain of concepts and data, they necessarily imposed a different albeit equally troubling form of reductionism on organizational inquiry. These limitations stem from the reliance upon natural language in interpretive research, the cognitive constraints of researchers and audience alike, and the extraordinary outlay of resources required to build and analyze appropriate data sets. For example, many primitives in interpretive theory such as "deep structure," "intersubjectivity," or "production and reproduction" obscure the very complexity they are meant to capture. Such simplifications become inescapable; there are limitations on the complexities and processes that the mind can discern and apprehend and that natural language can describe at any one time.

Although an interpretive account raises more questions than it answers, this heuristic value is overshadowed by the equally important questions that are neither asked nor answered due to the temporal and situational boundedness of interpretive investigations. How shared is a shared meaning? How long does it take for a meaning to be shared? Are the mechanisms that produce shared meaning similar across organizations? Is "shared meaning" a property of individuals or of organizations? In its present form, interpretive research lacks the frameworks and languages needed to adequately address these key problems of emergence, complexity, and temporal dynamics that have, in the main, gone unanswered across the field.

As *synthesis*, Poole suggested the development of higher order systems theories as a viable way to both model complex processes that interpretive research embraces but cannot fully apprehend and move systems research beyond the stale mechanism that characterized earlier work. Such an approach should be able to combine the rich universe of concepts found in interpretive research with the complexity, precision, and specification found in systems models while offering a way to incorporate dynamical and emergent properties into static 1960s vintage systems research. Finally, such an approach should not impose the limitations and constraints of one or another methodological mindset on empirical investigation and theory building but allow researchers the ability to combine a variety of analytic tools and perspectives within a coherent and flexible framework. In short, we suggest that what is required is not a return to old-style *systems practice*, but a new awareness of *systems thinking*. The following section describes how such an approach fits into previously developed systems frameworks.

THE SYSTEMS FRAMEWORK

One of the more influential systems frameworks advanced has been Boulding's (1968) "system of systems," an effort to lend structure to the hazy conceptual and empirical domains of General Systems Theory and cross-disciplinary research. Boulding attempted to arrange theoretical systems and constructs into a hierarchy of complexity corresponding to the complexity of the system in those domains. Boulding identified nine levels of systems, ranging from simple frameworks to systems of unspecified complexity. As described in Table 5.1, at each successive level in the hierarchy new capacities for control and adaptiveness are added as systems become increasingly complex, self-reflexive, and lifelike. Boulding pointed out that an additional value of such a framework lies in directing the attention of theorists in individual fields towards gaps in their own theoretical models, and may even point towards methods of filling them. Pondy and Mitroff (1979) applied this idea to a survey of systems research in organizational studies.

Table 5.1. A Hierarchy of Systems Complexity.

	System Description	Key Features	Examples
Level 1	Frameworks	Description of a static structure	Crystal structures, an organizational chart
Level 2	Clockworks	Simple dynamic system with predetermined, necessary motions	Clocks, machines, the solar system
Level 3	Control systems	Transmission and interpretation of information, closed loop control	Thermostats
Level 4	Open systems	self maintenance of structure, self-reproduction	Biological cells
Level 5	Blueprinted growth systems	Division of labor, differentiated and mutually interdependent parts	Plants
Level 6	Internal imaging systems	A brain to guide total behavior, teleological behavior, the ability to learn	Animals
Level 7	Symbol processing systems	Self-consciousness, knowledge of knowledge, symbolic language	Human beings
Level 8	Multicephalous systems	Roles, the transmission of values	Societies, cultures, organizations, families
Level 9	Systems of unspecified complexity	Inescapable unknowables	The idea of God

Pondy and Mitroff (1979) drew two general conclusions. First, they noted that although all human organizations are level-eight phenomena, our conceptual models of them are fixed at level four and our formal models and data collection techniques are rooted at levels one and two. That is, although organizations have been *conceived of* as "open systems" (however inadequately, as the authors point out), researchers have failed to *encounter* them as anything more complex than clockworks and frameworks. This conclusion may certainly be extended to systems research in organizational communication where organizations were assumed to have more or less set goals, attempted to maintain equilibrium through meeting certain communication functions, and emphasized regulation of equilibrium rather than the growth of system complexity (Poole, 1997).

Although we agree with these authors' contention that organizational research needs to move beyond the inherent limitations of this variety of "open" systems modeling, their second conclusion is more problematic. Pondy and Mitroff (1979) suggested that the key implication of their position for organizational research is the abandonment of "brute empiricism," comparative analyses, and cross-organizational generalization in favor of thick description, cultural and linguistic analyses, and the use of ethnographic techniques for documenting individual cases of meaning and belief systems. Again, such approaches bring with them their own set of constraints that in no way ensure an explicit focus on the highly complex, sensemaking, emergent, and dynamic nature of organizational communication.

How can researchers investigate those properties of organizations that cast them, in Boulding's terms, as level-eight phenomena without (paradoxically) abandoning the systems paradigm altogether? For organizational communication theory and research to advance, the goal of future work in the field should be to explicate these intervening levels of complexity in Boulding's systems hierarchy. Such research should explore the diverse generative mechanisms for organizational birth and growth, detailed environmental awareness, self-conscious symbolic processing, and emergent shared systems of meaning. We suggest that this goal may be realized through the practice of systems thinking. The following section describes foundations for systems thinking: dynamism, complexity, and emergence.

SYSTEMS THINKING

The concept of "system" involves the idea of a set of elements connected together to form a "whole" showing properties that are unique to the whole rather than to the properties of its component parts. Although systems thinking is concerned with wholes and the properties of wholes, it is equally concerned with the arrangement of subsystem elements, their dynamic interaction and interdependence, and an account of the explicit mechanisms that generate and sustain the emergence of wholes (Checkland, 1981). A *systems model* is a symbolic formulation, mathematical, semimathematical or verbal, that aims to represent the basic workings of some phenomenon to be explained. Within its explanatory framework, the model can be used to explore the phenomenon, to see how it behaves under various circumstances, or make predictions (McPhee & Poole, 1981). *Systems thinking* is an analytic stance that lies at the intersection of substantive and methodological concerns in theory building.

At the core of systems thinking lies a preoccupation with social dynamics, complexity, and emergence as one attempts to construct explanations for and about organizational communication. System thinking operates as a heuristic, or *topoi*, directing one not only to the sorts of questions one should ask, but also to the form appropriate answers should take. The tools and methodologies used to address these questions are at the discretion of individual investigators. Although concepts such as "complex" and "dynamic" are frequently invoked as inherent principles of organized human activity systems, it is usually less clear to many what specifically these ideas imply as well as how their implications may be realized in both research and in theory building about organizations. Both these issues are addressed next.

Dynamics

Systems thinking implies a concern with the role of social dynamics in theory building. In the context of organizational studies, an explicit concern with dynamics necessarily leads one to a conceptualization of "organization" as a process in action rather than "organization" as an object with attributes. This argument is more clearly made by contrasting statements of comparative statics with statements of comparative dynamics. A statement of comparative statics is an assertion about hypothesized patterns of covariation among the properties described by some system. In contrast, statements about social dynamics focus on the process of change as the thing to be explained rather than the thing itself. Hence, the assertion "The greater the X, the greater the Y" is more appropriately stated as "An increase in X leads to an increase in Y," and one is immediately more interested in the causal mechanism that produced such a change and the nature of that change (i.e., the shape or rate of change) rather than the pattern of covariation itself (Hanneman, 1988). Further specification may involve describing not only the rate of change (e. g., velocity) but also second-order change, that is, change in the rate of change (e.g., acceleration).

Still, however, statements of comparative statics play both a useful and important role in theory building and systems thinking. Static comparisons are implicitly grounded in dynamical theories although their dynamical underpinnings are too often poorly developed. Hanneman (1988) pointed out:

> While the focus of theories of comparative statistics is not on the processes that produce and reproduce the structures, such theories almost always (but often implicitly) are accompanied by a mental model of where structures come from and how they change. . . . Similarly, theories that focus on "process" or social dynamics must have (at least implicitly) models of structure embedded in them. (p. 18)

Thus, although theorizing about comparative statics is usefully seen as complementary to studies of social dynamics, the latter has been given far less attention. This disparity becomes problematic when it is the case that that the phenomena needing explanation is the rate of change in some pattern of social action and not variability within the pattern itself. For example, Contractor and Baldwin (1993) noted that although many studies in the adoption of innovation have extensively catalogued patterns of covariation among the attributes of innovations, adopters, and organizations involved in innovation processes, the specific nature of the change process itself, for example, rates of adoption at different point in time, has itself gone largely unexamined.

The construction of an explanation of a phenomenon, rather than simply a description, is a defining aspect of theory construction. It requires that one model causal processes, the mechanisms that undergird and produce these processes, and the shape and nature of the change processes themselves as they unfold over time. Systems thinking, via its concern with dynamics, encourages one to directly address these issues, forcing one to look beyond statements of comparative statics to addressing the role of comparative dynamics and prompting one to ask those questions critical to organizational analysis relating to growth, decline, transition, modification, and transformation over time. Such dynamic theories necessarily tend to become quite complex.

Complexity

A system, or by extension a theory, is "complex" to the extent that additional information is required in order to make accurate predictions about system behavior and possible outcomes. Simple systems are capable of only a limited variety of behaviors, hence it is relatively easy to predict their behavior without much additional information or analysis. For example, given a theoretical proposition of the form "Increased group cohesion leads to increased group effectiveness," to the extent that we note increases in cohesion, effectiveness is not difficult to discern. Although this is obviously an extremely simple system, ease of analyzability still applies when one considers theories with a greater number of axioms positing simple relationships between several terms, or qualitative accounts that can be reduced to simple logical expressions (Hanneman, 1988). More complex theories expressing more complex relationships are still amenable to direct analysis with the use of various tools and calculi (i.e., path analysis; direct solution of multivariate simultaneous equations).

In contrast, truly complex systems are able to produce a wide variety of responses to stimuli and truly complex theories often exceed our capacity to immediately understand them. The effects of changing one variable may be impossible to trace if that variable is interconnected in dynamic ways with several other variables. It becomes difficult to immediately discern possible behaviors and outcomes of complex systems, and it frequently may require the use of tools that are relatively less familiar than, for example, path analysis. But by constructing and analyzing complex systems one gains a far more complete insight into the nature of the systems being modeled with our theories and the dynamics that produce system behavior. How, then, do we make theories about organization and communication more complex?

There are two basic ways to incorporate complexity in a system: first, through increasing the number of elements considered in a system and second, by manipulating the nature of the relationships between elements in a system. Organizational scholars have proved themselves to be far more adept at the former than the latter. Weick (1987) has observed that many organizational theories, with their bewildering arrays of boxes, loops, and arrows, more closely resemble plumbing diagrams for Scottish castles than anything immediately recognizable in the social realm. Systems thinking suggests that the more appropriate avenue for apprehending and expressing organizational complexity is found by exploring the latter option: specifying the nature of the relationship between system elements. This strategy implies more than drawing authoritative arrows between boxes. The nature of such arrows is usually highly ambiguous, difficult to interpret, and hence does more to obscure system complexity than to coherently define complex system behavior. The nature of the relationship between system elements can be expanded on and specified in several ways.

First, the relationships between elements in complex systems tend to be defined by more complex functional relationships, for example, a complex polynomial or nonlinear equation rather than simple linear equation, implying that the shape of functional relationships may change over time. Second, functional relationships may have complex time–shape interactions. That is, elapsed time itself may serve to define the relationships between system elements. The key point here is that if one wants to understand how variables interact over time, one cannot necessarily assume that the role of "time" in "change over time" is either immediate or continuous. Speed-ups, slow-downs, delays, crises, and cyclical behaviors may be modeled with attention to the potential forms that time–shape relationships may take.

Even incorporating a few of these ideas renders a simple system immediately complex. For example, returning to the earlier hypothesized simple linear relationship between group cohesiveness and effectiveness, to cast this theory in more complex terms one could ask if the relationship is perhaps nonlinear; perhaps it becomes negative over time. Or, perhaps the positive relationship is not continuous as either cohesiveness or effectiveness increase or decrease; at certain times a change in one "unit" of cohesiveness may imply a change of three "units" of effectiveness. Perhaps the relationship between cohesiveness and effectiveness accelerates or decelerates at different points in the history of a group. Or, perhaps we have our arrow pointing in the wrong direction. We might consider the relationship between effectiveness and cohesiveness, illustrating yet another way to build complexity into theories and models by positing recursive relationships between system elements.

Recursiveness becomes a necessary feature of complex dynamic models when change within a system implies, as the system reproduces itself, change in the initial conditions of system elements producing a different set of system behaviors and possible outcomes. Such alterations in initial system values may in turn trigger variation in the rate of future change in the system and, again, the values system elements assume (and so on and so on). From this perspective, an otherwise largely static "box-and-arrow" model that posits a connection between a final system element and an initial system element (which is certainly common enough) becomes startlingly incomplete and to some extent incomprehensible if the implications for future system values and behaviors are not traced out (which is equally common). Although the implications of recursive relationships that unfold in dynamic ways over time are often exceedingly difficult to trace without the aid of simulation techniques and other modeling methodologies, it is necessary to begin making the attempt to do so in order to build more complete, more authentic, and more valid pictures of the organizations.

Systems thinking acknowledges the need to build complexity into models of organization. A first step in developing truly complex theories lies in expanding on the notion of complexity and exploring the different forms complexity may take in our implicit and explicit models about organizations. To summarize the different ways that complexity may be expressed, systems or theories that are considered more complex tend to (a) contain more elements, (b) have elements that are more densely interconnected, (c) incorporate change over time, (d) posit complex time–shape relationships between elements in the system, (e) relate system elements using higher order functional forms, and (f) suggest recursive relationships between system elements. Note that these strategies need not be expressed via mathematical formalisms. Whereas the first and second strategies listed have been extensively applied in organizational analysis, the remainder have been noticeably underused. Incorporating these novel forms of complexity into our models and theories of organizational communication will contribute a great deal toward overcoming the implicit assumptions of persistence, continuity, equilibrium, linearity that have characterized much of traditional quantitative and qualitative organizational communication theory.

Emergence

As previously defined, the notion of "system" involves the idea of a set of elements connected together to form a "whole" showing properties that are unique to the whole rather than to properties of its component parts. The previous discussions of dynamics and complexity have focused primarily on the arrangement and connection of systems elements, the first part of the definition. The second part of the definition explicitly indexes emergence which is "the tendency for a complex system to display global characteristics which are lacking at the level of individual components that comprise the system" (S.H. Kim, 1994, p. 171). The concept of emergence is inextricably tied to system complexity and system dynamics. It is the complex expression and dynamic interaction of system elements that give rise to systems as emergent and coherent "wholes."

The quality of emergence is also a key part of Boulding's (1968) hierarchy of systems. An assumption of this model is that unique emergent properties are assumed to arise at each defined system level, and that although all characteristics of lower level systems are found within higher level systems, the emergent properties of those higher level systems are not reducible to lower level system elements. This assumption reflects the historical foundations of the concept of emergence that took the form of a debate about the status of the organism as either a complicated machine reducible to and governed by the laws of chemistry and physics, or as a nonreducible whole. Of course, biology has gained status as an independent discipline, and although no biologist would claim that biological phenomena contradict the laws of chemistry and physics, neither are they "nothing but" chemistry and physics. They constitute wholes characterized by emergent qualities:

> The fact is that the existence of organisms having properties of wholes calls for different levels of description which correspond to different levels of reality. This is so even if the properties of parts, together with laws of combination, can explain the mechanism of the whole. The point is, the whole was there to be explained in the first place. (Checkland, 1981, p. 78)

The preceding quotation points to a critical dimension of emergence: a description of the global characteristics of wholes using language appropriate to that emergent level. Emergent system properties are meaningless in language appropriate to a lower level of system analysis. For example, although the taste of water probably has something to do with properties of hydrogen and oxygen, it cannot be meaningfully expressed in the language of molecular chemistry. It is this property of systems thinking that Poole (1997) referred to when he suggested that "different orders of data are required for higher level systems analysis" (p. 52). The meaningful articulation of emergent system behavior requires different orders of data to describe higher level system properties at higher levels of system analysis. Static cross-sectional studies, longitudinal research using variables that "reduce action to motion," and the aggregation of lower level system behaviors as supposed indices of global system behavior will not meet this requirement.

One obvious strategy is to augment higher order systems analysis with interpretive accounts of structure and meaning, or alternately, interpretive-critical assumptions could form the basis for higher order systems development. Other novel forms of higher order data should also be explored, such as the use of scientific visualization techniques (Forrest, 1991). The role of system interpretation, however framed, is critical in developing accounts of emergent organizational properties. At the same time, any such interpretive account is necessarily incomplete divorced from the complex and dynamical system behavior that undergirds emergent organizational properties.

To conclude, a conceptualization of emergence in systems thinking requires that one provide not only an account of system elements, their complex and dynamic relationships, and the mechanisms that generate and sustain the emergence of wholes, but that one does so at a qualitatively different level of analysis. Although this is certainly no small task, reframing traditionally amorphous constructs such as "structure," "structuration," "climate," and "intersubjectivity" as complex emergent communication processes with clearly articulated systemic and dynamic underpinnings would be a powerful strategy in advancing theory construction in the field. The next section illustrates systems thinking in action using research exemplars drawn from dynamic organizational simulation, emergent computational modeling, and an interpretive model of organization as the production of multiply authored text. Although none is necessarily either complete or ideal, each in a different way and to a different extent illustrates how systems thinking may be realized in organizational analyses via approaches than consciously emphasize the dynamic, complex, and emergent properties of organized human behavior.

SYSTEMS THINKING IN PRACTICE

Recent advances in computational modeling, network analytic, and simulation techniques have made tools which explore and apply the concepts that drive systems thinking readily accessible to most researchers. Examples from all these domains are described and discussed below. Yet systems thinking does not necessarily imply a preoccupation with the use of computers in computational modeling, problem solving, or organizational simulation. This assumption appears to be yet another case of conflating the analytic tools and methods used in theory construction with the substance and content of theory itself — exactly a conclusion we wish to avoid. However, it is also the case that the application of such methodologies can serve as tremendous aids in tracing out the Gordian implications and behaviors (as well as the possibly unforeseen and unintended consequences) of the complex models systems thinking encourages one to develop.

The Adoption of New Communication Technologies

Contractor and Baldwin's (1992) dynamic simulation of Burt's (1982) Structural Theory of Action illustrates the how the complex and dynamic implications of the process of innovation adoption can be strategically addressed via the use of computer simulation methodology. The execution of models using simulation techniques offers several valuable strategies in theory construction. First, model building through the design and execution of computer simulations forces one to make theories and their underlying assumptions extremely explicit before moving into the validation phase of hypothesis testing in organizational settings. Second, the methodology used in this study demonstrates the ability to subsume multiple levels of analysis within an internally consistent and coherent framework. Finally, the analysis of simulation data offers an opportunity to parcel out the differential and combined effects of individual and structural determinants on the process under investigation. This helps to identify those differences in initial system conditions that make a difference in an emergent process, and potentially allows the researcher to derive more useful and potentially more valid hypotheses that may not be immediately obvious via casual inspection.

The central theme of Burt's Structural Theory of Action is that actors are purposive under structural constraint. In this investigation, "action" is an individual's adoption of a new communication technology. The premises of this theory suggest that individuals evaluate the utility of adopting (or not adopting) partly in consideration of their individual preferences, and partly in regard to the preferences of other actors in the social system. Thus, action and structure are considered simultaneously as mutually constituting and constitutive; ongoing patterns of communication are both conditions and consequences of adoption decisions. This mutuality assumption causes the analysis to take on an emphatically recursive flavor as the decision to adopt a communication technology changes the structure of the communication network in which individuals are situated, thus altering the form of future decisions made under new conditions of structural constraint and thus differentially affecting both one's individual preferences and the preferences of others via social influence processes over time. The nature of the dynamic relationships between system elements in the model is clearly specified through the algorithms that drive the simulation.

Using this formulation, Contractor and Baldwin examined the effect of an actor's differential levels of interest in the new communication technology (high vs. low) and an actor's differential levels of access to resources in the communication network (high vs. low) on the adoption process. They created the four conditions and executed the simulation a total of 1,200 times. The results suggested that although individual interest heterogeneity does not influence the total number of new links emerging from the adoption process, it does influence when the new links are added to the network. That is, groups with low interest heterogeneity are more likely to be early adopters of the communication technology, whereas groups characterized by wide differences in initial interest in the technology are slower in adopting the technology. Finally, the results suggest that groups characterized by larger differences between members in their access to resources are always less likely to adopt new communication technologies.

This example illustrates how the dynamic implications of the complex relationships between a relatively few number of elements allows one to draw interesting conclusions about global system behavior stated in terms of comparative dynamics rather than comparative statics. Although the generative mechanisms of the Structural Theory of Action are clearly and unambiguously stated by Burt, the relationships posited are both cyclical and nonlinear, and hence their implications over time are not immediately evident. This is potentially true for many other social scientific theories that could also be usefully adapted to simulation techniques, leading to an increased understanding of their implications for emergent communication processes.

The Evolution of New Organizational Forms

Crowston (1994) used an emergent computational method to explore the emergence of new organizational forms via the use of a genetic evolutionary algorithm. By operationalizing organizational form as an emergent outcome of the interdependent actions of organizational subunits under differential conditions of task environment, he was able to test the viability of emergent forms. Furthermore, his operationalization allows him to explore the implications of widely held theoretical assumptions in organizational design about the clustering of related tasks.

Emergent computational models cast the behavior of the system as a whole as more than the sum of the operation of individual system elements. It is also important to note that not all computational models, however complex, are necessarily emergent models. The requirements for an emergent computational system of some phenomena are: (a) a collection of agents, each following explicit instructions; (b) interaction among the agents (according to the instructions), which form implicit global patterns at higher system levels; and (c) an interpretation of the epiphemonena at the higher system level usually by using a graphics-based or other visualization technique, or through direct perception and interpretation by the system designer. The notion of system levels is an important one. In emergent models, information that is present at higher levels of the system is neither present at nor reducible to lower level system operations.

The development of these models has been a response to more familiar models that employ parallel computing or processing. In these models complex systems are decomposed into independent subsystems operating simultaneously with minimal interdependence or interaction.

Parallel computing models frame communication between system elements as the necessary "cost" of managing multiple synchronous yet independent processes, and a centralized source of control minimizes this "cost" as much as possible by synchronizing system elements. In contrast, in emergent computational models, communication and coordination have been recast as inherent system properties that have been redistributed among and between system elements. In these models interesting system behavior at a global level emerges from multiple local interdependent interactions. By exploiting the interdependencies between simultaneous computational subprocesses, emergent computational models can be used to increase a modeled system's flexibility, efficiency, and allow for a more natural or valid approximation of the empirical system being modeled (Forrest, 1991).

Operationalizing organizations and organizational behavior as emergent computational processes has many of the same analytic advantages that dynamic simulation offers, with the added focus on the emergence and interpretation of higher level system properties as implicit outcomes of lower level system interaction and interdependencies. This becomes a powerful assumption in understanding the role of communication in organization. For example, the claim is frequently made that micro-level interaction and behavior produces emergent organizational structures or patterns of collective action. Although this is not a wholly unreasonable assumption to make, it remains only an assumption without an explicit account of the mechanisms that purportedly produce and/or reproduce qualitatively unique global system properties. It becomes an uncomfortable assumption when, as is frequently the case, statistical aggregation of local (i.e., message, individual, group) system behavior is taken as an index of "emergent" organizational properties.

A commonly adopted stance that communication is or realizes organization may stem from a cognitive, functional, critical, or cultural perspective. The detailed explications of the mechanisms that link microlevel accounts of organizational behavior with emergent organizational structures and properties is a crucial tasks for organizational communication theorists, regardless of their perspective. Emergent computational models address exactly this issue.

Crowston (1994) argued that an important role for organizational theory is to not only to study extant organizational forms, but also to suggest possible new forms. There is widespread concern that the business environment is changing, and that the properties of new communication and information technologies have the ability to make feasible new organizational forms. He used simulation to search for novel organizational forms based on the mechanics of evolution, noting that "the metaphor of organizations competing and being selected on the basis of their fitness is a compelling one [and] is also the basis of a computer technique known as the genetic algorithm" (pp. 20–21).

A genetic algorithm works by first randomly generating a population of possible solutions to a problem. The most successful solutions at solving the problem are used as the basis for the evolution of the next generation of solutions. These new populations are bred by crossover, by taking two existing solutions, splitting them, and exchanging the parts to create two new solutions. The processes is repeated for some fixed number of iterations or until the problem is solved by one of the solutions.

The use of the genetic algorithm to simulate organizational behavior requires that one (a) select the phenomenon that will be evolved at an appropriate level of analysis (i.e., individuals, groups, or entire organizations), (b) develop a representation of the phenomenon general enough to represent many possible organizational forms, and (c) develop a representation of the environment in which the organization performs and a fit function to identify "good" or viable organizational forms and behavior. This simulation used as the basis for its design well-developed theoretical suggestions about clustering related tasks in organizational design. Two parameters of the model were varied: the extent of overlap between tasks performed by different organizational subunits, and the coordination penalty actors paid for performing multiple tasks. In the simulation, organizations were modeled as a set of N actors that perform M tasks, represented as an NM-bit string that encoded the assignment of actors to tasks ("1" if the task was assigned to a particular actor and "0" otherwise). The task environment was modeled as a set of 10 overlapping subtasks, which could each be part of multiple tasks. The extent of task overlap or interdependence was varied from no overlap (subtasks are only part of one task) to complete overlap (all subtasks are part of all tasks). Fitness was defined as the extent to which all tasks were performed. If, for example, some required subtask was not performed by any actor, then that organizational form's viability is zero. The simulation generated 106 different organizational forms that were then evaluated for fit.

Results of the simulation were generally consistent with predictions, but with several interesting deviations. For example, even under conditions of high penalties for coordination and low task overlap, viable organizational forms still assigned two actors to each task. This result may reflect the vulnerability of organizational forms with only one actor per task in an environment characterized by many subtasks. Also, under conditions of high task overlap, actors were not necessarily assigned related subtasks, suggesting that the model (and perhaps the theory) does not capture the synergies between subtasks, tasks, and interdependent actors.

This example illustrates the possibilities that computational models offer for examining the emergent structural outcomes of dynamic interdependent and coordinated organizational behavior via a recursive evolutionary process. It also illustrates the critical role of interpretation on the part of the investigator as the implications of emergent computations are usually more implicit than explicit. Finally, as in the previous example, this modeling strategy allows one to meaningfully move between multiple levels of analysis, examine the implications of theoretical assumptions under different conditions over repeated observations, and generate new hypotheses from the unexpected outcomes of dynamic processes (Whicker & Sigelman, 1991).

Organization as Multiply Authored Text

The previous example implicitly relied on an information-theoretic model of communication where the focus is on communication as transmission of information (e.g., whether or not a task assignment was successfully completed) rather than communication as a process of meaning construction and social influence. Taylor (1993) rejected the information-theory view of communication, and claimed that it is this poorly developed and impoverished model of organizational communication that lies at the root of the field's failure to adequately account for the role of technology in the communication process. His mandate is to replace a model of organizational communication based on information with one that is not. His model implicitly invokes many of the properties of systems thinking previously discussed.

Taylor took as his starting point the various disasters he has observed in the implementation of office automation technologies (OA). Their information processing capabilities were assumed to have the ability to transform the workplace on the order of the industrial revolution. He suggested that their abysmal failure was, in fact, the only possible outcome because human communication is in no way and at no time reducible to "information processing." He referred to OA's built-in capacity for failure as "the office automation paradox": Instead of OA systems being modeled after organizations as communication systems, implementation of OA forced human communication systems to model themselves after the information-processing architectures of computers. This simply doesn't work.

Taylor's (1993) rejection of most things information-theoretic lead him to posit an alternate view of organizational communication as the accomplishment of action, "a fusion, not a concatenation; a dance, not a cause followed by an effect . . . resulting in *coordinated involvement relations"* (p. 167; emphasis in the original). This model of communication uses speech-act theory as a springboard to develop both the notion of communication-as-action, and the roles of actors involved in ongoing coordinated relationships. The model assumes communication has a deep structure whereby primitive agent/agent and agent/beneficiary relationships construct webs of mutual obligation and meaning. This deep structure corresponds to ideas in organizational theory about organizational coupling and coordination; hence "organization" is conceived as an emergent composition of elementary communicative relationships. He used as a metaphor of organization as a "text" produced by a set of authors through conversation. For Taylor, text is any systematic symbolic construction that has meaning to the participants, and text includes the set of all the structured events and artifacts that make up the matter and activities of an organization including an office, a meeting, or more "exotic" phenomena such as quality circles and office parties.

Taylor's (1993) theory posits that these (micro)conversational processes and the construction of organizational (macro)text structures mutually reproduce one another in an emergent process. Bridging the levels in this dynamic model is a mechanism which postulates that text structures are not only the emergent outcome of natural conversation, but that both communication and organization are mutually defined in a reflexive relationship. The performance of speech acts, the "quanta of human activity" are able to accomplish two things: the communication of information (a transitive function) and the structuring of interagent functions (an interactive function): "Conversation is thus a means to realize coordination, and by doing so make organization a reality. . . . Conversation effectively expresses hypothesized deep structural [organizational] relationships" (p. 208). Taylor later considers the implications of such a model of organization and communication for understanding the role of communication technologies in organizations, with novel results.

Taylor's model of organization as text supported by conversation in action illustrates an intriguing application of systems thinking. In the model, "text" is a coherent whole emerging from the natural conversations of actors embedded in mutually defining and interdependent relationships. Taylor made an effort to posit mechanisms for the emergence of higher order systems properties of texts, such as their moral and institutional dimensions, as well as offering mechanisms that account for conflict and change in the process of text construction. But this theory has some obvious limitations as well, stemming from the author's reliance on natural language as the only medium by which the content and mechanisms of the theory are (imprecisely) conveyed (Hanneman, 1988). Still, however, throughout Taylor's discussion the systemic and dynamcal underpinnings of his model remain the primary focus.

CONCLUSION

What we are calling for is not a return to the systems theory of the past, but a new awareness of systems thinking. Systems thinking is an analytic stance and not a "new and improved" version of functionalism. Functionalism emphasized equilibrium, giving it a conservative bias, did not have the ability to model conflict and disruption in social systems, and its failed to propose mechanisms that relate parts to the whole (Checkland, 1981). The foundational assumptions that drive systems thinking, dynamism, complexity, and emergence explicitly counter these shortcomings.

The goal of this chapter was to make clear not only the nature and content of systems thinking but also to illustrate the ways that it may be realized in research and theory building about organizational communication. The impetus for the development of systems thinking is found in the limitations and constraints that have characterized both early systems models and critical-interpretive research. Systems thinking, by way of conscious attention to the dynamic, complex, and emergent properties of organizational communication, offers a powerful framework to give both cultural-interpretive analyses as well as quantitative research broader reach, flexibility, and insight. Systems thinking forces one to fully articulate the systemic underpinnings of static organizational theory while lending precision and focus to descriptive accounts of communication processes.

Systems thinking may be realized through a variety of strategies, as illustrated earlier. Some, such as simulation techniques, require that researchers take the initiative in mastering new tools and languages. Poole has also pointed out that old prejudices against systems research must be shed, particularly that the use of qualitative approaches require the rejection of systems theories. Similarly, those with a quantitative orientation should consider integrating interpretive accounts into their own models. Newer systems approaches are highly flexible and not only suggest the interaction of multiple forms of analysis, they require it. Systems thinking thus has the ability to cut across traditional, albeit arbitrary, divisions that have historically characterized the field while indicating those critical foci that should undergird future theory development in organizational communication.

six

COMMUNICATION FOR ORGANIZING: A TYPOLOGY OF COORDINATION FORMATS

Bonnie Johnson

Interval Research Corporation

Organization theory throughout its brief history has been focused on issues related to the practical coordination of efforts to achieve common ends. Prior to the industrial revolution there was no evident need for a body of knowledge about how to organize for work. Work relationships were extensions of ingrained family patterns, as in cottage industries, and community relationships, as in guilds. Industrialization made it necessary for large numbers of strangers with no established patterns of interaction to learn to coordinate their actions in relatively brief periods of time. The coordination patterns learned at an early age that served well for such total organizations as the family or the guild were not adequate for the less than total involvement of large numbers of strangers in the limited-purpose organizations of an industrial society. In the latter, environmental coordination could not be taken for granted. The market for organization theory was created when people became conscious that organizing actions into cooperative systems was problematic, and that some ways of organizing might be better than others. Regardless of their disciplinary affiliations, organizational theorists speak to—ultimately if not directly—the practical question, "How can people work together better?"

The purpose of this chapter is to provide a framework for understanding and improving the methods by which people organize themselves into cooperative systems. Although most of the examples I use concern work-oriented systems, my analytical categories describe communication as the method by which people accomplish cooperation and coordination regardless of the setting. The tradition in organizational communication is to study communication within (or in relation to) the context of "formal" or "complex" organizations. In contrast, my conceptual framework concerns communication that functions to organize human activity.

The chapter has two major divisions. In the first section I describe the differences between the study of organizational communication as an organizing function and organizational communication as only one of the processes that occur within a complex organization. Here I argue the utility of premising a theory of organization on a theory of communication. In the next section I offer concepts for analyzing communicative methods of organizing. I call these methods "coordination formats." I suggest that although there is one basic process of organizing, each format functions somewhat differently in constructing systems of cooperation and coordination. I describe some of these functions. I also indicate some practical questions about coordination for researchers that are implied by this conceptual framework.

CONCEPTUAL FOUNDATIONS

Most texts on organization theory contain some statement about the importance of communication in organizations. Davis' (1972) metaphors are typical:

> Communication is as necessary to an organization as the bloodstream is to a person. Just as a man gets arteriosclerosis, a hardening of the arteries which impairs his efficiency, so may an organization get "infosclerosis," a hardening of the communication arteries which produces similar impaired efficiency. (p. 379)

In explaining why communication is important in an organization Davis stated "All management passes through the bottleneck of communication" (p. 380).

Although organization theorists such as K. Davis (1972) acknowledge the importance of communication within organizations, they tend to view it as one of a number of processes that happens because there are organizations. Note the function of communication in Figure 6.1 .

Communication is the process of transmitting information about other aspects of the organization—planning, designing, and so forth—and more often than not it is viewed as transmission of information from superiors to subordinates, manager to work group. In this traditional conception, the communication researcher's task is to study such questions as "How accurately are the intentions of *managers* transmitted to *workgroups* (downward communication)?" or "Are there adequate opportunities for managers to learn the responses of workgroups (upward communication or feedback)?" Although communication is acknowledged as a means of achieving coordination, this perspective on information transmission implicitly directs attention to improving messages or channels or both in order to improve coordination. Thus the implicit bias is for one-directional (top to bottom) control as the primary method of coordination.

K. Davis is typical of mainstream organizational theorists who begin by taking the existence of organizations as accomplished fact. They devise categories for explaining the processes that go on within organizations—planning, decision making, motivation, leadership, and so forth. Communication is one of these categories. Taking for granted the existence of the organization, some of the practical questions for organizational communications research are: How can the planners sell their ideas to the nonplanners? What kind of information system will prevent distortion? What kind of control system will prevent authority leakage?

An alternative perspective neither takes for granted the existence of organization nor looks at communications within that context. Rather, the focus is on the processes—communication processes—by which organizations are accomplished. The key concept in this approach is organizing.

```
               Planning
               Organizing
Manager ──▶ Staffing ──▶ Communication ──▶ Workgroup ──▶ Productivity
               Directing
               Controlling
```

Figure 6.1. Davis' model

Organizing is not a brief period that occurs in the history of an organization; rather, it is a continual process by which relationships are accomplished. Weick (1969) defined this view of organization succinctly: "Assume that there are processes that create, maintain, and dissolve social collectivities, that these processes constitute the work of organizing, and that the ways in which these processes are continuously executed are the organization" (p. 1). To understand organizations from this perspective, one must understand the communicative processes by which organizations are accomplished. The theorist's task is to study how organizing is accomplished. When communication theory is the starting point for explaining organizations, attention is on coordination through reciprocal relationships rather than formal control systems. From this perspective questions regarding span of control, information distortion, and authority leakage are not the most important practical questions to be addressed by the organization theorist. The practical questions concern how humans continuously create relationships through coordination of their actions.

To answer questions about constructing human relationships, one does not begin by considering how to create relationships on paper and then impose them on others. Rather, one investigates how people communicate with one another to create patterns of cooperation. If one assumes that interaction patterns are the substance of coordination and control networks, then one can study interaction patterns wherever they occur. Researchers are investigating organizing as a process rather than organizations as a context. Weick (1969) emphasized this point:

> These basic control and authority relationships are the essential ones in large as well as small groups. If we can understand how nine people go about the work of getting organized, producing, dissolving, and restructuring, then we shouldn't find many surprises when we watch 1,000 people go through the same activities. (p. 25)

Organizational communication is thus not contextually limited. It is functionally defined and becomes the conceptual arrangement by which we understand the variety of human interactions that coordinate individual actions.

In this section I have contrasted the traditional conception of organizational communication as something that happens inside creatures we call organizations with a perspective that considers communication as the process by which we create, maintain, and destroy coordination. The traditional perspective may limit organizational communication to the transmission of information. The logical problems for the theorist then are problems the communications engineer would call "noise." Better messages, more messages, more channels, and so forth will produce better communications and, at least implicitly, better organizations.[1] Coordination of actions is achieved through better information transmission that seems to mean some people clearly telling others what they are to do and then making sure it is done.

COORDINATION FORMATS

In the preceding section I argued the utility of premising a theory of organization on a theory of communication. Such a theory would begin with categories of communication and then examine some organizing potentials of each. In this section I describe four kinds of communication that I call "coordination formats." These are ways in which organizing processes may be executed. Each of the four provides one answer to the question, "How do people *take others into account* so that they may coordinate their actions?"

The first of these four ways I call "programmed interaction." Programmed interaction is largely "nonconscious." The second format is "planned interaction." People plan their interaction when they consciously attend to the norms, roles, agendas, and motivations of a *future* interaction with particular people. The distinguishing characteristics of this format is the *intra*personal planning period that precedes a given interaction. Planned interaction takes place when people are consciously attempting to influence particular others to act on their behalf. The third format I call collective decision-building. There is also planning for interaction in this format. The distinguishing characteristic here is that planning is *interpersonal*. Planning the interaction is explicit; it is carried out through interaction. A fourth format is formalizing or documentation. The first three formats are all kinds of oral communication. Formalizing is the creation of relatively permanent messages, written messages in particular, that are addressed "to whom it may concern" and signed "the organization." Let us now examine these formats in detail and consider the potential of each for accomplishing social systems.

---

[1] I recognize that theorists of organizational communication do not ignore the concept of human relationships. Goldhaber (1974), for example, devotes an entire chapter to "Human Relations in Organizations." Nor am I arguing that problems of information transmission are not practical or important. I am arguing that theorists of organizational communication need to tie their study of information transmission more closely to the study of how human relationships are developed. We need to study more often questions of the mode: "What kinds of communication function to organize what kinds of cooperative systems?"

Programmed Interaction

Everybody has an automatic pilot. When we drive down a familiar road, we steer, accelerate, and decelerate according to expectations learned from many times of driving over that road. Only when the unexpected occurs, such as a cat crossing in front of us, does our attention become problematic. That is, the question of what actions to take becomes a cause of concern. Even then, we may only have time to switch from one "program" (highway driving) to another (emergency stop). We may not have time to weigh the probabilities and consequences of hitting the cat versus being hit in the rear by a car four lengths behind us. We operate on "automatic pilot" when we are not conscious of the reasons and possible consequences of our actions. There is no "problem" toward which we are directing attention. We act "naturally" without any reflective thought of why or how. The program for driving a car is largely a solitary program. The objects to be maneuvered around—the road, the car—are not themselves acts. Social scientists have also described social or interaction programs. Goffman (1967) described interaction programs. Knapp, Hart, Frederick, and Shulman (1973) have described the program governing leavetaking. Organization theorists March and Simon (1958) used the term *program* to describe all routinized interactions in formal organizations. They defined the term:

> An environmental stimulus may evoke immediately from the organization a highly complex and organized set of responses. Such a set of responses we call a *performance program*, or simply a *program*. For example, the sounding of the alarm in a fire station initiates such a program. So does the appearance of a relief applicant at a social worker's desk. So does the appearance of an automobile chassis in front of the work station of a worker on the assembly line. Situations in which a relatively simple stimulus sets off an elaborate program of activity without any apparent internal of search, problem-solving or choice are not rare. They account for a very large part of the behavior of all persons, and for almost all of the behavior of persons in relatively routine positions. Most behavior, and particularly most behavior in organizations, is governed by performance programs. (pp. 141–142)

A program is a set of relatively elaborate responses set off by the appearance of a simple stimulus. When an old friend appears within talking distance, we respond with a relatively elaborate set of "How have you been?" responses. We take the other person into account by responding with a set of behaviors learned to be appropriate with that person and in that kind of situation. If we are simply enacting a *program*, by definition, we do not weigh possible consequences of our actions on the other. We do not consciously wonder why the other person is acting in a particular way. The other's intentions are taken for granted. In so doing we act with the other to create organized activity. March and Simon (1958) implicitly equated such organized action with "organization" when they stated that an environmental stimulus evokes from the organization a set of responses.

There are two prerequisites for programmed interaction. First, actors must be committed to a set of rules or a formula as the basis of their interaction. Second, actors must be monitoring the line of the interaction to provide cybernetic control of the relationship. A set of rules or a formula for interaction is a system of equivalent expectations held by all participants.[2] Any number of labels can be applied to the kinds of expectations that govern interaction. Michigan State researchers distinguish between "content" (what may be said) and "procedural" (how, when, and by whom) rules (Farace, Monge, & Russell, 1974). I find it useful to divide procedural rules or expectations into four categories: norms, roles, agendas, and intentions. Norms refer to those actions that are appropriate or obligatory for all members of a social system. Roles are those patterns of behavior by which people are expected to differentiate themselves from one another while complementing one another. Agendas are expectations about what is to happen when. Intentions are taken-for-granted expectations about why people are doing what they are doing. A good deal of research on "organizational behavior" may be classified into these categories.

Whatever classification scheme one uses to describe kinds of expectations, they are central to understanding organized activity. They are central because it is through expectations that individual behavior becomes "collective action." Katz and Kahn's (1966) use of the term *role* is functionally equivalent to expectations. They stated that, "It is at once the building block of social systems and the summation of the requirements with which the system confronts the individual member" (p. 171). The process of organizing is accomplished as people develop

---

[2]The term "equivalence" is used by anthropologist Anthony Wallace (1961) to describe the minimal conditions for psychic unity of human groups. Wallace offered the following example of equivalence in expectations:

Consider a group of airmen at a defense airbase. At the sound of claxon, they run to their aircraft, each taking an assigned seat, and commence the performance of their various highly specialized roles. There is one stimulus—the claxon—but its meaning, and the consequent responses, are different for each man. Nevertheless, the meanings—and the responses—can be defined as equivalent because whenever the claxon sounds, each responds in the same way that he has before. It is this equivalence of meanings which makes possible that coordinated specialization of responses to standard stimuli which is achieved in culturally organized societies. (p. 151)

expectations for one another's behavior. Individuals take others into account by acting as others expect. Expectations are the basis for organization in each of the four coordination formats I am discussing. In programmed interaction, actors do as expected; they do not think about what is expected.

When planning an interaction, in collective decision building, and in documentation, actors think about the future; in programmed interaction actors attend only to the present. They simply monitor what is happening. I use the term *monitor* as an analogy to the practice of television technicians who monitor an image on a screen to make sure the equipment is operating as expected. A deviation from the expected signal will throw them into a search for the cause of the disruption. Monitoring itself is not problem-searching or solving behavior. We monitor our programmed interactions to check out that others are using programs that are equivalent to ours. If we detect unexpected actions by another, we either change to another program or begin to plan the interaction.

There are a number of predictable consequences or functions of programmed interaction. The most obvious of these is stability in a social system. Programmed interactions contribute to stability because they render behaviors more predictable. March and Simon (1958) wrote: "Knowledge of the program of an organization permits one to predict in considerable detail the behavior of members of the organization. The greater the programming of individual activities, the greater the predictability" (p. 143). March and Simon are referring here to programmed actions, but the same inference can be made about interaction programs. The more individuals communicate with one another on the basis of taken-for-granted expectations, the more stable their interaction must be.

Programming of interaction can function to increase efficiency. It reduces decision costs by eliminating frequent but trivial decisions. Performance programs, for example, govern a good deal of the interaction between men and women. Two people do not need to figure out which one should open a door if one is a man and one is a woman. There is an interaction program governing that situation. In most American families the husband assumes the driver's role without a conscious thought by husband or wife. The interaction of the two people as they approach their car is programmed.

The case of intergender communication illustrates that we learn to use the same programs in many social systems. Programs thus function to permit stability across social systems. Sarason (1972) described how the existence of interaction programs function so that people organize new social systems largely like others in which they have been members. He said, in part:

> From time to time I have asked a class of my students to imagine that they want to start a new school for children. . . . They come up with all kinds of ideas and plans but they invariably have one thing in common: in the new school all the children are in one place. When I point this out to them with the statement that one could image a school in which different groups of children were in very different locations, the response is usually one of puzzlement or surprise. The characteristic common to their plans is a reflection of their previous experience with the existing organization we call school. [The commonality results from] categories [that] are not obvious; they are the unquestioned, even unverbalized aspects of thinking that insure that the new will have some features of the old. (p. 35)

We see in this example people attempting to plan interaction; they are thinking about the interactions that will constitute their "new schools." But their taken-for-granted expectations—their "categories of thought"—function so that their new social system will be comprised of many of their old interaction programs.

Programmed interaction can be a source of autonomy for members of an organization because programs cannot be mandated by organizational designers. At best, designers provide constraints within which organizational members develop their interpersonal programs. Designers can destroy programs by changing official regulations so that routine behavior is no longer routine. However, the process of creating a program can only be accomplished through direct communication of the interactants. Organizational literature is full of examples of the disruption of programmed interaction caused by the imposition of new regulations. W. M. Jones' (1964) study of decision making in the Defense Department is one example demonstrating that interaction programs are affected but not created by official regulations:

> The introduction of the new budgeting procedure in the Department of Defense is an excellent case study that demonstrates some of the difficulties. Without describing either the prior procedures or commenting on their merits and failings, one can simply observe that there was a sharp change in the formal organizational arrangements for handling this (budgeting) procedure. The old procedure had, over time, developed a well-recognized pattern of organization and communication at the subformal level. The sharp change in the formal system shattered many of the subformal arrangements and necessitated a rather unpleasant period of adjustment. [The personnel in charge of budget proposals] knew [the personnel] with whom they should interact in an attempt to "sell" their package. Without suggesting that they were always pleased with the results of such interactions, it can be noted they generally understood the subformal operations they had to perform in the attempt to accomplish their job. With the advent of the

new system this knowledge of operations was removed and a period of trial and error, false starts and general confusion ensued. It is worth noting that the pace with which the new system gained operating efficiency has been closely related to (and in the view of this writer, dependent upon), the rate at which a new subformal pattern has developed. (p. 7)

Personnel in the Department of Defense had established interaction programs ("subformal patterns") for accomplishing the budgeting process. They knew whom to contact for certain kinds of information. When they received information, they knew to whom it might be useful. They knew what kinds of questions they might ask others and what kinds would be considered out of line. The requirements of the new procedure could not be met with the old interaction programs. But neither could the formal procedures create new programs. The result was somewhat chaotic until the interactants themselves developed new expectations—new programs.

Another function of programmed interaction is the creation of organizational climate. McCroskey, Larson, and Knapp (1971) defined organizational climate as "a reflection of the prevailing assumptions about human behavior" (p. 189). Dehumanized climates, for example, result from interaction norms that prohibit overt expressions of feelings but permit distrust. Interaction roles are clearly divided by hierarchical function so that supervisors and subordinates base what they say and how they say it more on the official position of the other than on any other measure of competence or interest. Most important, participants take for granted that people are motivated only by money or other extrinsic reward. Expectations become climates as people enact interaction programs.

I have thus far limited my discussion to functions that have direct organizational consequences. Programmed interactions have functions that most directly affect individuals, but that have indirect organizational consequences. Programmed interactions are the means by which people define their common situation, clarify their roles, and thereby develop their self conceptions. Becker (1971) pointed out our individual stake (and implicitly our collective stake) in the interaction programs by which we do our work:

Usually we think of man's life in society as a rather routine thing, people going about their business so that the work can be done, saying what they have to say on the job or at the union hall. Even if we know about roles and statuses, how they structure social life, we tend to consider the whole thing as matter-of-fact; there shouldn't be much at stake in social encounters, since everything is fairly well pre-coded and automatic. So many of us may think—and we would be wrong. . . . In the social encounter each member exposes for public scrutiny, and possible intolerable undermining, the one thing he needs most: the positive self-evaluation he has so laboriously fashioned. With stakes of this magnitude there can be nothing routine about social life. Each social encounter is a hallowed event. (p. 88)

Because interactional programs have direct and indirect organizing consequences, it seems reasonable that theorists of organizational communication should be investigating their nature and function. Many organization theorists have called for the investigation of organizational programs. In general, the programs they describe are interaction programs (see Mintzberg, 1971). In addition, we should be investigating programs that are dysfunctional both for organizing and for the people who organize. Examples of these are programs based on norms of superrationality, impoverished roles, egocentric roles, and rigid agendas (e.g., Argyris, 1971).

I have suggested that interactional programs are relatively stable. If particular programs are determined to be dysfunctional, how could they be changed? One way to "change" a program is to wait for conditions to change. This is the passive way: you do not try to change. Instead, you tell yourself to wait for unforeseen circumstances to introduce uncertainty, for the routine to become nonroutine. This method "works." Change is inevitable, but often change is slight. And you can never count on changes in the direction you desire to occur on their own. In the following subsections I describe three more active way of directing change: planned interactions, collective decision-building, and documentation.

Planned Interactions

In planned interactions, you are conscious of your goals and you choose your own behaviors to influence the direction of change. Salesmen do this. They go to parties where everyone is acting normally on their established party programs. They pick out likely sales targets and choose communicative strategies to get what they want. When people recognize this ("Hey, this guy is not making small talk; he is trying to sell us something!"), they become more conscious of the interaction and their own motives. They start to respond by planning their own communications. The conversational program is up for grabs. Everyone is analyzing and adapting to the other.

A book that describes changing social formulas through the process of planned interaction is Alinsky's (1971) *Rules for Radicals: A Practical Primer for Realistic Radicals.* Alinsky described principles and methods for changing social systems where you are deprived, impoverished, and dehumanized. The method is essentially this: Analyze the other (enemy) members of the system, change your behavior in selected ways, and they will have to change theirs. In other words, be tactical. Alinsky defined *tactics:*

> Tactics means doing what you can with what you have. Tactics are those consciously deliberate acts by which human beings live with each other and deal with the world around them. In the world of give and take, tactics is the art of how to take and how to give. (p. 126)

The important words for us are "consciously deliberate." To be tactical, to plan interaction, means that you no longer take behavior for granted. You choose what to do on the basis of what you want (although you may not be clear about what you want) and what you have (although you may not know everything you have).

Planning is one of the processes most often linked with commonsense notions of organizing. For the classical organization theorists "organizing" was exclusively a process of planning or designing structure. They conceived of planning as an activity carried on by a select group of organizational members. The result of the process—the plan—was then "sent down" (communicated) to those who were to implement it. In this section I describe the organizing function of intrapersonal planning that precedes some interactions. I am concerned here with people planning their own interactions. I take up three questions: What is the nature of planning activity? What is the nature of interaction plans? What are some organizing functions of interaction planning?

The process of planning is the imaginative projection of consequences and justifications. Intrapersonal planning is displaying imagined futures to oneself. Collective planning involves displaying imagined futures to others. Planning is part of the process by which people make conscious choices. However, the term *choice* may be applied to actions even when there is no planning. Actions may be routinized or programmed so that the choice is obscure; actors may seem to make choices even when they are unaware of alternatives. For example, the executive who calls a staff meeting every Monday afternoon regards such meetings as routine. He or she may have chosen to hold the meetings during a period of rapid change. After a while the meeting time began to be filled with mundane announcements that could be made through other channels. An observer could conclude that the choice to hold the meeting on November 5th was a poor one. The executive and staff probably would be unaware when and why they chose to hold the meeting. Holding staff meetings became part of their interaction program. It was not a conscious choice on the part of the interactants. But an observer, by considering alternatives, could consider the action the result of choice.

"Planning," unlike "choice" is not a concept that an observer may use to describe another's nonconscious behavior. By definition planning is always deliberative, or conscious. We can say, indeed, that to plan is to be conscious. The philosopher Alfred Schutz (1967) distinguished conscious "action" from nondeliberative "behavior" in a way that helps us understand the nature of planned interactions and how they differ from programmed interactions in organizations;

> An action is conscious in the sense that, before we carry it out, we have a picture in our mind of what we are going to do. This is the "projected act." Then as we do proceed to action, we are either continuously holding the picture before our inner eye, or we are from time to time recalling it to mind. The total experience of action is a very complex one, consisting of experiences of the activity as it occurs, the various kinds of attention to that activity, retention of the projected act, reproduction of the projected act, and so on. This "map-consulting" is what we are referring to when we call the action conscious. Behavior without the map or picture is unconscious. . . . Our actions are conscious if we have previously mapped them out "in the future perfect tense." (p. 63)

Several ideas in Schutz's statement warrant elaboration. First, he equated what I am calling "planning" with consciousness when he insists that conscious action is guided by a "picture in the mind." This picture is formulated before the action. People often turn routine conversations into planned interactions in process. That is, they begin to imagine possible future actions of a conversation that they had been improvising on a program. Planned interactions may be woven into conversations that are largely routine. Most conversations, in fact, begin and end with interaction rituals; greetings and leave takings are generally unplanned. In the process of conducting a programmed conversation it may become more than routine. Actors begin to consider their own words and those of others before the words are spoken. When this occurs, the casual or routine conversation becomes "planned interaction."

Schutz's description of conscious action also helps us to understand the nature of plans. One commonsense understanding of "plan" is a step-by-step, how-to-do-it guide to construction. "Plans" for constructing furniture are examples of this kind. However, the construction of human relationships is not analogous to the construction of physical objects. Interaction plans are not step-by-step guides. Schutz used the term *projected act* to describe plans for human encounters. A projected act is "the goal of the action . . . which is brought into being by the action" (p. 141). He insists that "only the completed act can be pictured in phantasy" because it is only the total or completed act that is meaningful (p. 141). The kind of plan I am describing is a fantasized picture of completed human action. The meaning of any action can only be seen in retrospect. What, then, of actions that are not yet completed? Even incomplete actions are pictured as completed acts. We are able to imagine justifications and consequences of actions as if we had completed them. Through our imagination we "look back on" what we have not yet done. We think of possibilities in the future perfect tense (p. 141).

To say, therefore, that an interaction is "planned" means that, at least, one party has an image of the completed interaction. The plan is this imagined future state. Precisely because it is imagined, the plan is vague. It necessarily lacks significant details. Plans are symbolic representations of the future. They are "displays in the mind." They are dynamic, fluid, and abstract. As such they can never be realized. The feeling of unfulfilled expectations is a common one to all of us. We anticipate "what it will be like when. . . ." We have pictures of what it will be like to have graduated, to be working on a new job, or to live in a new house. Most important, we picture what human interactions will have been like. When the actions and interactions we plan actually come into existence, the lived experience is never exactly as we had thought it would be.

Interactions as objects of plans are unique because they concern interactions—that is, they are the product of the actions of more than one person. If a person plans her solitary actions, she can be reasonably confident of the projected outcome though the experience will be different from the projected image. If she notices that it is time to change the oil in her car, she may plan her actions beginning with buying the new oil and ending with discarding the oil she has drained from the crankcase. Any number of unanticipated events may intrude to motivate a change of plans—the store may be out of oil or she may fall and break an arm. However, such accidents would literally be intrusions into a sequence of events that would otherwise be somewhat predictable. The events would be predictable because they are solitary actions; they do not require much active participation by others. Once we begin to speak of participation of others—interaction rather than action—we must confront the fact that others have plans of their own. We cannot predict interactions as we can solitary actions because the actions of others are relatively unpredictable. Unpredictable events are accidental intrusions into our planned actions. However, unpredictable events are the very substance of our interactions regardless of how well they are "planned." If a person unscrews a crankcase plug she can be sure that oil will flow out. The oil is subject to the law of gravity. If a wife plans to convince her husband that he should change the oil, the results are characteristically uncertain.

Whenever we speak of a planned interaction, then, it is proper to ask "whose plan?" The existence of multiple plans for interaction means that no one plan will be enacted. Instead of the metaphor of building construction guided by visual plans, a more appropriate metaphor is a game in which each opposing party has plans for the mutual interaction, and each person's plan must take into account the plans and actions of the other. Seen in light of this metaphor, plans are strategies. Planned interaction is what Goffman called "strategic interaction." The game metaphor helps us to understand the role of planning in interaction. In particular, it helps us to understand the role of "the other" in the planning process—in other words, how planning an interaction is different than planning an action. It also helps to explain how people enact their plans through interactions in which others are simultaneously enacting their plans.

To explain the features of a "game situation," Goffman (1969) used a series of scenarios involving a fictious hero named Harry. The first scenario is of a planned action. Harry is a forest ranger who is "caught in a bush fire and perceives that to his right there is a tall tree that might be possible to climb and may survive the flames, and to his left a high bridge already beginning to burn." Harry plays out in his mind four possible courses of action: make for the bridge, make for the tree, call on the gods to save him, vacillate in an attempt to think of other escapes. Using the language of the game, it is Harry's "turn"; the opportunity for choice is his. The action he decides upon is his "move." To take a rational, game-like approach or to "plan his action," Harry would list all the possibilities, attach a success probability to each one, and solve his problem by selecting which one seems to offer his best chance for survival. He has got to figure whether the bridge will burn before he gets across or whether he has a better chance to survive the high fall into the water. This is a complicated situation. But Harry is planning only his solitary actions. The tree will not move itself in anticipation of Harry's climbing it.

The situation is different when Harry must plan an interaction. Contrast the planning of action with Goffman's (1969) scenario of planning interaction:

> Harry, the native spearman, having strayed from the territory populated by his tribesmen, comes into a small clearing to find that another spearman from a hostile tribe is facing him from what would otherwise be the safe side. Since each finds himself backed by the other's territory, retreat is cut off. Only by incapacitating the other can

either safely cross the clearing and escape into his own part of the forest. Now the game. If there were no chance of missing a throw, then the first spearsman to throw would win. However, the likelihood of missing a fixed target increases with the distance of the throw. In addition, a throw, as a move, involves a spear easily seen to be on its way by the target. And the target itself isn't quite fixed. It is able to dodge and will certainly try to do so. The greater the distance of the throw, the more time to dodge and the greater the chance of doing so. And to miss a throw while the other still has his spear allows the other to approach at will for an easy win. Thus, each player begins at a point where it does not pay to chance a throw and presumably approaches a point where it does not pay not to. *And each player, in deciding what to do, must decide knowing the other is engaged in exactly the same sort of decision, and knowing that they both appreciate this.* (pp. 93-94)

The crucial process involved in planning interaction that distinguishes it from planning action is figuring out the intentions on which the others will base their actions. This is done by starting with what we see (for example, an enemy with a spear blocking the path home). We then imagine what we would do if we were he. We attempt consciously to "take the role of the other." In effect we imagine what our goal would be in the situation and project the presumed goal of the other as if it were our own. Then we imagine what actions we would take if that presumed goal of the other were our goal. We may do this by remembering what we actually have done in situations we think to be comparable. We then use these pictures of imagined consequences as information in deciding what we should do. Or as Goffman (1969) explained: Once Harry sees the need to assess his apparent view of the situation, game theory gives him a way of being systematic. He should exhaustively enumerate the distinctively different courses of action open to the opponent as a response to each of his own moves, and in light of these settle on his best course of action (p. 100).

A plan for interaction is a strategy, a "framework of different courses of action each linked in advance to a possible choice of the opponent." A plan is a complex picture of "if–then" relationships. If I do "A," then he will do "B." But the "if's" and the "then's" that constitute strategies, or plans for interaction, are vague guesses of what the future will be like. We have incomplete pictures of what others will do in response to our actions. We cannot possibly think of all the alternatives and calculate probabilities. We cannot even know what our own actions will be like until we actually do them.

Although the outcome of any particular planned interaction is relatively unpredictable, the planning process itself has several predictable organizing functions. One of its functions is stability of the system and predictability for individual members of the system.

Stability is largely the result of programmed interaction, but programs are constantly disrupted by a turbulent environment. Plans simplify the complexity of the world so that people can decide what they should do. Becker (1971) observed that everyone poses to himself or herself the question, "How are they going to act next?" And that a person's answer to this question "allows one to frame an adequate response based upon a reasonable inference" (p. 84). One function of plans is that they act as stabilizers of nonroutine interaction. In planning we devise categories for understanding others' actions and for relating our actions to theirs, thus permitting coordinated actions.

A second function is related to the first. Plans not only permit us to simplify complex stimuli so that we can decide how to act, they permit us to act with deliberate purpose. Programmed interaction is "intentional communication." An observer could determine the "goal-directedness" of a programmed interaction. However, planned interaction is more than intentional. Actors have given thought to the purpose of their communication. The interaction is rhetorical. It proceeds from a prior planning period in which actors clarify their goals (by imagining them in the future perfect tense) and choose communication strategies on the basis of their goals and their information about the other interactants. It is characterized by "mapconsulting" in which people modify their actions (and often their planned goals) to meet unfolding contingencies. Purposeful interaction, directed toward particular goals and constrained by the expectations of particular people is a second function of this coordination format.

A third function is organizational change. I mentioned this function briefly in the previous section. In planned interactions communicative actions are deliberately chosen. Therefore, changes in patterns of planned interaction may be both more rapid and more suited to task requirements and individual preferences than changes in programmed interactions because actions in programmed interactions are not deliberately chosen. Interactions that are largely planned rather than programmed function to permit organizational change by creating a "situational climate." According to McCroskey et al. (1971), people in a situational climates attempt "to elicit the 'appropriate' responses for a given situation." Those authors suggest that in such climates people learn to "generalize from their previous experiences while continually watching for unique elements in a given situation" (pp. 202–203). Therefore, organizing accomplished through planned interaction should be more informed and have greater capacity for innovation.

Collective Decision Building

Another way to change is to make a collective decision to change.

Because a program requires the participation of all interactants, one person can stimulate renegotiation of the contract. One person can force others to treat him differently, but he cannot always force them to treat him in some particular way. If a group of people want a new set of expectations they can explicitly—in words—attempt to renegotiate those expectations.

An interesting book that describes how to change a social formula through collective decision is N. O'Neill and G. O'Neill's (1972) *Open Marriage: A New Life Style for Couples*. O'Neill and O'Neill proposed a change strategy that calls for the marriage partners to discuss their assumptions and explicitly to renegotiate their contract, especially the marriage formula they call an unconscious contract:

> Instead of surrendering to the hidden clauses of the old, closed contract, you can write your own, individual, open contract. You can agree to look honestly and openly at what you are doing and why you are doing it— whether you are going to get married today or have been married ten years. The power of the hidden clauses of the old contract to construct your marriage lies in the very fact that they are hidden. We have seen how those clauses operate through our examination of the relationship between John and Sue. We have seen the dangers of unconsciously accepting those hidden clauses. Look at your own marriage. Get the hidden clauses out into the open. Then you can begin to rewrite your contract *as you go along* starting new, from scratch, today. (p. 126)

Of course, rewriting the hidden assumptions about who should do what in a relationship is not a simple matter. The dishes get dirty every day. It is a routine occurrence. It is efficient to have a general assumption about who will do them. Few people want to spend the effort to do collective decision making every time the dishes need washing. It is harder to change an interaction program than to quit smoking.

There are two characteristics that distinguish collective decision building from other coordination formats. First, the planning process is interpersonal, and it is verbal. Second, the result of the process is a set of symbols that a group of people announces as its "decision." Thus, in coordination through collective decision building the process, and the product are symbolic. For example, two men may cooperate in the building of a cabinet without talking much about what they are doing. Their cooperation may result from a program. That is, after making 20 or so such cabinets together, they each know exactly what is expected of each. Their coordination does not require talk. The cabinet is their product which need not be symbolic. If they are learning to work together, each may be quite conscious of his actions and the impact of his actions on the others. They are planning. They may talk about their actions, but talk is not mandatory.

If the two engaged in collective decision building with regard to the cabinet they would necessarily talk. The outcome of their talk would be a more or less explicit agreement about how the cabinet is to be built. This agreement might specify what the cabinet should look like (their goal), the general procedures to be followed (the norms), who is to do what (the roles), and in what order the subtasks are to be done (the agenda). One output of the process is the verbalized agreement, but this agreement is not the whole decision. The plan is necessarily vague just like the outcome of individual planning. It does not represent all the decisions necessary to build the cabinet, and vague symbols must be translated into actions. This translation is part of the whole decision-building process. The plan provides a common point of reference that each person uses in making decisions about the cabinet. These "translating" decisions are not individual decisions because they are made with reference to a set of verbalized agreements. Let us look in slightly more detail at the two characteristics of collective decision-building: (a) talk about expectations or procedures and (b) symbolic or announced decisions.

In normative texts on group discussion, authors usually suggest that people begin with an orientation phase. In this phase talk is largely "metadiscussional." People talk about content rules (topics to be discussed) and procedures (norms such as whether smoking is to be permitted, roles such as who will moderate, the agenda, and the goals). Those who have analyzed the context of discussions empirically report that in most groups there is some initial period of metadiscussional or "orienting" talk. Whether or not there is a particular time or phase in which much of the talk concerns rules or expectations for the interaction, there is metadiscussional talk throughout collective decision-building processes. Seen from this perspective, metadiscussional talk such as summarizing and reality testing are kinds of interpersonal planning. Group members offer one another verbalized images of what is happening and will be happening in the discussion. People construct through talk a collective and ongoing "map" of their interaction. Some of their talk functions in part as collective "map consulting."

Collective decisions are "announced," though often announced only to the group making the decision. Such a decision is "collective" in the same way that any symbol or message is shared collectively. The announced decision provides a focus for individual interpretations, and the symbols serve as guides individuals use in making personal decisions about how to act. Collective decisions are the coordinated actions of people (perhaps a few, perhaps millions) motivated in part by a set of symbols devised and announced by that group of people. The total process of decision building includes both methods by which a group produces an "announced decision" and the methods by which people interpret the symbols through their actions.

Collective decision building, like programmed and planned interaction, is a process for reducing uncertainty about action choices, and this functions to permit coordinated activity. Unlike the other two forms, coordination is premised on verbalized agreements that serve as guides to coordination. Thus, one function of collective decision building that differs from functions of the other two formats is commitment. The practice called "participatory management" is an attempt to replace one-directional control with coordination through collective decision building. The rationale is supported by research demonstrating that the greater the verbal involvement of a person in constructing an announced decision, the more that individual will be committed to implementing the decision (J. Hall, 1969).

Change is a second function of collective decision building. It facilitates change because it replaces the unstated expectations of interaction programs with stated expectations. Once expectations are verbalized, they become objects of attention. Of course, expectations do not automatically change because people decide they should be changed, but expressed agreement to change encourages commitment to change and permits the possibility of individuals supporting one another in their attempts to change.

The area of collective decision building has been the subject of considerable organizational research. Most of it is referenced under the term *small-group decision making*. Some researchers have investigated the function of informal small groups within large organizations. We have a good deal to learn about the function of metadiscussional talk in the process of organizing. Specific research questions might concern the following general question. How does talk about the process of organizing change the process?

Documentation

In the first section of this chapter I suggested that the processes of organizing are the same regardless of the size or complexity of the resulting organization. This view is shared by other organization theorists, but is not widely accepted. In arguing for this perspective with some who reject it, I have found great resistance to equating discussion between a father and a son concerning who is to cut the lawn and negotiation between the head of the Fisher Body Division of General Motors and the G. M. Chairman of the Board concerning how cost centers are to be delineated. The two situations are so obviously different that the essential similarities of organizing function are not evident. The situations are essentially the same because they both involve people who are learning to coordinate their work. Each pair has the possibility of using programmed interaction, planned interaction, and collective decision building as a means of coordination. However, the second pair consists of members of a "formal organization"; the first pair does not. Both formal and informal organizations are systems of expectations. In this section I discuss the process of documenting or formalizing as a coordination format.

Often those who want interaction programs changed are not the interactants themselves, but others. Typically, we think of higher executives or planners who want to change the actions of those far below themselves in an organization. Their aim is for tighter control as a means of better coordination. Because those who want the change are not part of the face-to-face communication system, they cannot use planned interaction or collective decision building. They may use an indirect method for effecting the change—organizational document or written regulation.

The first three formats discussed are constructed through the use of oral communication—speech. Of the three formats, expectations are least expressed (not verbalized) in programmed interaction. They are most clearly expressed (verbalized) in collective decision building. Organizations are formalized through the use of non-oral communication—documents—to express expectations. Thus, the distinguishing characteristic of documentation is the creation of expectations through messages that are not oral. Let us examine some differences between speech and documentation as a means of understanding how each creates different organizing possibilities.

I use the term *speech* to refer not simply to spoken, verbal messages, but to all the visual and other stimuli that accompany messages. Smiles, frowns, body positioning, and distance between people are all ways in which we speak about our feelings and thoughts. We speak our feelings as we feel them by smiling, laughing and touching. Our speech behavior is constantly changing with our changing mental and emotional states. By contrast, documents are relatively static. I use the term *document* to refer not only to written messages, but to anything that has a permanent structure and that can have symbolic meaning. Thus, office furniture is a document. It acts as a nonverbal message about the status of the occupant. It can be changed, but unlike a smile, it cannot be changed instantaneously.

Organizations we call "informal" are created through speech alone. No one writes down anything about how people should relate to one another. Organizations are "formalized" by documenting how people should relate to one another. Written expectations may take such forms as job descriptions (who does what), organizational charts (who has authority over whom), budgets (who gets what), procedures (what happens when), and goal or objective statements (where are we going). Speech is the primary means of organizing in any social system, but, in those which we call "formal," there is an additional process of documentation.

Much has been researched and written about the differences between speech and written communication as means of transmitting information within organizations. However, almost no work has been done in investigating how they function differently in creating human relationships. The writings of C. C. Arnold (1974, 1980) distinguishing oral from written rhetoric are suggestive of differences between organizing through speech and organizing through documentation. I discuss these differences under four headings: personality, adaptiveness, informativeness, and potential for editing.

Speech is a personal means of communication. According to Arnold (1974, 1980), a speaker's personality "stands with" his or her message. We cannot listen to another person talk without making judgments about the speaker's personality. When we talk face to face with another we experience that other as a person, not a series of disembodied symbols. This means that the ethos of a person's message is personal ethos. Judgments of the credibility of the message are confounded with judgments of the person as he or she appears to be when presenting the message. Impressions change as the message unfolds. Because we "stand with" our spoken messages, it is risky to speak. We must observe negative responses to our message.

Documents are nonpersonal by design, They are addressed "to whom it may concern" and signed "the organization." They carry the ethos of the organization. Signing with the name of the organization does not involve much personal risk. The executive who sends an official memo ordering a budget cut is saved from experiencing the initial hostility he or she would have felt if the message had been delivered in person.

Despite the risks, most of us prefer to talk with another face to face than to exchange written messages. One reason is that in oral communication we can adapt our message. Watch an adult who is talking with another adult when a 4-year-old approaches and demands his attention. He will turn his head, change the expression on his face, change his tone of voice, and the complexity of his vocabulary. In short, he will adapt to his new audience. Moreover, whereas he will, in part, be adapting to his audience as a member of a class of humans called "child," he will also adapt to his *particular* child at this *particular* time. If she is his offspring and he thinks she is unduly interrupting, he will probably scold her in a manner he has found to be effective with her.

Skillful oral communicators are those best able to adapt to particular others *in process*. Even clumsy communicators can be more adaptive to a particular audience if they are speaking directly with the audience rather than writing or otherwise "documenting" their messages.

When we are engaged in oral communication with another, we get and give a great deal more information than when we communicate with documents. When we see a person, his facial expressions display his intentions. We use eye contact as a clue to sincerity. When he stands very close, we interpret the intentions of messages differently. Even if we only hear a person, his tone of voice, rate, inflection and pauses are cues to what he way saying.

When communicating with documents, the language, the form, even the timing of messages become important as cues of the source's intentions. Awkward phrases that would have been overlooked in oral communication become causes of great frustration because the readers are unable to figure out what is being said.

The creators of documents edit their messages to express their intentions more clearly. Speakers also make feeble attempts at editing. When we hear people say, "What I meant to say was" or "yesterday, no, day before yesterday" we are observing oral editing. But when we are speaking, all of our editing—errors included—is displayed to our listener. One reason that oral communication is so "risky" is that we show the other our "thoughts in process." We reveal ourselves to the other at the same time that we are seeing ourselves. We cannot erase our mistakes from the minds of our audiences.

Spoken communication is edited by the listener. Without a document to "prove" what happened or what someone was supposed to do, it is difficult to hold people to account for their actions. A. Downs (1967) observed that oral messages are important precisely because they can be withdrawn, altered, adjusted, magnified or canceled without any official record being made. We have more freedom in interpreting (editing) another's intentions and in reinterpreting out past behavior when there is no record.

These differences between speech and documentation function to permit quite different kinds of coordination. The four differences I have suggested—personality, adaptiveness, informativeness, and editing—center on the theme of rigidity. Speech is more "fluid" than documents. Speech constantly changes as our "mood" changes, as we adapt to the changing of the other, as we get more information about the other, as we attempt to adjust what we are saying because we are dissatisfied with how it is "coming out." Those organizations that are created almost totally by speech are very fluid. They have a great capacity to adapt because members cannot hold one another to account to behave in accordance with written rules. The rules of interaction are potentially being renegotiated all the time. When members of an organization begin writing their expectations they stabilize the patterns of interaction by introducing some rigidity. The message form—the document—stays the same, although, of course, individuals still interpret the same overt messages differently.

There are several differences in function that are more or less related to the difference in rigidity. First, of course, use of documents permits much larger systems of coordination. Organizations such as we have today would be impossible if there were no documents to provide rigidity across large numbers of people (A. Downs, 1967). A second and related function is centralized control. The more organizing takes place through programmed and planned interaction and through face-to-face collective decision-building, the more groups of people will develop idiosyncratic systems of expectations. Because these expectations are learned through speech, they will vary from one group to another. Use of documents brings some uniformity among different groups because they provide a focus for interpretation. The more specific the document in describing who is to do what and when, the more uniformity there may be.

Documents are not means of mindless control. However, because central authorities do not observe firsthand the responses to their messages, there is less reciprocity in control by documentation than in control through speech. This is another way of saying documents are less adaptive than speech and consequently the organizations they create are less adaptive. Organizing through documentation functions to permit a kind of blind impartiality. Members of an organization respond to each not as live personalities, but as paper categories. Individuals may receive the same treatment as everyone else in their category. Such decision rules permit quick decisions as well as a kind of "fairness."

Documentation also permits a kind of "visual design" applied to human relationships. "The organization" may appear to exist on paper. If the organization is represented on paper, then it may be redesigned on paper. Thus, managers and planners "design" organizations to be more rational. They "edit" the structure. Of course, they can directly change the symbolic representation of the organization. The process of formalizing involves creating constraints so that interpersonal structures are "rationalized" in accordance with a paper design of human coordination.

One avenue of organizational research has concerned how to control people (create constraints). to assure that they will act in accordance with "official expectations." This is one way to answer the question "How can people work together better?" But is there only one way? I have suggested here that because documentation is less personal, less adaptive, and less informative, its possibilities for creating coordination are limited. A complete research program would also investigate how people use oral communication to learn to coordinate their work.

CONCLUSION

In this chapter I have argued for a functional approach to the study of organizational communication. I have offered an alternative to defining organizational communication as that communication which takes place within a formal organization. I have suggested that communication is the method or process by which people accomplish coordination of their activity. I have said that differences in organizations result from differences in the formats people use to execute organizing methods. I have distinguished four coordination formats on the basis of the extent to which expectations are deliberated and expressed in the form of verbalized messages. Thus "expectations" and "messages" are central concepts.

seven

TRANSFORMING ORGANIZATIONS THROUGH COMMUNICATION

Eric M. Eisenberg, Linda Andrews, Alexandra Murphy, and Linda Laine-Timmerman
University of South Florida

"Man is a singular creature. He has a set of gifts which make him unique among the animals: so that, unlike them, he is not a figure of the landscape—he is a shaper of the landscape. In body and in mind he is the explorer of nature, the ubiquitous animal, who did not find but has made his home in every continent."
—J. Bronowski, *The Ascent of Man*

"This is a strange world, and it promises to get stranger. . . . So we must live with the strange and the bizarre, even as we climb stairs that we want to bring us to a clearer vantage point. Every step requires that we stay comfortable with uncertainty, and confident of confusion's role. After all is said and done, we will have to muddle our way through. But in the midst of the muddle—and I hope I remember this—we can walk with a sure step. For these stairs we climb only take us deeper and deeper into a universe of inherent order."
—Margaret Wheatley, *Leadership and the New Science*

Ishmael said, "We know what happens if you take the Taker premise, that the world belongs to man." "Yes, that's a disaster." "And what happens if you take the Leaver premise, that man belongs to the world?" "Then creation goes on forever." "How does that sound?" "It has my vote."
—Daniel Quinn, *Ishmael*

The natural state of the universe is one of constant change—of transformation and mutation, degradation and decay. Each life form is challenged to adapt to these changing conditions. Adaptation, for most species, takes place over many generations. Order is introduced by trial and error. Human organizing, however, is qualitatively different. For human beings, language and communication offer a relatively speedy tool for creating order. Communication is such a powerful organizing force that a very few people communicating in particular ways can and have had enormous influence on the species, and on the planet.

Attempts at organization are made against a backdrop of unlimited variation and possibility. For this reason, what is most remarkable is not change, but stability—how certain patterns of thought, talk, and behavior persist over time. For example, when we contrast Classical approaches to organizing with Human Resources approaches (cf., Eisenberg & Goodall, 1997), we are characterizing distinct world views and interaction patterns, each of which dominated consciousness and practice for decades before yielding to other patterns. But how did each scheme gain prominence? How is it that people achieve routine through communication? How do we organize in ways that construct the "taken for granted" across a series of historical moments?

Posed at this level of abstraction, the question of what makes for persistent patterns seems straightforward. But when we move to consider the enduring nature of specific organizational changes—and to questions of why, how, and when they might be made—we are cast immediately into an ocean of complexity. The complication comes about for at least two reasons. First, all patterns and structures favor some individuals and species over others. Consequently, we must attend to the *political* consequences of all change efforts. Second, people generally *resist* change, particularly when initiated by someone other than themselves. The combined result of these two tendencies is that most planned change efforts fail, as people resist them both because they are uncomfortable with new forms of behavior and because they perceive that the proposed change may not be in their best interest.

The purpose of this chapter is to outline some basic elements of a theory of organizational communication and change. We begin with a review of what is by now familiar territory, a discussion of how the collapse of traditional paradigms has created a special urgency for holistic thinking and for revolutionary, second-order change. Next, we reframe the challenge of coping with organizational stability and change as a special case of the more general human problem of negentropy— creating order out of chaos. Third, we consider in detail the pragmatics of organizational transformation, revealing parallels between evolving conceptions of communication and changing models of organization.

Our favored approach features dialogue as a driving force in promoting lasting organizational transformation.

WHY CHANGE?

This century has been characterized as a period of rapid, radical and dramatic change—perhaps the most profound revolution ever experienced (Osterberg, 1993). Discoveries in quantum mechanics have shifted our picture of the universe from one consisting of solid, discrete objects separated by space to a field of constantly varying and intimately connected energy. The universe vibrates and flows in unbroken waves. When we perceive the universe as complex, creative, and whole, we can conceptualize organizations as the same—communities of people interpreting complex and interconnected stimuli to respond creatively to continual change (Bohm, 1980; Henderson, 1993; Isaacs, 1993a, 1993b; Ray, 1993; Wheatley, 1992).

In a world undergoing enormous technological, economic, and political change, many of the established ways we have of living together are not working well (Bellah, Madsen, Sullivan, Swidler, & Tipton, 1992). The source of many of our problems is the fragmented way in which we conceive of our world. This fragmentation results in nations that consider themselves separate from others, and members of nations divided from other members (Bohm & Edwards, 1991). Fragmented ways of thinking create organizations that function as discrete entities scrambling for resources, innovation, and customers. Within this competitive context, organizational members refuse to share information. They construct boundaries to protect perceived power bases. Organizations react to crises without considering the global consequences of their actions. In contrast, holistic thinking can create organizations that exist primarily as "structures within which people come together to learn cooperatively" (Osterberg, 1993, p. 69).

To become more civil, humans must become ever more conscious of themselves, of others, and of the organizations that bring us together (Peck, 1993). We live on a planet that demands we develop better ways of living and working together. Searching for ways to structure interdependent lives more responsibly is no longer, if it ever was, the province of idealism—it has become the fundamental need we all share (Bellah et al. 1992). We tend to believe that somebody else's part of the boat is sinking and that it will not affect us. Instead we must talk together, cooperate, or we will destroy ourselves. Our problems are not "out there," they are "in here" (Bohm & Edwards, 1991).

Although there have been major crises on Earth in the past, it now seems that we face a unique historical moment in which most if not all traditional paradigms are collapsing simultaneously (Lyotard, 1984; Ventura, 1993). This situation is both terrifying and exhilarating. The need for change has never been greater, but the process of organizational transformation is in no sense easy or straightforward. The difficulties of altering routine, of challenging the taken-for-granted assumptions and practices of any culture are formidable. Many people are reluctant to abandon routines for psychological reasons, preferring *certain* dysfunctionality to an *uncertain* future. A less apparent source of resistance comes from the larger framework of justifications and constraints that runs through every society and culture. In this way, any proposed new pattern of organizational behavior (e.g., building daycare centers at work sites; inviting employees to participate in decision making) can only be understood within a set of cultural stories and assumptions concerning appropriate behavior for mothers, fathers, workers, bosses, businesses, and countries.

Having said this, the usual conclusion is that organizational behavior is hard to change precisely because these various cultural stories have significant staying power or inertia. Today, however, *growing fissures in each of these canonical stories diminishes resistance to change at the organizational level.* This is why the current moment is one of great possibility, and even suggests that changes made at the organizational level may in turn have significant consequences for the reshaping of larger, taken-for-granted stories about society as a whole.

One recent example of the interaction between organizational change and broader social developments can be found in the decline of the "old social contract" between employers and employees in America (Chilton & Weidenbaum, 1994). Researchers observe that until a few years ago, employees were loyal to their employers and expected loyalty in return—stable employment, benefits, and decent treatment. Increased global competition, advanced technology, and the development of a global workforce created conditions that made possible the termination of this invisible contract; workers who had been employed by a company for years were unceremoniously replaced by employees from another country at a fraction of the cost (cf. Goodall & Eisenberg, 1997). By now, even the pretense of loyalty is gone from most companies, as employees are hired and fired (or used as independent contractors) in accord with rapidly fluctuating business conditions. These changes have resulted in a widespread questioning of the nature of jobs, work, human rights, and capitalism.

Pursuing Second-Order Change

The nature of this questioning—of considering our current predicament and deciding how to best move forward—varies considerably. Although it is clear that the era of ever-expanding growth and limited competition is over, management models developed in the waning years of that era continue to enjoy popularity. Total Quality Management, with its emphasis on continuous improvement, is notable for its reliance on evolutionary or first-order change. For many of today's organizations, however, the choices to be made are more similar to the situation facing boat transport companies at the dawn of commercial air travel. The first response of these companies to the invention of the airplane was denial, followed by desperate attempts at improvement (e.g., faster boats, better food, cheaper prices). In the end, *no amount of continuous improvement can save a company with an obsolete goal.* Even the speediest boats with the tastiest food could not compete with affordable overseas travel by air. Second-order change involves reexamining and changing your goals, not just the effectiveness with which you reach them. Those boat companies that did survive redefined their business as entertainment, not transportation, and created the cruise industry. This is not an isolated story. In organizations around the world, radical ideas about the purpose and organization of schools, churches, and government are facing heated discussion.

But how do you imagine the first person who suggested the idea of a "cruise to nowhere" was received by his or her peers? Timing and readiness for change is crucial, and most people's natural tendencies toward resistance often mean that second-order change, when it comes at all, comes too late (Handy, 1993). The best time to make second-order change is sooner—and the change required more dramatic—than most of us are prepared to face. If we wait until our current pattern no longer works, however, we will most likely have missed the boat.

Although a specific organizational arrangement may work today, our hypercompetitive business environment dictates that no single configuration can be successful for long. This is a marked departure from generations past, when placid organizational environments allowed companies to conduct "business as usual" for years, even decades. In 1980, for example, banking, air transportation, and fast food were all relatively stable industries in placid environments. Today, sea changes in technology, customer preferences, global competition, and employee expectations challenge organizations to be in a continual state of reinvention and renewal. This is one reason why TQM approaches have been in large part usurped by "reengineering" approaches (Hammer & Champy, 1993) that begin with a clean sheet of paper in redesigning work processes.

The lessons of reinvention and second-order change echo outside the world of organizations. In the realm of children's toys, the most popular action figures no longer use conventional weaponry. Instead, in responding to threat, Ninja Turtles mutate, Transformers transform, and Power Rangers morph. Our children and grandchildren receive the clear message that speedy, structural change is the optimal response to adversity. We may in time thank the toy manufacturers for propagating this orientation. After all, the organism currently atop the food chain—the virus—succeeds by second-order change. Viruses are enormously difficult to fight because they change structure in response to attack. Perhaps the only way we will learn to compete with such organisms is through second-order thinking—by designing "smart" medicines that can morph along with viruses as they change structure.

Courting Holism in an Era of Limits

We have thus far maintained that change is essential to survival, and that second-order change—the reexamination of our aims and goals—is especially critical today. What we have not yet mentioned is a unifying theme behind many if not most change efforts, both in and outside of organizations. This theme has to do with the rediscovery of our radical interdependence, and with it the recognition that social problems can only be addressed by taking into account whole systems (Senge, 1990). The nuclear destruction at the close of World War II made clear how devastating our technological attempts at adaptation could turn out; the world has not been the same since. In the near future, we predict that any system which does violence to the species or planet as a whole (e.g., nationalism, capitalism) will come under suspicion, if not attack.

One might call this situation a crisis of habitat, or perhaps a crisis of identity. At the same time that we assemble in small (ethnic, gender, religious, professional, socioeconomic) groups to assert our differences, we are being pushed daily to discover our common concerns. Recall that the "tragedy of the commons" occurred when farmers sought foolishly to maximize their individual gains at the expense of the common pasture. Today, multinational corporations and national governments do similar harm to human rights and ecosystems in the name of profitability and survival. How will this strategy play out in the long run? The time has come to begin thinking in a planetary way about issues of employment, human rights, and habitat.

Evidence of such a capacity emerging in either the political or organizational arenas has been minimal. What is more, many observers maintain that leadership of this sort will not come from a single source, or in even a unified way. Instead, they claim that new models of organization are emerging at a grass-roots level, through the efforts of like-minded people focused on organizing in ways that are protective of "the commons" (Barnet & Cavanaugh, 1993; Handy, 1994).

CHAOS, ORDER, AND MANAGEMENT

One reason why the types of changes we are proposing are so hard to consider is that current patterns of organizational behavior are deeply rooted in the fundamental characteristics of our species, and specifically in the ways in which language and rationality construct our relationship to the rest of the world. Particularly in the West, language and reflexive consciousness lead us to conceive of ourselves as *separate* and apart from the world, despite vivid sensory evidence to the contrary (Watts, 1967). The enduring belief that we are somehow "in" rather than "of" the world results in two related responses. On the one hand, we tend to behave *irresponsibly*, destroying other species and habitats (and as a consequence seriously depleting our own). On the other, we claim *responsibility* for managing the future of the Earth, and in this role engage in various projects of ecological repair and planetary escape (e.g., cleaning up bodies of water, planning to colonize other planets, building underground communities and international space stations).

This ambivalent relationship between humans and the world is written into Western culture's best known story, the book of Genesis in the Old Testament. There it is told that God gave order to the world before humans came on the scene, but that when man appeared, he was given "dominion" over the world. But what is meant by dominion? The charge to human beings from such a statement is ambiguous. One way of interpreting this passage is that we have been selected as *managers of the world*. Most Westerners probably do interpret the Genesis story in this way.

However, there is at least one alternative interpretation worth considering. In her book *The Chalice and the Blade*, Eisler (1987) offered a different reading of human history, exploring times past in which not all cultures sought to dominate the world. In other, partnership societies, women played a more central role and people lived in harmony with the Earth. Similarly, in his book about a teacher (who also happens to be a gorilla!), Quinn (1992) traced our species' current challenges to the critical difference between apprehending order and taking control. He argued that before there were human beings, there was already an order in the world, and consequently effective "dominion" must mean *learning this order and guiding behavior within it*. This interpretation has not been popular, however, at least in Western history. Instead, convinced that creation ends with us and that the world was made for humans and humans made to manage it, we seek to take control. With few exceptions, these attempts to manage the world are failures, rife with unanticipated consequences and ironies resulting from ignorance of the natural order.

Recent developments in organizational theory have witnessed a growing sensitivity to this distinction between order and control. Notably, Wheatley's (1992) application of chaos theory to organizations presents a forceful case for creating order in human behavior through the development of guiding principles and other "conceptual controls" (such as organizational vision and values), as opposed to through supervision or surveillance. Senge's (1990) description of the "learning organization" further promotes the idea that people do best when enrolled in a common vision and given sufficient autonomy to accomplish the vision in their own way.

As we noted earlier, the development of language and rationality provides humans with a powerful tool for creating routine patterns of behavior. Unfortunately, we have for the most part become convinced either that the patterns we create take precedence over nonhuman patterns, or worse yet, fail to see the existence of patterns other than the ones we have created. In so doing, we cast ourselves as managers of the world, a job no single species is equipped to perform. An alternative that has received limited consideration thus far would be to seek out patterns of order already present in the world and to live within them in ways that preserve life and the planet as a whole.

However you see the role of humankind, the story of Genesis is itself fundamentally one of creating order out of chaos. If we were to extend the story to imagine creation continuing through the present day, perhaps we can also see humans' role in the story differently. Rather than being called on to manage the world, we might instead become benevolent and enlightened guardians or facilitators of a creative process that *does not end with our species* (Quinn, 1992).

CONTRASTING MODELS OF COMMUNICATION AND CHANGE

We have argued so far for the necessity of holistic thinking and second-order change, and situated such change within a set of canonical stories that function to construct and reinforce current practices and routines. We have also suggested that the moment is ripe for change in a whole system of stories, and furthermore that specific changes in organizational life may have implications for more widespread transformation in social life. What we have not as yet discussed are the specific ways such changes can be achieved in real organizations through communication. The remainder of this chapter is dedicated to identifying the various models relating communication to organizational change, exploring their underlying assumptions, and comparing their likely effectiveness.

Our main point is that models of organizational change are inextricably linked to models of communication. To demonstrate this relationship, we begin with an early model of change—that of the charismatic leader—and show how it corresponds to the conduit model of communication. Next, we show how transformational models of leadership align with transactional models of communication. Finally, we describe how facilitative models of change parallel dialogic communication processes. We present the relationship between these existing theories of organizational change and communication as a kind of paradox—the simultaneous existence of what appear to be opposing and even contradictory forces.

Figure 7.1 reflects the relationship between organizational communication and organizational change through parallel continua. The top line represents the tension between approaches that see communication as a tool and those that see communication as generative or constitutive of social reality. The bottom line represents the tension between theories that view organizational change as a discrete event and those that see it as an ongoing process. The arrows indicate the general flow of communication efforts.

The left side of the figure, where communication is viewed as a tool and change as an event, is labeled monologic approaches to organizational change. Seen this way, change happens to an organization in the form of an event which a strong leader must manage and control. The event can take place either through naturally occurring events or through strategic intervention on the part of the leader or management team. In a monologic model, communication is the process of information transfer from the top down or informational orientation (Deetz, 1995b). The manager attempts to control the change process using a linear model of communication. There are some situations in which such an approach may be most effective. For example, a monologic orientation may prove useful for dealing with first-order changes—incremental changes that occur within a constant framework (Bartunek & Louis, 1988). It may also work well for solving convergent problems for which there is only one right answer (Senge, 1990), and in emergencies when a quick response is vital.

The lines begin to converge in the middle, marking transactional perspectives in which employee participation is encouraged.

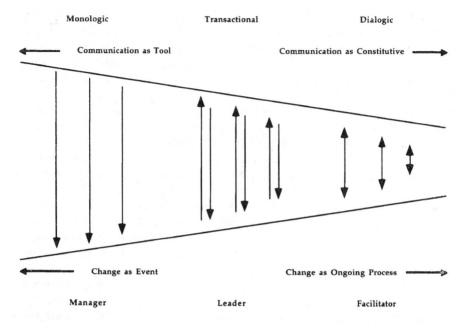

Figure 7.1. Parallels between theories of organizational communication and organizational change

Transformational change models focus on second-order organizational change—transforming organizational frameworks and structures. Organizational transformation emerges as "large scale changes in organizational form that occur throughout an organization's life cycle" (Bartunek & Louis, 1988, p. 98). In contrast to the monologic approach, transformational change parallels a more transactional communication model represented by arrows in each direction in the figure. With increased employee participation, the boundaries between senders and receivers blur as each simultaneously influences the other. Nevertheless, transformational approaches still require ongoing managerial direction.

On the right side of the diagram, where change is continual and communication is constitutive of meaning, the lines converge, representing dialogic approaches to change. This approach is most consistent with the notion of eliciting order out of chaos, rather than imposing a pattern by taking control. Dialogic models challenge conceptions of change as a "thing" that happens "in" or "to" an organization. Outside pressures do not instigate change, the *perception* or enactment of these pressures do (Kanter, 1983; Weick, 1979). Ongoing change is more difficult to delineate, demarcate, or define. "Change is bound to meanings that are attached to events and action possibilities that follow from those meanings" (Kanter, 1983, p. 281). If we believe that communication is fundamentally the process of creating meaning, it follows that perception of change is tightly bound to communication, hence the two-headed arrows.

[In most of the literature on organizational change, scholars do not explicitly address communication. We assert that communication forms the implied but neglected foundation of the change literature. Explicit or not, this literature reflects a paradox through which communication is presented both as a tool through which leaders promote change "events" and as an ongoing process through which new meanings and new practices are collaboratively generated. We next go into more detail about each of the three approaches in the model.

The Monologic Approach

Within the monologic approach, change is conceived as something that happens to an organization. Change is largely seen as an event such as a budget cut, a restructuring, a shift in the market, or a new governmental regulation rather than as an outgrowth of everyday activity. From this perspective, change is something to be managed. Important change management tools include the behavior of the manager, the vision, and the strategic use of communication.

Managers play the central role in monologic approaches—from this perspective, leadership drives change (Bass, 1981). First, managers execute and control change by scanning the environment, assessing needs, and creating strategies (Kanter, Stein, & Jick, 1992). In other words, they decide which changes they will address and create strategies to predict and control the environment. Managers, sometimes with the help of experts, facilitate change for their employees to help them adapt quickly and remain productive. The leader's task is to make change as smooth as possible for employees. For change to be effective, production, profits, and service must remain at high levels.

Second, these managers must have a clear vision of what the organization is going to become. They know where they are going and how to get there:

> If there is a spark of genius in the leadership function at all, it must lie in this transcending ability, a kind of magic, to assemble—out of all the variety of images, signals, forecasts and alternatives—a clearly articulated vision of the future that is at once simple, easily understood, clearly desirable, and energizing. (Bennis & Nanus, 1985, p. 103)

Furthermore, managers must create a vision that will be inspiring to their members:

They breathe life into what are the hopes and dreams of others and enable them to see the exciting possibilities that the future holds. Leaders get others to buy into their dreams by showing how all will be served by a common purpose. (Kouzes & Posner, 1987, p. 9)

The CEO creates the vision and hands it down to organizational members (Kanter et al., 1992; Stata, 1988). To keep the employees productive and the organization profitable through change events, managers must continually communicate and inspire.

From the monologic perspective, communication functions as a tool, and is used to disseminate the managers' vision for change. The messages managers choose to communicate generally flow downward and can be described according to a linear or conduit model of information transfer (Shannon & Weaver, 1949). At times, these communication strategies may be assessed and changed in order to increase efficiency and productivity. To increase effectiveness, managers continually sharpen their communication skills.

In one well-known model of change, communication shapes how organizations "adapt to the environment, make sense of external changes and implement strategic initiatives" (Daft, Bettenhausen, & Tyler, 1993, p. 143). Daft et al. offered a four-cell model that differentiates the type of information the leader should communicate to employees in response to varying environmental conditions. When the volume of external information is low and ambiguity is high (cell 1), managers develop common grammar, gather opinions, and define questions and actions. When the volume and ambiguity of information from the environment are both high (cell 2), managers gather opinions and analyze data to establish common grammar and answer explicit questions. When volume and ambiguity are both low (cell 3), managers gather and analyze routine objective data and answer objective questions. However, in an environmental state of rapid change with low ambiguity and high volume of information (cell 4), managers use scanning systems and high technology to answer explicit questions. *Different types of changes demand that managers use different channels and types of information.*

Another way of managing change which falls within the monologic perspective suggests that communication strategies depend on the type of movement (macroevolutionary, microevolutionary, or revolutionary); the type of change (identity, coordination, or control); and who is involved (change strategists, implementors, or recipients; (Kanter et al., 1992). Finally, a related model recommends tailoring communication strategies to potential psychological reactions (of employees) to change. This approach helps managers deal with employee denial, dodging, doing, and sustaining change (Rashford &

Coghlan, 1994). Each of these models assumes the manager who communicates in appropriate ways promotes change with the least interruption to the organization.

For many years now, both in communication and organizational studies, writers have sought to revise the monologic perspective. For example, it has been observed that to be effective, employees must participate in making the leader's vision a reality (Beer, Eisenstat, & Spector, 1990; Bennis & Nanus, 1985). The process for doing so can hardly be monologic. People enroll in organizational visions only when they are ready (Senge, 1990). Managers must persuade employees and encourage participation, information sharing, and shop-floor-level decision making to implement their vision (Beer et al., 1990). Tension emerges as leaders seek to drive organizational change, but at the same time require employee participation and involvement to make it happen.

This tension is felt by managers and employees alike. For example, many employees want quick solutions in the form of managerial decision making and directives. However, they may also wish to be involved in shaping their work by participating in decisions that affect them. Relatedly, the leader may experience discomfort and frustration as he or she attempts to involve organizational members and is met with distrust, lack of decision making and communication skills, or resistance to taking accountability.

Thus emerges the tension between change as located in leadership or management and change as located throughout the organization. The tension lies between wanting the sense of control and predictability that comes from a monologic, manager-focused approach to change, and realizing the need for participation and order—order that managers do not, and in fact, *cannot* control. This tension is played out as managers recognize the employees' powerful role in promoting successful change. In the transactional approach we begin to widen our focus on the sender (leader) and message (vision) to further include the receiver (employee). The monologic stance gives way to a more transactional one as the need for employee input in the form of feedback is recognized (Kanter et al., 1992).

The Transactional Approach

Perhaps the best example of an approach to planned change that incorporates employee involvement but maintains the leadership role for managers is the theory of transformational leadership. In this section, we first define transformational leadership and explore the transactional role of communication in the transformed organization. Next, we present the leader and follower(s) as participants in effecting system-wide change.

Transformational Leadership. Contemporary organizations seek leadership that can guide them through the enormous social changes described earlier. Leadership is rapidly being redefined as having the capacity for transforming social systems, and new relationships between leaders and followers are emerging. From this perspective, the leader's job is to *transform* organizations and mobilize them to create something new out of something old (Bass, 1981; Tichy & Ulrich, 1984; Zaleznik, 1977, 1990). Whereas many managers seek to make marginal improvements in quantity and quality of performance, transformational leaders inspire and motivate followers to perform above clearly communicated expectations. Accordingly, transformational leadership is based on more than the compliance of followers: it involves shifts in their beliefs, needs, and values. "The result of transforming leadership is a relationship of mutual stimulation and elevation that converts followers into leaders and may convert leaders into moral agents" (Burns, 1978, p. 4). The transformational leader raises followers' level of consciousness about the values of outcomes, and persuades followers to transcend self-interest.

In contrast to the managerial emphasis in the monologic perspective, transformational leadership recognizes that "one great man (or woman)" is not sufficient to accomplish any vision. Leaders and followers must develop new ways of working together which transform their organizations into safe learning environments equipped to respond to a turbulent world. This challenge requires leadership which recognizes the value of followers and encourages both innovation and independent decision making.

Transformational leadership is well known and has been widely researched across a variety of disciplines (Conger & Kanungo, 1987; Deluga, 1988; House, 1977; Kuhnert & Lewis, 1987; O. F. White & McSwain, 1983). The notion of transformational leadership developed from Downton's idea of "Rebel leadership," to political leadership (Burns, 1978), to its application in corporations (Bass, 1985; Bennis & Nanus, 1985; Tichy & Devanna, 1986), to a concept that includes the entire "learning organization" (Senge, 1990) as a dynamic system in which leadership is but one element in the set.

Close examination of research on transformational leadership reveals the following findings:

1. Significant and positive relationships exist between transformational leadership and organizational effectiveness (Avolio, Waldman, & Einstein, 1988; Hater & Bass, 1988; Seltzer & Bass, 1990; Yammarino & Bass, 1990).

2. Multiple levels of analysis in leader-follower interaction reveal that transformational leadership as compared to traditional forms was related more strongly to followers' extra effort and satisfaction (Yammarino & Bass, 1990). Transformational leaders were viewed as being more effective, and team members had greater levels of satisfaction with their leadership (Avolio & Bass, 1988).

3. The degree of transformational leadership behavior observed at one level of management tended also to be seen at the next lower level of management—called the "falling dominoes effect" (Bass, Waldman, Avolio, & Bebb, 1987).

4. In general, transformational leaders have more effective organizations (Avolio & Bass, 1988; Avolio et al., 1988).

As these findings reveal, for transformational leaders change is less an event to be managed than a process that requires leaders and followers to work and learn together. Communication is less monologic and more interactive. The next section continues to explore how a transformed organization requires the participation of followers and leaders in a transactional communication process.

Transactional Communication and Systems of Change. Transformational leaders simultaneously want control and participation. Toward this end, communication functions to "align attitudes, share knowledge, and manage information" (Quirke, 1995, p. 32). Leaders are responsible for communication; however, employees must simultaneously participate in organizational decision making. As the degree of change increases, so too does the level of involvement needed. When the degree of change is low, involvement can be limited to creating employee awareness. As the degree of desired change increases, employee understanding, support, and commitment are required. As the degree of involvement increases, the communication model employed must proceed from a one-way model to a more dynamic, transactional one.

The transformational leader is a perpetual learner. "The most marked characteristic of self-actualizers as potential leaders is their capacity to learn from others and the environment—the capacity to be taught" (Burns, 1978, p. 380). Learning is a system-wide activity as members obtain feedback from the environment and anticipate further changes. "At all levels, newly learned knowledge is translated into new goals, procedures, expectations, role structures, and measures of success" (Bennis & Nanus, 1985, p. 191). Innovative learning moves through six processes: reinterpreting history, experimenting, observing experiences of analogous organizations, using analytical processes, thinking and educating, and unlearning. These interdependent processes bring leaders and members of the organization closer together. They "nurture each other, guiding the process of creative self-discovery by which each learns how to be most effective in a complex and changing environment" (p. 205).

Transformational leadership features constant change, innovation, and entrepreneurship. Its advocates claim that this approach to leadership can be learned and managed; that it is "systemic, consisting of purposeful and organized search for changes, systematic analysis, and the capacity to move resources from areas of lesser to greater productivity" (Tichy & Devanna, 1986, p. vii). Only recently has literature focused specifically on the leader as part of a system that explicitly includes followers and their contributions. Within the transformational leadership approach, vision, purposes, beliefs, and other aspects of organizational culture assume prime importance (Bennis, 1984). Symbolic expression becomes the major tool of leadership, as leadership effectiveness is:

> no longer defined as a "9–9 grid score" or a "system 4" position. Effectiveness is instead measured by the extent to which a "compelling vision" empowers others to excel; the extent to which meanings are found in one's work; and the extent to which individual and organization are bonded together by common commitment in a mutually rewarding symbiotic relationship. (p. 70)

Leadership reveals itself in interaction between people and necessarily implies its complement, "followership." The leader is simultaneously a follower serving the interest of multiple groups, such as shareholders, subordinates, and customers. For one to influence, another must permit him or herself to be influenced—reflecting a transactional communication model where interactants become involved in an interdependent relationship with no clearly defined senders or receivers. Moreover, leader and follower(s) must be at least loosely organized around some common or agreed-on purpose or mission, the achievement of which depends in part on the quality of the leader-follower relationship.

Related to the inspirational, visionary, and innovative aspects of transformational leadership, our traditional views of leaders—as special people who set the direction, make the key decisions, and energize the troops—are deeply rooted in an individualistic and fragmented world view. Especially in the West, leaders are usually heroes—great men (and occasionally women) who rise up in times of crises. Our prevailing leadership myths are still captured by the westernized image of the cavalry captain leading the charge to rescue settlers from attackers. So long as such myths prevail, they reinforce a focus on short-term success and charismatic heroes rather than on systemic forces and collective learning. At its heart, traditional views of leadership are based on assumptions of people's powerlessness, their lack of personal vision, and inability to master the forces of change, deficits that can be remedied only by a few great leaders (Senge, 1990).

When organizations emphasize learning together, leaders function as designers, stewards, coaches, and teachers who grow organizations through which people expand their capacities. This concept of leadership drastically alters the rationale for and the roles of managers. Communication and change become even more closely intertwined as lines of our model converge. The transformational leader helps create a space for members of the organization to create, learn, and build individual meaning in work. However, these tensions between control and creativity, authority and democracy, individuality and collectivity continue to pull in opposite directions (Eisenberg & Goodall, 1997).

For example, many attempts at implementing Total Quality Management have failed because of these conflicting tensions. Leaders have encouraged individuality and creativity and have devoted countless resources to team meetings only to override, ignore, or sabotage the resultant suggestions for change. These moments of disillusionment deflate the growing excitement and participation at work and can cause alienation between manager and managed. All too often organizational members participate in decision making and visioning only to find their voices go unheard. Transformational leaders usually discover that trust is hard to win and easy to lose. This type of leader must consistently value and practice the inclusion of members in complex decision making that affects the entire organization.

The Dialogic Approach

In our third approach, communication and change are so closely intertwined that they are nearly indistinguishable. Communication generates the organization's interpretations, contexts, and practices. Emphasis shifts from management to facilitation as the literature challenges and redefines images of leadership. Organizations, seen as dynamic work communities, continually develop and change as people interact interdependently. The right side of the figure pictures this close connection between constitutive communication and continual change. Nonetheless, those with power can disproportionately shape organizational symbols and meanings.

Co-constructing Organizations Through Dialogue. As organizational members work together, talk through daily situations, and act interdependently, the organization is continually under construction. Communication generates the organization's interpretation of its context, its identity, and its practices. In doing so communication generates the organization itself. Put another way, "our symbol systems construct what we call the reality of a given situation, and words are the most taken-for-granted facts of those constructions" (Cheney & Tompkins, 1988, p. 466). Many organizational studies explore how symbolism creates organizational realities and environments (Berg, 1985; Goodall & Eisenberg, 1997). When we conceptualize communication as the core process which generates the organization, organizational change appears as "a transformation of the underlying symbolic field" (Berg, 1985, p. 289).

An organization's environments serve as symbolic contexts that provide meaning for members. These collective meanings are made manifest in the practices of the organization's members and effectively structure the organization. Strategy emerges as a "collective image that can be acted upon" (Berg, 1985, p. 295). Change is "bound to meanings attached to events and action possibilities that flow from those meanings" (Kanter, 1983, p. 281).

Organizational members engaged in dialogue recognize heterogeneity and face significant points of contention. They confront the tensions between authority and democracy, profit and caring, creating and constraining. "As we are increasingly challenged to change our ways or perish, we must begin to entertain questions that, even in the asking, will open us to new possibilities" (Mandel, 1993, p. 169). When people balance advocacy and inquiry by explaining their reasoning and inquiring into that of others, they are able to create a safe space for learning and risking together (Senge, 1990). Communication of this sort allows "dialogic, collaborative constructions of self, other, and world in the process of making collective decisions" (Deetz, 1995b, p. 107). When we listen both individually and collectively, we can build lasting relationships as the foundation of work. "Instead of glorifying transactions at the expense of relationships, business can re-energize itself as a high voltage conduit of human connectedness" (Mandel, 1993, p. 170). In the dialogic approach to communication, people function as essential information and idea resources, creating solutions we have never seen before. Human labor is no longer "a disposable commodity, but a creative resource, in which an individual's development is as valuable as the organization's growth" (Land & Jarman, 1993, p. 265).

Assumptions and Practices of Dialogic Approaches to Organization. Laying out some of the "ground rules" of dialogue may be helpful here. Bohm and Edwards (1991) discussed these in their book, *Changing Consciousness*, and Senge (1990) elaborated in *The Fifth Discipline*. The following is a summary:

1. Before beginning talk, we need to talk about the meaning of dialogue and its importance, usefulness, and risks.
2. We buy into the belief that our opinions and those of others are discussable and alterable. We are willing to hang them in front of us for consideration and questions. We listen seriously to opinion whether or not we agree. Only in this way can we learn to think together.
3. We recognize that dialogue is a commitment to time, to the group, and to the process.
4. Having no leader, no hierarchy, and no predetermined agenda enhances spontaneity. Imposing a question on the group is unnecessary—questions will grow out of the dialogue.
5. Exploring meanings together bonds the group and creates new ways of knowing.

Dialogic inquiry can lead to transformation. Generally speaking, the process leads from impersonal fellowship to friendship. Our emotions are integral. We change the nature of consciousness as we share content and think together. "I suggest that if we can sustain a real dialogue, we will find in the end that talking and thinking together is very like a kind of improvised singing and dancing together" (Bohm & Edwards, 1991, p. 192). We must be able to talk about and acknowledge our differences in a negotiable way if we are to stay together.

"The way people talk together in organizations is rapidly becoming acknowledged as central to the creation and management of knowledge" (Isaacs, 1993a, p. 1). Because complex issues require the combined intelligence of multiple individuals, dialogue is essential to the survival of today's organizations. In the tradition of dialogue as a way of knowing, William Isaacs of the MIT Dialogue Project asserts that dialogue is a discipline of collective learning and inquiry. It leads to new levels of understanding as well as to coordinated action. Although dialogue allows greater coherence among people, it does not impose it. People can agree on a direction but for different reasons. Dialogue is inquiry that can lead to a common vision. "The core of the theory of dialogue builds on the premise that changes in people's *shared attention* can alter the quality and level of inquiry that is possible" (p. 3). More than a mere problem-solving technique, dialogue is a means of exploring incoherent thoughts that underlie our problems.

In dialogue, people become observers of their own thinking (Senge, 1990). The suspension of assumptions, of hanging them in the air apart from specific egos, allows members to question and examine how and why they think the way they do. The collective conversation of colleagues who can question their own thinking is a powerful way of discovering new possibilities. In another popular management book, *The 7 Habits of Highly Effective People*, Covey (1989) called the highest level of communication *synergy*. At this level of openness and communication, creativity is exciting and differences are both valued and transcended.

Dialogue and the Experience of Work. What does this kind of communication mean in our experience of work? "Most . . . people desperately want to do more than just bring home a paycheck; they want to believe in their work. They want work they can feel good about when they get up in the morning, that they look forward to and that they think is worthwhile" (J. C. Collins & Porras, 1993, p. 83). An organization's vision or direction ought be a reflection of the needs, values, and motivations of organizational members; it must be a personal commitment; and it must be communicated and reinforced. Implementing a coherent strategy and effective tactical decisions requires a clear overarching goal which all organizational members can keep in sight.

Engaging in dialogue requires more than clearly phrased directives, open discussions, or polite greetings. It requires a different kind of attention to and awareness of others. James Autry (1991), a CEO and poet, talks about how his organization lives within the paradoxes of profit and caring. In his poem, *"Threads,"* Autry wrote about leadership in turbulent times:

> Listen.
> In every office
> you hear the threads
> of love and joy and fear and guilt,
> the cries of celebration and reassurance,
> and somehow you know that connecting those threads
> is what you are supposed to do
> and business takes care of itself. (p. 26)

Although most leaders want reform, they are not certain how to go about making it. How best can a leader who speaks from a position of power significantly affect the power distribution in the organization? The literature offers several proposals. One such proposal is organizational stewardship. "Stewardship, the exercise of accountability as an act of service, requires a balance of power to be credible" (Block, 1993, p. 28). Stewardship questions our assumptions that accountability and control are synonymous. Although managers step back, they continue to struggle with the managerial control they and others expect them to wield. Caught within webs of power, organizations free themselves by first changing the thinking of those in power. "What is unique about this revolution—and gives us hope—is that it is being initiated by the ruling class, the managerial class. Stewardship is a revolution initiated and designed by those in power" (p. 45).

A managerial revolution reveals the paradoxical tension between wanting partnership, yet needing those currently in power to change. Block (1993) wrote his book for organizational executives, yet his advice runs counter to conventional managerial wisdom. For Block, organizations are not made up of parents and children, but rather "adults making decisions together with full responsibility and accountability, but without systems of control and compliance" (Deetz, 1995b, p. 169). Echoing Eisler, the stewardship relationship moves leaders from a parental role to that of a partner. This change characterizes the dialogic approach and distinguishes it most clearly from the monologic and the transactional. In dialogue, everyone has an equal right to voice their experience. Similarly:

> Partnership means each of us at every level is responsible for defining vision and values. Purpose gets defined through dialogue. Let people at every level communicate about what they want to create, with each person having to make a declaration. *Let the dialogue be the outcome.* (Block 1993, p. 29; emphasis added)

Experiencing work as community reflects a particular view of communication and change, one that takes a long-term perspective and struggles to make some kind of democratic governance work. Such organizations are challenged to develop structures of democratic learning that check the "tendency of any human organization to develop factions which hoard power" (Bellah et al. 1992, p. 100). In this kind of work community, we may in fact see more socially grounded people in a more democratic economy. "Community, in its basic form, involves a group of people who have committed themselves to a process of ever-deepening levels of communication" (Gozdz, 1993, p. 111). This committed group communicates in uncharacteristically respectful and risky ways. In the process of building community, people learn to take greater responsibility for their own behavior.

However, a lasting organizational community requires more than commitment and communication. It requires discipline and mastery. This mastery is achieved as each person makes his or her contributions and assumes responsibility for them. Instead of a solitary leader responsible for performance, each member becomes the leader depending on the skills, knowledge, and experience needed in each situation. "Leadership in community is more a context than a person" (Gozdz 1993, p. 113). Because each member makes his or her own contribution, the experience of work in community becomes a creative and enriching part of life.

How does a dialogic perspective on communication and change differ from the monologic and transactional perspectives? Taking a monologic approach, the manager or leader is responsible for creating a vision and then clearly interpreting it for the organization. "The leader's goal is not mere explanation or clarification but the creation of meaning" (Bennis, 1993, p. 78). In other words, the vision and its interpretation are constructed by the leader. Although the transformational leader does encourage the two-way flow of communication, he or she is still the instigator and power behind change efforts. He or she has the first, final, and most powerful voice. In contrast, dialogue shifts control from any one person to the community. For organizations to move from dominance to partnership and from dependency to empowerment, managers must give up control and recognize order in its many present forms. A dialogic relationship requires give and take; as a result, it can inspire creativity. Conversely, monologue minimizes risk and surprise, and hence stifles creativity.

Complex decision making requires employee participation in generating ideas, suggestions, and innovative thinking. This kind of participation encourages better social choices, builds better citizens, and provides important economic benefits. Yet we need to be suspicious of programmatic solutions to reach these democratic goals. Simply implementing new management programs won't work because these programs are managerially imposed. Words like empowerment, participation, and quality become mere slogans (Deetz, 1995b), and they increase the effectiveness of bureaucracy, rather than change the system. Empowerment and participatory management programs have been tainted with elements of consent or concertive control. Paradoxically, employees want to make decisions about their workplace, yet they must conform to managerial programs that reward the current faddish behavior or work processes. The greatest threat to genuine participation comes in subtle control or consent, rather than in lack of opportunity for involvement which would most likely be resisted. To counteract the forces of consent, organizations must be open to a discourse of resistance:

> The existence of consent in pluralistic society calls for different kinds of activities, the force of more participatory discourse and the studies that

> aid it can no longer be a discourse of affirmation and
> must be a discourse of resistance on the way to co-detern
> would be a micro-practice of resistance to consent and
> discussion closure. (p. 171)

In other words, organization members at every level must speak up and ask questions to create a new kind of discourse which seeks to question rather than to convince.

Despite our obvious appreciation for the dialogic approach, we are nonetheless left with some questions. Most important, under what circumstances is dialogue most effective? When is it more trouble than it's worth? What place do skill and expertise play in a dialogic organization? Are all voices equally skilled in speaking (clearly not), and what difference does this make in the outcome? What about those who are not comfortable talking? Do all voices carry the same authority and weight? Are we attempting to substitute community at work for community at home or in our neighborhood? What about those who prefer silence?

CONCLUSION

This chapter began with the idea that in approaching organizational change, it is stability that most needs explanation. Furthermore, in describing reasons for resistance to change and the persistence of current patterns, we observed that our present day is unique in its openness to revision of canonical stories both in and outside of work. The path this revision ought to take is toward holistic, second-order change.

We continued by maintaining that the problem of organizational change management resides within a larger context of control traceable to the heart of Western culture. By entertaining alternatives to taking control of the change process—such as identifying sources of order that are already there and capitalizing on them—we may not only change the field of organizational behavior but the larger domain of social life.

The final section of the chapter sought to contrast three models of organizational change based on differing models of communication: monologic, transactional, and dialogic. Each of these models is progressively less directive in its approach to control and change management, so much so that in dialogue, change emerges through the joint collaboration of empowered managers and employees talking and acting together. Although all three models are in place today, we wish to argue for the special relevance of the dialogic approach in the development of environmentally adaptive, holistically oriented, high-involvement work communities.

part four

ORGANIZATIONAL COMMUNICATION RESEARCH METHODS

eight

NEURAL NETWORKS APPLICATIONS
IN SOCIAL SCIENCE RESEARCH*

Ofer Meilich

Washington University, St. Louis

Neural networks have been touted by popular science writers as machines that are capable of human-like reasoning (B. O'Reilly, 1989; Port, 1995). They are presented as powerful, yet simple, tools for achieving results. One needs to specify a minimal set of parameters, and then just wait and let the network "wrangle" the data. Neural networks are "hype," and as we shall see, are of great use for professionals and business people. But are neural networks such a "big hammer" that can "nail" all, if any, of the researcher's problems?

In this chapter I define neural networks, compare them to statistical approaches, and discuss issues in the design of the most popular type of neural networks—back-propagation networks. I then use a case study to illustrate how back-propagation networks compare with the statistical methods of discriminant analysis and linear regression, and discuss the results. I conclude with some thoughts about the general applicability of neural networks in social science research.

*The helpful comments of Moshe Fridman, Nandini Rajagopalan, and Patti Riley are gratefully acknowledged.

WHAT ARE NEURAL NETWORKS?

Definition

An (artificial) neural network is a processing device, operationalized as an algorithm or in actual hardware, whose design is motivated by the arrangement and functioning of human brains. It is "an information processing system that is nonalgorithmic, nondigital, and intensely parallel" (Caudill & Butler, 1992, p. 3). A typical network (see Figure 8.1) consists of several simple, highly interconnected processing units (which are referred to as the "neurons" of the network). Each neuron determines a single output value based on several input values. The network itself consists of layers of interconnected neurons. The network "learns" from examples, without requiring the user to specify a model for the data. It can handle very complex, nonlinear, "model-less" problems by recognizing the hidden patterns in the data.

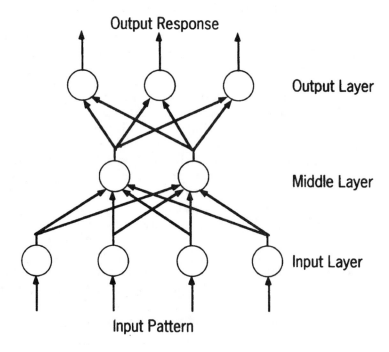

From Caudill and Butler (1992, p. 172). Adapted with permission.

Figure 8.1. Typical three layer back-propagation network

What Can Neural Networks Do?

Neural networks are of interest to quite a few disciplines, ranging from computer science and engineering, through physics, biology, psychology, and neuroscience, to business, and even philosophy. Neural networks' main strength lies in solving complex, practical problems. As such, they have three major uses: classifying data, modeling complex relationships, and processing signals (Lyons, 1993). In classifying data, neural networks typically replace statistical analysis (such as discriminant analysis and logistic regression). Lyons noted that the performance improvements provided by neural networks may range from 5% to 50% reduction in error. In modeling complex relations neural networks have been used to uncover relations between several continuous (online) inputs and outputs in areas such as forecasting, resource allocation, and operations control. Here neural networks substitute for linear and polynomial regression techniques. In signal processing, neural networks are useful in removing noise and clutter from signals, or for constructing patterns from partial data. They have been used for signal filtering, speech recognition, and diagnosis.

Listed in the following are a few examples of the diverse uses of neural networks in business and other fields: identification of fraudulent use of credit cards (C. J. Smith, 1990); processing credit applications (C. J. Smith, 1990); allocating airline seats (Kinoshita, 1988); identification of target groups for telemarketing (M. Smith, 1988); prediction of Standard & Poor's bond rating (Humpert, 1989); forecasting Standard & Poor's 500 index and currency trading (Chithelen, 1989); prediction of thrift failures (Salchenberger, Cinar, & Lash, 1992); detection of psychological profiles of criminals (B. O'Reilly, 1989); signature verification (Glatzer, 1988); detection of explosives in airports (Brody, 1990); evaluation of electrocardiograms (Glatzer, 1988); analyses of changes in chemical ingredients (Francett, 1989); detection of faulty paint finish, determination of optimal bulb manufacturing conditions, and reading Zip codes (B. O'Reilly, 1989). Cheng and Titterington (1994) reported diverse applications in pattern classification and recognition, among others: speech recognition and generation, location of radar point sources, identification of cancerous cells, recognition of chromosomal abnormalities, prediction of re-entry trajectories of spacecraft, sexing of faces, recognition of coins of different denomination, and discrimination of chaos from noise in the prediction of time series. Neural networks are, indisputably, of great use in diverse real-life applications.

ELEMENTS OF A NEURAL NETWORK

The Neuron

Each processing unit ("neuron") produces an output value based on its inputs (see Figure 8.2). It performs two operations. First, it computes a weighted sum of the inputs. Then the neuron applies a transfer function that maps the summed input value into a corresponding output value. Transforming the weighted sum allows for an improved learning mechanism (by reducing computation time and by converging on the best solution) and allows for a better representation of non-linearities. The most common transfer function is the sigmoidal function:

$$y = 1/\{1 + \exp \text{ (weighted sum of inputs)}\}.$$

There are also several other transfer functions (this issue is discussed in the section dealing with neural networks design).

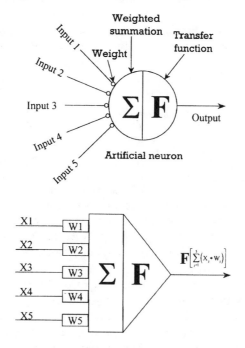

From Li (1994, p. 304). Adapted with permission.

Figure 8.2. The functions of an artificial neuron

Network Architecture

The architecture of a neural network describes how a group of processing units are organized. The two primary parameters that define a network's architecture are the number of layers and the type of connectivity. A typical network, such as that depicted in Figure 8.1, consists of three kinds of layers: an input layer, one or more hidden layers, and an output layer. "The art of network construction in ANNs [Artificial Neural Networks]," as Bing and Titterington (1994) noted, "is to use simple individual units but to link together enough of them in a suitable manner to solve a particular problem" (p. 7).

The Network Layers. The input layer simply distributes the inputs to the neurons in the middle (hidden) layer. Each neuron in the input layer corresponds to one type of input, that is, to a single "independent variable" in statistical analysis. The output layer produces the output for use by the "outside world." Each neuron corresponds to one output ("dependent") variable. The hidden layer consists of neurons that receive the entire input pattern; this pattern is modified by the weighted connections leading to each neuron in the hidden layer. The hidden layer allows the network to handle nonlinear patterns. Caudill and Butler (1992) noted:

> Since the weights on the connections are typically different for each middle-layer neurode [i.e., neuron], each of these neurodes sees a somewhat different version of the input pattern that its neighbors do. As a result, some combinations of middle-layer neurodes will become active to varying degrees, depending on the exact collection of weights on their input connections. This results in a variety of output responses from the middle-layer neurodes, ranging from no output at all to, possibly, an extremely strong output. (pp. 6–7)

We have some freedom in choosing the number of hidden layers and the number of neurons in each hidden layer. These issues are discussed further in the section dealing with neural networks design.

Types of Connectivity. Connectivity refers to the way the neurons are connected between and within layers. There are three types of connectivity: feedforward, feedback, and lateral. *Feedforward* connectivity allows connections from a lower layer to a higher one only (e.g., from the input layer to the first hidden layer). There are no connections among neurons in the same layer or from a higher layer to a lower one. This type of connectivity is the basic and most common in neural network design. Figure 8.1 describes a typical feedforward configuration. In *feedback* connectivity there is a connection from a higher layer to a lower layer. In *lateral* connectivity, there are connections between neurons in the same layer. A network may be feedforward only, or any combination of feedforward with one of or both feedback and lateral connections. The discussion in this chapter is limited to one type of feedforward-only networks—back-propagation. This network type is, as Caudill and Butler (1992) noted, "the workhorse of applications development today, used, according to one vendor's poll, in about 80 percent of all current neural network projects" (p. 173).

The Learning Mechanism

A neural network "learns" by changing the weights on the interconnections between neurons in the network. The learning process is called "training" the network. The network is trained with a set of examples, called the "training set." Training can be done in three distinct ways: supervised, graded, and unsupervised training:

Supervised training. The network is provided with sets of inputs with their corresponding desired (i.e., observed) outputs. The network compares these target outputs with the network output, computes an error term, and adjusts the network weights to reduce the difference. The process is repeated until the difference between the computed and desired output reaches an acceptably low value. This procedure is akin to statistical methods that minimize an error function (e.g., RMS) such as linear regression and discriminant analysis.

Graded training. Here the process is similar to supervised training, but instead of having a precise desired output, only a "grade" on how well the network is doing is available. For example, an output may be pass/fail, or a more informative "too high" or "too low" feedback. This method is also called "reinforcement training."

Unsupervised training. In this case, the network has only a series of input patterns, with no feedback at all. The input patterns are classified according to their similarity, with similar patterns activating the same output pattern. This process (also called "self-organization") is analogous to cluster analysis. Unsupervised training has been used in computerized text processing (called "connectionist natural language processing").

HOW DO NEURAL NETWORKS COMPARE WITH STATISTICAL METHODS

Both neural networks and statistical regression methods (such as linear regression and discriminant analysis) are correlational techniques aiming at reducing the mean square error (J. M. Collins & Clark, 1993). Neural networks "are simply weak models that combine much flexibility with a (developing) insight into how to manage their complexity," concluded Refenes (1994, p. 46). They are multivariate, nonlinear, nonparametric (i.e., the distribution of the error function need not be specified), stochastic approximations with dynamic feature extraction/selection. On the other hand, statistical methods are primarily designed for solving linear and parametric problems. In this section I examine the advantages and the problems associated with neural networks.

Advantages of Neural Networks

No restricting assumptions on the distribution of the data. There are no restricting assumptions or requirements from the inputs of the neural network, such as linearity, homogeneity of variance, independence, or normality. No transformations are needed, and the training patterns can be run almost "as is" (sometimes with a simple rescaling). No functional restrictions are imposed on the error distribution function either (e.g., there is no requirement for normal distribution).

No a priori, limited-complexity model is needed. Neural networks allow great flexibility in generating input–output relationships allowing the representation of complex relations (Wang, 1995). Neural networks assume no prespecified type of relationship. Whereas regression models require the researcher to prespecify the model (linear, interactive, quadratic, etc.), a neural network is capable of discovering data relationships by itself, as it maps whole patterns from the input space to the output domain.

Accurate approximation of any complex function. Neural networks allow "complex relationships to be accommodated" easily (Collins & Clark, 1993, p. 510). Cybenko (1989) and Hornik, Stinchcombe, and White (1989) have shown that neural networks can provide an accurate approximation to any function of the input vector. The function can be nonlinear and even discontinuous. No data transformations are needed and the network can accommodate complex relationships. This allows the network to extract more information from complex functional forms (Hill, Marquez, O'Connor, & Remus, 1994).

Robustness in treatment of missing or partial data. Whereas regular statistical methods have problems in incorporating missing or partial data (leading to either dropping variables or observations from the analysis), neural networks can recognize and match "complicated, vague, or incomplete patterns" (Zahedi, 1991, p. 27). Moreover, neural networks "degrade gracefully," that is, they continue to function even when part of the network fails.

Smaller cross-validation sample size. Neural networks require, as a rule of thumb, about 10% of the observations to be used for cross-validation as reported by J. M. Collins and Clark (1993). On the other hand, the recommended validation sample size for regression methods is between 30% and 50% (Snee, 1977).

Provision of overall performance statistics. Because both statistical and neural network models minimize the error function, we can compare RMS (Root Mean Square) and R^2 values. If a cross-validation set is used, we can compare the shrinkage rates. The shrinkage rate is the difference in the goodness of fit measures (such as RMS or R^2) between the training and the cross-validation sets. For classification problems, we can use the miss-classification rates in both statistical and neural networks models. Note that these measures indicate the overall performance of the models, not the significance of the components of the model (such as significance levels of the coefficients/weights).

Disadvantages of Neural Networks

Lack of network architecture guidelines. There is currently no formal method to derive a network configuration for a given task, beyond some very general directions (Tam & Kiang, 1992). Li (1994) argued that "there is no structured methodology available for choosing, developing, training, and verifying" a neural network (p. 311).

Low explanatory capability. Neural networks inner function is close to a "black box." It is difficult (if not impossible) to construct a formal model out of the network's multitude of weights. Moreover, there may be several solutions (i.e., sets of weights) for a given problem (Wang, 1995). There are no ways to test the significance of individual inputs, nor to derive the relative importance of an input from the weights (Tam & Kiang, 1992). Hence, there is no practical way to interpret cause-effect relationships in a neural network. Gorr (1994) advocated using graphic representations as a partial solution. He suggested, for example, using "graphs showing the impact of variation in one or two independent variables on the dependent variables" (p. 2).

No parametric statistical properties. No significance tests are available for the individual coefficients or the whole model, hence, as J. M. Collins and Clark (1993) noted, comparison with regression analysis based on *t* or *F* tests is impossible.

Danger of convergence on local minima. The use of nonlinear optimization (i.e., training) algorithms may result in the network converging on a local instead of global minima (Gorr, Nagin, & Szczypula, 1994). There is no theoretical way to ensure that the network would converge on the global minimum of the error function. However, there are some practical solutions to this problem (see the section on the learning parameters of back-propagation later).

Overfitting tendency. When regular statistical models are used we can control the complexity of the model to avoid overfitting (we can fit perfectly any N observations to an Nth power polynomial function using Taylor series, for example, and get $R^2 = 1$). However, in neural network modeling, the complexity of the model is harder to control (see network architecture section). Prechelt (1995) noted that in many cases a network gets worse instead of better after a certain point during training. This is because the network overfits—the long training may make the network memorize the training patterns, including all their peculiarities. There are two methods to control overfitting: early stopping and weight decay (forcing the net to "forget" some of its learning by restricting the values of the weights). However, there are currently no clear-cut guidelines for avoiding overfitting.

Low computational efficiency. Neural networks require more computation time than statistical methods. Neural networks find the solution by computing many iterations, whereas statistical methods generally require only one computation cycle.

ISSUES IN THE DESIGN OF BACK-PROPAGATION NEURAL NETWORKS

Back-Propagation Networks

As noted before, this chapter focuses on the most prevalent type of neural network—back-propagation networks. This type is the most studied, with many successful applications (Maren, 1990). Back-propagation networks perform classifications similar to discriminant analyses, and complex data modeling comparable to multiple regression in statistics. These networks are feedforward, supervised-learning neural networks, employing a maximum-gradient method for error reduction, also called "generalized delta rule" learning.

The generalized delta rule moves the weight vector (i.e., all the current weights in the network) in such a manner as to make the error reduction in the steepest descent toward the minimum-error weight configuration, usually minimizing the network's sum of squared errors (SSE). Graphically, the SSE function plot looks like a bowl (see Figure 8.3). The bowl's bottom corresponds to the set of weights that produces the lowest amount of error. At any point on the surface of the bowl, the derivative of the error function corresponds to the slope of the surface with respect to the weights. The back-propagation algorithm adjusts the weights in the direction of the steepest slope, such that we reach the bottom of the bowl. More issues concerning the learning parameters of back-propagation are discussed under "learning parameters" in a later section. The design issues concerning the neuron's transfer function and the architecture are in major part the result of research on back-propagation networks.

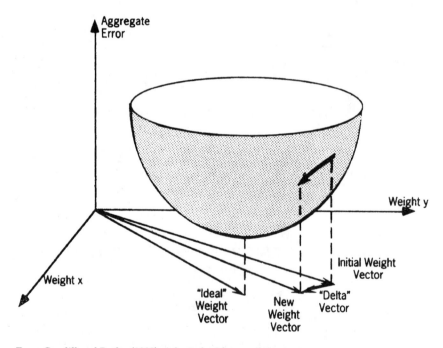

From Caudill and Butler (1992). Adapted with permission.

Figure 8.3. Generalized Delta rule: Gradient descent system

The Neuron: The Transfer Function

The most common transfer function used is the sigmoidal function:

$$F = 1/\{1 + \exp(\text{weighted sum of inputs})\}$$

The greatest advantage of this function is the ease of computing its derivative (which is equal to $F*(1-F)$). Other functions that have been suggested are hyperbolic tangent, linear, and Gaussian. Fahlman (1988) reported considerable improvement in training time by an addition of 0.1 to the sigmoid derivative.

The Architecture

Because the size of both the input and the output layers is dictated by the problem itself, the only details that are left for the designer of the net concern the number of hidden layers and the number of neurons in each hidden layer:

The required number of hidden layers. Cybenko (1989) and Lippmann (1987) have shown that two hidden layers are sufficient to compute any arbitrary function of the inputs. Maren, Jones, and Franklin (1990) reported that empirical tests have not demonstrated significant advantage in moving from one to two hidden layers compared to the increased computation time. They recommended using only a single hidden layer for all classification problems and in most continuous output applications.

The required number of neurons in the hidden layers. It has been proved theoretically that $2N+1$ hidden neurons (where N is the number of inputs) are sufficient for estimating any arbitrary function (Hecht-Nielsen, 1987). Of course, using so many neurons in the hidden layer would result in overfitting by encapsulating all the peculiarities of the training set. On the other hand, with too few hidden neurons the net would not be able to represent the inherent complexity of the data and will not converge to a satisfactory solution. Ripley (1993) reported that a common rule of thumb is to take the average of the numbers of inputs and outputs as the number of neurons in each hidden layer. Maren et al. (1990) suggested taking the geometric mean of the number of inputs and outputs. Prechelt (1995) argues that these rules of thumb are irrelevant, as the number of hidden neurons depends critically on the number of training examples and complexity of the problem. Maren et al. (1990) recommend changing (either increasing or decreasing) the number of hidden neurons when the network fails to train satisfactorily. For example, Gorr et al. (1994) performed a grid search. That is, they ran a large number of network configurations and chose the one that provided the lowest prediction error.

Learning/Training Parameters of Back-Propagation Networks

Here we are mainly concerned with two parameters: the learning parameter (η), and the momentum (α). Both determine the way the weights are updated between iterations (training cycles).

The Learning Parameter (η). As discussed earlier, in each iteration the network's weights are being updated using the generalized delta rule. The learning parameter (η) sets the proportional effect of the error derivative. That is,

$W_{(new)} = W_{(old)} + \eta*$ (error derivative with respect to the specific connection weight)

When the error decreases (i.e., we are getting closer to a minimum), the error derivative decreases, too, as we approach flatter areas on the "error bowl" (see Figure 8.3). This is why sometimes the convergence time can be reduced by increasing the value of η as the error derivative decreases. J. A. Freeman and Skapura (1991) noted that the network may bounce around the minima if η gets too high, and they recommended using values between 0.05 and 0.25 for η. Another alternative is using Fahlman's (1988) QuickProp algorithm, which purports to optimize the training parameter for each weight in a continuous manner. Fahlman reported that QuickProp reduced the convergence time to between half to quarter compared to back propagation.

The Momentum Term (α). Because the error surface tends to be "rough," with large dents on the sides, we may get stuck in local minima instead of reaching the true, "absolute" minimum. A common method used to somewhat overcome this phenomenon is to add to the new weight vector a fraction of the previous change. This additional term tends to keep the weight changes going in the same direction—hence the term momentum. Brown, Coakley, and Phillips (1995) illustrate this process:

> A marble rolling down the side of a bowl gains momentum and will actually start up the other side. If the marble hits a dent in the side of the bowl, it usually will continue through the dent towards the bottom, eventually, the marble will stop rolling at the lowest part of in the bowl. (p. 55)

The marble behaves in this way because of its mass—the heavier the marble, the more inertial it is. The modified weight is then:

$$W_{(new)} = W_{(old)} + \eta^* \text{ (error derivative)} + \alpha^* \text{ (previous error derivative)}$$

Caudill and Butler (1992) noted that the momentum term "has become nearly universal in applications" (p. 208). Ripley (1993) reported that most back-propagation applications use a momentum term, with $\alpha = 0.9$ as a frequent choice.

Other Training Parameters.

Weight noise. Another solution to the local minima problem is to add random amounts of noise to the weights (Caudill & Butler, 1992). This has an effect similar to the momentum term—by not letting the network to settle down easily around any minima, we hope to avoid being "trapped" in a local minimum. This process is figuratively equivalent to "shaking" the error surface.

Input noise. Adding a random noise term to the input patterns makes the network less sensitive to changes in the input values. Like adding weight noise, this procedure trades longer convergence time for reducing the risk of being trapped in a local minimum (Caudill & Butler, 1992).

Training set order. J.A. Freeman and Skapura (1991) recommended presenting the training set observations in a random order in each training cycle. Otherwise, the network may fail to generalize and may partially "forget" the first observations in the training set.

Tolerance term for errors. By placing a threshold on the error, so that only errors above that threshold are considered, we can ensure that "the pattern elements that are already learned are not disturbed much, thus permitting the overall learning to be raised for quicker learning on those elements that are still not understood" by the network (Caudill & Butler, 1992, p. 210).

CASE STUDY: CLASSIFYING MANAGEMENT PROFESSORS AS HIGH OR LOW POST-TENURE PERFORMERS

In this section I use a database of publication rates of management professors to compare the statistical methods of discriminant analysis and linear regression with various neural networks models. I describe the database, report the results, and then discuss them.

The Database

Population and Sample. The population from which the sample was drawn consisted of all the full professors in the management departments of the top 50 universities (i.e., the most prolific institutions in the area of management as ranked by Stahl, Leap, & Wei, 1988). In cases in which no separate department existed, professors were included in the population if their area of interest was organizational behavior, human resource management, organizational theory, strategy, industrial relations, international management, and/or public policy. Data were collected for 279 full professors representing 30 institutions of the top 50. Performance records of 55 professors of management in the top 50 business schools were obtained, which is about 20% of the population (the 279 full professors). The performance measures were aggregated by tenure status (before tenure, and 1 to 5 years after tenure).[1]

Performance Measures.

Pre-tenure measures. Yearly publications and citations were obtained from the Social Sciences Citation Index (SSCI) from 1956 until 1992. For each professor the following yearly data were recorded: (a) number of sole-authored articles; (b) number of jointly published articles in which the professor was first author; (c) number of joint articles in which the professor was not first author; (d) number of citations; and (e) number of books (taken from the Library of Congress Catalogue). Edited books and nonfirst editions were excluded. A sixth variable, the total number of articles, was computed by summing up the three article publication measures (single-, first-, and non-first-authored articles). Only journal articles were

---

[1]Detailed description of the database is given in Meilich (1995).

counted; all other types of publications were excluded (i.e., book reviews, editorials, letters, or notes) as only new contributions to science were sought to be recorded. Book chapters are not covered by the SSCI and were not considered in the analysis. All types of citations were counted, as a measure of the impact a professor had in a certain year, except for self citations (of publications in which the professor was the sole or the first author[2]).

Post-tenure publications: Determining the high performers after tenure. Before discriminant analyses could be performed, there was a need to separate the sample into two groups—high and low post-tenure publishers. "After tenure" was defined as the first 5 years after being granted tenure; this allowed inclusion of the maximal number of observations. A principal components analysis was carried out to find the maximum variability dimension using all five variables (in the years 1 to 5 after tenure). The professors were ranked according to the first principal component. They were ranked also by total number of articles. Kendall's coefficient of concordance (Kerlinger, 1986) was calculated. The resulting value of 0.95 suggests that we can use the simple measure of number of articles to distinguish between the "high" and "low" post-tenure publishers. The separation threshold was chosen to be *five post-tenure* articles (i.e., any professor that published a total of at least five articles was classified as high performer). This threshold divided the sample as evenly as possible, while being a "reasonable" expectation (i.e., publishing one article every year).

Methods

Statistical Methods.

Discriminant analyses. Three discriminant analyses were employed. Each computed a linear discriminant function (Fisher's). The dependent variable was the classification of a professor as low (value = 0) or high (value = 1) post-tenure performer (as explained in the preceding paragraph).

---

[2]Citations are recorded only by first author in the SSCI.

Three sets of independent variables were used. The first set (set 1) consisted of five variables: (a) total number of articles published, (b) total number of jointly-authored articles, (c) number of joint-first-authored articles, (d) number of books published, and (e) number of citations. All variables reflect *pre-tenure totals* (summed over the years between earning one's PhD and the tenure year, inclusive). Set 2 consisted of four variables (all were manipulations of the original five variables of set 1). These were identified by stepwise regression on all the five original variables and their second-order interactions, a total of 18 variables. The four best variables were: (a) articles x citations, (b) citations, (c) jointly authored x citations, and (d) jointly authored x first-authored. All these four variables' coefficients were (statistically) significant at $p < .001$. Set 3 consisted, in addition to the four variables of set 2, a fifth variable: Articles. This variable was identified by the stepwise regression as the next variable for inclusion (although its p-value was 0.6).

Linear regressions. Because the output data were continuous (the number of articles published in the 5 years after tenure was granted), a two-step procedure was also used for discrimination between the high and the low performers. First, a regression was run. Then the fitted values were classified according to the original classification rule (i.e., to be included in the high-performers group one had to publish at least five after-tenure articles). This enabled using as much information as possible for the classification. It was expected that this procedure would yield better classification rates. I refer to this classification procedure as *cut-point regression*.

Three regressions were computed, each with a different independent variables set (i.e., set 1, 2, or 3). As explained earlier, the second and third sets were identified by a stepwise regression procedure. The dependent variable was the actual number of articles published in the 5 years succeeding the year the sampled professor was granted tenure.

Neural Network Models.

Inputs and outputs. The more complex the network is (i.e., with more neurons in the hidden layers), the higher its ability to represent complex combinations of the inputs. Because neural networks reconstruct intricate relationships from the data, all models had the five original independent variables as inputs (i.e., set 1). The output (target) variable was dichotomous (0/1) for the discriminant analysis simulations and the actual number of post-tenure articles (years 1 to 5) for the regression simulations.

Transfer function. In all runs a "sigmoid + 0.1" function was used following Fahlman's (1988) recommendation. That is, the transfer function was $F(x) = 1/[1 + \exp(-x)]$, and a value of 0.1 was added to the derivative of $F(x)$.

Network architecture. In all runs the input layer consisted of five neurons, one for each variable. The output layer had only one neuron. The neural network minimized the discrepancies between this neuron's output and the dichotomous target values of the classification (for discriminant analysis simulations) or between the neuron's output and the continuous values of the target (for the regression simulations).

Number of hidden layers. The number of hidden layers was one in all the discriminant simulations and one or two for the regression simulations, following Maren et al.'s (1990) recommendation .

The number of neurons in the (first) hidden layer. Three configurations were tested. The first had only three neurons in the hidden layer, heeding the average number of inputs and outputs rule of thumb (Ripley, 1993). The second configuration employed eleven neurons in the middle layer, following Hecht-Nielsen's (1987) theorem. Hecht-Nielsen showed that no more than $2N + 1$ neurons (where N is the number of inputs) are required for full representation of any function. A "degraded" configuration was also run, employing only 10 neurons. This configuration was used for comparison with the performance of the other two configurations.

Hence, for the discriminant simulations three configurations were employed: 5–3–1,[3] 5–10–1, and 5–11–1. The first configuration was run twice, again, for comparison. Three configurations were used for the regression simulations: 5–3–1, 5–10–5–1, and 5–11–5–1.

---

[3] The network's architecture notation is in the form *I-H1-(H2)-O*, where *I* indicates the number of input neurons (equals five in all runs), *O* is the number of output neurons (equals 1 in all runs), *H1* is the number of neurons in the first hidden layer, and, if there is a second hidden layer, *H2* is the number of neurons in this layer.

Learning parameters. In all the runs the momentum (α) was set to 0.9 (Ripley, 1993). The training examples (i.e., the observations) were presented to the network in random order each training cycle (Freeman & Skapura, 1991). Because the number of observations was too small ($n = 55$), it was not possible to evaluate the generalizability of the models by employing the trained network on a separate observations set.[4] All the 5–3–1 models used learning parameter (η) = 0.2. The more complex models (with either 10 or 11 neurons in the first hidden layer) employed values around 0.02, because the higher value was extremely sensitive to the initial (random) set of weights and led to local minima.

Equipment: Software and Hardware. Statistical analyses were run on Minitab for Windows release 10.2 (Minitab Inc., 1994). Neural network models were run on WinNN version 0.97 (Danon, 1995). All analyses were run on a PC machine.

Results

The results of all the analyses (both statistical and neural networks) are listed in the Table 8.1.

Statistical Methods.

Discriminant analyses. The best model was the one using the original set of independent variables (run 1). It achieved 82% correct classification rate, compared to about 70% of the two other runs (runs 2 and 3). Hence the "insight" gained in the stepwise regression, by identifying the best combinations of first- and second-order variables through the stepwise regression, was not reflected in the linear discriminant analyses.

Linear regressions. The original set of variables (set 1) yielded an R^2 of 35% and was successful in discrimination between the high and low post-tenure performers in only 60.6% of the cases. The best second-order four-variable regression, identified by the stepwise regression procedure, raised the R^2 to 42% and gave 67.3% correct classification rate. This was the best rate of the three

---

[4]To reflect a similar "overfitting" bias, the statistical discriminant analysis were run *without* cross-validation.

Table 8.1. Comparison Between Statistical Methods and Neural Network Analyses.

Run	Analysis Type	Input Set	Architecture[a]/Cycles	% classified accurately	# of misclassified observations	R^2	Correct to Nearest integer
1	Discriminant	1	Fisher's linear function	81.8	10		
2	Discriminant	2	Fisher's linear function	69.1	17		
3	Discriminant	3	Fisher's linear function	70.9	16		
4	Linear Regression	1	---	60.6	22	35.0	4/55 (7.3%)
5	Linear Regression	2	---	67.3	18	42.0	6/55 (10.9%)
6	Linear Regression	3	---	65.5	19	42.3	8/55 (14.5%)
7	NN[b] Discriminant	1	5-3-1 (7000) (run 1)	85.5	8		
8	NN Discriminant	1	5-10-1 (7000) (run 2)	83.6	9		
9	NN Discriminant	1	5-10-1 (10,000)	87.3	7		
10	NN Discriminant	1	5-11-1 (50,000)	98.2	1		
11	NN regression	1	5-3-1 (10,000)	70.9	16	59.6	14/55 (25.5%)
12	NN regression	1	5-3-1 (100,000)	78.2	12	60.9	13/55 (23.6%)
13	NN regression	1	5-10-5-1 (10,000)	81.8	10		27/55 (49.1%)
14	NN regression	1	5-11-5-1 (10,000)	89.1	6	94.5	39/55 (70.9%)
15	NN regression	1	5-11-5-1 (50,000)	94.5	3	95.7	32/55 (58.2%)
16	NN regression	1	5-11-5-1 (70,000)	98.2	1	98.2	43/55 (78.2%)
17	NN regression	1	5-11-5-1 (4,250,000)	100	0	99.7	53/55 (94.5%)

[a]The network's architecture notation is in the form I-$H1$-($H2$)-O, where I indicates the number of input neurons (equals five in all runs), O is the number of output neurons (equals 1 in all runs), $H1$ is the number of neurons in the first hidden layer, and, if there is a second hidden layer, $H2$ is the number of neurons in this layer.

[b]"NN" stands for Neural Network; all other analyses (runs 1 through 6) are "statistical."

regressions runs. The third regression (best second-order five-variable regression) increased the R^2 slightly but was less successful in classifying the observations.

Comparing the two statistical methods. The best model is the discriminant analysis model with the original five variables. Surprisingly, all the regression models performed worse than any of the discriminant analyses. We may conclude that the added information employed by the regression models only "confused" the discriminating ability. Knowing exactly how many articles one published did not help us in classifying him or her as high or low post-tenure performer.

Neural Networks Models. Hecht-Nielsen (1987) predicted that the more complex models (with 2*inputs + 1 neurons in the first hidden layer; runs 10 and 17) would achieve almost perfect fit. This is the less interesting case because with so many hidden neurons the network is simply overfitting the data.

Discriminant analysis simulations. Both run 7 and 8 (5–3–1 architecture) achieved similar classification rates (about 84%). The more complex model of run 9 (5–10–1 architecture) gained only slight improvement over a comparable number of training cycles. A comparison of the weight sets connecting the input layer to the middle layer uncovered an average discrepancy of 142% between paired weights from runs 7 and 8, with differences ranging from as little as 0.2% to as high as 740%. This reaffirmed Wang's (1995) argument that the resulting weight set is unstable. Although the most complex model (run 10) was able to converge on near-perfect classification, it was found that successive runs of the simpler model (5–3–1), derived from the average (inputs + outputs) rule of thumb, did not improve the classification rate even after extended training.

Regression simulations. In comparing runs 11, 13, and 14, we notice that even with the same amount of training (i.e., same number of cycles) the more complex models outperform the simpler ones. Extending the training of the 5–3–1 configuration to 100,000 cycles (run 12) brought the success rate to 78%, which appeared to be close to the maximal discriminating power this configuration could give. Runs 14 through 17 show that the $2N + 1$ hidden neurons configuration (Hecht-Nielsen, 1987) approaches perfect data fitting rather slowly. Ten thousand training cycles were required to achieve 89% success rate, yet the additional 5.5% improvement required another 40,000 cycles.

Comparing the two neural networks simulations. Examination of the two minimal architecture runs (7 and 12) indicates that, again, the direct approach to classification outperformed the regression-based classification.

How Did the Neural Networks Simulations Compare with the Statistical Methods? Comparing our best statistical classification model (run 1) with the least-complex neural network (runs 7 and 8), it appears that the neural network performed only slightly better than the statistical model (about 84% vs. 82%). This may indicate that the added complexity of the neural network did not contribute much discriminating power.

Further examination of the misclassified cases have shown consistent behavior of the neural networks used for discriminant simulation. In all the cases that a neural network failed, the statistical discriminant analyses failed too. There was also consistency among the neural network simulations. The more complex architecture "corrected" the errors made by the less complex configurations—where the more complex failed, the simpler configurations failed too.

A comparison of the statistical regressions (runs 4 through 6) with the least complex neural network regression simulation (run 12) does indicate that the relationships between the five input variables and the (continuous) independent variable are rather intricate. The neural network brings the R^2 to almost 61%, compared with 42% of the best second-order linear model (run 6).

The reasons as to why the cut-point regression classifications performed worse than the direct classification approaches (i.e., statistical and neural discriminant analyses) are still unclear. Yet the phenomenon seems to be unrelated to the method of computation, as it recurred in both the statistical analyses and the neural networks simulations.

Discussion

How can we make use of neural networks in the context of traditional statistical methods such as linear regression and discriminant analysis? Without a validation set, a performance comparison of the statistical methods with the most complex neural network configurations is meaningless, due to the overfitting problem. However, we can still make use of the less complex neural networks, the ones that employ the rule of thumb for the hidden layer (i.e., where the number of hidden neurons is equal to the average number input and output neurons).

I suggest that neural networks, in their simple rule-of-thumb architecture, can provide us with an approximation of the amount of information our data contain. Compared with statistical methods, such neural networks allow better separation between model complexity and the amount of information contained in the data. When we perform statistical regression, for example, a low R^2 value may be interpreted in two ways. First, it is possible that not enough independent variables have been included, that is, more information is required. Second, the model may have been misspecified. It is possible that higher level interaction terms were missing or that the functional form may have been inappropriate (for example, trying to fit an exponential function with a linear combination of the variables). The neural networks approach "takes care" of the complexity issue.

Recall that neural networks do not require the user to specify a model. Whereas in statistical models we limit the number and order of interactions, in the neural networks approach we only limit the number of interactions and the form of the transfer function. We then let the network itself select the appropriate combinations of units (Rumelhart, Durbin, Golden, & Chauvin, 1995), however intricate it may be.

By running a limited-complexity neural network we allow for the introduction of (yet unknown) higher level interactions and nonlinear functional forms, while avoiding overfitting. Note that the most complex neural network architecture is comparable to the approximation of any arbitrary function by a polynomial, for example, by Taylor series. In a sense, what the most complex neural network does is produce a higher level polynomial that passes through all the observations (which is, by definition, overfitting). Hence, increased complexity can substitute for gaining more information. This is why we need to employ the limited-complexity neural network.

We can obtain a partial separation between model complexity and data richness by comparing the performance of our initial statistical model with a limited-complexity neural network. Possible output performance measures are R^2, SSE (Sum of Squares), or RMS (Root Mean Square) of the error terms. First, we can examine the difference between the values obtained by the two methods. If we obtain similar R^2 (or SSE) values for both methods, then we can be confident that our model, as currently specified, is practically complete (i.e., it is complex enough). If, on the other hand, we get considerably higher R^2 (lower SSE) value for the neural network simulation, it is indicative that we need to introduce more complexity into our model, in the form of interaction terms, higher powers of the variables, or different functional form. Second, we can inspect the values of each of the performance measures obtained by the limited-complexity neural network. This would be an indication of the overall amount of information the data contain. If we obtain low R^2 then we need to introduce more independent variables to the model. We can be more confident that the low R^2 is not a result of insufficient complexity.

Neural networks can be used for preliminary analysis of a database, as the neural network performance measures can give us some separation between model complexity and the richness of our data. Large performance differences between the neural network and the statistical model is indicative of inadequate model complexity. High R^2 (or low RMS) of the neural network simulation is indicative of a rich enough database. This interpretation concurs with Rumelhart et al.'s (1995) contention that neural networks are useful when we have rich data (many examples) but not much theory or structure, so a first-order variables model can not be specified. This way, the use of limited-complexity neural networks may serve as a quick substitute for an examination of the myriad combinations of the original variables set with their higher level interactions.

However, the network behaves as a "black box." That is, the resulting set of weights is not unique—for example, two consecutive runs (7 and 8) produced different weight sets. This uninterpretability of the inner workings of the network allows only limited usefulness in more advanced phases of a research. This is because, unlike in business application and other practical problems, as researchers we are primarily interested in an interpretable model and only secondarily in its performance. Until neural networks will provide us with model decomposition and interpretability comparable to the ones given by the established statistical modeling methods, the latter can rest assured— they have no replacement for academic researchers.

CONCLUSION

Neural networks are outstanding "black boxes." They can "deliver" results in cases where our run-of-the-mill statistical methods encounter great difficulties. Neural networks are inherently multivariate, nonlinear, and nonparametric. The question is whether we, as researchers, are interested in "black boxes" that do the job. Whereas in business application and in other practical problems we are content to have a good "black box," academic research has limited use of such machine, because the most important element of any research is in explaining phenomena. In this area neural networks are poor performers. However, theory is still developing, giving us some hope that interpretation of neural networks' inner working is within reach.

The best approach, I believe, is to use both methods. Specifically, as discussed in the previous section, back-propagation neural networks can be of considerable help in the initial phases of the data analysis, when data are abundant, but the specific theory is underdeveloped or yet unknown (Rumelhart et al., 1995). If the neural network analyses show that our data is rich enough, we can then proceed with the traditional statistical methods.

It is hoped that this review and data analysis illustration helped to demystify neural networks, by showing their strengths and weaknesses, and by outlining how, and more importantly, when to use them.

nine

WIDENING THE LENS: THE USE OF HISTORICAL DATA IN ORGANIZATIONAL COMMUNICATION THEORIZING

Katherine Miller
University of Kansas

"History, the evidence of time, the light of truth, the life of memory, the directness of life, the herald of antiquity, committed to immortality."
—Cicero

"I don't know much about history, and I wouldn't give a nickel for all the history in the world. History is more or less bunk. It is tradition. We want to live in the present, and the only history that is worth a tinker's damn is the history we make today."
—Henry Ford

In recent years, it has become a truism in communication, and throughout disciplines of social scholarship, that social behavior is culturally and historically situated. And, to a large extent, theorists and researchers in organizational communication have heeded the implications of this truism by considering a variety of cultural contexts in their work. In addition to work on the diversity of "organizational cultures" (e.g., Pacanowsky & O'Donnell-Trujillo, 1982; R. C. Smith & Eisenberg, 1987; Trujillo, 1992), scholars are also now considering organizational communication processes across national boundaries (e.g., Papa, Auwal, & Singhal, 1995; Stohl, 1993; Wiseman & Shuter, 1994). However, with regard to the historical context of social behavior, organizational communication scholars have tended to eschew the sentiments of Cicero and endorse the mentality of Henry Ford. By keeping our theory and research almost exclusively in the present tense, we have, implicitly or explicitly, supported the notion that the only important history—and the only relevant data for organizational communication theorizing—is the history we make today.

This chapter is a call for organizational communication theorists and researchers to widen their scholarly vision to extend not just across boundaries of geography and culture, but across boundaries of time. Specifically, I argue that the study of organizational communication would benefit from further consideration of historical events in the process of contemporary theory development. In this chapter, I first make the argument for the importance of using historical data in theory development. I then consider some theoretical frameworks useful for developing theory through historical data and discuss some of the challenges inherent in the use of historical data. Finally, I consider three examples of historical theorizing—two from the extant literature and one in the formative stages of development.

THE IMPORTANCE OF HISTORICAL DATA IN THEORY DEVELOPMENT

In 1993, *Communication Theory* published a forum on "Communication, Theory, and History" (Hardt & Brennen, 1993). Included in this forum were discussions of the role of history in theorizing within mass communications (Nerone, 1993), rhetoric (Whalen, 1993), women's studies (Jansen, 1993), and interpersonal communication (Stephen & Harrison, 1993). All of these authors outlined ways in which "communication research has been largely ahistorical" (Jansen, 1993, p. 136), and considered possible palliatives to this state of affairs. Notably absent from the discussion, however, were scholars of organizational communication.

To some extent, the absence of organizational communication from this forum was surprising. Organizational communication scholars have always been very concerned with history in terms of disciplinary background. This is seen clearly in the structure of our textbooks (e.g., Daniels & Spiker, 1994; Eisenberg & Goodall, 1993; Kreps, 1990b; K. Miller, 1995), in which the opening chapters are typically devoted to historical developments in management and organizational theory from scientific management to systems theory to postmodern approaches. Our absorption with our own history is also evident in genealogical reviews of the discipline (e.g., Redding & Tompkins, 1988). However, with few exceptions, our consideration of the past has been limited to these somewhat inward-looking pursuits. I would argue, however, that looking at a broader range of historical data would serve to enrich contemporary theorizing about organizational communication processes. In this section, I outline several reasons why we should use historical data in the development of contemporary organizational communication theory.

It is undeniable, of course, that context plays a critical role in the operation of organizational communication processes. Because of the importance of context, it would be ludicrous to suggest that the workings of a turn-of-the-century factory are comparable to activities in one of today's high-technology firms. It is likely, though, that many basic processes through which we organize communicatively are comparable across historical periods. Consider, for example, the process of negotiation. In exploring a negotiation incident from a long-past era, it is likely that the context of the negotiation and the resources available to the negotiators differed substantially from those in present-day negotiations. However, the process through which organizational actors transact the negotiation process may well be similar today and in times past. At a more abstract level, Abrams (1980) has argued that the basic problem of "structuring" is one that has confronted social actors throughout history. As he stated:

> It is the problem of finding a way of accounting for human experience which recognizes simultaneously and in equal measure that history and society are made by constant, more or less purposeful, individual action and that individual action, however purposeful, is made by history and society. (p. 7)

If structuring is, indeed, a central aspect of society, this process could be investigated using both contemporary and historical events. Thus, the functioning of a number of organizational processes might be similar across historical eras.

The notion of phenomenal similarity would suggest that historical events can be used as data for organizational communication theorizing. Beyond this mere possibility, however, the use of historical data can also provide "added value" to contemporary ideas about organizational communication. Specifically, by using historical data, we have a wider range of contexts to consider in our theorizing. The mere placement of contemporary organizations within the modern (or postmodern) era limits the variety of situations in which organizational communication processes occur. However, by looking at historical data, we are able to look at how these processes differ given a contrasting historical situation.

Consider, for example, a theory about the adoption of communication technology in organizations. A theorist might be concerned about whether the framework proposed to explain adoption is general enough to work across a variety of technological innovations or only for the technologies of the late 20th century. One way to investigate this theoretical concern would be through historical accounts of the adoption of the telephone, the telegraph, the copy machine, carbon paper, or other technologies that are accepted as commonplace in today's organizations. This notion is akin to the process of "theoretical sampling" advocated by proponents of grounded theory (Strauss & Corbin, 1990). This idea suggests that sampling should be designed "on the basis of concepts that have proven theoretical relevance to the evolving theory" (p. 176). Although grounded theorists are generally concerned with sampling in terms of contemporary research sites, individuals, and documents (see Lincoln & Guba, 1985), a theorist's concern with relevant theoretical issues could also involve focusing sampling efforts on historical events.

Finally, theorists in our field have long been concerned with the processual nature of organizational communication (see, e.g., Monge, Farace, Eisenberg, Miller, & White, 1984). It has also been long noted, however, that our scholarship rarely captures the complex processual nature of organizational phenomena. One way to deal with this shortcoming is through the consideration of historical data in our theorizing. Through the hindsight of a historical view, we can know "how things happened," and "how things turned out." We have a wider lens with which to consider the evolving nature of the organizational communication processes we're considering. We can look at the life cycles of organizations throughout the entire cycle, rather than simply using our knowledge of life cycles to contextualize the particular "slice" of organizational life we're studying.

FRAMEWORKS FOR DEVELOPING THEORY WITH HISTORICAL DATA

If we accept the premise that historical data might provide a useful avenue for contemporary organizational theorizing, the next question becomes how we can combine historical data with organizational communication theory in a fruitful way. Nerone (1993) argued that there is an essential tension between history and theory that results from the conflicting goals of historians and theorists. Specifically, historians see themselves as "blue-collar workers who mine archives and craft narratives [which are] true in as much as they describe what actually happened with fidelity" (pp. 148–149). In contrast, theoretical knowledge "is generally understood as being true in as much as it describes (or predicts) a broad range of phenomena" (p. 149). Thus, the challenges facing organizational communication theorists involve (a) learning how to mine history effectively and (b) finding tools that will link historical narratives with contemporary theory.

With regard to the first of these challenges, a detailed discussion of specific methods of historical analysis is beyond the scope of this chapter (for a classic discussion of these methods see Barzun & Graff, 1985). Suffice to say that historical data gathering involves "the examination of data provided in diaries, letters, newspapers, autobiographies, and other accounts of participants and observers" (Stephen & Harrison, 1993, p. 164) and that the historian must make choices regarding "the means of interpreting, contextualizing, organizing, legitimizing, and judging sources" (Blair & Kaul, 1990, p. 148). With regard to the second challenge, however, several theoretical frameworks developed within the social sciences might provide useful bridges between historical data and contemporary theory for the organizational communication scholar.

A framework capable of bridging substantive communication theory with historical data must allow the scholar to deal with the confluence of three factors—time, meaning, and social interaction. Although a variety of frameworks might assist in this endeavor, three are briefly considered here. These are structuration theory (Giddens, 1979, 1984), symbolic convergence theory (Bormann, 1972, 1980), and social movement theory (Simons, Mechling, & Schreier, 1984). All three of these theoretical frameworks provide overarching structures through which more specific organizational communication processes can be considered. They differ in emphasis, but each considers the ways in which communicative interaction influences the shaping of social meanings over time.

Structuration theory (Giddens, 1979, 1984; see Poole, Seibold, & McPhee, 1986 for useful summary) considers the ways in which the practices of a social collective are produced and reproduced in interaction. The analysis of social practices is accomplished through a distinction between the observable behaviors of social actors (the "system") and the unobservable rules and resources drawn on in producing those behaviors (the "structure"). Central to structuration theory is the notion of "duality of structure." That is:

> Structures are at once the medium and the outcome of social action. They are its medium because members draw on rules and resources to interact within and produce practices. They are its outcome because rules and resource exist only by virtue of being used in a practice. (Poole et al., 1986, p. 247)

Thus, structuration theory provides a framework through which a theorist can explore the processual creation and recreation of social norms, practices, and institutions.

Symbolic convergence theory (SCT; Bormann, 1972, 1980) is a second theoretical framework that deals with the intersection of time, interaction, and meaning. SCT (and its attendant methodology, fantasy theme analysis) considers the ways in which recurring communicative forms and patterns contribute to and indicate the evolution of a shared group consciousness. According to proponents of SCT, actors within social systems develop and maintain a sense of community through the use of rhetorical devices such as "dramatizing messages," "fantasy themes," and "rhetorical vision." According to Bormann (1982; see also Bormann, Cragan, & Shields, 1994), SCT is appropriate as a framework for understanding symbolic convergence both in face-to-face interaction and across larger communities separated by geography and time. Thus, the combined consideration of time, meaning, and communication in symbolic convergence theory makes it another useful framework for the theorist using historical data in theory development.

Finally, a variety of social movement approaches have been proposed by rhetorical scholars over the past 50 years (e.g., Riches & Sillars, 1980; Simons et al., 1984). These approaches, beginning with Griffin (1952), are all concerned with "the process through which history and rhetoric combine to study the inception, crisis, and consummation of movements designed to achieve change" (Joraanstad, 1992, p. 7). As Joraanstad argued, social movement theorists can be differentiated in terms of the focus of the analysis, especially the degree to which the rhetors within the movement are conceptualized as working against or within a dominant social system (see Smith & Windes, 1975). However, all social movement theorists again look at the ways in which communication, meaning, and time come together within the context of societal change.

CHALLENGES IN THE USE OF HISTORICAL DATA

The preceding section of this chapter presented three frameworks that could be used in the development of substantive organizational communication theories. Even under the enabling umbrella of these theories, however, there are a number of challenges inherent in the use of historical data that do not confront the researcher or theorist working in the present tense. The first of these, of course, is the challenge of finding information relevant to the theoretical problem at hand. The historian attempts to craft a factual narrative that "can presumably be established as empirically verifiable on the basis of a critical reading of documentary records" (Nerone, 1993, p. 149). Thus, historical archives provide the mine from which relevant data can be excavated. However, because the organizational communication scholar is dealing with data collection retrospectively rather than prospectively, there are clearly limits to what data can be gathered. As Webb, Campbell, Schwartz, Sechrest, and Grove (1981) pointed out, the researcher using archival data sources must deal with the dilemmas of "selective deposit" (not all archives are kept) and "selective survival" (not all archives are maintained or survive over time).

Beyond this difficulty in gathering full and relevant historical data, however, lies the challenges of interpreting those data. The most basic aspect of this dilemma stems from the bias inherent in any "reporting" of the empirical world. Based on developments in the philosophy of science ranging from Heisenberg's Uncertainty Principle (Heisenberg, 1958) to Berger and Luckmann's (1966) treatise on the social construction of reality, many social scholars now conclude "that whatever is seen is always preceded by, or seen through, a construction that entails certain expected perceptions" (Krippendorff, 1989, p. 76). This bias in observation hold for both the original "recorder" of the historical events and for the social researcher investigating these reportings through historical archives. Nerrone (1993) discussed this problem in some detail:

> First, when historians encounter the sources, they are already narrativized in some form. So in the process of ascertaining the facts historians must actively denarrativize the sources. Then, in the process of letting the facts speak for themselves, historians must again actively narrativize the facts. Naturally all of this denarrativizing and renarrativizing involves more than empirical science. And historians have always recognized this, since they have always known that, while History may not change, histories go out of currency very quickly. (p. 150)

These interpretive challenges are especially daunting for the contemporary social researcher using historical data. As Stephen and Harrison (1993) noted, "researchers cannot produce historical accounts of communication phenomena without drawing upon their own processes of meaning construction" (p. 164). Thus, the interpretation of historical accounts of communication events will always be colored by our modern-day interpretations of both history and communication. Stephen and Harrison suggested that these interpretive challenges can be approached through the hermeneutic process of "tacking" between "experience-near" and "experience-distant" concepts (Geertz, 1983). For the organizational communication theorist, the "experience-near" concepts are those that comprise the theoretical framework of interest; the "experience-distant" concepts are the historical materials under examination. This juxtaposition of history and theory allows the scholar to "treat modern conceptions of communication as implicit foils for understanding historical actors' experiences of communication within their economic, political, and sociocultural contexts" (Stephen & Harrison, 1993, p. 164).

There are limits, of course, to the success of the hermeneutic project. As Diesing (1991) argued, the two major limits on the hermeneutic process are "our ability to find or produce additional texts or nonverbal communications for further testing, and our ability to question our own assumptions and conceive of alternatives" (pp. 110–111). The first limit is accentuated by the use of historical data. As noted, we cannot find data that were not recorded or that have been lost over time. Further, with regard to our interpretive account of history, we cannot do "member checks" to ascertain whether our interpretations are "recognizable to audience members as adequate representations of their own (and multiple) realities" (Lincoln & Guba, 1985, p. 314). Second, the hermeneutic process is limited when the scholar "is unable to imagine a different theoretical perspective" (Diesing, 1991, p. 111). As with any academic work, the investigation of historical data can be hampered by theoretical determinism in which all observations are force-fit into the theorist's framework of choice.

TWO EXAMPLES FROM THE LITERATURE

To this point, I have argued that organizational communication scholars could enhance theory-development efforts by "widening the lens" and considering historical events as data in the theory development process. Although such efforts have been largely missing from our theory development efforts, there are several exceptions to this pattern. In this section, I discuss two published examples of the use of historical data in the development of organizational theory. I then consider a project that is now in the formative stages of development.

Sensemaking and the Mann Gulch Disaster

In 1949, a fire engulfed the Mann Gulch area in Montana. A group of fire jumpers were flown in to fight the fire. Although they expected a "routine" fire, the flames crossed the gulch and threatened the fire jumpers. The foreman of the group, Wagner Dodge, lit a fire in the path of the flames and yelled at his crew to lie down in the burned area. The incredulous crew ignored this directive and instead attempted to run to safety. Dodge survived the fire by staying in the ashes of the burned area. Two other fire fighters made it through a crevice and escaped the ridge. All of the other fire jumpers perished in the fire.

In 1992, Norman MacLean chronicled the Mann Gulch disaster in his book *Young Men and Fire*. MacLean essentially worked as a historian, documenting the incident through archives, trace evidence, interviews, and observation of the Mann Gulch site. In 1993, Weick used MacLean's historical account as data for theorizing about "the collapse of sensemaking in organizations." Weick used the events of August 4, 1949 to build a case about how the fire-fighters' role structure and the "cosmology episode" (Weick, 1985) that ensued made it impossible for the fire-jumpers to make sense of the happenings around them. Weick then built on this analysis by considering ways in which organizations can develop resilence to sensemaking collapses through the use of improvisation, virtual role systems, an attitude of wisdom, and respectful interaction.

Weick's analysis of the Mann Gulch disaster is an excellent example of the use of historical events in the development of organizational theory, and it is noteworthy for several reasons. First, Weick (1979) used the Mann Gulch disaster to confirm and develop contemporary ideas about organizational sensemaking. The use of this historical incident supports other case studies on sensemaking (e.g., Weick, 1990) but provides added value through the investigation of a well-documented incident in which sensemaking collapsed. It is the historical nature of the case that allows Weick the retrospective distance necessary to make theoretical sense of the incident. Second, Weick took care to argue for the high quality of the historical data used in the case analysis. He outlines the methods used by Maclean in investigating the fire and argued that Maclean's historical research techniques were effective in combatting most recognized threats to research validity. Thus, Weick avoided many of the pitfalls of historical data analysis while reaping the benefits of an illustrious and well-documented historical incident.

Structuration and the Development of the Memo Genre

A second example of the use of historical data in contemporary theorizing is the research program currently being developed by Yates and Orlikowski. This line of research began with Yates' 1989 book, *Control Through Communication: The Rise of System in American Management*. This book is a detailed and carefully researched treatise that considers the historical development of organizational communication systems and their contribution to management. Yates and Orlikowski then used these and similar historical data to make several important theoretical arguments about organizational communication (Yates, 1989b; Yates & Orlikowski, 1992). Specifically, Yates and Orlikowski have argued from a structurational framework that it is useful to consider organizational communication "genres." Using the development of the memo as an exemplar, Yates and Orlikowski (1992) illustrated the ways in which historical events and human action work reciprocally to create and recreate genres, defined as "typified communication action invoked in response to a recurrent situation" (p. 301). For example, they traced the influence of workplace innovations such as the vertical file on the development of the memo genre and speculate about the future of memos in the age of electronic communication.

Like Weick's work on sensemaking, Yates and Orlikowski's work on organizational communication genres is an exemplary program of research in its combination of historical data and contemporary theory. Several aspects of this research program stand out. First, Yates and Orlikowski's work demonstrates an intricate combination of history and theory at a variety of levels. These scholars wove together substantive theory regarding communication technologies with metatheoretical positions regarding structuration and genres. They then used this complex theoretical fabric to understand the historical development of organizational communication systems and allowed the historical data to speak to the further development of their theoretical positions. This work clearly demonstrates the value of using multiple theoretical positions in the hermeneutic project of understanding historical texts. Second, Orlikowski and Yates combined their investigation of historical events with research on communication genres in contemporary organizations. Thus, these scholars use historical events as one piece of a larger theory development project. Finally, like Weick, Yates and Orlikowski demonstrate strong concern with historical documentation (see Yates, 1989a). Thus, this work makes a contribution both as historical narrative and as social science theory.

ONE EXAMPLE IN PROGRESS

In the final section of this chapter, I discuss a work in progress that again seeks to use historical events as data for the development of contemporary organizational communication theory. In this project, I am attempting to use methods of historical research to craft a narrative about the communicative development and maintenance of occupational identity within the profession of osteopathic medicine. This historical narrative will then be analyzed in light of two strands of communication theory. The first theoretical framework—symbolic convergence theory—will provide a vocabulary for understanding the process through which a community of professionals converge and diverge in statements of "who we are" and "what we do." The second theoretical framework—organizational identification—will provide a vehicle for understanding the substance of textual material regarding occupational identity. Some of the details of this project are outlined in the following.

The Theoretical Domain—Identification and Communication

The notions of commitment and identification have long been areas of interest to organizational scholars (see, e.g., Albert & Whetten, 1985; Salancik, 1982; Steers, 1977). In the field of communication, Cheney and Tompkins (1987) have argued that commitment and identification are "distinct but interdependent concepts" (p. 9) in which identification is the "substance" of action patterns and commitment is the "form" that action patterns take in behavior. As Cheney and Tompkins conceptualized these issues, identification is particularly central for communication scholars, for identification is "attuned to the ways one's talk about him/herself becomes him/herself" (p. 6) and that identity must be approached through the consideration of the "common language" of a "community of communicators" (p. 5).

Research on identification in organizational contexts has typically considered the connection between individuals and organizations, sometimes considering the ways in which individuals must negotiate identification with multiple entities within an "organizational society" (see Cheney, 1991). The individual is seen as appropriating identification from institutions that are implicitly assumed to have relatively stable identities. However, these approaches miss several critical features of organizational life that are central to the Cheney and Tompkins conceptualization of identification. First, identity is articulated in a community, not by individuals. That is, identification is not a process in which an individual assimilates an objective organizational identity to a greater or lesser extent. Rather, it is a process through which a group of communicators negotiate an identity for the institution with both internal and external constituencies (Cheney, 1991). Second, organizational identity is not a fixed concept. Rather, identity is fluid—changing as an institution moves through its life cycle (Kimberly, Miles, and Associates 1980) and adapts its culture to internal exigencies and the external environment (Schein, 1985). Thus, a comprehensive approach to identification must consider the ways in which an institutional community negotiates an identity over time with both internal constituencies and the larger environment.

The Historical Case—The Osteopathic Profession

The profession of osteopathic medicine (see Baer, 1981; Gevitz, 1982) was founded by Andrew Taylor Still, a frontier physician who was disturbed by the excesses of traditional medicine (e.g., drugs, bleeding, surgery). Still proposed a system of healing based on the tenets of holism, the primacy of health over disease, and the systemic unity and dynamic homeostasis of the body. Originally, osteopathic medical practice relied almost entirely on the manual manipulation of the musculoskeletal system. When first introduced, osteopathy was viewed as one of many alternative healing systems by proponents and as a "cult" by practitioners of traditional medicine. In its over century-long existence, the osteopathic profession has engaged in many "struggles" for recognition and acceptance, including fights for full practicing rights, hospital priveleges, and medical school accreditation. Today, osteopathic medicine is an accepted part of the medical scene. Doctors of Osteopathy (who represent 5% of all physicians and serve more than 10% of U.S. patients) have full practicing rights in all 50 states, 19 medical schools, and many osteopathic hospitals as well as privileges at a huge number of mixed staff hospitals. In other words, members of the profession have accomplished their goals of acceptance by the larger society.

Through an ongoing research relationship with the American Osteopathic Association (AOA) and several colleges of osteopathic medicine, I have been able to collect a great deal of archival data on the historical development of the osteopathic profession. Most of these data were collected in Kirksville, MO (the "birthplace" of osteopathic medicine) at the Kirksville College of Osteopathic Medicine Library. Additional materials were gathered at three other medical schools and from other AOA sources. To this point, data collected include (a) historical documentation of early statements of identity in the osteopathic profession from turn-of-the-century journals and publications, (b) formal statements of osteopathic mission and identity in the form of speeches by AOA presidents and others in the profession, (c) informal comments regarding the history of the profession in the form of videotaped interviews with osteopathic "insiders" during the last 20 years, (d) ethnographic materials collected via interviews and observations during the college's centennial celebrations, (e) academic work on the history of osteopathy, and (f) scholarship regarding professional identity in osteopathy, other medical fields, and professions in general. Additional historical data will be collected as the needs of the project dictate.

Theory and History—The Symbolic Convergence of Osteopathic Identity

Initial analyses of these historical data paint a complex picture of identity within the osteopathic profession. The various facets of data collected point to an evolving conversation within the profession with regard to "who we are" and "what do we do," especially vis-à-vis other relevant professions (e.g., allopathy and chiropracty). More detailed analyses of these data are planned in which symbolic convergence theory will be used to identify the patterns of rhetoric through which constituencies within the osteopathic profession created and sustained a vision of what it means to be an osteopathic physician.

One area of promise in this research is a consideration of some of the defining events within the osteopathic profession that have punctuated the evolving conversation about identity. For example, A.T. Still strongly advocated a medical system that was totally drugless. His devotion to this aspect of osteopathy is clear in his supposed dying words—"Tell the boys to keep it pure." However, initial analyses indicate that rhetoric regarding osteopathic identity changed substantially after Still's death in 1917, and soon the notion of a drug-free system was no longer a core concept for osteopathic physicians. Other "punctuating events" emerging from initial analyses include battles over professional licensure, and "turf wars" with the allopathic profession in key states such as California.

SUMMARY

"That men (sic) do not learn very much from the lessons of history is the most important of all the lessons of history."
—Aldous Huxley

The call for papers for this conference urged us to consider "the challenges facing organizational communication in the next century."

My argument throughout this chapter has been that one of the best ways to meet the challenges of the future is to look to the past, and learn from organizational communication events that have come before us. By using historical data in theory development, we gain the ability to look at different social contexts, the ability to consider processes of organizational communication over long periods of time, and the retrospective distance to use these events in contemporary theory building. This type of theory development is not easy, of course, as the examples of sensemaking at Mann Gulch, the structuration of the memo genre, and the development of osteopathic identity illustrate. However, by using frameworks such as structuration theory, social movement theory, and symbolic convergence theory to enhance the interpretive interplay between history and theory, we can both construct revealing narratives about organizational communication in times past and use those narratives to enhance our understanding of organizational communication processes both then and now.

ten

RECONSTRUCTING METHODOLOGY: GIVING VOICE TO STICKY WEBS *AND* FUZZY RIGOR

Patricia Riley
University of Southern California

> He had bought a large map representing the sea,
> Without the least vestige of land:
> And the crew were much pleased when they found it to be
> A map they could all understand.
>
> 'What's the good of Mercator's North Pole and Equators.
> Tropics, Zones, and Meridian Lines?'
> So the Bellman would cry: and the crew would reply,
> 'They are merely conventional signs!
>
> 'Other maps are such shapes, with their islands and capes!
> But we've got our Captain to thank'
> (So the crew would protest) 'that he's bought us the best—
> A perfect and absolute blank!
> —Lewis Carroll "The Hunting of the Snark"

> "In the beginner's mind there are many possibilities. In the expert's mind there are few."
> —Shunryu Suzi Zen Mind, Beginners Mind

I love methods—most kinds, orientations, and tools. I teach multivariate statistics, ethnography, computer-assisted content analysis; you name it, I'm fascinated by how we might make interesting meanings with it. I'm unapologetically eclectic across studies yet rule-governed within projects. Having begun my career at the University of Minnesota, and heavily influenced by Ernest Bormann, I took for granted that critical, humanistic, qualitative, and quantitative approaches to communication research were but different frames on our pictures of social life. Thus my job in the discipline was to be part curator, part apprentice, part artisan, part historian, part tutor, part critic, and in large part, audience.

So what is this that we call methodology and why is it once again being problematized? Is it because methodology is inherently a political statement as we bind together our theories and research questions with the rules and norms of data gathering in order to consecrate our particular world view? Is it because we create maps and models and procedures arcane enough to insulate us from the uninitiated (the great unwashed as one of my statistics professors used to say without malice but much ignorance) and thus increase our value in the marketplace of academia or the larger circles of the intellectual elite? I guess the answer depends on whom you are asking, although many of my colleagues would respond that nothing so cynical or political is at hand. Methodology, most social scientists claim, is "merely" the philosophy that underlies the application of methods or tools, like sampling statistics, or content analysis, or the guidelines of a process like ethnography.

In organizational communication, as in the social sciences generally, this notion of a philosophy of methods has always been more than a little murky. As a student, I was exposed to many of the methodological debates such as positivism/humanism, value-free versus researcher's values, and data-driven versus theory-laden conflicts. The solution of the time, using the word "solution" loosely, was to understand the ontological assumptions and epistemological requirements of the framework in which you chose to do your research and then follow the conventions. To accomplish this task, I was taught several category schemes that guided method choice. For example, in the first column there would be a list of paradigms—not all positivistic—and then you picked yours out and moved across the columns to see what methods were deemed appropriate (e.g., K. D. Bailey, 1982). The categories may have been too generic and not always mutually exclusive, and the recommendations imperfect for a variety of reasons, but the matrix did help explicate the relationships and the differences between various methods and their respective theoretical frameworks. Some of the decision-tree approaches could also help with other annoying issues researchers must contend with like resource availability. The utility of such devices probably invited oversimplifications and drew attention away from the philosophical debates.

This pluralistic spirit, however, was not for everyone. There were/are locales of communication study where only one paradigm was allowed to rule and other approaches not given equal welcome. I remember quite vividly that during my first day as a visiting professor at Michigan State I was given a tour of the department. On the door to the graduate student lounge was a sign that read, "Qualitative research is an oxymoron."

Well, we are all being encouraged to rethink our relationship to our methods and methodological issues because of the scrutiny under which all the social sciences have recently been placed. Much of this attention has been spurred by the philosophical issues involved in what is known as the "interpretive turn," including the challenges of postmodern thinking, but there are also pragmatic concerns that could be methodologically significant and I believe deserve some attention. The description of the issues that follow is necessarily limited but should begin/continue the conversation on methods and their philosophies.

PHILOSOPHICAL ISSUES

There are many philosophical issues that need to be part of this discussion, but the dissolution of both the "interpretation versus explanation" and the "objectivity/subjectivity" bifurcations are among the most profound.

Interpretation versus Explanation

This methodological conflict was often defined as having its roots in the German historiography concepts of *Verstehen and Erklären*: understanding versus explanation (Putnam, 1983). It was pretty much accepted in the academy that the natural sciences had to do with explanation, whereas much of the scholarship of the social sciences was concerned primarily with understanding. There has been a fairly radical reappraisal in communication, as in the rest of the social sciences (anthropology, history, and sociology in particular), of this epistemological division. There appears to be a good deal of agreement (especially in the social sciences) that interpretation is just as elemental to the natural sciences as the social sciences. Although the philosophical conversation about interpretation can get quite complicated, one of the more obvious shifts in thinking is the wide acceptance of the claim that we are born into an already interpreted/interpreting world, and that much of our language, concepts (including math and scientific terms), cultural practices, and societal concerns existed before we did and continue to be reinterpreted.

There is also a companion argument that although generalizations in the social sciences are constituted differently than those of the natural sciences, they nonetheless involve causal attributions (e.g., Giddens, 1987). This is consistent with Bhaskar's dictum that agents' reasons are themselves causes in social life. This position is more controversial, when combined with the previous argument it appears that the causal/interpretation and explanation/understanding bifurcations are no longer generally accepted across large portions of the social sciences.

Objectivity versus Subjectivity

There is also today a much greater appreciation of the problems inherent in observing human action, especially communication (assuming for the moment that we want to reify communication as a phenomenon). The key issue is reflexivity, and most modern research is seen as ignoring the reflexive sense of its own production. It is odd that this should occur in a field like communication where many of its members have at least some exposure to rhetorical theory, but Plato's teachings on the relationship between the knower and the known were misplaced somewhere on the path toward scientific methods (Giddens, 1987). Although the natural sciences are also willing to be self-reflexive and revise what they think they know on the basis of new information (perhaps more slowly than the social sciences) they do not, to the same degree, have the methodological problem of separating the observer from the observed. In communication, as in the social sciences more generally, the interactions we observe are in part informed by the concepts we are studying. For example, the use of power and authority, empathy, and intercultural communication practices are to some degree stable enough concepts that they are used both by academic researchers and "nonexperts." Yet the people in the organizations we study (as well as the organizing communication we study) are constantly changing, both in the invention of new forms of interaction and strategies and through the conscious appropriation of communicative and social knowledge. This means that while we are studying the impact of the authority relationship on communication practices, the relationship and the practices can be changing.

At its core, this recognition of what Giddens (1984) inelegantly called the "double hermeneutic" (the appropriation or constitutive use of research concepts by those who are being studied), as well as a better understanding of issues like identifiably different speech communities, and other historical and cultural differences, have obvious implications for concepts like "replication," "the object of study," "testability," and midlevel theory development. As Taylor (1995) noted, the ideal of objectivity as the progressive elimination of error through successive corrections is a chimera. It appears more than unlikely that we could ever approach the laboratory success of the natural sciences or have the ability to aggregate research results in that manner.

Although some researchers in our and other related fields find this conclusion disappointing or downright unpalatable (especially those who refer to themselves as scientists), one of the interpretivist and postmodern arguments against social science is that we should have never wanted to emulate the objectivity of the natural sciences in the first place. My reading of this claim is that beyond the well-discussed difficulties with ever being "objective," the philosophy of the natural sciences is inherently logocentric in a Derridean sense (this is the notion that language is at its best when it is transparent to reality, or identical with its object in an Aristotelian sense) among other wrongs, and therefore an impoverished model for intellectual endeavor. So, at its best, objectivity is impossible to achieve and at worst a meaningless or ridiculous notion.

Does this imply that we should promote only interpretive scholarship that is careful to privilege nothing? Or that our universities should not continue to teach quantitative research methods or encourage detailed and rigorous social scientific research? That is not my conclusion (I can just hear the internal groan from both the math haters and the postmodernists, sometimes in the same bodies), but before I turn to that discussion here are some of the pragmatic and political concerns that also impinge on our discussion.

PRAGMATIC AND POLITICAL ISSUES—TIME, MONEY, POLITICS, AND PURPOSE

First, the loudest complaint is most likely that given all the time and energy and money put into social scientific research, the results have been disappointing, especially when compared to the natural sciences. The common responses from our discipline and the other social sciences are of two types: one, that social phenomena are much more complex and less uniform, and two, that there are far fewer resources devoted to their study. I agree that human behavior and social action are less uniform than much of what is investigated in the natural sciences, but I seriously doubt the complexity argument—DNA and the AIDS virus quickly come to mind. The second issue, however, is an empirical question and I suspect that most campuses are like ours where the vast majority of grant and contract money belongs to the natural sciences, engineering, and the health sciences. And what is the result? The pictures coming from the new and improved Hubble telescope—the one showing the birth of a universe? Or how about the ones indicating that billions of galaxies are out there? How about the computer mapping of the human genome? Pretty exciting stuff!

In organizational communication, we can add insights about sexual harassment, the use and abuse of power and control, investigate how decisions are really made in hallway conversations or on Lotus Notes, or increase organizational members' awareness of the difficulties of communicating in multicultural environments or teams, but those may not always be the kinds of projects that capture the fancy of congressional committees who set federal research budgets, or university administrators who put new resources into applied natural and health sciences. There has been a good deal of press surrounding the new freshmen congressional members, and their constituencies, who are vocally opposed to having their tax dollars go to the "ivory tower" and to research that has no useful application. The vice president for research on our campus believes universities could be facing huge downsizings if even half of the proposed cuts in research, scholarships, and other funding to education come to pass over the next decade. Given that our discipline is often the target of such downsizings these concerns need to be part of the dialogue about research and our methodology.

Second, in a completely different vein, for close to a century the natural science model of the study of humans and human behavior has been attacked as part of the plot for political control and subjugation of the masses (J. O'Neill, 1995). For organizational communication the specific argument was that we existed only to further management's goals. Now we can console ourselves that in response to this complaint organizational communication disavowed its purpose as a handmaiden to management and that most of these attacks were designed for sociology, political science, economics and psychology—communication not being visible enough to draw much of the brunt. Nonetheless we are implicated in this argument as our members, like other social scientists, are engaged in activities like communication campaigns, counseling, consulting, and data gathering and in administering governments and corporations as well as teaching in institutions like universities.

Regardless of our self-images as "free-floating, intellectual elite" (O'Neill, 1995) who challenge the system, question authority and convention, and are friends of the poor and the exploited, we are primarily middle-class folks whose lifestyle depends on large establishment institutions, mostly paid for by taxing those large corporations we love to hate, and our research is paid for directly or indirectly by these same institutions. It would be quite a conceit to see ourselves as not part of the "system" or exempt from these questions. I do, however, find perverse humor in juxtaposing this position with the previous one—that we might simultaneously know little of any value yet be able to use this knowledge to aid management in a conscious or unconscious conspiracy to control workers.

The third argument is the generalized attack that universities have lost their original purpose. As spokesperson for the back to the basics movement in higher education, Bloom (1987) led the battle cry for a return to the days when universities taught content and students learned the canon—what educated people needed to know in order to be termed educated. The academy today is described as an unhappy mixture of self-indulgent and inner-directed notions of human growth coupled with the additional problem that universities have little respect for teaching undergraduates. Bloom articulated the avowedly elitist position that in democratizing our universities we have allowed the masses to dictate what should and should not be taught. The result is incoherence of purpose, creeping careerism, and noneducation. Of particular importance to our discussion is that the growing use in organizational communication of critical and interpretive methods are thought to be politically correct methodological devices that sanctify the values of the cultural left. The back-to-basics movement also views postmodern perspectives as simple-minded imports from the dispossessed humanities—a set of approaches that flatters both the creative fantasies of the professors and the democratic tastes of students in the search for the humanities' imaginary empire (Bloom, 1987). Although more thoughtful critiques and detailed readings of postmodern positions abound (e.g., Rorty, 1991), this particular perspective is less philosophical than it is political, but more than anything it is loud.

The cultural left dismisses Bloom and other neo-conservatives as having misguided nostalgia attacks for the Eurocentric legacy of dead white males (as if the cultural left is not Eurocentric). My reading of Bloom and his colleagues always conjures up a vision of barbarians at the gate meeting a kinder, gentler Nietzsche. Yet anyone who reads the newspaper or watches 60 Minutes is aware that the academy has forfeited its honored position in our society (although some argue that respect only breeds complacency) and is under almost daily assault in the media for having lost its purpose and relevance.

METHODOLOGICAL CONVERSATIONS

Now, these are by no means the only issues we have to contend with; they are just my minimalist reading of the ones with the most compelling stories. A synopsis of the problematizing discourse indicates that the scientific model could be (choose one) methodologically flawed, useless, corrupt, or misguided; and the critical interpretive method might be self-indulgent, biased, noninformative, or politically motivated. Love those options! It seems to me that the fundamental question is what kind of conversation do we want to create involving the methodological issues that concern us—that fuzzy set of activities we call "doing" organizational communication research. This presumes, of course, that we participate as well in other ongoing conversations in the discipline and in the university about the nature of theorizing, the philosophy of communication, the challenges to epistemology, and our role in the academy and society(ies).

I suggest that this conversation needs at least four threads in order to adequately "work" on the problematic relationship between our theories and our methods. One conversational thread needs to be the obvious one: If we believe social knowledge is reflexively constituted, what parameters does this place on concepts like reliability, testability, and the accumulation of knowledge? Just as a starting point in the conversation, validity might be recast as a highly contextual "meaning," generated by the speech community whose members are participating in some inquiry or analysis, subject to transformation over time and space, and not concerned with representing some true concept or idea or process. The accuracy component of traditional conceptions of validity could either not change—as in the case where a researcher is interested in the pure recall of a vision statement or some other discrete organizational message—or be dramatically different and consist of the breadth of metaphors or symbols, or some new measure of the comfort level organization members have with a researcher's descriptions of their interactions (perhaps a content analytic concept of coherence).

Instead of thinking of reliability as the consistent measurement of some issue, idea, discourse, or interaction over time, we focus instead on the relative change over time of some practice or metaphor. The assumption would be that anything worth studying is likely not static and may even be transformative, in which case the lack of reliability in a traditional sense is not necessarily indicative of some investigator error but that something interesting could be underway (this position, of course, does not condone thoughtlessly worded interview questions, etc.). Similarly, the changing notion of "variable" should enter into the conversation. Pushed by feminist scholars who believe that treating gender as a variable is the result of unreflexive replication of compulsory heterosexuality in our society, researchers have posited a number of alternative strategies such as Dervin's (1989) sensemaking approach.

I expect that these ideas are likely to be heretical to some. In a fairly recent issue of the *Academy of Management Journal*, Bartunek, Bobko, and Venkatraman (1993) suggested three themes which need to be considered when evaluating research methods: (a) a need for significant methodological contributions, (b) a need for adequate conceptual grounding, and (c) a need for adherence to methodologically sound and accurate strategies. The first theme of significance, they argue, has many facets, one of the most important being its "value-added contribution," either by demonstrating that the chosen method generates knowledge that previous, traditional methods cannot or by moving along some particular content domain. The second theme's concern with conceptual grounding is to ensure that epistemological incommensurabilities are avoided when borrowing methods from other disciplines and that the approach not be overly narrow in its conceptual or statistical assumptions. The third theme of sound and accurate strategies is designed to focus on all the underlying issues, like reliability, validity, sampling, bias, and replication. This multifaceted lens was actually used to evaluate several regression based articles as well as a symbolic interactionist study, a textual analysis, and a critical hermeneutic piece—go figure.

The second thread of conversation should be, I think, about pedagogy. How do we teach methods and what should we teach? A number of us have reduced the time and emphasis on experimental design and dramatically increased our attention to field methodologies from time series analysis to ethnography. Do we ever spend enough time on ethics or field notes or reporting back to the organizations where so much of our research takes place? My impression from the group discussion at the organizational narrative conference hosted by the University of Colorado a few years ago was that we are shifting to a position that the individuals who produce the discursive practices that constitute much of our data are the "owners" of that data and have to be coupled much more tightly into the research process.

Other issues include the relationship between quantitative and qualitative approaches. Early notions of qualitative research placed this research practice in a subservient place with respect to quantitative studies (e.g., the preliminary interviews that were needed to develop the variables or constructs needed for more rigorous analysis). The pendulum has now swung the other way, and interpretive approaches are seen as not in need of further elaboration but as stories that stand on their own, and increasingly the argument is that they are superior constructions of communication phenomena or practices. Perhaps we would be "enlightened" by careful juxtapositions of qualitative and interpretive techniques to inform a particular study? This suggestion would ask us initially to train our students very broadly. We would then need to create opportunities for students to specialize in techniques appropriate to the types of interactions or meaning constructions that interest them. Someone intrigued by multinational corporate decision making on a computer communications network may be able to examine an aspect of those interactions through ethnography and a very large travel grant, but I can envision a need to know some alternative approaches as well as an understanding of the limitations of the data they construct and utilize. This is an important part of the conversation because unlike literary criticism, where an essay may never stray from Rousseau, interpretive studies in communication are replete with historical "facts" and statistics about the organization, society (e.g., downturns in an industry), and so forth that were produced through the social scientific model. Although we may problematize quantitative research and its assumptions, its constitutive nature in our environment is likely inescapable.

A good book to use as an entree into this pedagogical conversation is Frost and Stablein's (1992) treatise on doing research. They looked at a truly diverse set of research projects that were nominated as good exemplars of organizational research: a linguistic/content analysis, an observational field study, a case analysis, a series of qualitative studies, a series of laboratory studies, an archival/historical analysis, and a journalistic/anthropological study. Although the exemplars often seem to deal with communication naively, a number of themes emerged from their examination of these studies that may serve as interesting conversational gambits. First, they recommend that students should stay close to the phenomena—there were a number of examples where a more distanced observer would have missed important issues. Second, when confronted with apparently inconsistent results or anomalies, don't stop. Keep looking at the context and figure out why and under what conditions should you find specific results. Third, they argued that the research methods should be driven by the research questions which might lead to a combination of methods. Fourth, look at all possible alternative explanations, and if you have chosen an explanation to defend, you had better be able to rule out the alternatives as better choices. Fifth, learn to write well. Sixth, don't let innovative ideas get crushed under the specter of some particular journal's preferences. Good work will find an outlet. Seventh, take advantage of your colleagues and talk to people about your ideas, especially before you begin a study. It is hard to repair a fatal flaw once the data are collected. Last, invest the time it takes to learn new things. Their list does not encompass all the concerns that need to be discussed and does not deal explicitly with communication studies, but it cogently poses an interesting set of issues.

We could, of course, discuss whether this game is worth improving and simply accept the postmodern position that epistemology is often a vacant concept, that research is without value as are all methods except perhaps philosophical ones, and go home and not teach any social science methods. However, before we replace the devil science with the hegemony of deconstruction or any other method, I think we should consider the paradox created as the current proponents of *authorial* death try to develop a monopoly on social and political theorizing.

I propose that the third thread in our conversation be about political and pragmatic concerns. This might be the most difficult conversation because it presupposes ideas about the future and the role our research might play. At issue are our beliefs about our value to others versus the idea that we need only feel valuable to ourselves. There are survival issues at stake, but they affect people differently. One way is to view the creativity and self-learning of scholarship (whether it is written, aural/visual or performative) as the goal and assume that academic freedom protects this avenue of work. Another is to attempt to articulate a much more public defense of interpretive/critical and postmodern scholarship. We might also look at the power structures of universities and their inclination to approve hiring lines where they see potential grant money. Part of this discussion should be about the ways to value scholarship that "cost" money, as well as developing opportunities to conduct scholarship that can achieve external funding. Inherent in this discussion is the relationship between research methodologies and money—an unhappy topic for some, but one that cannot be ignored in the era of revenue center budgeting. This dialogue could question an administrative decision-making process that overprivileges research methodologies (typically scientific/quantitative) that generate grant money. At the same time, a number of communication departments threatened with dissolution argued that they were cost effective now and that they would soon be more so as the likely recipients of upcoming funding to explore the communication revolution and the social impact of new communication technologies. We need to think about nurturing young scholars who will be able to conduct this research.

The fourth thread of this conversation should be about developing and carefully molding other methods and techniques/tools. The question is what do we want to know, feel, live, and how can we best accomplish this? Shotter has said that communication research is often considered an activity where "being true to science is more important than being true to the phenomena" (cited in Bochner & Ellis, 1992, p. 166). Bochner and Ellis used the example of research on relationships that transform the passionate process of falling in love into a cooler, more rational state of being that substitutes product for process. They suggested that it will be necessary to create research practices that conform more closely to the practices of relationships than to the practices of mainstream social science.

Pearce (1989) argued that researchers need to learn to speak "so that the natives hear you talking as they do" (p. 173)—in this way we might marginalize the central instead of centralizing the marginal. This is how ethnographies of communication problematize the taken-for-granted means of creating a sense of shared meaning and coordinating action in various speech communities:

> If we wish to understand the deepest and most universal of human experiences, if we wish our work to be faithful to the lived experiences of people, if we wish for a union between poetics and science, or if we wish to use our privileges and skills to empower the people we study, then we should value the narrative. (Richardson, 1990, quoted in Bochner & Ellis, 1992, p. 165)

Organizational communication has forged ahead with this belief using ethnographic, narrative and cultural studies (see Eisenberg & Riley, in press; Riley, 1991, for examples) but other techniques will be needed and valued. A possibility is radical empiricism—where one makes "oneself an experimental subject and then takes the biographical experience as primary data. This is one way to take reflexivity seriously and to provide a methodology for bringing lived experience into the center of research" (Bochner & Ellis, 1992, p. 170). Taylor (1995) suggested that as we move from what he called a heteronomous paradigm of organizations (the typical way of thinking of an organization as a structured entity coupled to an environment) to an autonomous one, where organizations are made of conversations, that research which is conducted in naturalistic circumstances and idiographic in its emphasis will be even more salient than it is now. In addition, he argued that we will need to develop new instruments for the analysis of discourse that will enable us to recognize boundaries of conversation and the coupling of discourses, all of which will lead to a new emphasis on the phenomena of stability and change.

Possibilities abound. Examples include Carley and Kaufer's (1993) approach for analyzing symbols in semantic networks (looking beyond density to include conductivity and consensus). Although I have some difficulty with their nomenclature, and a proclivity to overcompartmentalize, 1 found it thought-provoking. And a project underway at Harvard Business School uses computer-generated images to explore the root metaphors people use in decision making.

The other chapters in this section were equally intriguing. In her paper on "Widening the Lens: The Use of Historical data in Organizational Communication Theorizing," Miller called for us to change our methods and begin using historical data in our theorizing and research. Her well-articulated position is that although organizational communication is interested in its own history and all of our textbooks and handbooks look at the emergence of our subdiscipline in the context of the development of management theory, we rarely look at the phenomena of organizational communication in anything other than the present.

There are at least two additional problems to add to those she presents. First, most scholars are interested in studying "communication processes," and this has been interpreted primarily as studying talk, symbol use, networks, and practices. None of these are easily examined historically although many studies incorporate historical data to contextualize their interpretation of events and discourse. Second, professional historians are much less comfortable with the notion of theory than are communication scholars, who are much more enamored with grand narratives (Nerone, 1993). Even those organizational communication scholars who oppose deductive theories are often comfortable with cultural theories or feminist theories or dramatistic theories. In the discipline of history, the methods that have developed are largely the result of normative conventions within that discipline and my reading is that they privilege information differently. As Nerone indicated, "In practice, it is still the empirical work that is thought to give history merit. Sound research can save a theoretically naive work, but no amount of conceptual sophistication will protect a historian who gets dates wrong" (p. 152). Now, I would never argue that organizational communication scholarship would ignore or be sloppy about the ways we construct "facts" like important dates, but I think our normative conventions of late have privileged theoretical sophistication.

Miller's chapter is indicative of this perspective because part of her argument is that we need to ground our work in the theoretical perspectives that incorporate time, meaning, and social interaction. She presented three frameworks that should enable this practice: structuration, symbolic convergence theory, and social movement theory. My reading of those related literatures suggests that the methodological implications are clearest in symbolic convergence theory. Bormann (1983) has a well-developed method he called *fantasy theme analysis* that can guide interpretations of either ongoing interactions or historical situations where evidence of the fantasies and visions remain. Fantasy theme analysis and the companion concept of rhetorical vision are particularly apt for organizational communication study. Grounded in a dramatistic conception of sensemaking (see Eisenberg & Riley, 1988), the method is also informed by empirical studies of small group interactions. The interplay of fantasy themes and their combination into rhetorical visions would be a particularly insightful way to interpret the clash of visions that appear so regularly in large organizations and institutions. Although the framework has its detractors. over the last two decades a wealth of studies have been conducted that have contributed both to the development of symbolic convergence theory and to an understanding of the method (see Bormann, Cragan, & Shields, 1994).

Structuration theory and social movement theory are not as tightly bound to methodological convention. Structuration theory is often used as a metatheoretical perspective that envelopes another approach and social movement theory is more akin to an umbrella term for a wide variety of approaches—historical, psychological, rhetorical, symbolic interactionist, ethnographic—to the particular construction of social phenomena. Methodological approaches are quite varied in structurationist accounts as several organizational and group communication studies indicate. For example, Keough (1989) embedded an argumentation coding scheme for contract negotiations in a structurationist framework. In small group research, Poole and DeSanctis (1990) developed what they called adaptive structuration theory with its own methodological implications. Banks and Riley (1993) offered a structurationist research exemplar that demonstrated how a method emerges from a structurationist ontology, but there are many additional issues to be worked out. Structuration theory is also not without its critics (see Conrad, 1993), and because it is highly reflective of sociological concerns it continually needs to be problematized in theoretical as well as methodological conversations with respect to the study of communication. Similarly, although there is an obvious rhetorical tradition in social movement studies, the concept and framework were initially sociological, and the notion that scholars should investigate radical change in the social order binds us tightly to conversations in sociology and psychology as well.

I found both of the organizational studies Miller cited in the last chapter as exemplars of historical data use as well as her own project very interesting. I would add that an outstanding example of both detailed historical analysis and communication practice is Cheney's (1995) investigation of workplace democracy in Mondragón, Spain. Cheney's findings are innervating and thoughtful. Of particular import to this discussion is his conclusion that trying to develop a chronicle of workplace democracy is problematic since the concept predates the professionalization of knowledge. This brings us back to questions of method, of practice. How do we decide what constitutes history?

As an example, the subfield of organizational communication, like much of the discipline, is believed to have emerged less as a research-based community than as a skills-based activity. Most texts locate the "beginning" of organizational communication in the 1940s and 1950s as something called "business and industrial communication," however, that is just another place to draw the line. Although there is a reasonable argument that this time frame was indeed a turning point due to the war efforts and the rapidly expanding literature in the area of management and organizations, I believe that Tompkins and Redding's (1988) story is equally compelling when they describe our history as "the illusion of novelty" (p. 7). To frame for us the length of time organizational communication issues have been of concern, they cited passages from a self-help manual for those aspiring bureaucrats who wished to work for the Egyptian Pharaohs—circa 2700 or 2600 B.C. For those of you unfamiliar with this reference, the advice from the *Precepts*, often referred to as the oldest book in the world, includes such wisdom as:

> If thou art one to whom petition is made, be calm as thou listenest to what the petitioner has to say. . . . It is not [necessary] that everything about which he has petitioned should come to pass, [but] a good hearing is soothing to the heart.

and:

> If you are the guest of a superior, speak only when he addresses you, for you do not know what will offend him. . .

and:

> If you carry a message from one noble to another, be exact in the repetition. (cited in Tompkins & Redding, 1988, p. 7)

The many recommendations found in the *Precepts* and similar manuals from that era are today called guidelines for empathic listening, superior-subordinate communication, information accuracy, and managing up (Tompkins & Redding, 1988). We think of organizational communication today as complex phenomena, but imagine the added difficulties three and four thousand years ago, when legions of scribes and messengers were required to transmit or record decisions and any information or conversation of importance. Having read Michner's *The Source*, however, I suspect these manuals were developed not only to help bureaucrats use their heads, but also to keep them. My suggestion, of course, is that history, as opposed to being a compilation of historical "facts" could be viewed as narratives—constructed by individuals who are reproducing/recrafting those events or aspects of community, or discourse that they have learned to find important. As such these narratives are not sacrosanct but culturally positioned.

Meilich's chapter on neural networks is also an intriguing topic albeit quite different from the call for using historical data. This paper is about coping with complexity and our need for sensemaking devices in the face of this complexity. To deal with large amounts of data or to see patterns in relationships across time and space that we could not see on our own, our discipline has borrowed or developed numerous statistical/mathematical techniques. Neural networks approaches are one of the new advancements of basic correlational techniques. Successful applications of neural networks abound in business and industry, and social science researchers are attempting to figure out how the tool might be useful to them, especially in situations where we have a great deal of data. I was especially interested in neural networks because the reengineering study that I have been engaged in for the last 3 years has data from 10 industry groups and the five researchers involved in this project have observations and recorded discourse from literally thousands of meetings—boxes and boxes of field notes and transcripts. Interpretive case studies are already emerging from the data, but we also hoped to investigate communicative practices through a larger lens and had been looking at neural networks as a possible sensemaking device. The "learning" attributes of the networks appeared at first glance to be potentially useful to the study of change.

According to Meilich, our search is to continue. Meilich cogently detailed the working of the networks and positions it next to techniques with which most of us are quite familiar. He carefully explained the advantages and the limitations, particularly the problems of overtraining the network and interpreting the weights (the black box feature). The suggestion that researchers with large, complex data sets should think of using a neural network application to help determine the construction of the model that will be used in further investigation, (for example, in a subsequent regression or discriminant analysis) is a valuable contribution to our continuing conversations about statistical tools and their aid in our interpretations.

CONCLUSIONS

Our love–hate relationship with quantitative research is amusing. It is similar to the way we demonize science but want someone's head to roll when the phone lines are down. We in organizational communication are not just trying to understand the philosophical and pragmatic implications of our scholarship, but many of us are also desperately trying to deal with the rapidly multiplying issues of the institutions, corporations, agencies, churches, and other groupings of people that we study (not to mention our own lived experiences). We learn techniques to help manage the complexity created by the juggernaut of modernity like computer-mediated communication, and rely heavily on the expertise of others just to go on. At our universities these experts include benefits counselors, air conditioning mechanics, information systems engineers, and budget officers, just to name a few of those whose science or social science "knowledge" make an ordinary day happen. Consider the additional communicative implications in healthcare organizations, high-tech electronics or the justice department. Add to the everyday chaos issues of globalization, mediated communication, and rapid shifts in the location of jobs, and the concerns are palpable and sometimes bloody, as organizational change enhances some lives and disenfranchises others. And believe it or not, there are people asking for our help, help in understanding and explaining organizational communication.

The methods we use to investigate these institutions of sedimented discursive practices, or the local enactments of innovative talk, or whatever, will need continuing thought and redesign with respect to the myriad of issues in this large conversation but especially with respect to change. Those of us who study organizations and social life may hold many differing opinions, but admitting to the rapidity and magnitude of change in these environments is not one of them.

In *Fuzzy Thinking*, Kosko (1993) told us that science has been wrong, that the world is ambiguous and socially constructed: "We know things change. . . . More precision does not take the gray out of things—it pins down the gray. Medical advances have not made it easier to draw the line between life and not-life at birth or death" (p. 5). As more and more scientists embrace fuzzy logic the notions of exactitude and finite understanding disappear and appreciation for the messiness of life appears. Neural networks may not do for organizational communication what they have done for Toshiba, at least not yet, but looking for fuzzy rigor may not be a bad idea in the face of gargantuan complexity. Just as surveys were not the solution to all organizational communication questions, neither, in my opinion, is ethnography or discourse analysis or poetry.

Eisenberg likes to remind us that those "webs of significance" we speak of so fondly are also sticky—they bind us to our sensemaking practices and to those who see the world the way we do. As we reconstitute our methodologies in an attempt to learn from advances in social knowledge, there should be a place for all voices in the dialogue. I believe that the longstanding tension in the social sciences between the mathematically based natural science model and the more idiographic and interpretive perspectives misses the point in communication research—meanings are both idiosyncratic *and* general.

Beyond the expert's learned blinders and the beginner's naiveté I believe we can conceive of a methodological space that lies somewhere between aimless pondering and static representation. In this place and manner we are open to the diversity of human life and our communicative constructions and to the myriad of ways we are able to provide insight, information, critique or pleasure. Social science methodologies may have taken some wrong turns, and the enlightenment vision may have been ill-conceived, but the need for knowledge has not abated because Lyotard said so. I agree with J. O'Neill (1995) that there are too many problems, and too much injustice for those of us who enjoy literacy, health, knowledge, and regular access to food to abandon the enlargement of these gifts to the rest of society.

part five

ORGANIZATIONAL
COMMUNICATION APPLICATIONS

eleven

CHANGES IN WRITING IN THE WORKPLACE: CYCLES OF DISCUSSION AND TEXT

Lisette van Gemert and Egbert Woudstra
University of Twente, The Netherlands

The business communication literature emphasizes documents and the skills professionals need to write memos, reports, letters, and proposals. Indeed, most professionals regard writing as an important skill (Anderson, 1985; van Gemert & Woudstra, 1996; Kirtz & Reep, 1990). In one survey 69% of respondents reported spending more than 10% of working time on writing, 38% reported writing more than one day a week, and 15% reported writing more than two days a week (Anderson, 1985).

Although it is clear from this research that writing documents is an important organizational activity, it is at the same time unclear what the respondents meant by writing. Were they thinking about writing as an individual activity only or were interactions with others taken into account? For example, in one survey, the most frequently mentioned writing tasks for engineers and technicians were reports, memos, and executive summaries, followed by letters, procedures, and descriptions of mechanisms (see Durfee, cited in Glover Campbell, 1991). The most important oral communication skills were speaking before large groups, preparing informal messages for small groups, eliciting information during conversations and committee meetings, and conveying highly technical information to those not trained in the discipline. The results suggest that writing and speaking may be linked in some way, but the connections are not clear.

This kind of research does not describe the way writing is embedded in an organizational context. Although organizational communication literature suggests that organizational context is important (e.g., Goldhaber, 1993; Jablin et al., 1987), there has been little attention to the role of documents, how they are created in organizations, and the effect of the process on the organization. More recently, writing researchers have tried to understand the mutual interactions between organizational aspects and the writing process (Kleiman, 1993).

The next section describes the literature about writing in the workplace. First we examine the shift in research from a mainly cognitive to a more sociocognitive approach. We then look at the influence of structure and culture, interpersonal relations, interaction, and computer-mediated communication. The literature survey closes with a description of the review process.

The description serves to link the literature to the case study that follows. In this case we provide an analysis of the document design process in an engineering consultancy responding to a government contract. The case study focuses on oral and written interaction in the document design process. The discussion section of the chapter contains implications for the design process.

RESEARCH ON WRITING

The Shift from Individual Writing to Document Design

Over the last decade there has been growing interest in "real-life" writing studies. The reason for paying increased attention to real-life writing research is related to changes in organizations. Today, more organizations delegate responsibilities to employees, and more employees work together in project teams to ensure that quality standards are met. Working together has an impact on written products and also on the socialization and acculturation process in the organization itself (Bacon, 1990). As Winsor (1989) said:

> Writing at work is firmly embedded in a social web. This social network is most visible in organizations like workplaces . . . where actions are aimed at a collective goal. Within these organizations, writing is visibly used not just to record decisions and events but to do the organization's work, to build its shared understanding, and construct its knowledge. (p. 271)

Organizational changes that have significant impacts on writing in real-life situations include:

- Writers do not work alone; they interact with others (reviewers, managers, the client) during the whole design process to shape ideas about the text that is to be produced (Kleimann, 1991; Paradis, Dobrin, & Miller, 1985).
- Writing is depersonalized: The organization wants an institutional product "that speaks with the voice of the organization" (Kleimann, 1991; Paré, 1993; Shirk, 1991).
- The writing process is often embedded in a larger umbrella project, such as a quality project (van Gemert & Woudstra, 1996). Goals and conditions that relate to such projects also apply to the writing process.
- The writing process extends over a long period related to the umbrella project (Cross, 1993; van Gemert & Woudstra, 1996).
- Writers often use other documents (such as genre models, policy documents, proposals) to provide them with goals and constraints for their own documents (van Gemert & Woudstra, 1996).

In general, workplace writing is a social process, rather than an individual cognitive process. To express this, we use the term *document design* to indicate writing as a collaborative activity with shared responsibilities, conscious consideration of alternatives for the presentation of the design, and an institutional product.

There is a growing recognition of the importance of collaborative writing. In particular, in the literature about safety regulations in industry there is a much stronger emphasis on documents as part of a system (Elling, 1994). For instance, in the nuclear industry (Brune & Weinstein, 1981; Reason, 1987; Swain & Guttmann, 1983), the chemical industry (Covello, 1989), transportation (Fenell, 1988), and in the aircraft industry, writing has almost always been an integral part of working life, and documents function as a system. A well-known observation is that in the process of developing a new aircraft, the weight of the documents is often equal to the weight of the aircraft.

There has been a movement from research on writing as a strictly cognitive process (Flower & Hayes, 1981) to research on writing as a social and contextual process (Odell & Goswami, 1985). For example, cognitive writing research (Flower & Hayes, 1981) defined the environment as the task environment. Through this task environment, the writer formed an initial representation of the writing task by specifying the rhetorical problem. However, the task environment was also the "external storage" of texts and available tools (schemata, computer, writing aids, library, people). Research about the context contrasts with cognitive writing research emphasizing the internal process of the writer in problem solving.

Writing can be seen as a social act consisting of a series of activities, some of which imply interaction with others to reach a common view on the document design process (Bazerman, 1983; Faigley & Miller, 1982; Knoblauch, 1989; Odell & Goswami, 1985; van Pelt & Gillam, 1991; Piazza, 1987; Spilka, 1988, 1993a; J. R. Weber, 1991). Writers communicate both orally and in writing with fellow writers and/or managers during the process (see Couture & Rymer, 1989; Lay & Karis, 1991; Locker, 1992). The oral and written interactions occur during planning, drafting, and revising.

These new concepts have led to various research approaches: social and psychological approaches seeking to ascertain the impact of relationships between collaborating actors (writers, colleagues, managers), especially their impact on the job satisfaction of the writer; studies that examine the influence of the organizational context on the writing process, and vice versa; and studies that focus on the activities performed during writing, in order to gain an understanding of matters such as the use of sources. In recent years the various approaches have produced interesting but ultimately heterogeneous studies.

What have these studies contributed to understanding the document design process? First, there has been a mutually causal relationship between document design and the more macroscopic organizational factors such as organizational structure and organizational climate. For example, when staff members discussed the goals of the organization and its mission throughout the development of a business plan, the collaborative writing effort contributed to a flatter structure (Doheny-Farina, 1985). In a hierarchical, more vertical organization the document design process was slower than in a flatter organization (Kleimann, 1993), There were also more conflicts over the competencies of writers, because the writers were more tightly bound to the regulations of the organization, and there was often less room for the writers to consult among themselves about the criteria the document should meet (see also Odell & Goswami, 1985; Paré, 1993). While writing procedures, writers formed new ideas about the desired production process, and sometimes the results included a different division of tasks and responsibilities and different attitudes toward organizational processes (van Gemert & Woudstra, 1996).

Second, several social-psychological factors have predicted the success and failure of collaborative writing efforts. These factors included the hierarchical relationship between actors (Kleimann, 1993), the degree of autonomy enjoyed by the writer (Debs, 1985; Paradis et al., 1985; Weber, 1991), the experience of writers (Couture & Rymer, 1991; Paradis et al., 1985), their competence in handling conflicts and managing the writing task (Hackos, 1994; Morgan & Murray, 1991, Weber, 1991). For example, in groups with equal responsibilities and a clear definition of tasks there was less conflict about the goals and content of the document (Forman & Katsky, 1986; Weber, 1991), but in more formal relationships supervisors and managers dictated more restrictions and procedures for the writers, and there were conflicts about the autonomy of the writers (Ede & Lunsford, 1990). Conflict handling and negotiating have been skills writers needed to reach consensus on the purposes of the document (Cross, 1993; Doheny-Farina, 1986; Weber, 1991). In some situations it is particularly important to reach consensus, because consensus would be the basis for policy or tasks.

Third, the document design process has involved a variety of both written and oral symbolic activities. Writers communicate with fellow writers and/or managers during the design process both in writing and oral methods (see Lay & Karis, 1991; Locker, 1992). Oral and written interactions have occurred during planning, drafting, and revising. In some instances, professionals who seldom write together have cooperated in planning groups and wrote individually (see Couture & Rymer, 1989; Farkas, 1991). This cooperation involved oral and written communication about goals and constraints for the document (Kogen, 1989). In some interaction studies, the focus of research was the interaction of the various activities that resulted in a document (see Plowman, 1993; Spilka, 1993b). However, there has been little research describing the whole design, the interactions that take place, the purpose and time of interactions, or the relationships between these interactions and the document that is produced.

Fourth, technology has been changing the document design process. Technologies include the now familiar group decision support systems; computer networking, email, and internet; and video-conferencing, fax, voice-mail, multimedia and hypertext systems, but they also include the EMS (Electronic Meeting System), which allows members to work together in real time on a document (Easton, Eickelmann & Flatley, 1994), the Group Decision Support system known as "Group Forum" (Aikin & Martin, 1994), and hypertext and hypermedia (D. C. Smith & Nelson, 1994). The newer media will allow for the use of common communication genre such as technical documentation, repair and maintenance manuals, and, of course, contracts and encyclopedias (Sheiderman, 1989), but they are also important for internet use.

Studies on writing in organizations have provided impressions of writing in organizations and there has been a shift from the cognitive approach to the study of the writing process to a social-cognitive approach. This suggests, the researcher should take into account various factors influencing the design process, such as the organizational context, interpersonal relationships between actors, the interaction between writers, the individual cognitive writing process, and the characteristics of a specific document.

Some research has used methods drawn mainly from ethnological studies rather than the "conventional" survey or experimental designs (Bouldin & Odell, 1993). Although this has widened the horizons of possible research methods, it has also led to an enormous diversity and multiple perspectives. In a short time, many different impressions of the writing processes in an organization have been gathered, but this has produced few usable conclusions because the results are not comparable. It is not clear in any case how different the results would be if the research was done in another organizational context, in relation to different tasks (routine, nonroutine), with different subjects (career or professional writers, experienced or inexperienced writers, etc.; see Bouldin & Odell, 1993). Moreover, these studies often do not trace a longitudinal process from the proposal to the completion of the final document. They often rely on retrospective interviews, and so there is a lack of methodological triangulation.

Many of the interaction studies focus on some part of the process, but they ignore the outcome of the design process: the written product and its quality. Document design research should not focus on the forms of interaction between actors, but should find the connections between interactions, the completed text, and the effectiveness of that text. The completed documents are an indicator of the quality of the design process, especially where the document is the core product of the organization, as in consultancies that contract for research with the government.

Rhetorical research often limits quality to internal features of the text, such as cohesion and correctness. In practice, quality is also determined by interactions between textual and external factors such as the organizational culture and structure. The fact that this sort of quality has not been considered in research to date may be related to rather limited conceptions of the meaning of quality. The "quality" of the document is then its usability in decision making. The same applies where some action must be taken on the basis of a document, such as directions for the use of an apparatus. Quality can then be expressed in terms of a reduction in the number of incorrect actions.

Future research should clarify the precise connection between the factors mentioned and the efficiency and effectiveness of the collaborative writing process. Because in practice, writers write alone but interact with their colleagues, supervisor, or client to shape ideas about the document, it would be fruitful to concentrate on those relationships and to study, for instance, what the effect of a specific negotiating strategy is on the efficiency (writing and production time) and effectiveness (reaching culture goals and the usability of the document) of the design process.

The Review Process

The interaction between a document design process and the organizational context is particularly evident during the review of draft versions. During such reviews, the document is always the object of the evaluation. Various people share knowledge, and they often discuss organizational norms and values (Shirk, 1991). Review provides the writer with the knowledge needed to prevent the document from becoming "a work of fiction." The discussion tests the norms and values as the basis of texts as they are being produced. This testing may lead to a reevaluation of these norms and values, and this can lead to changes in the organizational culture (see Paré, 1993). Moreover, review can influence the consultative structure in the organization, when the reviewers comprise a unit that is not bound by departmental lines (Kleimann, 1993).

The value of studies of this kind depends on how far it is possible to identify distinct variables in the context, so that their influence on a document can be ascertained. For example, a government running a publicity campaign about separating rubbish by types sets standards for the campaign on the basis of waste control legislation. Thus businesses must be told, in comprehensible language, the goal of the legislation and the sanctions for failing to comply. These requirements lead in turn to criteria determining the appearance of the brochures in the campaign. By distinguishing such contextual demands, it is possible to make connections between the context and the document. The identification of these demands is visible in the review of the draft versions of a document. The organization must also provide the conditions to make a smoothly functioning document design process. That means, for example, that the organization must attach sufficient value to the writing process, allowing writers and reviewers sufficient time, and providing opportunities for them to undertake any required training, especially for newcomers.

A study of the review process could provide insight into social-psychological processes. When writing involves cooperation, a clear division of tasks and deadlines for each phase of the work is necessary. Actors are dependent on each other's drafts and comments. One of them must keep an eye on project planning to ensure that the necessary information is available and that deadlines are met (Hackos, 1994; Farkas, 1991; Weber, 1991). Many collaborative studies have concluded that writers with work experience are more aware of the organizational values that should be incorporated in the document. They interact more with managers and users about the purpose of the document than inexperienced members of the organization (Paradis et al.,1985). Teamwork seems to foster insight into corporate values (Forman & Katsky, 1986). This implies that newcomers in an organization will acclimatize more quickly if they are incorporated in a writing team with work experience.

Furthermore, a study of the review process involves gaining an understanding of the sequence of actions and interactions that characterize the production of the document. An analysis of these interactions would include descriptions of the use of technology. Naturally the way in which these interactions are combined should be related to the environment in which the design process takes place, because the environment influences the interactions.

Therefore the study of document design processes should not be limited to a study of the written interactions between the people involved. To study workplace writing with the aim of gaining insight into the actual writing practice, while avoiding anecdotal research, the methods should investigate:

- The actors involved.
- The writing-related activities performed by the actors.
- All kind of texts produced (memos, notes, letters, written comments, drafts).
- The sources of information used (genre models, proposals, project plan, policy documents, mission statements).
- A description of the organization culture and structure.
- The chronological order of activities and text production.

The goal of the research was to examine both text production and discussion that is part of the document design process. A subsidiary aim was to illustrate how a design process in the workplace could be studied and the methodological problems encountered. More specifically, this research sought to answer these questions:

1. Who is involved in the design process (the actors) and what is their role in the design process?
2. What is the pattern of written and oral communication during the design process?

    a. What forms of written and oral communication do the internal and external actors use during the design process?

    b. What connection exists between oral and written communication?

    c. Do both forms of communication contribute to the progress of the project?

3. How do oral and written communication contribute to making the document appropriate to its ultimate use and to the target group?
4. How can the design process be improved?

METHODS

The Organization

The organization selected for the case study is a small engineering consultancy competing with larger bureaus to produce high-quality reports at short notice. Founded in 1977, it specializes in carrying out risk analyses and is a leader in this field in the Netherlands. The firm distinguishes itself from other similar consultancies by the fact that it does not adopt a formal approach with potential clients, nor does it work in a routine way. It prides itself on producing manageable and readable reports, and working closely with a design studio located in the same building.

    Most clients (80%) are national, regional and municipal government agencies. Assignments are received on the basis of word-of-mouth recommendation and as follow-ups to work the company has done previously. The firm currently employs 10 men, of whom 8 are university trained and 2 have a polytechnic background. All are engineers. Although there are no formal guidelines for the skills required, employees are expected to work on multiple assignments simultaneously and to be flexible. In peak periods the staff works overtime, and if problems arise with a particular project they are expected to help each other. More than one employee is responsible for most reports. In 70% of the cases colleagues supply data, and one person is responsible for writing the text. Individuals are held responsible for the quality of the individual work they contribute.

    The firm's motto is that if a job is worth doing, it is worth doing properly. The staff would rather work overtime than produce an unreliable analysis of a problem. At the moment an internal quality system is being developed to help the firm become more effective (produce better products) and more efficient. One of the methods that will be adopted is an internal review procedure for reports.

The Task

The firm contracted to produce a section of an environmental policy plan for a Dutch province. This section of the plan (the "section document") concerned "external safety", that is, the risks to residents from LPG stations, toxic goods transport, industrial installations, and so forth. A 1989 version of the document served as the starting point. The updated document should provide information about the execution of the safety policy and present an up-to-date overview of potentially risky situations in tables and maps. The aim of the document is to inform local authorities about current policy and how it is applied at the local level.

On the basis of its internal objectives and the results of a pilot study, the consultancy decided to appoint one staff member with a great deal of knowledge and experience as an internal reviewer for one of the coming contracts. Text versions would only be sent to the clier s if they had been evaluated internally and revisions had been made on the basis of that evaluation. In this way the organization hoped to incorporate more systematic quality control into the document design process. Moreover an editor would also run checks with the target group to assess the document's usability.

Data Gathering Techniques

A pilot study was conducted from November 1993 to March 1994. The choice of instruments in the pilot study was based on studies in which comparable processes have been examined (Couture & Rymer, 1991; Doheny-Farina, 1985; Kleimann, 1989; Spilka, 1988). After evaluating the implementation of these procedures, the following instruments were used to answer the research questions:

- Activity logs provided to the internal reviewer and to the writers to determine how much (extra) time was involved in the internal review.
- Audiotape recordings of the meetings and telephone calls concerning the project (within the consultancy and with the client). The telephone was connected to an audio recorder.
- Comparison of successive drafts (only the revised draft based on internal comments and the draft that was sent to the client for review) to examine whether problems were detected and solved before the draft was sent to the client (i.e., to ascertain the effect of internal review) and to

establish what kind of changes were made. These comparisons were the input for the interviews. We also collected supplementary documents such as the proposal, the project plan, minutes, and memos to track statements about the use and users of the final product.

- Taped interviews with the client, writers, internal reviewer, and editor. At the start of the project, we interviewed all persons involved about the purpose and use of the new document, their contribution to it, and about the planning of both product and process. A few days after a draft was offered for review to the internal reviewer we interviewed the reviewer about his comments. After the writers had received internal or external comments, we interviewed them about their interpretation of the comments and the purpose of any changes. We also interviewed the writers about these activities, who they had interacted with, and what problems had occurred.

The tapes of interviews, meetings and telephone calls were all transcribed and analyzed to detect utterances directly related to the usability of the final product, or related to sections of the document intended to increase its usability, such as an index of the terms used. However, we have limited ourselves, in this chapter, to those comments relevant to the purpose of the project and the target group; other comments relating to the document (including, for example, the index of terms) are not discussed further here. These utterances were related to the texts produced (e.g., proposals, memos, letters, and drafts).

It is important for researchers to learn from each others' experiences. This can be achieved by describing the instruments used in detail, and indicating any problem areas that have been encountered. One problem is that studies of the writing process in the workplace are difficult to manage. The fact that WR1 dropped out of the project and that there was no time for an internal review had immediate consequences for the course of the study, which was originally started to determine the effectiveness of the internal reviewer. It also became apparent that the bureau had estimated the time required too optimistically. The project exceeded the time allocated by more than half a year. Nevertheless, the structure adopted in this study was more manageable than the pilot, because not all versions of the text had to be collected and analyzed. It did prove more difficult to maintain an overview of the project when the times of interviews were widely separated.

Another problem was the dependence on the cooperation and alertness of the writers. Every time they discussed something with the client, the writers had to ensure that the tape recorder was switched on and that there was a tape available. Moreover, the writers had to be prepared to make time for the interviews.

As regards the instruments, it can be noted that:

- The actors did not complete the activity logs very often. This instrument proved, once again, to be unreliable. Thus indications of the actual use of time had to be obtained in the interviews.
- Audiotape recordings of the meetings and telephone calls concerning the project (within the engineering firms and with the client) did require the cooperation of the writers and the client, but the recordings were necessary, because the document developed through both consultation and the text production.
- Comparison of successive drafts (only the revised draft based on internal comments and the draft which was sent to the client for review) proved to take a lot of time, and in the course of the process we found that writers seldom made low-level changes in the text, and that comments were mainly made in consultation or by letter. We then decided to ask the writer concerned how he had interpreted the comments, how he had revised the relevant version, what documents he had used in the process, what was available to him, and so forth.
- Taped interviews with the client, writers, internal reviewer, and editor at the start of the project provided a lot of information about the purpose, use, and users of the document. The interviews with the writers were problematic when a lot of time had passed between the revision and the interview. Their reconstruction of the writing process is then likely to be less reliable. A great deal has already been written in the literature about the reliability of this instrument. We have used the interviews only to corroborate statements made in consultations or texts, and to gain some insight into the activities that had been carried out and the time they had taken. We are conscious that the interviews could have the effect of guiding the writers approach. For now, the only possible solution is to be alert for possible influences.
- Making the transcripts of the tapes ready for analysis is one of the problems we encountered. Initially we tried to use a software program to construct a database of all the sources,

to make it possible to keep track of relationships between the various sources (memos, letters and tapes). This proved to be very time-consuming work, and it was not clear whether it would ultimately be more efficient. At this point, how all the data can most efficiently be made accessible remains an open question for us.

There is an additional problem of interpreting the comments. We have not used a comprehensive encoding system. Studies by Kleimann (1989) and Broadhead and Freed (1986) have also shown that encoding is not only a great deal of work, but also gives rise to numerous overlaps between categories. We have therefore introduced one restriction, by focusing on the relationship between the process of composition and how the document is made to match its purpose, use and users. This means we selected comments that had some direct match, or with components of the document that could increase its usability (such as an index of terms, a case study in which an illustrative question was dealt with), and by relating these comments to the produced texts.

It remains difficult to carry out qualitative research into document design processes, because there are many uncontrollable factors influencing the process. In fact many are dependent on the cooperation of the actors involved in the research. If they do not keep good records, are not conscientious in recording conversations, and do not make time for interviews, the study is not really practicable. The researcher's schedule is entirely dependent on the writers' production. Because we could carry out the research in our own hometowns, it was still possible to follow the whole course of the projects.

RESULTS

The Role of the Actors

We limited our definition of the actors to those who made verifiable comments about the document, or who were directly involved in its composition. A senior consultant who talked to writers during coffee breaks may well have contributed to the document, but we considered this person to be one of the "persons involved" only if we were able to trace these contributions in other ways such as in the form of comments on texts. Without this limitation it would not be practicable to study the design process. The persons involved have been designated as "the actors," and their interactions are the focus of this study.

The internal actors were three writers and an internal reviewer, all of whom were qualified engineers, equivalent to a master's degree in a technical field. Two writers were shareholders of the bureau. The first writer (WR1) was the head of the bureau. He communicated with the client about the project from the start, prepared the quotation and the contents list for the new document, and wrote the first three chapters. He managed the project and controlled all the documents produced. Writer 2 (WR2) had worked 11 years in the bureau. He was required to finish another project before he could begin work on the document in question. However, he was involved in the project from September 1994. From the outset, both writers took part in planning. WR2 also served as an internal reviewer, when the person chosen for that task had no time. Because WR1 fell sick halfway through the project, the project was continued by WR2 alone. WR3 worked on the project base for the firm. He was responsible for creating the risk charts. He could begin work on the document only when it was clear what charts were needed. The internal reviewer (IR) was a senior consultant with the bureau for 17 years. He had the task of providing a critical commentary before the texts were sent to the client. The comments were made on the basis of review guidelines created by WR1. At the outset of the project, they discussed the goals of the document and the review procedure. Because WR1 fell sick there was extra time pressure on the project, and no more time could be made for the internal review. WR2 did make some efforts to carry through with the internal review, but this proved impossible. The IR contributed only to drawing up the contents list and a provisional text of Chapters 1 to 3 from July 1994 to the end of November 1994. The editor was contracted by WR1. WR1 arranged with the editor to check the language of the document, and to test the document with the target group.

The client, a Dutch province, had engaged the consultancy because it had developed special expertise in risk-assessment studies of the transport of dangerous materials and because of personal contacts. The provincial administration assembled a project group (PG) of five people (PG1 to PG5) to update the 1989 document. These were all specialists in the field of external safety. PG1 was the secretary of the project group. She was responsible for communication between the writers and the project group. PG2 and PG3 were technical experts in the field of external safety working for the provincial administration in the Office of Water and Environment. PG4 and PG5 were engineers working for the province where most of the risk sites were located. The task of all of the members of the project group was to comment on the writers' drafts. Some of the members of the project group wrote proposals for particular parts of the document.

When a draft was sent to the PG, an advisory committee consisting of representatives of the users (local and provincial administrations) first commented on the draft. The PG discussed those comments in their meetings. The writers never communicated directly with the advisory committee, and never saw the committee comments. Because there were no direct interactions between the writers and the advisory committee, we have not included their actions in our observations.

The actors did not write their material jointly (i.e., face to face). WR1 and WR2 worked individually on particular parts of the document, and the members of the project group who wrote particular pieces did so as individuals. The cooperation consisted of commenting on each other's pieces, and of discussions about the texts.

All of the actors discussed content problems, but no conflicts arose between writers or between writers and their client. They all saw each other as experts in a specific field with their own expertise. The writers were free to make their own decisions although all actors felt responsible for the quality of the document.

Many case studies have examined the relationships between writers and supervisors or managers with a special focus on conflicts arising because of power differences (see Paradis et al., 1985; Weber, 1991). In our case hierarchical differences were not an issue or part of the way power was exercised. There were also no conflicts between the writers and the client. The actors regarded each other with equal status; all were experts in a particular aspect of external safety. Failure to meet the deadlines also seemed to be no problem for the client: The project group was apparently not under pressure from the provincial administration. Because the project group was part of writing the document, the cooperation was not limited to just writers delivering products and the client evaluating them. The client's function was greater than just checking the output, and the project group made decisions concerning changes in text versions, in response to problems.

It was striking that there was no "social talk" between actors during their consultations; this could be because their discussions were all by telephone. WR1 and WR2 knew a number of members of the project group previously, but neither knew the spokesperson of the project group, PG1.

The lack of conflicts and of a clear authority relationship means that remaining results are not generalizable to situations having such a relationship. In this study there was no authority relationship within the bureau nor was there one between the firm and the client. This may be inherent to engineering firms working for the government.

Written and Oral Communication

Forms of Communication. In our study it appeared that there was face-to-face contact with the client on only two occasions. In April 1994 WR1 and the PG discussed the project, and this contact resulted in a project plan from the client in June 1994 and a proposal for the project prepared by WR1. In July 1994 there was again face-to-face contact between WR1 and the PG about planning and the subjects to be covered in the document. This discussion was based on a preliminary proposal for the contents list. During that discussion it was agreed to consult by telephone as much as possible. After September 1994 there was no face-to-face contact between WR1 and the client, and WR2 had no face-to-face contact with the members of the PG at all.

There was also face-to-face contact between WR1 and WR2 and the editor in September 1994 about the editor's contribution to the project. This discussion resulted in a structure for final editing and the pretesting of the document. There were internal face-to-face contacts between WR1 and the IR as part of the review process. When WR1 withdrew from the project, internal review ceased.

The external face-to-face contacts took place mainly in the orientation phase of the project, in that the focus was on project realization, the allocation of tasks, and the subjects that would have to be covered. The oral communication between the client and writers was largely made by telephone, usually once per month and lasting an average of 1–2 hours and about the various versions, letters, commentaries, agreements and source material which had been sent. This consultation was usually initiated by the project group. Internal face-to-face contacts arose mainly because of the review.

None of the actors expressed any need in the course of the project for more face-to-face contacts. The interviews showed that this group looked at the document mainly in the light of its practical utility. In retrospect, WR2 would have liked to have been part of the advisory committee because their commentary was delivered via PG1, and he had no opportunity to ask about the reasons behind that commentary.

Written communication was mainly external. There was communication with the client about the structure of the project, the planning of the contents list, source materials, and any problems. This resulted in the following products: the quotation, project plan, versions of the text, and accompanying documents such as letters and memos. The quotation and the project plan were written in June 1994. At that time it was agreed that the versions of the text would be sent to the client by post or fax.

In February 1995, email and text on floppies were also used. The comments on the various versions were sent in letters to the writers.

When the versions were sent on floppies, changes were made in the text at the microlevel (sentence and paragraph level). The text was accompanied by a letter with an explanation and justification of the commentary plus a plan of activities for the sections remaining to be written. Email was not used as a medium for sending comments.

Any problems were communicated in letters and memos appended to the text versions or accompanying the commentaries. The PG sent minutes of their meetings with the PG about the versions. Once WR1 had left the project and the desired structure of the document had been clarified, WR2 sent no more external memos or letters.

There was little internal written communication about the project. In September 1994 WR1 completed review guidelines for the internal reviewer. These guidelines stipulated the purpose of the document and the points to which the internal reviewer should give attention and those that should be ignored. On one occasion (9/20/94) WR2 composed an internal memo regarding the objective and use of the document.

Thus oral communication was used both internally and externally, with the internal oral communication arising mainly from the review process. External face-to-face communication occurred only in the initial phase of the project. With a few exceptions, written communication was not used internally, and once WR1's contribution to the project had ceased, there was no internal written communication about the project, or arising from the project. External communication was chiefly by telephone or in writing.

Connections Between Forms of Communication. In this case text production and oral consultation alternated over the whole course of the project and the frequency of the interactions depended on the problems that arose. The writers and PG1 met to discuss written commentary on a version of the text by the PG and memos and letters sent by the writers to clarify the structure and goal of the document. Normally, the client (PG1) initiated oral consultations. A text (draft, letter or memo) would normally generate consultations, and the consultation itself would again stimulate the production of a text (draft, letter or memo).

Table 11.1 shows how version 2 of the document developed through a process of interwoven cycles of discussion and text production during the period from October 1994 to January 1995. The cycles comprise a part of the chain of text, commentary, and accompanying letters and memos. During this period there was little reference to earlier versions of the text or to earlier decisions about the purpose, use and users of the document. For example, in the planning meeting that took place in September the writers did not refer to the

Table 11.1. Cycles of Discussion and Text Production

Communication	Actors and activities	Output	Date
Text production	IR gives comments on V2	Written comments on V2	10/94
Face-face talk	WR1 & WR2 discuss comments	Audiotape of comments	10/27/94
Face-face talk	WR1 & WR2 discuss revised V2	Audiotape of comments	11/2/94
Text production	WR2 writes a proposal: about structure	Letter with proposal	11/3/94
Text production	WR1 sends V2 and letter with proposal to PG	V2 and letter with proposal	11/9/94
Text production	PG writes a letter: proposal outline	Letter with comments	11/29/94
Telephone talk	PG discusses comments on letter with WR1	Audiotape of comments	11/30/94
Telephone talk	PG discusses comments on letter and V2	Audiotape of comments	12/2/94
Face-face talk	WR1 & WR2 discuss comments of PG	Audiotape of discussion	12/7/94
Text production	PG gives comments on V2	Letter with comments, planning	1/11/95

Note. IR = internal reviewer, WR = a writer on the project, PG = a project group, V2 = the 2nd version of the document proposal and project plan made in June. From the interviews (9/22/94) with the writers and IR it appeared that WR2 had not seen the proposal or project plan, and that the IR perceived these documents as "agreements on procedures rather than on contents."

It was also apparent in later phases that the actors did not "look far behind them" in their discussions and texts. Neither writers nor client made frequent use of the memos and letters produced in the initial phase of the project. At most, they had all source material that had been provided earlier:

> WR2
> Maybe with some things there are comments that I didn't understand, where I thought, hey I've read an old version of this somewhere, Then I get hold of it to see if I can work out what they meant. But that would have been some background pieces about physical planning, etc. Otherwise not.

The frequency of discussions and letters and memos depended on the nature of problems. When a written product was sent to the reviewer or the client, the actors usually talked with each other. On average the client (via PG1) and the writers consulted once per month. When problems arose internal and external discussions were more frequent, and memos and letters were produced to elucidate the problems.

For example, during the internal review after the production of the first three chapters, the writers noticed a significant problem with the structure of the document. At that time the writers discussed the desired structure with each other more frequently. That consultation resulted in a letter (7/11/94) explaining that the structure of the document was not appropriate for its intended use and suggesting a new structure. The writers felt that the document was developing too much in the direction of being a policy document, rather than a practical manual. As a result of this letter, over a period of 2 weeks there were a number of telephone conversations with the client discussing a new chapter structure and a new activities plan. Written and oral communication continued in the period after November 1994, when WR2 was directing the project. When problems arose with the last chapter, there was more intense telephone contact between WR2 and PG1. Thus our results show that oral communication and the production of texts are interwoven in the design process of a technical report, and that the frequency of oral communication depends on the problems the actors encounter.

Communication and Project Functions. In this case both oral and written communications were used in planning and developing the project. The quotation and project plan included a planning summary of the whole process. The final document had to be at the printer in January 1995. The project plan listed the activities associated with this and stipulated what activities should take place in each week, with a diagram showing the duration of each activity. The plan extended from week 25 through week 52 of 1994. For example, the project plan called for the activity "compile the contents list" to be started in week 26 and to be completed in week 29. The quotation included time for the editor to make her evaluation and test the document among the target group. This time was in addition to the schedule as shown in the project plan. No time was set aside for the internal review. There was also no time indicated for the external review of each version, and no indication of whether there was a maximum number of times that a version might be reviewed, although it was stated that there would be a total of three or possibly four review rounds whenever a section was sent to the client. The project plan allowed one week for supplying comments on each version. However, from the interviews with the writers it was apparent that the planning was continuously modified during discussions and that it was already clear by the end of October that the January deadline could not be achieved.

The quotation document implied that the detailed planning would take place in consultation with the planning group. The July discussions produced a plan for the whole process based on the parts of the contents list. The external review procedure was also discussed at this time, but the time required for the review was not covered. There was also no agreement as to whether they would need to reserve time for the discussion of texts other than versions of the document (e.g., letters with questions, or memos).

There was much more discussion and written communication than had been planned. Every time a text (version, letter or memo) was followed by the PG's written responses, there was discussion by telephone with the PG (via PG1). Thus, in planning, the PG was in fact dependent on the writers. There were internal discussions arising from the review and the reactions of the PG (while WR1 was active in the project). During every consultation between PG1 and WR1 or WR2 a plan was made for the remaining parts of the document. The writers were informed of the results in writing.

Thus, based on our results we cannot separate a specific part in the design process in which oral communication is more important. It seems that oral and written communication are strongly interwoven. When problems were encountered, the actors talked to each other more frequently, but the same was true of written communication. The two forms influence and supplement one another. Because they are so bound up with one another, it appears to us impossible to assign separate functions exclusively for spoken or written text production.

Communication and Document Development. Case studies seldom make any connection to the texts being produced. Plowman (1993) has shown that there is a relationship between notes made during face-to-face communication and text versions, but our case dealt with professionals who had to write a piece jointly. The mutual dependence of oral and written communication, in relation to the texts produced, has thus far been examined mainly in research focusing on computer support for the process of composition. If suitable software to support the design process is to be developed, it is necessary to have a detailed understanding of how consultation and text production influence one another.

In this case both oral communication (discussion) and text production (drafts, memos, letters, written comments and minutes) adjusted the document to conform to its purpose and ultimate use. As an illustration we describe the period from July to early November during which the reviewer and both writers were involved in the project internally, and during which all the actors realized that a different structure was desirable for the document.

In June WR1 had prepared an outline based on the 1989 sector document, and PG1 had approved it. Except for a couple of items, the outline of the new document was the same as that of 1989. However, the document would now have to serve more as a means of providing information to local authorities regarding the practical implementation of the safety policy.

In July WR1 and the PG met to divide the subjects into the various chapters and to plan the realization of the chapters. During the consultation WR1 and the PG decided the subjects to be covered without reference to the ultimate use of the document. There were different ideas about the target group. WR1 seemed to assume that civil servants in local government would be the users. He thought that the document should be accessible for them. The PG believed local government or the provincial administration would be the primary target group:

7/26/1994

446   PG1   What you actually try to do is to write the sector document on external safety from the point of view of the provincial administration and then I reckon, not so much at the level of municipalities.

449   WR1   But municipalities have to use it.

450   PG1   Yes municipalities do have to use it, but . . .

451   PG2   It must be logical for whoever eventually has to use it. And then the question is: should they look under the heading "municipalities" or under "province."

479   PG3   And ideally municipalities and provincial authorities should have the same safety policy. So you shouldn't put too much emphasis on that distinction

The consultation about the target group led to discussion about the use of the document, and PG1 realized that the document would have to be a handbook:

513   PG1   But have I got it right that the sector document should also be a sort of manual for the municipalities?

516   PG2   No, but it is in any case for companies. What does that mean and what about the zoning aspects? The way I tackled it then was to look in which set of rules zoning was recorded for third parties. That was the initial approach.

In the report that PG1 made of this meeting there is no mention of the purpose, future use, or users of the document. From the consultation it was apparent that there was still no agreement within the PG about the purpose of the document. The structure of the 1989 document was retained even though the purpose was not clear. PG2 commented on this on one occasion:

7/27/94

339   PG2   So why are we putting out the new sector document? We're doing it because we have certain ideas about how safety should influence other policy fields. And then you have to provide a resume or some representation of your own instruments. Shouldn't you put that somewhere in the beginning? In a paragraph immediately after the introduction?

Despite this lack of clarity, none of the PGs considered a new document as an alternative to an update of the previous one. WR1, in contrast, was thinking of a new document with local government as the primary target group. He regarded the outline as no more than an indication: he would see later how the various elements would fit together.

9/30/94

WR1: . . . the most important thing is that we have a total picture of what has to be dealt with; at a later stage it may become clear that the division as it is now must be partly restructured.

It became clear to the writers that a more exact specification of the target group was necessary during a planning meeting on September 5, 1994, during which they discussed the editor's contribution to the project with her. As they spoke, WR1 and WR2 realized that they did not really know who the users in local government would be.

9/5/94

17   WR1   That is what I have understood so far about the objectives, in terms of the province. But I actually think that's a bit limited. Because there are of course a number of questions about what precisely you want to say to the municipalities. How far you should go. So I think that it is simply handy to define such objectives. Because if you want to write—and how you write—it depends on the target group, which is clearly the province itself, i.e., the policymakers, the municipalities and third parties, ministries and so forth. OK. I reckon I need to know and I think that it makes sense. WR2?

33   WR1   Or to clarify. Get it on paper and then with some feedback.

36   WR2   Yes, but that is not clear enough here.

The editor then asked who would actually be the local government officers.

90   Editor   Let's see, who was the most important target group? In the objectives, you mentioned the municipality. But what does that mean? Are these technical people or are they policymakers or officials in the safety field or in public information or what? I think that it is important for us to know that more precisely.

97   WR1   We can tell them that in our memo. I think that they are in fact both policymakers and executive officials.

98   WR2   Yes, I agree.

99   Editor   And executive officials in which sector?

99   WR1   Environmental permits.

100   WR2   Environmental permits.

100   WR1   And Physical Planning too?

101   WR2   Yes.

101   WR1   That they have to approve or evaluate zoning plans.

101   WR2   And give out permits.

102   WR2   These are planners and project developers.

103   Editor   So mostly people with a reasonable technical background. In any case they're technically clued up. It is of course important to find out what technical level these people are at to know how much you have to explain things in everyday language or if you can assume that the audience has enough basic knowledge to understand what you're saying.

111   WR1   Maybe we have to make an educated guess.

112   WR2   Yes, but it is a good idea if we make the aim very explicit. Because you often have lawyers involved in disaster management, don't you? Or members of the cabinet. Should they also be able to read it, or is that not necessary?

During the consultation WR1 had the idea of modifying the document to suit a range of different readers, with and without prior knowledge of the field:

119   WR1   Because I have now written down this and that, I realise that it's handy to give a bit more background for people who lack basic knowledge—which makes it more difficult for them to follow. My idea was that if you put everything in the main text, then it's a drag for those who know about the subject to plough through it all. So I actually wanted to try to split essential information from "nice to know" stuff that could be skipped while following the main lines. But it's there if you want to read it. Or in order to give some extra details. Which can be pretty relevant. Or an explanation somewhere of things that can be very useful for people who perhaps lack some background knowledge.

The consultation resulted in a memo from WR2 to the client (9/20/94). The memo explained the problems during this consultation and defined more precisely the purpose, use, and user. From our interview with WR2 it was apparent that the memo was intended to check whether the picture that the writers had of the ultimate users matched with the client's ideas. From the memo it appears that both of the writers assumed the users would be local government officers with various levels of background knowledge relating to the external safety policy:

The purpose of the document is to convince the user of the "reasonableness of the provincial policy."

The reading level must be suitable for staff members educated to the level of Higher Vocational Education, who might or might not have a background in technical fields, such as town and country planning, members of the cabinet, environmental affairs, or the fire service.

The document should include a reader's guide for various types of users. The text should be short, with references to deeper levels according to the need of the reader.

In the meantime WR1 wrote the first draft based on the 1989 structure and the consultations that WR1 had had with the PG. He had discussed this draft with the reviewer. During the consultation with the IR, as part of the review, the IR for province and local government said:

8   IR   Now I found it difficult to say anything here because I
would simply spurt out the content of the report. The most important
comment is that if you stick to the main target group, then I miss the
other target group, let's say (in this case) the municipalities. How do
the issues that are important to the municipalities get expressed?
Personally, that's what I find most difficult.

At the end of September (9/30/94) PG1 responded to the memo
for the first time, by telephone. Meanwhile, the PG realized it would be
difficult to match the levels of information to the knowledge of the
various readers. Just who these readers would be was not specified. PG1
suggested indicating which chapters were important for the reader
without any background knowledge.

The PG's response (10/7/94) to the first draft (sent 9/20/94) did
not comment on the purpose and use of the text, or take note of any
problems with making the document suitable for local government
officers.

Finally, as part of the review of the second draft of the first
chapters (11/3/94) the writers found that the existing structure of the
document would not be appropriate for its future use in local
government:

8   WR1   OK. I actually prefer to make a decision simply as a result
of the structure. And then it is also linked to the content. Because I think
about it of course. And then you get a fresh angle on it. . . . Of course that
has a number of advantages. But that's why we must question whether
the division as it's made at the moment—that table of contents with its
sections—whether it's actually what's wanted. I have an idea that it may
not be. And perhaps, and I don't know where to begin, maybe we
should deal with this first and then look at the kind of pieces we have
and how they fit together. Should we take the structure for granted?

469   WR1   I think that we must simply opt for a structure that
follows from the main questions. That we must formulate them very
explicitly. Then we can present them clearly to the decision-makers at
the municipal level or to officials. They have to formulate a number of
questions. Even as far as the level of adjacent policy fields. Because they
might also be involved with disaster management at the municipality
level. Or with the official responsible for disaster management. Is he
going to get involved or not? And that's where you can bring together
all the other things we've written. Then it's easy.

482   WR2   No, I don't agree—I think we should simply write that in
the memo.

They reformulated the purpose and target group in a memo
(11/4/94) to the local governments and suggested a totally different
structure, based on "concrete questions arising from the practical

procedure of granting permits." Policies and laws could be described at various levels so that users could select the knowledge they needed for their particular problems. During consultations (in November 1994) the PG agreed to this change and created a list of contents for the new document on the basis of the memo. In a subsequent consultation (11/30/94) PG added more detail and created a new timetable. In January 1995 WR2 produced the first chapters for the new structure. PG1 reported by telephone that the PG was satisfied with the draft.

It can be seen from the aforementioned example that the document was suited to its purpose, use, and users through both consultation and the production of texts (drafts, memo). Actors communicated with each other repeatedly. This communication took place in consultation and through posing questions and making suggestions to the client. Problems with suiting the document to its use and user were first noted internally, during the review discussions and the consultation with the editor. The client was informed about problems by means of memos sent to the PG. These memos reported the problems and suggested solutions. The PG, especially in the initial phase of the project, was focused more on making the document conform to new developments in policies and the role provincial administration had in policy questions, rather than on matching the document to its ultimate use by local governments.

From the time that he produced the first version, WR1 had problems with making the document suitable for its final use. The consultations between WR1 and the PG did not result in substantial modifications in the document. For example, WR1 and the IR discussed modifications in September:

9/13/94

126   IR   What I find most difficult is in fact these first three sections. How to link those first three chapters. To get some structure into it.

129   WR1   Now, the introduction is OK, I think. Because that's where I have put the general concepts.

130   IR   Yes, OK, but you mustn't go into too much detail. Those external policy fields depend on those relationships, between the different backgrounds.

134   WR1   What have they got to do with each other?

134   IR   What have they got to do with each other? What kind of instruments can they use?

135   WR1   Let's be precise here.

136   IR   And then relate it specifically here to the province. And then you explain, what the province expects, or what you actually expect from the municipalities.

138   WR1   That's what I had in the back of my mind when you wrote that down. But it is clear now. I'll take a look at it.

140   IR   Apart from that, all those examples are focused on physical planning and living space.

WR1 reported the following reservations in one of our interviews:

9/27/94

330   WR1   Now, when I made those remarks, it was more of an observation. One remark was a warning: don't go into too much detail. That has mainly to do with Chapter 1. Yes that could be true. You do indeed have to keep an eye on that. As far as giving those three chapters a different structure is concerned, well, we'll see. These issues are all related. . . . If you're talking about the instruments, you could also put that in Chapter 2. You could. That's true. Yes, these are the kind of choices where I think, I don't know. I mean I could do it. I can't say anything more precise about it. With that sort of comment I can't say clearly that it is actually an improvement or this or that should be different or whatever. It is an option. And I haven't received enough information to be able to say: hold on, this really is a breakthrough—if you do it that way, then you'll have vastly improved it. It's more an expression of confirmation, also considering what IR says and I agree is, yes, there should be some attempt to create a structure. To get things into a certain order and to make sure they're mentioned. It's all relative. It could be quite different. But as to whether it's really a good idea, I actually don't know myself. I have my doubts. He expresses some doubt. Me too. But that's about as far as it goes. So, you can see—I can't do anything with it.

The internal reviewer also admitted that he found it difficult to give concrete pointers for the structure of the document at this early stage:

9/29/94

272   IR   In general terms, yes. That is clear, I think. Only at the stage we're in now it's simply difficult or problematic to act as reviewer because we now have a draft of the content, say some keywords or bits of text that could be important. To get some structure into the report. It is simply very difficult to say whether the texts can be clearly understood, for example. At this stage that is simply not relevant.

Although the early consultations did provide a stimulus to finding solutions, the writers made no changes in the document, but they represented the solutions in supplementary texts such as letters and memos. The writers delayed changing the document until they received responses from the PG. Decisions regarding changes in the versions were left to the PG. When the writers discussed problems, there was no time to make large-scale changes in the text and still meet the agreed timetable for the delivery of versions. WR1 wanted to meet the deadlines, despite the problems. He wanted to use cover letters with the versions, and to let the client decide whether changes were necessary

Once WR1 was no longer involved in the project and the internal review ended, WR2 could discuss the project only with the PG. The remaining problems involved the purposes of the last chapter. This chapter would have to contain all the background information on the external safety policy, content originally part of chapter 1. WR2 had problems with this chapter because, in his opinion, it had become a sort of "wastepaper basket for fragments of text compiled previously." When he found solutions, he made changes in the document rather than explain things in supplementary texts. He made his own decisions, and presented them to the PG for their reaction. This was because time was now pressing and because he did not find the comments made by the PG clear.

From September 1994 to late January 1995 it appears, first, that the document was matched to its purpose, use, and users through both oral and written communication. Second, oral and written communication complemented one another during this matching process. During consultations between the writers and the reviewer, problems were noted. These were first presented to the PG in the form of texts (memos). Suggestions for solutions to these problems were also first presented in text. Changes were only made in the drafts once the PG had reacted. PG1 normally responded first in writing, in memos and letters in which problems were mentioned and on the versions which had been sent, and later explained these comments and discussed the planning implications by telephone.

Improving Document Design

The Role of Internal Review. One of the purposes of the study was to ascertain the effect of an internal review. Unfortunately, the internal review actually functioned for only the first 3 months. From that period it was apparent that internal review makes a positive contribution to the process of composition. The internal review discussions were the first point to identify problems with matching the document to its goal, use and users, and the discussions also generated solutions. The internal review made it possible to communicate with the client more efficiently. Once WR1 had withdrawn and the internal review had ceased the PG and the advisory committee served as the only reviewers. The disadvantages of this were that the desired internal transmission of knowledge did not occur and that the writer was more dependent on the knowledge of the client. Both WR2 and WR1 found the internal review necessary, and the internal reviewer also considered it important, but no way was found within the bureau to continue with it. The difficulty was apparently due to indefinite project planning and management. Also, the usefulness of the comments may play a role here. From the interviews we know that the reviewer found it difficult to comment on rhetorical aspects (structure, language, etc.); and so, writer and reviewer had problems finding rhetorical solutions.

Project Planning and Document Management. When various actors contribute to a document, efficient planning and document management is important for the coordination and progress of the process (Hackos, 1994; J. R. Weber, 1991). In our case project planning was continually modified, planning was done on the basis of the texts, and the deadline was considerably exceeded. In the quotation document and the project plan too little time was allowed for internal and external consultation. This may have happened because the consultancy is a small bureau competing with larger consultancies to deliver quality at a competitive price. However, the failure to incorporate internal consultation makes internal planning even more important. The majority of the employees work on more than one project at a time, so rigorous planning is essential.

The internal management of the text production could be considerably improved. Failures in this respect might be due to the lack of a coordinator. J. R. Weber (1991) has shown that, if several writers contribute to an extensive document, there is a need for someone to coordinate the various contributions and ensure that they fit together. Harmony between the authors could be effected through the internal review, but document management and communication with the client can be better realized by working through a lead author. In the beginning this was WR1's function, and there was no more internal consultation and coordination once WR1 had withdrawn.

Both writers and client focused, in the initial phase, on planning the contents of the document. There was scarcely any rhetorical planning in these discussions. Couture and Rymer (1991) have shown that professionals who write have a tendency to see this task mainly as a demonstration of their professional expertise, in contrast to career writers (those for whom writing is their main job) who approach their task more as a question of solving rhetorical problems. Because the editor approached her contribution to the document in the light of her own expertise in rhetoric, it became clear to the writers that the objective and target group would have to be specified in more detail. Actors realized only too late that the planning meeting was the right place to reach consensus as to the goal and use of the document. Collaborative planning meetings at the outset would have reduced the likelihood for conflicts or a bias toward either rhetorical or technical aspects (see Burnett, 1991).

DISCUSSION: IMPLICATIONS FOR THE DESIGN PROCESS

More research about the relationship between oral and written communication during the design process has been conducted in recent years (Couture & Rymer, 1993; Locker, 1992; Plowman, 1993; Spilka, 1993b). The initial purpose of these studies was to examine how the two forms of communication can contribute to fulfilling rhetorical and social functions during the design process (Locker, 1992). Spilka (1993b) has shown that written and oral communication have an interdependent relationship that serves critical rhetorical functions, which, in turn, help fulfill social goals. These rhetorical functions include facilitating the progress of the composing process, facilitating the development of ideas, planning and problem resolution, encouraging cooperative dialogue between the speakers and their audience, and increasing the opportunities to exercise power.

Posner, Baecker, and Wellner (1990) found that solutions for text problems were found mainly in consultations. In our case study consultation included discussions about matching the document to its goal, use and users, and the ideas for solutions, but only forms of texts expressed specific solutions. Once again, this shows that oral and written communication influence one another and that both contribute to refining the document to its purpose and future use .

In our case consultation was not limited to planning in the initial phase of the design process, as van Pelt and Gillam (1991) found. There were both oral and written communication during the whole course of the project. It can be concluded that, in a document design process, consensus about purpose and use emerges from oral communication between actors and from text production (see also, Plowman, 1993). In a different study about writing ISO procedures (van Gemert & Woudstra, 1996) we also found that consultation was a continuous process during the whole course of the project.

A document design model should include the contribution of written and oral communication on the (re)definition of the writing problem and on the continuous consultation of people and other sources of information in an iterative process. One approach is to look at the process as one of obtaining information by means of consultation of people and from available documents, research reports or policy documents as activities to reduce uncertainty. This approach suggests Weick's (1979) process-oriented model of human interaction with the information as the central phenomenon of organizations. Weick introduced the concept of equivocality and of reducing equivocality by behavior cycles and rules. In the document design process writers process the information available from the organizational context. This information can be highly equivocal if the writer has a limited insight into the organizational and communication goals, structures and culture, on the one hand, and to communication means and skills on the other.

Reflecting on the case study, we think the initial available information was unsuitable to act on effectively and efficiently, and as a result there was a lot of interaction. What kind of rules could be distinguished? There were rules developed about the management of the project and about review; also the bureau was seeking rules to become a learning organization. The evaluation of the present way of working could lead to these rules. The problem in the case study may have been that the actors were not capable of recognizing the equivocality of the available information at an early stage. They tried to solve their problem by continuous interaction (review), but because there was no variety in actors, there was only slow progress.

One could also look at rules as a set of cognitive tools available for the actors. For instance, one should have knowledge about how to reduce uncertainty during interaction. Knowing how to behave in meetings, interviews, and review feedback and using the accompanying skills can be of great help. There also should be rules available to write and interpret documents. A writer has to know and apply certain rules (heuristics) during the writing process. Depending on his experience as a writer and a worker he has access to the information needed from his long-term memory, or he has to look for the right information in his environment. If the necessary knowledge and skills are not available, the organization needs to introduce another cycle through training programs.

We see rules not only as some kind of external "procedure" but also as an internal set of heuristics. This internal approach gives us the opportunity to add a more cognitive approach to the social-psychology approach of Weick. In cognitive psychology one distinguishes between declarative knowledge (content knowledge about, for instance, security norms, a manufacturing process, but also content knowledge about, for instance, textual structures and ways of formulating) and procedural knowledge (knowledge about how to use declarative knowledge). In addition we would like to introduce strategic knowledge because in communication (other than in learning situations) a writer has to know what is realizable in his or her organizational environment.

In the document design process having an unclear problem definition will be a natural situation. The search for knowledge by means of interaction can help the actors if the organization they work in gives them this opportunity. Within the framework of project planning certain milestones can be agreed on. Drafts of documents can serve as a source for consultation or review, and there are also informal consultations. Whenever the actors feel a need for information they should be able to consult each other. For the document design process this means that time must be available for consultation. From this case study, our study about writing ISO-procedures (van Gemert & Woudstra, 1996), and from literature, we know that time may not be available for consultation and review because time for writing, consultation, and review has no priority. Any document design model should contain some monitoring and managing of the process to include such time.

In the case study, there was no hierarchy differentiation expressed in the way power was exercised, and there were no conflicts reported between writers and client. However, conflict may be defined as "the interaction of interdependent people who perceive opposition of goals, aims, and values and who see the other party as potentially interfering with the realization of these goals" (Putnam & Poole, 1987, p. 552). The entire design process may be one of conflict and negotiation. The case study certainly included interaction between interdependent people.

Although these actors in our case treated each other as experts, they did have power over each other. The client had power because eventually he approved or disapproved, he paid the bill, and he could decide to contract the bureau for future projects. The writers had power over each other because they delivered parts of a coherent document to each other in time. The reviewer of the bureau had power according to his role as expert and colleague. Even the editor had some power because she had knowledge the writers did not have and because she had not worked with the previous outcomes of the project. The bureau could not easily ask for another editor because she worked for the bureau on a regular basis. The bureau also had some power over the client because the moment the parties had an agreement to start the process the client was dependent on the bureau. The client needed the bureau's expertise.

What about the incompatibility of the goals? Looking only at the client and the writers team as two possible parties with a conflict we did not see incompatible goals. What we saw was an evolution of ideas about objectives and users. Even the observation by the editor that a decision was needed about the primary users and goals was not a problem of incompatible goals but rather a logical stage in developing clearness between the two parties. From interviews with the writers we know that the development of the process was not due to some hidden strategy. Considering all this we doubt if it is worthwhile to look at the data as conflict although it might be possible that research on relational variables could lead to a richer interpretation.

Yin (1994) argued that case studies should be considered from the point of view of replication logic, rather than from that of sampling logic. This would give case studies something of the character of experimental studies. In this approach a researcher would conduct a case study "in the hope of confirming or refuting their claims and thereby contributing to a discipline's confidence that research is leading to objective truth about the world" (Bouldin & Odell, 1993, p. 280).

A problem in research into writing processes in an organizational context is that organizations are not closed. There is continuous interaction between the organization and its environment. One might conclude that it is impossible to draw any generalizable conclusions. Bouldin and Odell (1993), following Young, Berker, and Pike (1970), proposed doing research to determine the "range of variation" of concepts important for the document design process. This would enhance the explanatory power of these concepts, and so would prevent research from being reduced to simply "information collection." This criticism does not imply that replication research cannot serve any function. For example, it might be used to determine the range of variation in which a particular concept is relevant. In our opinion, if the conclusions are to have explanatory power, it must be clear from the research which concepts have been studied, their significance for document design research (theory, models), and the instruments used. This will substantiate the validity of the study.

ACKNOWLEDGMENTS

We thank our colleague Dr. T.M. van der Geest for her contribution to our research project.

twelve

CHALLENGES FOR THE APPLICATION
OF ORGANIZATIONAL
COMMUNICATION

Cal W. Downs
University of Kansas

The Organizational Communication Conference of 1976 made a very special contribution to the study of organizational communication. It was a time of great excitement as scholars pooled their information about theories and about methodologies. One of the principal goals was to design an approach to communication that could be applied practically to all those kinds of "real-life" organizations being studied. Audit procedures were formulated to generate information that could be applied by the organization. Those scholars also debated the future of "our discipline." At that time there were those in communication who questioned the legitimacy of organizational communication as a field of study, so it was good to meet people who were excited about what they were doing, who were excited about how they could contribute to the understanding of organizations, and who were supportive of one another.

Twenty years later it is useful to explore where organizational communication has been, where it is, and where it is going. For 2 days the conference explored contributions to theory and developments in methods, and it is time to examine the application of knowledge. Application is very important because it tests theories and formal and informal hypotheses in a real sense. Furthermore, it is precisely the possibility of application to practical situations that attracts many students to organizational communication.

My objectives in this chapter are (a) to look at some successes in organizational communication and (b) to investigate some of the special challenges associated with application. I have been an organizational communication professional for over 35 years, and I call on my own experiences and the experiences of colleagues in addition to typical published sources to exemplify my points. My analysis suggests there are still gaps that need to be overcome.

Like the Confucian model of change, I view the development of organizational communication as being continuous, without ever reaching the end but making contributions through the search itself. The fact that the future requires adaptations does not make the past accomplishments invalid or the present inadequate. In the future, the past always looks inadequate. So when I point out the challenges of application, it is not meant to indict the past.

WHAT HAS ORGANIZATIONAL COMMUNICATION ACHIEVED?

In general, there has been much academic success. The discipline is respected, and there are divisions of organizational communication in the International Communication Association, the Academy of Management, and the National Communication Association. Surveys of what will be needed by workers and managers in the next century list communication and teamwork near the top of the list. Department chairs have told me that anything they call "organizational communication" will sell to students, and the number of majors is up. The first success is that we have built a discipline.

For some, this discipline may appear fractured and confused. At different universities, organizational communication students learn different things, but that is also true of many majors. Furthermore, many of students still wonder what they are going to *do* with their major because many universities do not assist students to learn about application.

The domain for organizational communication has always been a bit elusive. At one of the early meetings of the Organizational Communication Division in the International Communication Association, a group met to write a charter. We tried to define organization and then tried to define communication. It was a rather hopeless task and so it is today. We are united by the label "organizational communication," but we certainly are not united in substance. In listening to the papers delivered in the first 2 days of the conference, I was aware that our family is rather loose. Some of us are brothers and sisters whose ideas resonate well with each other. Others of us are just cousins who barely recognize our relationship with what the others are doing. And then some of us are just in-laws to which you are not certain you want to be related. In this sense, we are not different than most other academic disciplines.

HOW IMPORTANT IS APPLICATION?

One of the consistent claims about organizational communication is that there is not enough theory. As scholars and practitioners in a boundary spanning discipline, professionals draw on both organizational and communication theories, but there have been few well-developed theories of organizational communication. In an effort to develop these theories, scholars may be moving slightly away from application, and this is unfortunate.

Application has an important role in developing knowledge for at least three important reasons. (a) Attempts to apply can test theories by giving feedback about the gaps in those theories. (b) Attempts to apply knowledge can give professionals new questions to address. Sometimes academic questions are not the ones that organizations are asking, and some of us may not have even heard the question. (c) Attempts to apply give a greater understanding of the ways that organizational communication actually works.

WHAT DOES ORGANIZATIONAL COMMUNICATION HAVE TO APPLY?

Most prominent scholars of organizational communication have some experience consulting, and most have found it invigorating. As consultants, they use many different theories, research, ethical points of view, and world views, and they use their own intuitions in limited ways. For example, applications vary from efforts focusing on internal communication to try to build better climates to looking at subsystems such as performance reviews or study group meetings. Some interventions deal with external communication and attempt to improve customer satisfaction or to build corporate citizenship.

As I listened to some of my colleagues at the conference I did not have a clear notion of how to apply some of what they presented. Maybe they do. And that is the point. The discipline does not make the application. I do. Application is as much the person as it is the knowledge and techniques employed by the person.

Leavett (1972) argued that we all define problems according to the solutions that we have available. As we travel through the academic rain forests, so many theories rain on us that we get soaked by some theories. Often it is difficult to reconcile all that we "know." For example, earlier in the conference Putnam (Chapter 3) advocated that organizational communication professionals move away from a means–end paradigm. This is a sharp contrast to the popular author Stephen Covey (1989), who advises individuals to start with the end in sight. The practitioner must make a choice.

What we apply depends on the theoretical and experience cards we are dealt and the choices we make about those cards. Table 13.1 displays the choices made by two different consultants. They are poker players, and they have been dealt different cards. They have made different choices about the draw, about what to keep and what to discard, and their hands are now complete. The game will not be complete until they play their cards, but their play will be different because of the cards they were dealt and the choices they have already made.

These two people will approach organizational problems very differently and, they will make vastly different applications. For example, Consultant One is likely to treat problems as deviations from a desirable model. The person who bases judgments of effectiveness on Covey and Maslow will be concerned about general principles, relationships, and opportunities for individual development. Consultant Two would base judgments on the fit between the organization, people, and rewards. Experiences at different management positions and the other knowledge bases would focus Consultant Two on contingencies. Although an outsider could not say that one approach to a particular problem would be more successful than the other, the two approaches are different. Consultant One wants an ideal, and Consultant Two is after the practical.

Table 13.1. Differing Knowledge Bases as Perceptual Filters Among Consultants.

Knowledge bases	Consultants	
	One	Two
Management theory	Stephen Covey	Paul Hersey
Communication	Bad experiences	Berlo
Motivation	Maslow	Herzberg
Experience	Graduate degree	Six different management jobs

HOW CAN WE BRIDGE THE GAP BETWEEN ACADEMIA AND OTHER ORGANIZATIONS?

The frames of reference for academics and managers are necessarily different because of the contexts in which they operate. The language, the approach to research, and the use of the results are all very different, and what readers value is are very different. Academics most often do research and publish for other academicians, but managers want action and they are concerned about financial matters. Some academicians show disdain for practicality or immediate problems, and some managers show disinterest in theory or long-term solutions. There is a huge gap between the academy and other organizations, and application of what scholars know requires them to bridge that gap somehow. Table 13.2 points to some of the features of that gap.

I want to elaborate some elements in the table to illustrate important differences. Academic research functions to gain acceptance by peers and to attain publication in a respected journal. The research designs get more complicated and rigorous, but the readership for most articles is low. In most cases, the author gains rewards for publication, regardless of the impact of the publication. A manager or consultant, on the other hand, is interested in ideas that work. The publication of the ideas is unimportant as long as the ideas work in a given situation.

Table 13.2. Gap Between Academy and Other Organizations Studied.

Area	Academy	Other organizations
Audience	Faculty, students, colleagues	Managers, consultants, specialists
Results	Discussion, analysis	Decisions, solutions
Purpose	Reinforce orgcom discipline	Holistic considerations, survival
Accountability	Loose, no loss if it does not work	Great responsibility
Approach	Description	Prescription
Context	Free, generalization	Specific organization
Emphasis	Theory, "truth"	Practical, what works
Process	Sense making	Policy
Rewards	Reputation: others read your work	Reputation and money
Pressures to	Publish and teach well	Survive and make money

Managers and consultants may rely more on insight and intuition honed over years of experience rather than well-documented published research. In some organizational contexts, the people who implement ideas are separate from the people who do research. For example, the people who run political campaigns are rarely the people who have done the research on them. Academics often gain notoriety for analyzing what managers have done without the benefit of research. The academician gets rewarded for description and explanation, and the manager gets rewarded for prescription and implementation.

Accountability in the academy is different from other organizations. Indeed there are differences between academics, consultants, and managers. An academic can propose a remedy and suffer no serious penalty if it does not work. Likewise a consultant risks only the loss of a client for poor recommendations. Managers, however, could lose their jobs. When a division of TRW was trying to develop teams, they hired many consultants outside the organization who would say, "Try this and let's see if it works." After several efforts that did not work, they decided to abandon this loose approach, and they fired all the consultants. In the end, the company developed a viable strategy from within.

Some academicians are unwilling to bridge the gap. Some may be unable to bridge the gap because adaptation to the academy makes it difficult to adapt to other organizations. A few may be proud of the gap. Most can bridge the gap easily.

The abilities to conduct research, to analyze cases, or to conduct audits may be one of the chief skills produced by the discipline. Such analysis can make students and faculty good consultants if they also develop good interpretive skills that enable them to make useful interventions. Indeed, many graduates do elect to become consultants and succeed. One of the tendencies I have noted is that once someone discovers something truly marketable, they often turn almost totally toward consulting and application.

WHAT ARE THE SPECIFIC CHALLENGES?

For those who wish to bridge the gap, there are specific issues to face. Effective application of knowledge is dynamic, and there are new challenges in our environments. Listed here are eight challenges, and facing these will strengthen our abilities to apply our discipline.

Challenge 1: Encourage More Application. Studying Organizational Communication Is Not the Same as Doing Organizational Communication

A few years ago at an ICA convention a person with a doctorate in communication revealed that IBM hired her to coordinate small groups because she had done an analysis of small groups for her dissertation. However, when she went to work, she said, "I realized that I knew how to study small groups but I did not know how to do them." She revealed her story in a call for more application. Just last year I received a call from someone with a doctorate in organizational communication from a prestigious school who said, "I have been asked to analyze the organizational communication in a company, but I don't know where to begin." Yet this person said, "This is what I want to do for my career."

In the past, people who worked in applied communication were often held suspect by their more theoretically driven peers. Now, however, application is one of the strongest appeals organizational communication has for students. One should not have to make a choice between theory and practice; they enhance one another. In a sense, this is the same point made by Cheney and Wilhelmsson (1996) to take learning out of the classroom. Doing so may be very necessary if one is to understand how organizational communication operates.

There is a special kind of development that accrues from application in either of its two forms: (a) applied research or (b) consulting. Applied research should be welcomed, even though the opportunities for publishing this within communication publications are limited. Such research often challenges the assumptions made in textbooks and provides feedback about the adequacy of commonly held theories or positions.

Opportunities for consulting abound, and they can contribute to understanding as they force a consultant to adapt to specific circumstances that fit no textbook. One makes choices and develops rationales beyond those acceptable in the classroom. In a classroom one typically covers models of change, of communication, and different orientations to leadership and management. These are good pieces of information, but at some point, it is useful to force people to choose what they can adapt. Good consultants often develop good theories, but they must translate their experiences into formal theories to publish them in academic journals.

Challenge 2: Move Outside the Box! Break Down the Walls!

Universities tend to carve up knowledge into disciplines or departments so that each can say, "This is yours and this mine and you should not touch my part of the world"—my box. Indeed, communication scholars seem to be more worried and concerned about the perimeters and parameters of their box. Recently, on the Comgrads Hotline, a computer bulletin board, people were asking questions such as, "Should I have friends outside the department?" "Should I have friends outside the university?" and "Should communication departments hire people with PhD in other fields?" Although one may understand some of their concerns stemming from academic pressures on departments, these questions reflect a kind of parochial sectarianism that make application almost impossible.

Organizations do not carve up knowledge into these same boxes, and communication is related to many other variables not always covered in the academic study of communication. In other words, to be really helpful in applying what we know, professionals can be most helpful when they view communication phenomena in a broader organizational context. Furthermore, less time should be spent defining the exact perimeters of communication.

Organizational communication will always be a boundary spanning discipline in a university, but organizations do not have those same boundaries. This means that application demands cross-fertilization of ideas from all organizational disciplines. Applied consulting contributes a great deal to one's career by demanding growth, and one of the greatest joys many experience is the freedom that consulting gives to move outside the box (DeWine, personal communication, 1996).

More can be done to encourage cross-fertilization within universities. A recent limit at the University of Kansas set the minimum number of students in graduate classes at six. This economic efficiency rule had the impact of forcing small PhD classes to look for people and opportunities outside their private preserves. Organizational communication academicians should welcome this diversity, but they should not wait for universities to impose it on their academic practices. Rather, they should be generating innovative methods of their own.

Challenge 3: Test Popular Assumptions

Some have been critical of organizational communication for lacking theory and for making statements on the basis of unsupported claims, value-laden principles, or just saying that this is the way it ought to be because it fits my values. I sometimes shudder when I think of some of the things I taught from books when I first started my career. That has caused me to ask in many doctoral orals, "What are we teaching that is wrong?" One may be critical for a lack of theory, but one may also be equally critical for the lack of application. Scholars may theorize about things that simply do not pan out. Fellow consultant and academician Ken Mackenzie has an orientation of "let me tell you my theory and you tell me what is wrong with it so I can refine it." Few take this orientation, and most of us listen only to what supports our own ideas.

Three examples illustrate the challenge. One assumption often made is that all people are good and people in organizations want to solve problems, want to resolve conflict equitably, and want excellence in communication. Overlook for the moment the fact that people will have vastly different definitions for, and orientations toward, problems. Both scholars and consultants sometimes think that they equip people to overcome difficulties by presenting information on active listening, open communication, win–win conflict resolution, diversity or sensitivity training, or set up off-site meetings to work through problems. Two things are wrong with this. First, clients are left to their own devices about how to apply such information and frequently the consultants have not thought much about future applications. Second, consultants and trainers often do not have a way of dealing with people who want conflict or who are basically unprincipled (DeWine, personal communication, 1996). In other words, the prevalent assumption miscasts the world.

Some also assume that certain types of communication climate or organizational climate are better than others. Recently, a group of graduate students analyzed an organization that has had an 83% turnover in 2 years, lives in a rather chaotic atmosphere, but outproduces most of its competitors. It did not fit any textbook description I have ever seen. This intervention forced all of us, students, professors, and clients, to revamp their notions of climate, system, and turnover. The usual pronouncements would not fit.

One of the greatest inhibitors to successful application is the assumption circulated widely in academia that all ideas are created equally and that it is unfair and unscholarly to be critical of an idea, particularly if it has been published in a journal. Professors may force students to pander to their pet theories. Instead, professors should expose people to diverse viewpoints, and teach people methods of evaluating these ideas for themselves. Application forces one to make choices among ideas. Organizations create a marketplace to test the utility of ideas, and utility is one criterion that will elevate some ideas and diminish others. Organizations will quickly reject ideas that do not help them accomplish their goals.

Challenge 4: Get Rid of the "One-Size-Fits-All" Dictums. Account for Individual Differences in Developing Effective Communication in Organizations

The "one-size-fits-all" approach to communication needs adaptation. Most experts have a litany of things that seem to work well generally, yet many also espouse individuals' differences both among organizations and among the people within a given organization.

One significant difference is in the communication styles that people exhibit in organizations. These style preferences become filters through which people with different communication styles expect vastly different things from the communication in their organizations. In a recent intervention in Scotland, I examined styles using the Jungian classifications of Thinker, Feeler, Sensor, and Intuitors. In three organizations there were significant differences among the people with different styles in how satisfied they were with communication in the organizations. Thinkers wanted the total organization and its processes to be rationalized through descriptions and rules, but this inhibited the freedom preferred by Intuitors and Sensors. All were not satisfied with a system or job descriptions and rules; all were not satisfied when general information was given so they could make their own decisions on how to do something. Some wanted exhaustive details; some did not.

Other examples can be found in other popular concepts. Empowerment is a positive value (or buzzword, depending on one's point of view), but how does one do this when some people don't want to be empowered? Teamwork is another popular organizational strategy, but some people prefer to work alone. Should professionals take these differences into account? If so, how do they do that? A review of the team literature has revealed (a) that there are so many different definitions for "teams" and so many different approaches to it that there was no "it" in teamwork and (b) that most prescriptions certainly did not take individual differences into consideration (C. W. Downs, 1989). How and when can individual differences be incorporated into organizational policies?

Challenge 5: Expand Horizons Beyond the United States

Organizations will have characteristics of their national cultures, even though one can recognize a great variety within any given culture. It has been an article of faith that a business's values are influenced by a national cultural environment that will determine many aspects of its operations (Wiio, 1988). Increasingly, however, organizational communication scholars have the challenge of seeing how a global company is influenced by the many cultures in which it operates.

Scholars can profit from looking at how communication principles are applied in different cultures. Almost always, there will be a concomitant increase in the understanding of one's own culture.

To their credit, academicians in general and many organizational communication scholars in particular have developed opportunities to investigate cultural comparisons. For example, Lee and Barnett (1995) conducted a symbols-and-meaning approach to the organizational cultures of banks in the United States, Japan, and Taiwan. They reported that the Taiwanese bank and Citibank are not very different. As a result of the analysis, "socializing with workers" can be considered as the crucial difference to compare the Taiwanese bank and Citibank with both the Japanese bank and the American bank. "Supervisor" and "money" are the concepts that differentiate the American bank from the Japanese bank, the Taiwanese bank, and Citibank. "Authority" was an important concept to distinguish the Japanese bank from the American bank, the Taiwanese bank, and Citibank.

Businesses in the United States, Japan, the United Kingdom, and South Korea have learned that good management practices need not be invented in their home culture. Ticehurst, Downs, and Ikeda (1994) investigated Japanese-managed companies in three different nations and found that people were more satisfied with Japanese management in Australia and Thailand than they were in Japan.

Hofstede (1980) has challenged the "silent assumption of universal validity" (p. 373) characteristic of management studies published in the United States. His Value Survey Module is a popular measure of cultural values that contrasts cultures on four dimensions: (a) individualism vs. collectivism, (b) uncertainty avoidance, (c) power distance, and (d) masculinity. C. W. Downs, Adrian, and Ticehurst (1995) investigated how communication factors predicted organizational commitment in four different cultures. Table 13.3 displays a summary of findings. The four had some communication phenomenon in common in that the relationship with the supervisor was an important predictor in all four cultures. This tells something about the role of the supervisor, but in order to apply this information well, one may have to understand much more about the four cultures than are indicated by this study. On the other hand, communication climate was an important predictor for highly individualistic cultures, whereas media quality was an important predictor in the collectivist societies. These findings challenge us to investigate the culture in order to know how these results can be applied.

Such results are interesting and begin to confirm or deny some basic precepts. They are helpful in supporting the claims that cultural

Table 13.3. Communication Predictors of Commitment in Power Distance and Individualism Quadrants.

| | Power Distance | |
Individualism	Small	Large
Low (collectivist)		Guatemala/Thailand Media Quality Rel. with supervisor Organizational integration/ Personal feedback
High	Australia/USA Communication climate Rel. with supervisor Horizontal communication	

differences are important. What the studies do not do, however, is indicate how these bits of information can be applied. In fact, cultural comparisons are instructive but to apply them well one would need to be more thoroughly grounded in the other cultures than most of us are.

It is important to note that comparisons across cultures are sometimes difficult because researchers have used different instruments and reported statistics which are not comparable. The diverse natures of the studies prevent actual cross-cultural theory development and, therefore, application of this information needs to be done carefully and cautiously.

Challenge 6: Connect Communication to Outcomes. Answer the Question: "So What Difference Does Communication Make?"

A few years ago I was conducting an executive training program when one executive came up during the coffee break to make the following statement: "You know, I am so uncomfortable. Our company is productive and is making so much money, but we just don't do it the right way." The right way? I am afraid that much of our teaching has been dedicated to teaching "the right way" without actually looking at the right goals or without asking, "Is this accomplishing what the organization wants to accomplish?" In fact, one of the stickiest problems in all of organizational communication is the determination of what criteria for effectiveness should be applied to the situation.

At most professional organizational communication conferences, scholars are primarily concerned with enhancing their legitimacy in academia. That is certainly a worthwhile concern, but it should not be the only concern. Anyone who emphasizes application must also be concerned with enhancing the legitimacy of the discipline with practitioners in organizations. One of the best ways of doing this is to demonstrate that organizational communication makes a difference when it is done well in the organization.

There are many outcomes that are important to organizations: productivity, healthy financial status, satisfaction of workers, organizational commitment, corporate citizenship, customer satisfaction, stockholder satisfaction, and union–management relations. Thousands of studies have looked at job satisfaction and commitment, but there are much fewer about other outcomes. Organizational communication professionals do a better job of connecting to some outcomes than others.

In particular, organizational communication professionals may have done the least well with financial concerns. Clampitt (personal communication, 1996) claimed that one of the biggest problems he saw with organizational communication is that "we do not value the dollar value of communication. Until we do, we cannot promote effective communication." For example, one of the most frequent remedies I hear is to have a meeting about something. How much does that meeting cost? That can be computed. Second, surveys are very dear to me. As a communication strategy, they are useful for getting feedback, but surveys can be expensive. What dollar value does that information have? Arlene Faulk, corporate director of research and training for United Airlines, once presented a case to a graduate class and had them analyze it. She congratulated them for doing a wonderful job of analyzing some dimensions but then pointed out that no one had mentioned money, the starting point for her in every decision. DeWine (personal communication, 1996) suggested *Costing Human Resources* (Cascio, 1987) as a book that directly ties communication and human resources to the bottom line.

Challenge 7: New Technologies Breed New Organizations. In Order to Understand the Organizations in Which Communication Occurs, Be Aware of the Implications of New Technologies

One of the greatest problems of application is that experts sometimes make prescriptions about organizational communication without a thorough understanding of the design of the work, without a comprehensive view of the design of the organizational structures such as the degree of hierarchy or centralization, and increasingly without an up-to-date understanding of the technologies being brought into the organizations. To understand the communication needs in an organization, one must strive to understand other organizational processes.

Writing about technology and organization, Nayaranan (1996) claimed "Not only were specific new technologies adopted, but the configuration of these technologies brought about a radical rethinking of the philosophy of management needed to operate organizations." Each change in the philosophy of management will have implications for changes in the way people communicate in organizations.

Goodman, Lye, and Gavaghan (1994) concluded from a survey of the United Kingdom that "communication professionals do not know enough about technology and become passive users rather than driving the process" (p. 6). However, there is a rush among academicians to fill the gap by providing all kinds of training in managing technology, not only in communication but in other disciplines as well. Given the fact that communication technology has become a driving force behind organizational change, organizational communication experts and scholars have no other choice than to learn to apply new technologies if they are to remain relevant.

Tucker, Meyer, and Westerman (1996) gave an excellent coverage of this challenge as they pointed out how new technologies revolutionize organizational strategies by releasing "the stranglehold of bureaucratic inertia" (p. 54), and how the developments accompanying this innovative period are taking place in a chaotic, probabilistic climate. The speed of the movement is fast, and the assumptions underlying organizations' experimentations have been largely unexamined and untested. This uncertainty provides organizational communication with a great opportunity to do valuable applied research. For example, Lawson's (1996) dissertation is investigating the introduction of Lotus Notes into an international organization. This move was driven by economic and efficiency objectives, but already people see subtle changes in how work gets done and how communication takes place. The organization is changing, and management is interested in how his applied research can help them understand their own organization better. His subsequent publications will also contribute to the field of organizational communication.

Challenge 8: Elevate Organizational Communication to the Level of Strategy

Many have considerable skill at applying organizational communication principles to a particular tactical problem in an organization. In fact, one of the criticisms of communication is that it is often applied merely as a Band-Aid. However, communication can be used strategically to implement core organizational values, or strategically to create an alignment of people and system. Tucker et al. (1996) described "communicated knowledge . . . as probably the single most important source of competitive advantage." They also described "the central role of communication in the development of firm-specific internal strategic capabilities which lead to sustainable strategic competitive advantage" (p. 58). There are good opportunities for organizational communicators to begin not only to investigate strategy but also to collaborate with those who specialize in it. Note the following comments from the call for papers from the Strategic Management Society's 16th International Conference:

> CEOs believe that "strategy is the easy part, implementation is the hard part." Economic value analysis, total quality, re-engineering, open-book management, teams, and time-based competition currently command more top management attention than strategy . . . diagnose what some believe is strategy's diminishing share of influence and suggest possible remedies.
>
> Human capital, rather than financial or physical capital, is the basic building block of the new economy. To what extent will the challenge of knowledge management force companies to rethink fundamental assumptions around organization, hierarchy and control?
>
> We look forward to considering your ideas that challenge the hegemony of the economic view of strategy and the firm.
>
> No one has yet reinvented the practice of management for the information age. There are, as yet, few answers. What we need are better questions.

The academic strategists seem very open to the applications communication might make. My experience has led me to believe that top managers are very receptive to strategic communication. Indeed, an advertising agency has now tied all of its executive bonuses to the results of periodic communication audits. Organizational communication has many opportunities.

CONCLUSION

Theories are readily shared and published, whereas adaptation of organizational communication principles is often an individual affair, not often published for people to see. Each person here has experience in applying some part of organizational communication to some organizations. This paper reflects the Downs's filter, shaped not only by 35 years of teaching but also by that many years of consulting. It is my personal conviction that organizational communication, like organizations in general, is in a period of rapid advancement. The discipline will improve and advance faster as it attempts to make applications of its shared information.

part six

ORGANIZATIONAL COMMUNICATION AND SOCIAL RESPONSIBILITY

thirteen

SOCIAL RESPONSIBILITY AND THE MODERN HEALTH CARE SYSTEM: PROMOTING A CONSUMER ORIENTATION TO HEALTH CARE

Gary L. Kreps

Hofstra University

HEGEMONY AND ALIENATION IN THE MODERN HEALTH CARE DELIVERY SYSTEM

The modern health care system seems to have forgotten how to care. It is rarely user-friendly and is often lined with peril (J. A. Jones, Kreps, & Phillips, 1995; Mendelsohn, 1979). It is a terrible paradox that seeking health care can be very dangerous to your health! Recent shocking and well-publicized health care delivery calamities are indicative of the most extreme dangers consumers face in the modern health care system (such as surgical errors, misdiagnoses, or incorrect use of medical equipment and prescribed drugs). There are also many less extreme, but also troublesome, problems that confront many consumers of health care. Consumers are routinely forced to wade through seas of health care system paperwork and red tape, endure unbearably long waiting periods to access care, and withstand callous and intrusive handling from health care providers. Many of these problems occur because the modern health care system has become overly complex, increasingly insensitive, and terribly bureaucratic (Geist & Hardesty, 1992; Landers, 1978; W. J. Smith, 1987). What is worse, the modern health care system is also terribly inequitable and often corrupt, favoring members of privileged dominant cultural groups over marginalized group members, such as the poor, disabled, elderly, those who suffer from stigmatized diseases such as AIDS or mental illness, minorities, and all too often women (Chesler, 1972; Corea, 1977; Diethrich & Cohan, 1992; Fuchs, 1974; J. A. Kelly, St. Lawrence, Smith, Hood, & Cook, 1987; Kosa & Zola, 1975; Kreps, 1986, 1993; Kreps & Kunimoto, 1994; Mendelsohn, 1981; Mondragon, Kirkmann-Liff, & Schneller, 1991; Pashkow & Libov, 1994; Quesada & Heller, 1977; Thornton, Marinelli, & Larson, 1993; Treichler, 1987; West & Dranov, 1994).

Many of the injustices prevalent in the delivery of health care are due to an ingrained hegemonic ideology about the nature of control in the modern health care system. This ideology legitimizes provider authority and control and limits consumer participation in and control over their own health care (Freidson, 1970; Haug & Lavin, 1983; Mendelsohn, 1979). This ideology grows out of widely accepted scientific, technological, and medical beliefs about the nature of health care (sometimes referred to as the "medicalization" of health care) that legitimizes and privileges health care "professionals" as being more important and credible than consumers, systematically disenfranchising and marginalizing the consumers of health care (Hyde, 1990; Kreps, 1993; Landers, 1978; Mendelsohn, 1979).

The modern health care system is designed to meet the needs of health care providers and not consumers. Landers (1978) suggested

> The ideology of modern medical practice has very little to do with the human experience of being sick. It has much more to do with the need of physicians for a conceptual framework that will focus and simplify their work and that will justify the segmented, episodic, superspecialized individualistic character of their work arrangements. (p. 78)

Instead of emphasizing the convenience and comfort of health care providers and administrators, the modern health care system should be designed to serve consumers. Health care delivery will benefit from a "consumer orientation" that focuses institutional attention and resources specifically on the needs and expectations of consumers. A consumer orientation clearly demonstrates respect for the consumer, encouraging active consumer involvement and control of their health care (Arntson, 1989; Haug & Lavin, 1983; Jones et al., 1995; D. H. Smith & Pettegrew, 1986, Sneider, 1986).

THE MARGINALIZATION OF WOMEN IN HEALTH CARE

Inequity in health care is clearly illustrated by widespread marginalization of female consumers by the health care system. Let us examine three major areas of prejudicial treatment of women in health care:

Women's health care complaints are not taken seriously (Corea, 1977; Thornton et al., 1993). Women are often patronized by a health care system that minimizes their symptoms, suggests psychosomatic causes for their health problems, and infers that women's health complaints are ploys for getting attention (Chesler, 1972; Wallis, 1994). There is a:

Pervasive stereotype of the woman as complainer, as someone who manifests her mental woes in physical symptoms, such as the hysteric, the neurasthenic, about whom the physician does not have to be too concerned; her headaches or her chest pains are imaginary. (Wallis, 1994, p. 20)

Because women's health care complaints are not always taken seriously by health care providers, treatment of these health problems are delayed and the health problems women experience often get worse through lack of attention, become quite serious, and demand complex and intensive treatments by many different specialists. This is one of the reasons why female consumers have become so dependent on the modern health care system.

Men are used as the standard in clinical health care research and practice (Matroianni, Faden, & Federman, 1994). Male health problems are taken more seriously than female health problems by the health care establishment, with more concern shown for risks to men's than women's health (Mahowald, 1993). Because of this bias against women, the medical establishment is less likely to be proactive in trying to prevent women's health problems. The history of treatment for heart disease is a stark example of this neglect, where for years heart disease was considered to be a male disease by the health care establishment (Diethrich & Cohan, 1992; Pashkow & Libov, 1994). Over the past 20 years almost all cardiovascular clinical research programs and health promotion efforts were designed for men. Yet deaths from cardiovascular diseases claim more than half a million women's lives each year; the truth of the matter is that today heart disease is a more dangerous and deadly disease for women than it is for men (Diethrich & Cohan, 1992). I wonder if heart disease would be such a serious threat to women if there had been more gender equity in cardiovascular research and treatment.

Women are often subjected to unnecessary and excessive surgical procedures. For example, there is a growing scandal concerning the overuse of hysterectomy as the fall-back treatment for virtually any reproductive tract complaint (West & Dranov, 1994; see also Boston Women's Health Collective, 1992; Fee, 1993; Payer, 1988):

> Hysterectomy has classically been treated as an operation of minor significance by the medical establishment even though recent studies suggest tremendous psychological impact including loss of libido, sexual dysfunction, and depression. . . . In France, approximately one-third the rate of hysterectomies are performed compared to the United States, yet morbidity and mortality rates are similar. (Thornton et al., 1993, p. 191)

It has been estimated that as many as 30% to 40% of all the hysterectomies performed in the United States are unnecessary, with better alternative treatments available (Ammer, 1989; Boston Women's Health Collective, 1992; Lowdermilk, 1995). There are similar scandals brewing concerning the excessive use of cesarean section and radical mastectomy surgical procedures in the Unites States (Dan, 1994; Fee, 1993; Thornton et al., 1993).

The fact that women comprise such a large segment of health care consumers only makes the scandal of gender bias and the fragmentation of women's health care a truly immense health care problem that must be addressed. Gender bias in health care is rooted in the systemic disenfranchisement of the consumer within the modern health care system. Human communication is the primary tool available to consumers to help them gain control of their health care.

COMMUNICATION, HEALTH INFORMATION, AND A CONSUMER ORIENTATION

Communication practices that limit consumers' access to relevant health information enforce hegemony in health care. Interestingly, communication is also the primary process that can equalize power between the providers and consumers of health care by disseminating health information more widely. Health care consumers and providers require relevant and accurate health information (Kreps, 1988a). It is their most important health care resource. With relevant health information, they can demystify many of the complexities and ambiguities of illness and improve the quality of their health care decisions. Information can help both consumers and providers interpret symptoms of illness to discover the causes of ailments. It facilitates diagnosis and helps consumers select from among available treatment options. Armed with relevant health information, consumers can better understand the actions and messages of health care practitioners and they can use this information in establishing cooperative working relationships with their health care providers (Kreps, 1988b). Similarly, relevant information about the health care delivery system can help consumers manage the many complex rules, regulations, and procedures that so often get in the way of effective health care delivery.

Human communication is the primary tool consumers have for gathering relevant health information (J. A. Jones et al., 1995; Kreps, 1988a). The quality of communication between health care providers and consumers dramatically influences the effectiveness of modern health care (Kreps, 1988b; Kreps & O'Hair, 1995). Yet, in current practice human communication is often poorly utilized. An important part of promoting a consumer orientation to health care involves both consumers and providers of health care recognizing the communicative demands of effective health care, coupled with their development of strategic communication skills and strategies to gain access to relevant health information needed to make sense of often complex health problems and health care options to get the most out of health care.

When people are ill, they want action, reassurance, and care without delay. They depend on their health care providers to help them. The more proactive consumers are in communicating and participating with their providers in the health care delivery process, the more the providers can do for them. Recent evidence suggests that the greater consumer involvement is the more likely it is that their health will improve (Greenfield, Kaplan, & Ware, 1985, 1988; Kreps & O'Hair, 1995). Health care consumers must stop being passive recipients of health care; they must stop being patient and start being active participants in the health care process! Consumers (and their advocates) must communicate strategically and assertively to gain relevant health information, share relevant health information, and use communication to fully participate in their health care (J. A. Jones et al., 1995; Kreps, 1993). This active participation in the health care delivery process is similar to what Arntson (1989) referred to as health care "citizenship," becoming a participating citizen of the modern health care system. Citizenship depends on our abilities to use communication as a tool for identifying and avoiding potential health care system perils, making informed health care decisions, and enlisting cooperation from providers in accomplishing our health care goals.

CONSUMERISM AND HEALTH CARE LITERACY

It is very difficult for consumers to participate effectively in health care if they are medically illiterate (J. A. Jones et al., 1995; G. M. Phillips & Jones, 1991). Using health care advice effectively means, at a minimum, that consumers must know the basics of human physiology, have a working medical vocabulary, be able to explain their symptoms accurately and clearly, and understand their conditions well enough to interpret what their health care providers tell them and ask their providers useful questions. Skilled health care consumers actively seek relevant health information. They read and listen in order to keep up to date with key health care innovations, especially those innovations that are most relevant to their specific health conditions.

There are many popular sources of inaccurate health information that act as barriers to health care literacy (J. A. Jones et al., 1995). Books and magazine articles routinely recommend unusual diets, compulsive exercise, megavitamins, and major life modifications as panaceas for all human miseries. Although some popular health promotion strategies may have some merit, uninformed health care recommendations can cause serious harm. Family members, friends, and coworkers routinely recommend remedies to each other, often erroneously, while paradoxically at the very same time well-informed health care professionals armed with state-of-the-art prevention and treatment strategies often fail to provide their clients with relevant health information (Kreps, 1990a).

Interestingly, in a national survey of a representative cross-section of the American public, primary care physicians were identified as the most preferred source of health information, with 84% of the 1,250 consumers surveyed identifying a discussion with their personal physician as potentially their most useful source of health information (Kreps, Ruben, Baker, & Rosenthal, 1987). A related survey conducted with primary care physicians found that while these providers were genuinely concerned with health education (providing their clients with relevant health information), a variety of communication barriers such as lack of training in health education and counseling skills were inhibiting their information dissemination efforts (Maibach & Kreps, 1986). In fact, there is abundant evidence that clearly suggests that current physician (and other health care provider) communication practices fail to supply consumers with satisfactory levels of health information (J. W. Hess, Liepman, & Ruane, 1983; Kreps, 1990a; Newell & Webber, 1983; Orleans, George, Houpt, & Brodie, 1985; Relman, 1982; Wechsler, Levine, Idelson, Rohman, & Taylor, 1983). This implies that to become well-informed, consumers need to actively seek out relevant health information from their doctors and from a variety of other sources.

PROMOTING A CONSUMER ORIENTATION TO HEALTH CARE

One way to emphasize caring in health care is to equalize the roles performed by consumers and providers, encouraging consumers and providers to really relate with one another as human beings (developing a consumer orientation to health care). The modern health care system revolves around the consumer. Without consumers there would be no health care system. Interdependent health care providers and support staff are employed by the health care system to serve consumers.

Professional education and in-service training for health care providers should emphasize the centrality of the consumer in the health care system, illustrating the mutual dependencies between providers and consumers in the delivery of health care. Providers should be trained to engage in sensitive, appropriate, and informative communication with their clients, fulfilling the specific information needs of consumers and empowering their consumers to take control of their health care. Health care providers should use their interactions with clients to identify different effective sources of relevant health information available to consumers, defuse the many challenges and constraints consumers face within the modern health care system, and provide health education for enhancing consumers' health care literacy, helping consumers negotiate their ways through health care bureaucracies and get the most out of health care.

COMMUNICATION AND TEAMWORK

A consumer orientation suggests strategic use of communication by both health care consumers and providers to promote cooperation and the sharing of relevant information. Health care providers depend on the information they can elicit from their clients to diagnose health care problems and to develop and monitor appropriate treatment strategies. Consumers depend on gathering relevant information from their providers to make sense of their health care problems and to evaluate different courses of treatment. Strategic communication must also be used to develop cooperation and coordination between these interdependent members of the health care team. To be effective health care providers and consumers must be able to work together as team members. They must recognize their interdependence and collaboratively work toward promoting health.

RELATIONSHIP DEVELOPMENT IN HEALTH CARE

A consumer orientation to health care also underscores the importance of establishing and maintaining effective health care relationships between the many interdependent participants in the modern health care system. The levels of relational communication competence engendered by health care providers, staff, and administrators performing interdependent health care roles often determines the effectiveness of health care delivery. Relational health communication competence embodies specific provider and consumer knowledge and skills, such as empathic listening, verbal and nonverbal sensitivity, encoding and decoding skills, and interaction management skills (Kreps, 1988b). Complex health care situations demand high levels of relational communication competence between providers and consumers to accomplish health communication goals such as increased interpersonal satisfaction, therapeutic communication outcomes, cooperation between providers and consumers, social support, and health education. Insufficient levels of communication competence will surely limit fulfillment of these important health care goals.

THE SENSITIVITY OF HEALTH COMMUNICATION

One of the most important relational communication competencies relevant to modern health care is the sensitivity of interpersonal communication. Personal communication (communication that demonstrates respect for others) is a humanizing form of interaction that encourages relationship development and cooperation, whereas object communication (communication that demonstrates disrespect for others) is dehumanizing, leads to relationship deterioration, and undermines interpersonal cooperation. There is far too much object communication in modern health care and participants in the health care system should work toward treating one another with respect to promote cooperation and relationship development (Kreps & Thornton, 1992).

CONSUMERISM AND A PROACTIVE APPROACH TO HEALTH CARE

When do we seek health care? Usually when a nagging problem, a pain, an injury, or a recurring discomfort becomes so troublesome that we can no longer ignore it. Most people would rather not deal with these problems; they'd prefer to ignore them, hoping the problems disappear, until pain and discomfort force them to seek care. Most people take a reactive view of health care (reacting to discomfort) rather than a proactive view (planning ahead, trying to avoid health problems, or, at the very least, trying to nip these problems in the bud before they become unmanageable).

J. A. Jones et al. (1995), in their book *Communicating With Your Doctor: Getting the Most Out of Health Care*, advocated a preventive model of health care based on a partnership between consumers and their personal physicians. Together, consumers and providers can plan ahead to avoid serious health problems and work together to address problems that arise. This preventive approach to health care should probably start at an early age with parents teaching their children about the importance of regular checkups and vaccinations to help prevent the onset of serious illnesses. Children should be encouraged to ask their physicians questions about health and health care, making sure they understand the health preserving activities their doctors and other health care providers perform for them, and helping them begin to feel comfortable about actively participating in the health care system and directing their own health care.

The process of choosing health care services is an act of consumership similar to selecting nutritious foods at the supermarket; it is not a simple act. People are rarely taught how to select health care or to use it well. The qualities a consumer should seek in a good doctor are partly personal, partly professional. Courtesy and respect are components of all successful interpersonal relationships. In the medical relationship knowledge and skill are also important.

SHARING RELEVANT HEALTH INFORMATION

Consistent with the consumer orientation to health care, the initial burden of providing information in the medical transaction falls on the consumer. The consumer's complaint should guide the doctor in subsequent investigation. The process of providing information is often complicated by the fact that clients may be worried and emotional about their condition. Doctors must adapt to the particular emotional state of their clients without subverting the accuracy of the examination procedure.

Health care providers should tell their clients where they can access relevant information about their conditions. For example, consumers can consult their public libraries, or if available a local university or medical library. In addition to reference books and health care journals, most libraries have access to computerized databases, like the National Library of Medicine's MEDLINE. There are a great many medical information services available on the internet. The government also has information on most serious diseases available from the Government Printing Office. Local librarians can advise consumers about these resources. In fact, it is the primary job of the reference librarian to help library patrons get the information they seek. If consumers don't understand what they read, they should feel free to ask their doctors to clarify matters, even if this requires another appointment.

Consumers can get information and pamphlets from organizations that provide information on specific conditions. For example the National Cancer Institute operates a toll-free telephone information system, the Cancer Information Service (CIS), which can be accessed from anywhere in the United States at 1-800-4-CANCER. CIS hotline telephone operators will try to answer any questions about cancer and provide referral and treatment information. These hotline telephone operators can also have PDQ database searches conducted for callers to access the latest information about cancer treatment and clinical research being conducted. The best tool in seeking the best health care treatment is relevant information, which will help consumers understand the nature of their health problems and the different treatment strategies available.

CONSUMER ORIENTATION AND HEALTH PROMOTION

A consumer orientation is not only a critical ingredient to effective health care delivery, it is also a prerequisite to successful health promotion efforts. To be effective, health promotion efforts should always begin with a clear consumer orientation (Kotler & Roberto, 1989; Lefebvre & Flora, 1988; Maibach, Kreps, & Bonaguro, 1993). The very best health promotion campaigns rise out of clear recognition of consumers' health needs, problems, beliefs, and behaviors so the campaigns are developed to reflect target audiences' specific concerns and cultural perspectives. Further:

> Effective campaigns appeal to the interests and orientations of target audience members to gain their attention, increase the likelihood they will comprehend and be moved by campaign messages, encourage their participation in campaign activities, and ultimately to enable them to adopt the campaign's strategies and recommendations. (Maibach et al., 1993, p. 20)

A CONSUMER ORIENTATION TO HEALTH CARE

There is a compelling need to firmly establish a consumer orientation in modern health care delivery organizations to address the troubling imbalance of power that systematically disenfranchises and marginalizes health care consumers. Adoption of a consumer orientation should focus institutional attention and resources specifically on fulfilling the physical and psychological needs of health care consumers, equalizing influence and control between providers and consumers, and empowering consumers to make informed decisions about their health care to help promote social justice within the modern health care system. This chapter examines the issue of control in health care and suggests communication strategies to help equalize power in health care by developing and promoting a consumer orientation in the modern health system.

IMPLICATIONS OF PROMOTING A CONSUMER ORIENTATION

Promoting a consumer orientation to health care and health promotion is likely to change the modern health care system in many ways. A consumer orientation should dramatically increase consumer participation in health care while decreasing providers' exclusive control over health care. Communication will undoubtedly become an increasingly important health care process. Providers will depend on their interpersonal communication skills to share relevant health information, make cooperative health care decisions, and coordinate health care activities with their clients. Provider–consumer interactions will become the primary means for conjointly determining health care treatment strategies. Similarly, health promotion campaign planners will depend on communication to gather relevant information from consumers in tailoring their campaigns to meet the specific needs, expectations, and orientations of target audiences of consumers. Effective health care providers and campaign planners will communicate strategic health education messages (through a range of different channels and media) to increase consumers' levels of health care literacy. These changes are very likely to increase the quality of health care and health promotion efforts by informing health care delivery, legitimizing consumer participation in health care, and empowering consumers to make proactive choices to resist health threats and seek health care.

fourteen

WOMEN IN ORGANIZATIONS: PERCEPTIONS OF POWER

Catherine B. Becker

Radford University

Steven R. Levitt

University of Texas at San Antonio

Power is one of the most frequently mentioned themes in organizational research. Research consistently shows that women have less power, status, and prestige in organizations than men (Brass, 1985; Fryer, 1994; Haslett, 1993). Only 6% of the directors of Fortune 1000 companies are women, and less than 5% hold senior management positions (Fryer, 1994). Women with a bachelor's degree or higher make an average of 65 cents for every dollar that men make (U.S. Department of Commerce, 1994). The less powerful positions of women may be a result of women's low accessibility to typical sources of power (Haslett, 1993). Brass (1985) stated that "despite an increased awareness of women's concerns, and associated effort by corporations to hire and promote women, studies still suggest that women have not acquired status and influence comparable to that of their male counterparts in organizations" (p. 327).

This study explores how women in organizations define power; how they perceive powerful men, women, and behaviors in their organizations; and how they relate power to information, computers, and new information and communication technologies (NICTs). A time-based model of power based on the classical scientific definition of

273

power as the rate of doing work is introduced. It also considers whether women with different levels of power perceive power, computers and NICTs similarly.

POWER

Perceptions

Although power is a popular theme in the study of organizations, the definition of power varies widely. Salancik and Pfeffer (1977) stated that power may be difficult to explain, but it "is easy enough to recognize by its consequences—the ability of those who possess power to bring about the outcomes they desire" (p. 3). That is, "Power is simply the ability to get things done the way one wants them to be done" (p. 4).

Discussions on power refer to two main types of power: behavioral and structural. Behavioral power is the actual use of power. In an organization, power is first and foremost a formal and informal structural phenomenon (Burkhardt & Brass, 1990; Pfeffer, 1981b; Smith & Grenier, 1982). One's position in the hierarchy provides access to people, information, and other important resources. Structural power allows individuals to have a wider repertoire of sources and resources using various behavioral tactics. Power also strengthens existing structural configurations. That is, those in power often seek to maintain power by reinforcing existing organizational structures (Burkhardt & Brass, 1990; Pfeffer, 1981b). Structural power is potential power, and behavioral power is its actual use (Brass & Burkhardt, 1993).

A person's power is only determined through perceptions of others who assess their behavior as powerful. As Brass and Burkhardt (1993) noted, "Power is a social phenomenon, dependent on the attributes of others. If behavior is consistent with attributions, then those perceived as powerful are powerful" (p. 121). This implies that an individual's power is only as strong as others perceive it to be and that perception is created either through structural position or interpersonal interactions.

Although there may be different explanations for the disparities between men's and women's organizational power, there are few if any differences in the behaviors of men and women (Brass & Burkhardt, 1993). Rather, women are *perceived* differently even when they perform similar behaviors to men. The same power use will be evaluated differently depending on whether it is enacted by a man or a woman, with the same power use by women being perceived more negatively (Haslett, 1993).

Popular opinion seems to recognize these perceptions. In an article in *Working Woman*, Kaye (1993) said, "For men power always had its rewards, for women its price." She asked, "Is that why we can't picture a powerful woman?" (p. 51). She went on to say, "Powerful women are bound to be isolated from other women" (p. 53). She attributed women's inhibitions about attaining power due to their "mixed feelings about it" and their preoccupation with its costs. The article quotes feminist author and scholar Carolyn Heilbrum, saying that women are afraid of attaining power, "because we have been taught that we are supposed to be loved. And when you have power you have to risk not being loved" (p. 53).

In an article in *Fortune*, Sellers (1996) described 15 leading women from a variety of fields as imbalanced, out of control, and dissatisfied. Her concluding statement reads, "No matter how spectacular the ascent, life at the top is never comfortable" (p. 56). Similarly, in a portrayal of successful women in *Computerworld* L. Wilson (1995) began, "Many women who make it to the top in IS [Information Systems] feel they have to work twice as hard as men to get there. Among the biggest challenges: juggling professional and personal success" (p. 419).

Information and Technology

In addition to perceptions regarding women obtaining and using power, another variable that is relevant to the study of women's power in organizations is information. Brass and Burkhardt (1993) stated that "much of the writing on power characterizes information as a critical resource and a potential power source" (p. 8). Knowledge in organizations has been described as an "inexhaustible source of power" and the ability to "turn knowledge into action and to learn from the consequences of action provides further competitive advantage" (D. Davis, 1995, p. 115). According to Blanchard (1995), "The first secret to empowering people is to share information with everybody" (pp. 11-12).

Those who have a central position in the communication network of an organization have access to an important source of power (Pfeffer, 1981). "Most empirical studies have found that an employee's centrality in an inter-organizational network is related to power" (Burkhardt & Brass, 1990, p. 6). People in central network positions have greater access to, and control over, resources such as information. People in control of resources have others depending on them and therefore are in a position to acquire power.

Network centrality is often an artifact of one's position in the structural hierarchy because one's position inherently gives one access to people and information. However, even people in low, relatively powerless formal structural positions have sources of power available to them. A individual's position in the communication network of an organization is an important source of "symbolic power" (Pfeffer, 1981b) or "relationship power," the power of associations with others and having inside connections (Blanchard, 1995). Such sources of power would include access to people, control over the flow of information, or expertise in an important area that may make them indispensable (Mechanic, 1962).

Women in organizations are believed to have less structural power than men due their systemic exclusion from networks of information (Benokraitis & Feagin, 1986; Haslett, 1993). Women are often not included in men's networks, and thus they are excluded from the dominant coalition (Brass, 1985). Consequently, "both supervisors and non-supervisors perceived women as less influential than men; in addition, women received disproportionately fewer promotions than men" (p. 340). Brass said this may be due to the fact that "men, as the typically dominant group in most business organizations, wish to maintain [their] dominance by intentionally excluding women from informal interactions" (p. 328).

Access to computers and new information and communication technologies (NICTs) have influenced the prominence of an individual in an organization (Contractor & Eisenberg, 1990; Leduc, 1979; Rice & Case, 1983; Sproull & Kiesler, 1986). Women may be able to increase their network centrality, and subsequently their power, by using computers and NICTs to their advantage (Burkhardt & Brass, 1990). Computers are assumed to bring relevant information to people who use it to make decisions and implement action (Clement, 1994). Computers and NICTs may flatten organizational structures and change network centrality, acting as a "democratizing agent" (Burkhardt & Brass, 1990; Fryer, 1994).

Although technology provides an opportunity for power redistribution, it does not guarantee it, as power distribution in organizations tends to be stable rather than dynamic (Burkhardt & Brass, 1990). However, the introduction of new technology creates a dramatic increase in uncertainty, and this may affect the distribution of power in addition to affecting structure. Uncertainty represents an opportunity for employees to gain influence. An individual who is able to reduce uncertainty for himself and others may increasingly be perceived to have expert power. "Thus, early adopters who have the ability to reduce technological uncertainty for others within the organization have what is tantamount to a recipe for increased centrality and power" (p. 107).

Computers and NICTs (such as the internet) may enable women to gain power by providing them access to important information and increasing their network centrality. Burkhardt and Brass (1990) found that early adopters of a new computer system did gain more power than late adopters, and adoption increased communication network centrality. This centrality was significantly related to power, and centrality preceded power. Therefore the total amount of individual influence increased as individual centrality increased. In addition, the new computer system gave individuals more control over their work outcomes. They conclude that early adopters of computing technology will increase power more than late adopters, as early adopters systematically change social networks to acquire information to reduce their uncertainty about the change. They can then increase power by reducing uncertainty for others.

On the other hand, when those already in central, powerful positions are early adopters, existing power structures will be reinforced. Sometimes more information translates into disempowerment. In one case, people at or below middle management were given access to more information that allowed them to make their own decisions without consultations with upper management. The ironic side effect of the new job empowerment was a disempowerment. A reduction of middle management was created as decision making was pushed down the hierarchy (Clement, 1994). Therefore, women may not advance beyond middle management because their jobs might either be phased out or their lower management position job descriptions might widen without the benefit of hierarchical advancement or the pay increases that result from such advancements.

Women and Technology

When women use computers and NICTs, it is frequently in lower paid and less prestigious jobs. For example, the majority of women employed by computer companies tend to cluster in less powerful staff jobs, as they often do in other industries (Fryer, 1994). Women appear to be over represented in word processing jobs in offices, whereas men are over represented in the higher paid design and programming jobs (Arnold, Burke, & Faulkner, 1982; Barker & Downing, 1985). Computer and technology innovation in the printing and insurance industries bifurcated women's work, creating lower power clusters and amplifying gender structural position inequalities (Baran, 1985; Cockburn, 1981).

In addition to negative perceptions regarding the relationship between women and power, the relationship between women and technology is also perceived negatively (Fryer, 1994; Turkle, 1988). A person's attitude toward new technology is partially forecasted by social information (Rice & Aydin, 1991), and women often find their technical competence questioned, whereas men do not (Fryer, 1994). Women seem to be afraid of using information technologies to their advantage (Frissen, 1992). Collins-Jarvis (1993) cited 10 studies which have found that "females are more likely than males to maintain negative attitudes toward the importance of computing and their own abilities to use computers." She also cited research that demonstrates the ways that the "socially constructed characteristics of computing technologies as well as the social practices which surround the implementations of these technologies act to limit their appeal to females" (p. 51).

There appear to be significant gender differences in expectations about new technology (Hackett, Mirvis, & Sales, 1991). Women are more skeptical about the effects of technology on worker benefits, job upgrading and pay increases, and also expectations regarding their chances to get ahead. Women may be opposed and adverse to information technology itself (Turkle, 1988). Hackett et al. (1991) suggested that existing gender inequalities might be heightened if women do not perceive that computers and new communication technologies can be used to their benefit. Thus, women may refrain from utilizing computers and NICTs to gain access to and control over information that could potentially increase their power.

Although some researchers are optimistic about the ways that women could use computers and NICTs to their benefit, others are not. Van Zoonen (1992) said that if we limit our analysis to reasons why women aren't adapting NICTs then the "technology is thought of as an independent factor affecting social relations without being affected by them. Such a mild form of technological determinism prevents an appreciation of the social relations in which technology is embedded" (p. 14). She pointed out that the relationship between gender and technology is as much a cultural issue as it is a social and economic phenomena of unequal access and recommends that new research concentrate on disclosing and analyzing the conditions in which NICTs and gender meet.

Frissen (1992) called for examining use patterns along with acknowledging that women are not passive victims in relation to technology. She further suggested examining the role technologies may play in the construction of gender relations. Other researchers tend to believe that any attempt by women to adapt to technology will merely replicate unequal power relations (Zmroczek, Henwood, & Wyatt, 1987).

However, neither the "adaptation" or the "gender/power" perspective adequately addresses the case of women in organizations where many women's jobs require them to use computers and NICTs. Women working in organizations are usually required or expected to use computers and new information technologies as part of their jobs due to office automation (Faulker & Arnold, 1985; Kramarae, 1988).

Time

In order for a woman in an organization to achieve the outcomes she desires, she must not only have the ability to get things done the way she wants, but she also must know how to get things done (information) and be able to get things done when she wants them to be done. That is, she needs control over time. Even if women working in an organization may desire to learn how to use computers and NICTs to increase their access to information and perhaps, their power, they may not have the time to do so. Women's desire for time may be also be indicative of the conflicts they encounter due to combining household and professional tasks. Although men's contributions to household work are increasing, the amount of time men spend contributing to the domestic workload is still significantly less then that of women; statistics show that women are working an average of 15 hours longer a week (Hochschild, 1989).

According to Hessing (1991), "The inability to control the duration and flexibility of office hours, the complexity of social relationships which must be negotiated, and the excessive time demands of a dual workload undermine women's autonomy and power in administering time use" (p. 629). She said, "Time can be perceived as a means by which contemporary organizations control clerical workers" and this functions "as potentially serving the needs of patriarchy as well in managing and facilitating men's schedules and their relative power, both in homes and offices" (p. 630).

Knights and Odih (1995) cited five studies that suggest that men and women tend to use time differently due to their distinct life situations. They said that all of these show that women's temporalities are different from those of men because women's time exists in relation to the time demands of significant others. This significantly inhibits women's power to make decisions about how their time is used (Davies, 1990). Due to negative perceptions women may have regarding power, they may be reluctant to admit that they want more power, but might easily admit that they want more information or time.

An operational definition of power based on Woelfel and Fink's (1980) suggestion that power be defined by using the classical scientific definition, "the rate of doing work" (p. 200) provides a useful time-based model for research. Qualitative researchers could use the model to analyze data for hidden indicators of women's aspirations for power. For example open-ended interviews could be analyzed for associations between words like power, information, time, and want. This is based on theories that claim word patterns are symbols that represent the shared beliefs and attitudes of a group (Whorf, 1956; Woelfel & Fink, 1980).

Woelfel (1992) developed a method, CATPAC, that systematically analyzes text for co-occurring words and patterns.

CATPAC generates a neural network of word patterns via cluster analysis (Doerfel & Barnett, 1996; Woelfel, 1992). Unlike traditional content analysis, which usually imposes categories on data, CATPAC uses the strength of relationships among the concepts to train a network that simulates human cognition.

CATPAC allows complex relationships to be represented while assuming no prespecified type of relationship. For example, if there is an association between information, time, and power, a neural network would generate patterns that might reveal this association whereas direct questioning may not. Furthermore, a neural network can discover relationships in the partial or missing data, allowing for smaller sample sizes (Meilich, 1996).

METHOD

This study explores women's perceptions of power and powerful behaviors in organizations, and their aspirations regarding power. Additionally, this research describes how women relate power to information, computers. and NICTs, and how they perceive powerful men and women. It also considers whether women with different levels of power perceive power, computers and NICTs similarly.

In order to begin to answer these questions, open-ended interviews were conducted with 30 women working at different levels in a variety of organizations in the Eastern and Western United States. Twelve of the women interviewed held clerical positions, 13 were managers, and 5 were executives. Table 14.1 describes the types of positions held by the respondents.

The women were asked to describe their experiences with computers and NICTs, to talk about power in their organizations, and to consider the ways that power and NICTs may be related. Each interview took approximately 30-40 minutes and was transcribed. Ninety pages of single-spaced transcripts were analyzed for frequently occurring words, patterns, and themes using the CATPAC computer program (Woelfel, 1992). Closely related terms such as "I" and "me," "company" and "organization," "work" and "job" were combined. Articles' interjections, conjections, and verbal fillers were removed from the analysis.

The combined data set was examined in order to identify important words and concepts. The time-based model allowed messages about needs for information and time to be analyzed as potential indicators of a desire for power. The responses of executive, management, and clerical women were analyzed separately to see if these women had different perceptions of power.

Table 14.1. Description of the Interviewees.

Organization	Role			Total
	Clerical	Managerial	Executive	
Insurance	5	3	1	9
Retail	3	2	2	7
Government	1	1	0	2
Education	1	2	0	3
Social service	0	1	0	1
Nonprofit	0	1	0	1
Medical	0	1	0	1
Legal	1	1	0	2
Investment	0	0	1	1
Real estate	1	0	0	1
Communication	0	1	1	2
Totals	12	13	5	30

RESULTS

Power and Time

The five most frequently mentioned terms included "make decisions," "recognition," "information," "unlimited communication," and "ability to move." Other words and phrases used to describe power include: "influence," "confidence," "responsibility," "control," "good management," "knowledge," "intelligent," "straightforward," "honest," "sensitive," "nicest people," "easy to get along with," "ability to get other people to do what you want," "to boss," "credibility," "task-oriented," "higher up," "monitoring," "have people with them," and "in control." These terms suggest the communicative styles associated with behavioral power, and this list is similar to the behaviors associated with interpersonal power (Brass & Burkhardt, 1993).

The relationship among 11 frequently used terms appears in Figure 14.1. The figure was generated using the Galileo system, a software program that provides a method to transform the strength of the associations between each pair of concepts into a set of coordinates that can be plotted in multidimensional space (Barnett & Woelfel, 1987; Woelfel & Fink, 1980). In the Galileo system the farther two concepts are away from one another, the less association there is between them.

Figure 14.1 shows that the terms "want" and "power" were the farthest from each other. Most of the women interviewed seemed

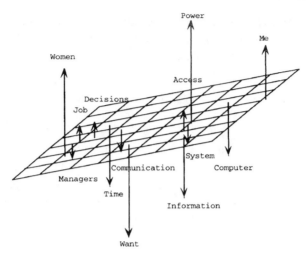

Figure 14.1. Galileo plot of associations among the 11 most frequently used terms

uncomfortable talking about power in general, and did not say that power was desirable, although one of the executives mentioned that she had become "comfortable" with it. When asked to define or describe power, the women frequently answered that they did not know or tried to avoid the question. For example:

> Can we skip to the next question? Lets see. Gosh, describe what it means? Hopefully we're not going to use up your whole tape while I stammer around for words. Can I come back to this one?

Responses such as these were common and support the assumption that women tend to perceive power negatively. The closest concept to "power" was "access." This association was made in narratives such as:

> And while we have access to quite a large number of systems, there's a lot of things that we're not authorized for. And I remember feeling very frustrated—there's a system I'm trying to get into, and I can't seem to get into it. And it's not that it's any secretive information; it's not that only certain people need to look at it. This is something that is vital that I need to use to get the job done, but I can't get the system security.

Stories about access referred not only to information but also to the ability to move through the organization both hierarchically and even physically:

I feel that a lot of times we're chained to our desks. And the way I recognize powerful behavior is, I guess, like my supervisors who are able to walk around.

When the data was analyzed separately, the strongest association made by both the clerical and managerial worker's was between the concepts "want" and "time." Executives made the strongest association between the words "want" and "information." However, women from the other groups also said they wanted information:

I don't know what secret this is about withholding information. Some people really do feel a lot of power from it. They make a point to let you know they have known this. I don't care, just let me know what's gonna impact us, but also if you want your people to develop so that they don't have microvision, they're just looking at that little tunnel. If you want them to be able to analyze the full picture, you have to give them the information.

In regard to time, the narratives show that these women did seem to perceive their time demands in relation to others. Furthermore, they seemed to discuss power itself in terms of the perceptions of others. For example:

Sometimes you're gonna have to *take time* off, because you have a sick child. There's pressure *not to take that time* off. There's a pressure to be at work. It's like, gee, you can't be here again. It's like, what do you do, you're trying to juggle it, *you want to be accepted* in your little world. And you want to *be thought of as effective.* (emphasis added)

and:

I think that sometimes women feel the pressure to change the way that they normally behave in terms of sensitivity, because it's almost *looked at* as not being professional, or maybe it's *looked at* as being a little weak, you're too easy, just get it done, get it done, we *don't have time for this.* (emphasis added)

and:

In my capacity as secretary to Mr. X, I feel at times I have *to take care of* Mr. X as well as my husband and home and all that. It can be stressful to find the balance [the time] and do everything perfectly. (emphasis added)

The ability to get things done quickly was also perceived to be an indicator of power:

For example if you need a light bulb changed an your in Mr. X's office and you call building maintenance they are right over . . . but if she needs her computer or light bulb changed it may be weeks before someone shows up.

Comparisons of Powerful Men and Women

Distinctions between powerful women and powerful men were made using terms that describe women managers as, "more sensitive," "more people-oriented," "not as pushy," and "more able to see the big picture." As with the narratives regarding time, narratives about powerful women were described from the point of view of significant others rather than the respondent herself:

A woman, if she's pushy, and tries to drive her point across, she's *seen* as pushy still.

or:

There is still a trend to feel that powerful women are aggressive, demanding, and that they, and these are negative qualities to me . . . they are back biting whereas the very same qualities in a man *would not be considered* so. (emphasis added)

or:

As long as you wear a skirt, you will always *be viewed* as a babe in a skirt, regardless of the qualifications you have . . . you have to be a hard woman . . . you have to present that demeanor. (emphasis added)

Rather than the norm, powerful women were described as extreme:

Career-oriented, goal-setting, overachievers a lot of women in the workplace feel they have to do an extremely good job because they are women and this places a lot of stress on them.

and:

Sometimes what I see in powerful women is that they have taken it to the extreme. They are so caught up with in the fact they are women, they are so into proving themselves they loose touch with who they are.

The association of the terms "women" and "managers" were often found in narratives about power differences between men and women and in regard to descriptions of what it means to be a powerful woman. The use of the term "women managers" may indicate that some women see the role of managers as one that separates female managers from other women providing some support for Kaye's (1993) claim that powerful women are perceived of as isolated from other women.

Women with Different Amounts of Organizational Power

Table 14.2 shows that the words "I/me" were the most frequently used terms by all three groups; executive women used them most often, followed by managerial women. This may indicate that power is related to a strong self-concept. Executive women used the word "I/me" the most, followed by the word "power." Executives also used the name of their organization the most frequently. The words "don't" and "know" were used most frequently by clerical women, followed by managers and least often by executives. This provides some support for the assumption that power is related to information.

Table 14.3 shows the unique words that appeared among the top 50 most frequently used terms of each group. Cluster analysis of the executive data revealed the following associations: "power me work," "don't computer," "comfortable top." Managerial clusters included: "send information down," "me computer," and "computer communication." Clerical clusters included "I don't know," "computer work," "different system," and "managers information."

Technology

Cluster analysis of the entire data set revealed other co-occurring terms, including "I don't know," "women managers," "women work," "work computer," "me computer," "little power," "feel good," "able learn," "meeting top," "decisions managers," "computer information," "don't access," and "system access." The most frequently occurring phrase, "I don't know," was typically used in responses to questions about the relationship between power, computers, and NICTs, as well as women's ability to use the technology to their satisfaction. The co-occurrences of words such as "don't access," "don't computer," and "able learn" also appeared in discussions of not being able to access a system or information due to security, a woman's position in the organizational hierarchy, or because she did not have enough time to learn how. This supports the analysis of Frissen (1992), who claimed, "One of the crucial points that has been made in feminist perspectives on technology is that women do not have the same access that men do" (pp. 34-35).

Markus (1990) said that "access devices" such as personal computers and modems are a precursor to women successfully adopting

Table 14.2. Comparison of Language: Ten Most Frequently Used Terms.

Terms	Role Clerical	Managerial	Executive
Me/I	24.0*	29.0	38.0
Power	2.5	3.3	6.2
People	5.2	5.1	4.7
Work	3.9	4.4	4.1
Women	3.0	3.1	3.6
Know	7.4	5.4	3.6
Organization	0.0	0.0	3.4
Don't	5.3	3.3	2.8
Technology	0.0	0.0	2.2
Computer	4.2	3.9	2.1
Information	2.6	2.5	0.0
Time	0.0	2.0	0.0
System	2.6	0.0	0.0

*Numbers represent the percentage of utterances from women playing a particular role that contained the term. For example, 24% of the utterances from women in clerical roles contained the terms "me" or "I."

Table 14.3. Unique Words Among the Three Groups.

Clerical	Role Managerial	Executive
Managers	Professional	President
Run	Internet	Meetings
New	Send	Group
Position	Students	Comfortable
		Top
		Terms
		Whole
		Example

an interactive technological system. Research has shown that males are more likely to gain access via computer classes and membership in computer-centered organizations, and to own or regularly use a personal computer (Chen, 1987; Dutton, Rogers, & Jun, 1987; R. D. Hess & Miura, 1985; Rogers, 1986). Collins-Jarvis (1993) explains that lack of access makes it difficult for females to try innovations (such as computers) without investing considerable time or money.

Although this study has provided evidence that power may be linked with information, the relationship between power and the use of computers or NICTs is not clear. Clerical workers used the word "computer" the most; executives used the word "computer" the least. Cluster analysis showed that the executives associated the terms "don't" and "computer." This is contrary to the assumption that computers and NICTs are directly related to power. Rather, some of the data suggest no relationship, and other data suggest an inverse relationship. This was discussed in several of the narratives. For example:

> The more powerful you are . . . the higher you are in the food chain, the less likely you are to use a computer.

and:

> Close supervisors, people just immediately above me who have power are very sensitive to regulations of Organization X and not very connected, I don't think, to those kind of new directions [the possibilities of the World Wide Web and the internet].

and:

> One day I told him, "Come on let me show you how to get on the computer." And he looked at me and said, "If I wanted to that, I wouldn't need you. I hire people to run computers for me."

She continued:

> In order to be a secretary you have to know how to use a computer, but in order to be a director its not a requirement . . . and so there's this ghettoization of technology users from decision makers who are up higher. If you put all the directors in the company on computers I would bet you some of them wouldn't know how to turn the damn thing on.

However, several of the women seemed to think that although computers and NICTs were not linked to power in the past, the next generation of powerful people will use them:

I think that information is power and that's what technology allows you to have your hands on. It's definitely the wave of the future. There's no going back and it's only going to get more and more that have the information have the power.

Although comments such as this were typical, none of the women reported that they could or would use computers or NICTs to empower themselves.

CONCLUSION

This chapter has examined the perceptions of women in organizations regarding power. Although it is not possible to make generalizations based on this research because the sample is not representative, the findings identify possible directions for future research. The study indicated that women with different levels of power might not perceive power similarly and that women with more power may have a stronger self-concept. Some women are reluctant to discuss power or they talk about power in terms of how significant others are likely to perceive them. Power may be associated with information, but not necessarily with computers and NICTs.

We have demonstrated how a time-based model of power could be used to analyze qualitative data. In this case, the model examined narratives for hidden desires for power. This study also showed that even if women in organizations tend to be reluctant to admit that they desire power, they still seek two of its main benefits: time and information.

A time-based model of power could also be used to analyze quantitative data. For example, quantitative researchers may ask women in organizations how much time they need to accomplish all their goals and compare it to the amount of time they report they have. Future researchers could apply the model to analyze the amount and kinds of information women need to accomplish their goals in the time that is available. A sample of men working in organizations at similar levels could be used as a baseline for comparison.

fifteen

MULTIPLE STAKEHOLDERS
AND SOCIAL RESPONSIBILITY
IN THE INTERNATIONAL
BUSINESS CONTEXT:
A CRITICAL PERSPECTIVE*

Stanley Deetz

University of Colorado

No one familiar with the international business situation today needs to be told that contemporary issues of responsibility are complex and critical. They range through important issues such as human rights, environmental protection, equal opportunity and pay for women and various disadvantaged minorities, and fair competition. Such broad issues become instantiated in activities such as using prisoners as workers, moving operations to environmentally less restrictive communities, offering and taking bribes and payoffs, creating environmentally unsound or wasteful products, closing of economically viable plants in takeover and merger games, growing income disparity, declining social safety nets, malingering harassment, maintaining unnecessary and unhealthy controls on employees, and advocating consumerism.

Many of these issues are complicated and heightened in impact owing to transportation and information technological developments

*Portions of this chapter have been adapted from the following prior publications: Deetz, 1995a, 1995b, 1996, 1998; Deetz, Cohen, & Edley, 1997.

289

and the concurrent growth of internationalization of business. The complex, high-speed business environment is not terribly conductive to value debate and the type of value-based decision making that benefits the wider community (see Deetz, 1995b). Further, both globalization and the rise of outsourcing and interlocked small businesses reduce many common means of encouraging or requiring business responsibility and create social surveillance nightmares. And further yet, the massive growth and consolidation of commercial corporate ownership and sponsorship of mass media restrict and distort public knowledge and discussion of responsibility issues.

At the same time the highly visible presence and importance of responsibility issues has created a much more acute academic, corporate and public interest in responsibility issues (e.g., Watson, 1991). Not since the late 1960s has responsibility been of such concern. Few today see business as either socially benign or benevolent. Even middle managers—the organization men—of a past period are questioning their own easy loyalty and are asking more serious social questions (Heckscher, 1995). Nevertheless, the popularity of such discussions are easily coopted into more or less responsible "green" and "social" marketing. Perhaps it should come as little surprise that in this situation value, moral, ethical, and aesthetic considerations are taking on additional significance. Organizations are beginning to be evaluated by criteria richer than profitability. And Gergen (1992) is hardly alone in arguing that organizational research and theory needs to be evaluated more by questions like "How shall we live?" than by verisimilitude and methodological rigor.

Until recently, organizational communication scholars generally have not shown much interest in responsibility issues. None of the texts and few of the scholarly articles prior to the 1990s offered any sustained discussion. Virtually no one in communication studies, until the emergence of the critical communication theory writings, situated responsibility as a central issue in the design and conduct of organizations. Nearly always responsibility was a personal choice issue for managers. Thus, nearly all the responsibility laments were directed toward the need for "good" as well as effective leaders and concern that the "good" social stewards of the past had somehow gone away.

Much of the problem in discussing ethics today rests in the continued reliance on conceptions of business and responsibility, which provide little guidance during a period involving fundamental social changes and the centering of much of life in the economic context. These conceptions and practices include both those based in traditional beliefs and values and those based in rational discussion and instrumental reasoning. The former assumed relatively stable and homogeneous communities and the latter relatively predictable relations between actions and consequences as well as equal opportunities to engage in such discussions. Neither of these conditions hold today in large areas of human endeavor.

When business leaders shared communities and community standards with workers and consumers, there were similar warrants in responsibility arguments. The complexity of multiple communities with multiple standards make discussions more difficult. Further, the links between cause and effects are strained. Most serious social problems have multiple interactive causes, only some of which are business decisions. Even the most clearly responsible choice can have negative unintended and unforeseen side effects. We must realize that all business decisions are made in conditions of complexity and uncertainty; responsibility issues are no exception.

My position is fairly straightforward but at some distance from most contemporary discussions. Our economic conceptions of the workplace are woefully inadequate for developing responsible and effective production. It is not that our leaders are irresponsible, nor that they lack moral guidance from others, nor that they have considered productivity at the expense of social values. The processes of organizational decision making, although heavily value-laden, do not include a sufficiently representative set of values to make responsible decisions for the community, nor to make the most productive use of resources. The call for greater responsibility is less the application of a new social standard than a transformation of organizations to allow more decisional voices and value debate and negotiation. Clearly to me responsibility rests in communication rather than in moral standards. Morality is based in communication practices rather than being a basis for them (Apel, 1979; Deetz, 1990, 1992a).

To develop this theme, I first argue that workplaces are appropriate places for value debate. Second, I show that individual ethics, marketplace choices, and government regulation all provide weak value guidance to workplace decision making. This is largely a result of looking external to the organization for moral guidance. Third, I review what critical communication theories of organizations have shown us regarding open value discussion in the workplace. And finally, I argue that a reformed "stakeholder" conception of workplaces can enhance the application of critical communication theory to the workplace for the sake of greater responsibility and more effective production. Such a conception can (a) provide a unified way of understanding the complex processes of organizational life, (b) direct the evaluation of existing organizational forms and activities, and (c) provide guidance for the education of members and redesign of organizational structures and practices.

Let me be clear from the start: I am not antibusiness nor antiprofit. I firmly believe that good business can be done in workplaces which are positive social institutions providing a forum for the articulation and resolution of important social conflicts regarding the use of natural resources, the production of desirable goods and services, the development of personal qualities, and the future direction of society. By focusing primarily on narrow economic outcomes (usually profitability), the broader social and economic effects of our way of making business decisions have been missed as well as creative (and adequately profitable) work processes.

THE WORKPLACE AS A SITE OF RESPONSIBILITY

The commercial business context is a significant site of responsibility. Within such sites, in most societies, crucial decisions are made for the public regarding the use of resources, development of technologies and products, and working relations among people. Increasingly social/political decision making in family, community, and state processes is replaced by economic decision making organized in corporate practices (Deetz, 1992a). Corporate practices and propaganda have significant affects on social conceptions, values, and personal self-definitions.

Organizations have inherited in society roles and effects far broader than their economic conception acknowledges. The presumption of a purely economic realm with the questions of moral and good passed off to the state, religion, or private person obscures these roles as does the conception of organizations as mere tools for the production of goods and services. Value questions on behalf of the world community rest at the heart of the contemporary business enterprise. The economic conception is misleading for several reasons.

First, neither managers nor market economy are economically rational (see Gorz, 1987; Schmookler, 1992). Dominant groups gain considerably from treating their conceptions and practices as economically rational and value neutral. Concepts such as efficiency, effectiveness, and performativity have been treated as if they were goods or ends in themselves without recognizing that their quality is grounded in the ends they serve and ultimately in relation to some conception of social good (Carter & Jackson, 1987). Effective and efficient toward what? And whose and what interests should count for how much in formulating goals (Cameron & Whetten, 1983)?

Second, although perhaps done for economic reasons, organizational colonization of the private realm and influence on the state have considerable social effects. Modern corporations have developed processes, some intentional and others not, for colonizing the life world through political action and various forms of cultural management, often soliciting employee's self-colonization on their behalf (see Deetz, 1992a, 1998). The problem is not just the instrumental reasoning of managers but their size and clout with no competing institutions to moderate or counterbalance their effects. Corporate economic effects are felt in worker's lives, childrearing practices, income distribution, and general economic cycles. Such public decisions in a democracy require public discussion. The home and community are dependent on corporate money, corporate goods, and corporate stability. The workplace does not just produce goods and services but meaning. In fact, given commercial dominance, the meaning of life has often been reduced to the accumulation of goods, the only apparent certain thing in an uncertain world.

Finally, commercial organizations in most Western societies have been given many of the legal rights and legal standing of persons. The rights of a person and citizen clearly carry some of the responsibilities.

THE WEAKNESS OF EXISTING SYSTEMS OF RESPONSIBILITY

With the international business situation, we have entered a new moral and ethical situation with new responsibilities, and we need a new discussion. The enlightenment legacy emphasized the sequestering of different realm of life. Values, emotions, and beliefs were placed in the private realm. With this positioning, traditional community-based values no longer directed the entire system but were relegated to the home and local communities, and ethical responsibilities where given to the individual (see Deetz, 1995a). Choices for the direction of society as a whole were placed in the public sphere largely organized in the state and guided by democratic principles. And science and commerce became conceptualized as value-neutral technical systems guided by instrumental reasoning. Although conceptually science and commerce could be guided by and placed in the service of private and public goals, the 20th century has witnessed the gradual "rationalization" of both the private and public realms and a reversal of these relations (Habermas, 1984; Lyotard 1984; MacIntyre, 1984; Weber, 1978). System goals replaced life goals, and performativity rather than social good became the primary means of evaluation of social practices. As I detailed in my discussion of corporate colonization (Deetz, 1992a), business activities were seen as rational and the individual and cultural values as well as the state became increasingly subservient to and enticed to support organizational goals.

Despite the evidence of disenchantment and corporate colonization, common sense, along with most popular discussion of responsibility, provide us with three enlightenment-style ways of accomplishing responsible workplace choices. Each are backed by legal statutes and social practices that make starting a new and more productive consideration of organizational responsibilities difficult. The first rests in the private realm, and is based on the inculcation of community values and reasoning processes in the leaders of organizations. The second rests in the public realm and is based on the development of shared values and systems of regulation. The third rests in the systems realm and is based on marketplace choices representing the values of specific consumers and collectively of the social community. In looking at these it is clear why common sense fails us so completely in discussions of responsibilities and why a thorough critique of each is necessary before we can start a more productive discussion.

RESPONSIBILITY IN INDIVIDUAL CHOICES

In traditional society, the community developed basic values and expectations and these were maintained through active socialization. In one account, the decline of business responsibility can be linked to the decline of communities. At the least, corporate leaders today appear to have little sense of allegiance to peoples or communities. Many studies of organizations have documented the development of a technocratic consciousness (e.g., see M. Alvesson, 1987; Fischer, 1990). Such studies indicate a narrowing of conceptions of rationality, a tightening of control systems, and a loss of social responsibility. Other studies have indicated that with the growth of multinationals a kind of manager "more distant, more economically driven . . . more coldly rational in their decisions, having shed the old affiliations with people and place" (Reich, 1991, p. 77). However, the apparent loss of responsibility, I would argue, arises more from the type of values pursued than the absence of values. The proclaimed presence of a new superrationality often hides the value-laden and personally interested rationalities that invade manager's decisions—economically rational for whom and in regard to what? It is not just the coldness and distance that is of issue, but their rationality. Managers have been excused from moral scrutiny based on their perceived neutrality or at least economic rationality, and they have carefully used their attachment to science to support this image. Clearly managers are not value-neutral nor simply economically rational; they make decisions in conditions of uncertainty and rely greatly on decisional routines.

However, can community values instilled in managers be advanced in workplace decisions? I doubt that we would want this even if we could. First, commercial organizations of the past have not been terribly responsible, perhaps even less so than the ones of today. Even if recovery were possible, I question the responsible character of many traditional communities. For example, owing to the vast oppression of women in many cultures, male domination has not only been accepted in many cultures but protected through generations of exclusion, institutional domination of women, and physical violence toward women (including rape, murder, and maiming of women and young girls). Even acknowledging the Western ethnocentrism of universal human rights claims, clearly most human rights "violations" occur in "strong" traditional communities. And industrial and postindustrial societies owe much of their continued "glass ceilings" and various relatively subtle forms of "human rights" violations in sexual, class, ethnic, racial, physical, and age discriminations maintained in their cultural traditions. Male domination is a characteristic of most traditional communities and community values have a decisive patriarchal character.

Even if strong traditional communities could provide positive ethical conceptions and action, however, such systems require three conditions rarely present today: agreement, surveillance, and social consequences. Especially in closed traditional communities, agreement was easy to come by. The community's way of seeing, thinking, valuing, and acting had little competition and the community's particular mode of being could easily be treated as the preferred way of nature itself. The growth of science and global contact undermines such a naive faith. If the community's way of being is understood as a set of historical choices and alternative communities are readily available to members, much of the spontaneous voluntary compliance disappears. As the arbitrary and discriminatory nature of many community standards becomes clear, legitimacy is often lost and embarrassing questions are asked regarding who benefits from these standards. Such issues are clearest in feminist writings.

It is not only agreement that is strained. Surveillance of member conduct is difficult in complex institutional settings, especially in workplaces that often maintain a proprietary cloak over member behaviors. Further, the private/public split developed in the Western world limited the domain in which community standards were considered relevant. Even if surveillance were possible, the social consequences associated with violation are weak. The large complex communities of today grant much anonymity and even if one were held accountable to a relevant community the possibilities of moving unscathed, or even as a hero, into a new communities are great—a lesson seen over and over again in looking at saving and loan officials, actors in the Watergate scandal, insider traders, and so forth. Even professional codes appear fairly weak as members slide from one profession to another in instances of violation.

Further, in the corporate context the increased importance of images and symbolic events leave individuals with little support for or faith in community standards. Jackell (1988) perhaps chronicled this best in his description of moral decision making in corporations:

> What, however, if men and women in the corporation no longer see success as necessarily connected to hard work? What becomes of the social morality of the corporation—the everyday rule-in-use that people play by—when there is thought to be no fixed or, one might say, objective standard of excellence to explain how and why winners are separated from also-rans, how and why some people succeed and others fail? What rules do people fashion to interact with one another when they feel that, instead of ability, talent, and dedicated service to an organization, politics, adroit talk, luck, connections, and self-promotion are the real sorters of people into sheep and goats? (1988, p. 3)

Not only are individuals in the corporate context in a difficult place regarding the possibility of rational choices, the same dilemmas exist for corporate officials on behalf of the corporations.

In the absence of surveillance and social enforcement, community standards have been augmented by a belief that good behavior pays off in the long run. Unfortunately in the international business world of today, there is no long run (see King & Cushman, 1994). In the open system of modern commerce, time is irreversible and relevant. Systems rapidly transform and no one is around to realize the long-term consequences. Not only is the notion of time difference from our classical and commonsense models, highly complex systems have highly complex action chains, hence the consequences of particular choices are virtually impossible to determine.

In conditions of community decline, homeless managers, cynical employees, reduced surveillance, and complex causal action chains, it is of little surprise that many businesses turned to "shared value" and "cultural management" programs. Largely, although these tried to replace values present in earlier times from strong communities, most have been developed more to increase compliance to corporate policies and self-surveillance than to increase larger responsibilities (Alvesson, 1987; Deetz, 1998).

RESPONSIBILITY IN PUBLIC CHOICES

Given the failure of community-based values and community inculcation of values, the enlightenment offers the public realm as the place of collective choices. If common goals and values can be found, governmental policies and policing can lead to greater business responsibility. This logic has led to the liberal alternative in most societies looking to governmental intervention to protect the environment, create economic stability, protect disadvantaged groups, provide health care and other social services, and stimulate appropriate growth. Although state political processes are significant and have provided important workplace protections, the hope that ethical and responsible decision making can be accomplished by value codification in governmental and other public regulation is dim. The problems exist at both ends of the equation: Universal or shared values and goals (and the commitment to them) are hard to find in the complex national and international communities of today, and even if they could be found, governmental interventions and regulations based on them are filled with difficulties.

The Problem of Universal Standards

For years people have sought a common set of values that could serve as guidance for social choices and grounding for social intervention. Generally three tacks were taken to found shared values—a universal religion, a human essence, and cultural universals. Owing to the rather obvious ethnocentrism of a privileged or universal religion, most scholars have pursued the latter two directions. Grounding values and responsibility in an essence sought an understanding of distinctly human qualities and argued that these served as categorical or inalienable rights. Kant's categorical imperative—that every person should be treated as an end and never as a means—represented the most discussed and advanced position. Much of the human rights discussion today maintains a similar reasoning process. Such principles have aided the development of civil liberties and granted protection to oppressed people, but have been rarely applied to international corporations. One can hardly imagine a strategic management program or personnel department where people are treated as anything but means. The search for cultural universals has fared little better. Universals have been difficult to find, to guard against claims of ethnocentrism, and to apply to commercial organizations (Waltzer, 1987).

For example, recently a "new foundationalist" literature has arisen focusing more on human tasks and bodily experiences (see M. Johnson, 1993). MacIntyre (1984) and his followers (see Mangham, 1995) have been most explicit in the applications to business enterprises. MacIntyre, in opposition to the individualistic, rational models of organizational ethics, suggested that one of the legacies of individualistic, enlightenment models is decreased emphasis on community as an essential part of life. In this way the "new foundational" literature has a clear communitarian quality. He hoped to recover some shared foundation in which individuals are grounded in a connected community of shared traditions. He suggested that it is within this connected community (local, national, and international) that organizational goals, as well as ethical and moral decisions, can be made by organizations and communities that will represent the values of the collectivity rather than merely the values and ethical concerns of "powerful" individuals. Integrated and complete people grounded in connectedness and tradition are able to engage in a discussion aimed at a more rational social order.

Frederick (1986) followed a similar analysis in considering business responsibility in his corporate social rectitude (CSR3) model. He suggested that moral and ethical questions arise principally during periods of social stress. The most significant stresses occur when "the norms or standards defining and controlling human consciousness, human community, and human continuity are affected" (p. 127). Frederick's strategy for dealing with the decisions that must be made (either by actions or inaction) in these contexts is to pursue core values and normative principles that are deeply embedded in general culture or humankind itself. The strategy seems to work in the right direction, but there are a number of difficulties in pursuing substantive values of this sort. Many of the moral platforms he discussed are distinctly Western and perhaps male in character and philosophers for generations have had difficulties in suggesting universal ones (see Mangham, 1995). Further, the problem remains of applying them to specific contexts where the same value is open to alternative interpretations, and different core values suggest different actions. Further still, the core values are often treated as if they were immune to the processes of everyday life, where the dominant speakers and messages of the time might have considerable influence on the nature of these values and their interpretation. And finally, rarely do these conceptions entail an adequate theory of power. How does one get from a concept of shared values to political action?

In the absence of shared core values, in an international context it is always unclear whose community standards are relevant. Neither ethnocentrism nor the cosmopolitan, "When in Rome do as the Romans" offer much help. Ethnocentrism arises whenever any community's values are made universal. Much of this arises in the contemporary discussion of human rights. Although those working from a "human rights" stance have exercised much clout in the reduction of practices that most of us consider repugnant, the concept of human rights is itself a kind of community standard. Most conceptions follow Western ideals and rarely have such conceptions taken on violations of democracy or mental and physical health by western corporate interests. In fact, the economic sanctions that are central to human rights advocates' clout would rarely be effective against these units. Ethnocentrism, even in the name of human rights, favors dominant groups in dominant societies. Further, when such standards have been applied to dominant groups, the intended ethnocentrism shows more clearly, as when the U.S. withdrew its support of UNESCO.

Of course, as is shown in discussions of market economy, the relativism of the cosmopolitan offers little more. Problems of violence and environmental damage stretch across communities. And unfortunately in the world of commerce, communities granting greater member protection are penalized as jobs and resources flow to areas encouraging more individual opportunism. International business by the least ethical standards is common, but offers little.

The Problems of Regulation

Even if common standards could be found, the hope of regulation based on them is not great. First, in regard to the internationalization of business, not only must the standards be universal, but so must the policies and enforcement. As we have already seen with piecemeal national and community policies and enforcement, the competition among communities and nation states for businesses (and their jobs) lessens the capacity of political units to regulate corporate activities. For example, tough environmental standards virtually assure that some companies will move to places with fewer standards rather than clean up their work processes. This condition leads to a downward spiral with communities lowering standards to compete with each other. The structure of competition assures corporate financial interest dominate political discussions and decisions without the business community having to coordinate their activities or exert any specific political force. Domination is structural rather than chosen, intentional, or conspiratorial. Communities world wide have eroded tax bases as they compete with each other to lure or hold businesses. As communities tax individuals to make up for this, they continue to lose legitimacy and reinforce the impression that corporations are more efficient. Positions supported in political processes consistently lose to specific corporate interests. Nations of crooks like Switzerland and Aruba in money market, Brazil in beef production, and China in manufacturing have international effects with weak international regulation.

Further, even if possible, regulation becomes a pricey way to accomplish ethical and responsible behaviors. Most often the attempt is not only expensive but a failure. As detailed elsewhere, governments usually lack the resources, microknowledge, capacity, or legitimacy to provide proactive value-based regulation (see Deetz, 1995b, 1995c). Most often they provide crude guidance at best and are left cleaning up the mess of socially irresponsible actions of others. Further, the entanglement of dominant groups (especially commercial ones) with regulatory agencies leaves little hope that policies and enforcements will match values more widely shared in a society (see Laumann & Knoke, 1987). And further yet, as anyone who has dealt with a building department knows, ultimately codification and regulation leads to red tape and generic solutions that defy good common sense in their particular applications. Each of these difficulties undermine any liberal hope of government successfully guiding responsible behavior.

No present government appears to have either the desire or power to make business responsible. Although the relation of governmental interventions and corporate decisions are not to be developed here, a brief list of problems can show why state intervention provides little hope. Even though regulation and incentives can influence system choices, most significant choices will remain within corporations themselves. Even if they wanted to, governments cannot micromanage companies. Government lacks both the popular legitimacy and capacity to make or require more proactive corporate choices, governmental policy is largely influenced by corporate leaders and lobbyists, and rarely do public agencies have enough information soon enough to participate actively in corporate processes to make them more publicly accountable. Additionally, regulation enviably leads to a costly double bureaucracy—a public one to establish guidelines and monitor compliance for public good, and a private one that struggles to keep up with the paperwork and find loopholes and avoid regulation. The application of endless bureaucratic rules constantly runs counter to good situational judgments and common sense and is only matched in social stupidity by the energy and imagination used by corporate managers in pursuing narrow self-interests at the expense of public health, public information, and positive social development.

Public ideology, highly publicized problems in a few public projects, corporate control of media, and government self-criticism all argue for a minimalist government. Not only is the government seen as corrupt and inefficient in contrast to private industry, the public defines the government in a supportive rather than competitive role regarding business. Increasingly the government is seen as appropriately supportive of managerial decision making under the guise of public economic well-being. The media "watchdog" function heightens the effect. Government criticism sells. Government as an institution is constantly criticized both for regulation and for failure to adequate protect the public, sometimes regarding the same issue on the same program. The public sees and understands welfare and visibly violent crime, but knows virtually nothing of corporate welfare and white collar crime.

Election politics aid this relation. Although governments make relatively few of the decisions that create or end recessions, they are clearly held accountable for them. Although consumers and managers make the decisions, the political party in power gets voted out. In relatively rare cases of economic dislocation the government has been able to direct development toward a proactive vision of the future. Companies have largely made the decisions and the government has mopped-up the problems. The growing problem of temporary workers is a good example. As companies increase flexibility and reduce costs by hiring temporary workers, the public is left with a growing price tag for retraining, health care, and other standard worker benefits. Profitability and legitimacy of business is advanced whereas the government is seen as more and more costly, and hence inefficient. And this is just the tip of the iceberg.

Corporate debt and economic dislocation from takeovers and mergers, the desertion of the cities, violent media content, unreasonable health care costs, and so forth have massive social effects and costs. In each case, professional and managerial groups have made fortunes, and governments to their demise have picked up the growing price tag. The public does not seem to understanding this relation. We all seem more bothered by big government than the corporate activities that require government regulation and cleanup. We all seem to understand that we pay for government actions, but we do not understand that we also pay for corporate bureaucracies and waste. Corporations effectively tax without representation for their mistakes, their own benefits, and managerial interests.

Further, as upper managers continue to use marketplace ideology to extend control to fulfill self-interests and redistribute income upward, governmental solutions are costly attempts to overcome the most damaging effects and support the most disadvantaged groups—small wonder that the average person feels cheated and drained. Unfortunately the cynicism often accompanying this leaves the average person a weaker, more reactive political participant and more self-interested employee, thus reinforcing the cycle of disempowerment and justifying control. As I argue later, acquiring meaningful and appropriate participation at work helps create better citizens as well as better social and economic decisions. One way to get government out of business is for business managers to become firmly committed to public values. However, available evidence leaves me with little faith in benevolent monopolies. The better alternative is to get the public into the decision-making process.

RESPONSIBILITY IN MARKET CHOICES

Given the difficulty of community-based standards of responsibility and the integration of different community values to direct a sense of global responsibility, many have looked to the marketplace as technical system directive of social choice. If this could work, we would not need to debate values or regulate social choices and the work process would not have to be actively participatory. Multiple value systems could be integrated into collective choices guided by individual action. The public would get what it is willing to pay for. If stakeholders were not happy with managerial decisions, they will eventually vote with their feet or dollars. If a dollar equals a vote and everything is either a cost or a resource expressed in monetary terms, as long as corporations wish to be competitive, and managers employed, they will be responsive to public desires. If the public does not respond, then it gets what it deserves.

In the redefinitions implicit in this solution, social and political relations are reduced to economic relations, democracy is reduced to capitalism, citizens to consumers, and discussion to buying and selling. Unfortunately, each of these transformation entail a constraining of people's capacity to make decisions together and reduce potential human choices to choices already available in the system as controlled by others. The marketplace does not work as a way of representing social values. As many have shown, free-market capitalism was never intended to represent the public well; it was intended to describe how to make a return on financial investment. The idea that market choices accomplish representation and money measures it is very naive. Markets are value-laden rather than neutral representation processes, but the values are rarely explored (see Schmookler, 1992). Market place decisions provide among the most thin and ethnocentric ethical systems available (Deetz, 1995b, 1995c). A few basic problems of using the market to represent stakeholder interests are readily apparent.

First, because money is not equally distributed, "dollar voting" is a highly skewed representation process. Do we want a democracy with some people having many more votes than others? Second, not all things translate equally well into monetary terms; therefore they are not well represented. The more humanistic qualities of service and the jobs of many women are good examples. Certain values thus are never expressed—they might be expressed politically in a democracy but not economically in the system. Third, hidden costs and longer term benefits get no expression. For example, long-term damage to the environment or people's skills are often not represented, the costs are absorbed by the community or person, and no one may provide things that are only beneficial in the long run. The underpricing of all natural resources until they are nearly depleted is a serious invisible social cost as are long-term negative effects on communities. Destroyed communities make bad markets. For example, as U.S. companies line up to get in on the Eastern European market, they seem to overlook the costly destruction of the inner-city economies back home (which often would provide a better investment).

Fourth, the market is a weak and biased system of representation for a number of reasons. Market pricings and accounting practices are often carefully controlled by groups in power and managers often choose personal gains over economically rational choices for the company. Mass advertising and information control inevitably distort "dollar voting" (e.g., vendor driven sales dominate many industries, and who can equally advocate nonpharmaceutical health care?). In addition, choice in markets is directed only toward existing products with no assurance that the public can influence what is available in the future (e.g., who assures the development of desired but probably unprofitable drugs?). The problem with the economic vote is that all the costs are not charged to the one who makes the money and alternative choices are not available for the community to buy.

Finally, consumers are rarely adequately informed of the relation of their purchases to social responsibility issues and many of the causal action chains are so complex that responsible choices are difficult to assess. Informed "politically correct" shoppers, for example, struggle over the use of paper or plastic bags only to be confronted with so many contingencies and unpredictable codeterminative elements that no preferred choice seems possible. Anyone who has been involved in social actions knows the rude awakenings that come with following out any action program. Some of this is actual complexity. The relative environmental costs of recycling versus new product production is hard to determine and many struggled to determine just what American-made entails (How much produced in the United States? Just assembled?). Some is informational. How many can tell the difference between old growth and renewable lumber or know which companies are run by all employees? And some is false complexity and deceit such as "recycled" paper which is 10% postconsumer, rain forest wood products labeled as "oak" in stores, or employee-"owned" companies that are run by managers.

The myth of market economy is that competing self-interests work themselves out for the benefit of all. However, in practice the domination by the market economy reverses the relation of economic and social relations making social relations subordinate to the presumed self-regulating market. In such a representation system all competing human interests become reduced to economic interests, and economic interests become organized in the sole direction of payoffs for financial investors. The market has not provided an invisible hand; rather, we have a selective, ideologically based, quite visible managerial hand. Despite managers' massive public relations campaigns for market-based decisions, they consistently attempt to control the market and limit its effects on them. Open markets are for others and the illusion of markets hides the real mechanisms of self-interested political control.

CRITICAL THEORY AND PLACING RESPONSIBILITY IN THE WORKPLACE

Following this discussion, I think that it is clear that one of our problems has been the attempt to situate responsibility issues and discussions outside the workplace. They are placed in the individual, community, market, or government with each impinging on workplaces as if workplaces were value neutral. Although gains in responsibility can be had by improving each of these systems, such as increasing social representation in market or providing more international regulation, ultimately the problem remains. Such changes do not get to the heart of the structure and practices of the workplace. It is for this reason that I believe that a critical theory of the workplace is essential to increasing social responsibility of business. The intent is not to advocate a particular conception of responsibility, but to transform the processes of decision making within workplaces. This leads to the focus on a critical communication theory. Allow me to briefly review what critical theory has offered the analysis for those who are less familiar with this body of work before I turn to my expanded "stakeholder" model (see Alvesson

& Willmott, 1992 and Alvesson & Deetz, 1996, for more extended reviews).

Critical researchers see organizations in general as social historical creations accomplished in conditions of struggle and power relations. Workplaces are largely described as political sites, thus general social theories and especially theories of decision making in the public sphere are seen as appropriate. Although organizations could be positive social institutions providing forums for the articulation and resolution of important group conflicts over the use of natural resources, distribution of income, production of desirable goods and services, the development of personal qualities, and the direction of society, various forms of power and domination have led to skewed decision making and fostered social harms and significant waste and inefficiency. Either explicit or implicit in their presentation is a goal to demonstrate and critique forms of domination, asymmetry, and distorted communication through showing how reality can become obscured and misrecognized. Such insights help produce forums where the conflicts can be reclaimed, openly discussed, and resolved with fairness and justice. The research aims at producing dissensus and providing forums for and models of discussion to aid in the building of more open consensus. Of special concern are forms of false consciousness, consent, systematically distorted communication, routines, and normalizations that produce partial interests and keep people from genuinely understanding or acting on their own interests.

The central goal of critical theory in organizational communication studies has been to create societies and workplaces that are free from domination and where all members can contribute equally to produce systems which meet human needs and lead to the progressive development of all. Studies have focused both on the relation of organizations to the wider society and their possible social effects of colonization (rationalization of society) and domination or destruction of the public sphere (Deetz, 1992a), and on internal processes in terms of the domination by instrumental reasoning, discursive closures, and consent processes (e.g., Alvesson & Willmott, 1995; Clair, 1993a; Forester, 1989, 1993; Mumby, 1987, 1988, 1993a). They tend to enter their studies with a priori theoretical commitments which aid them analytically to ferret out situations of domination and distortion. Critical studies includes a large group of researchers who are different in theory and conception but who share important discursive features in their writing. They include Frankfurt school critical theorists (see Alvesson & Willmott, 1992; Fischer & Sirianni, 1984; Mumby, 1988), conflict theorists (Dahrendorf, 1959), some structurationists (Banks & Riley, 1993; Giddens, 1984, 1991; Howard & Geist, 1995; Riley, 1983), some versions of feminist work (e.g.,

Ferguson, 1984, 1994; Iannello, 1993), some Burkeans (Barker & Cheney, 1994; Tompkins & Cheney, 1985), and most doing labor process theory (Braverman, 1974; Burawoy, 1979, 1985; Knights & Willmott, 1990).

Some critical theorists have a clear political agenda focused on the interests of specific identifiable groups such as women, workers, or people of color, but usually they address general issues of goals, values, forms of consciousness and communicative distortions within corporations. Their interest in ideologies considers disadvantaged groups' difficulties in understanding their own political interest, but is usually addressed to people in general, challenging consumerism, careerism, and exclusive concern with economic growth. Compared to Marxism, critical theory is not antimanagement per se, even though one tends to treat management as institutionalized and ideologies and practices of management as expressions of contemporary forms of domination. Two principle types of critical studies can be identified in organization studies: ideological critique and communicative action.

IDEOLOGY CRITIQUE

Most of the critical work has focused on ideology critique. Analyses of ideologies show how specific interests fail to be realized because of people's inability to understand or act on their own interests. Some identified ideologies are group specific and others are held by people in technological-capitalist society in general. Ideological critique is guided by a priori researcher conceptions and aims at producing dissensus with the hope that the recovered conflicts and explicit concern with values will enable people to choose more clearly in their own interests.

The earliest ideological critiques of the workplace were offered by Marx. In his analyses of the work process he focused primarily on practices of economic exploitation through direct coercion and structural differences in work relations between the owners of capital and the owners of their own labor. However, Marx also described the manner in which the exploitative relation is disguised and made to appear legitimate. This is the origin of ideology critique. Clearly the themes of domination and exploitation by owners and later by managers has been central to ideology critique of the workplace in this century (see works as varied as, Braverman, 1974; Clegg & Dunkerley, 1980; Edwards, 1979). These later analyses became less concerned with class-based coercion and economic explanations through focusing on why coercion was so rarely necessary and on how systemic processes produce active consent (e.g., Burawoy, 1979, 1985; Deetz & Mumby, 1990; Gramsci, 1971; Kunda, 1992; Vallas, 1993). Ideology produced in the workplace would supplement ideology present in the media and the growth of the consumer culture and the welfare state as accounting for worker's and other stakeholders failure to act on their own interests.

Four themes reoccur in the numerous and varied writings about organizations working from such a perspective: (a) concern with reification, or the way a socially/historically constructed world would be treated as necessary, natural, and self-evident; (b) the suppression of conflicting interests and universalization of managerial interest; (c) the eclipse of reason and domination by instrumental reasoning processes; and (d) the evidence of consent.

Reification

In reification a social formation is abstracted from the ongoing conflictual site of its origin and treated as a concrete, relatively fixed entity. The illusion that organizations and their processes are "natural" objects protects them from examination as produced under specific historical conditions (which are potentially passing) and out of specific power relations. Ideological critique is enabled by the elite-driven search for reifications in everyday life. The resultant critique demonstrates the arbitrary nature of "natural objects" and the power relations that result and sustain these forms for the sake of producing dissensus and discovering the remaining places of possible choice.

Universalization

Lukács (1971), among many others (see Giddens, 1979), has shown that particular sectional interests are often universalized and treated as if they were everyone's interests, thus producing a false consensus. In contemporary corporate practices, managerial groups are privileged in decision making and research. The interests of the corporation are frequently equated with management's interests. For example, worker, supplier, or host community interests can be interpreted in terms of their effect on corporate—universalized managerial—interests. As such they are exercised only occasionally and usually reactively and are often represented as simply economic commodities or "costs"—the price the "corporation" must pay for labor, supplies, or environmental cleanup (Deetz, 1995b). Central to the universalization of managerial interest is the reduction of the multiple claims of ownership to financial ownership. In ideological critique managerial advantages can be seen as produced historically and actively reproduced through ideological discursive practices in society and in corporations themselves (see Bullis & Tompkins, 1989; Deetz, 1992a; Mumby, 1987).

The Eclipse of Reason

Habermas (1971, 1984, 1987) has traced the social/historical emergence of technical rationality over competing forms of reason. Habermas described technical reasoning as instrumental, tending to be governed by the theoretical and hypothetical, and focusing on control through the development of means-ends chains. The natural opposite to this Habermas conceptualized as a practical interest. Practical reasoning focuses on the process of understanding and mutual determination of the ends to be sought rather than control and development of means of goal accomplishment. However, in the contemporary social situation, the form and content of modern social science and the social constitution of expertise align with organizational structures to produce the domination of technical reasoning (see Alvesson, 1988; Fischer, 1990; Mumby, 1988; Stablein & Nord, 1985). To the extent that technical reasoning dominates, it lays claim to the entire concept of rationality and alternative forms of reason appear irrational. To a large extent studies of the "human" side of organizations (climate, job enrichment, quality of work life, worker participation programs, and culture) have each been transformed from alternative ends into new means to be brought under technical control for extending the dominate group interests of the corporation (Alvesson, 1987). The productive tension between the two becomes submerged to the efficient accomplishment of often unknown but surely "rational" and "legitimate" corporate goals (see Wendt, 1994).

Consent

"Consent" processes occur through the variety of situations and activities in which someone actively, though often unknowingly, accomplishes the interests of others in the faulty attempt to fulfill his or her own. The person is complicit in his or her own victimization (Laclau & Mouffe, 1985; see Clair, 1993a, for examples). As a result, rather than having open discussions, discussions are foreclosed or there appears to be no need for discussion. The interaction processes reproduce fixed identities, relations, and knowledge, and the variety of possible differences are lost. Thus, important discussions do not take place because there appears to be no reason for them. Consent often appears in direct forms as members actively subordinate themselves to obtain money, security, meaning, or identity, things that should result from the work process rather than subordination. In fact, both the subordination and requirement of it hamper the accomplishment of these work goals. Critical organizational communication research during the 1980s and 1990s includes a rather wide body of studies showing where culture and cultural engineering may be described as hegemonic (e.g., Alvesson,

1987; Deetz, 1985; Knights & Willmott, 1987; Mumby, 1988). Other researchers have shown how normative, unobtrusive, or concertive control processes develop in organizations and subvert employee participation programs (see Barker, 1993; Barker & Cheney, 1994; Barker, Melville, & Pacanowsky, 1993; Barley & Kunda, 1992; Bullis, 1991; Bullis & Tompkins, 1989; Kunda, 1992).

Several limitations of ideology critique have been demonstrated. Three criticisms appear most common. First, ideology critique appears ad hoc and reactive. It largely explains after the fact why something didn't happen. Second, the elitist is often criticized. Common concepts like false needs and false consciousness presume a basic weakness in insight and reasoning processes in the very same people it hopes to empower. The irony of an advocate of greater equality pronouncing what others should want or how they should perceive the world "better" is apparent to both dominant and dominated groups. Third, the accounts from ideology critique appear far too simplistic. Many studies appear to claim a single dominant group that has intentionally worked out a system whereby domination through control of ideas could occur and its interest could be secured. Clearly domination is not so simple. Certainly the power of ideology critique can be maintained without falling to these criticisms, and most studies today carefully avoid each problem. Largely this has become possible with the development of Habermas' theory of communicative action.

COMMUNICATIVE ACTION

Whereas earlier critical studies focused on distortions of consciousness, thought and meanings, Habermas' (1984, 1987) work since the late 1970s has concentrated on distortions in communication processes. This project retains many of the features of ideology critique, including the ideal of sorting out constraining social ideas from those grounded in reason, but it envisages procedural ideals rather than substantive critique and thus becomes quite different from traditional ideology critique. It also introduces an affirmative agenda, not based on a utopia, but still a hope of how we might reform institutions along the lines of morally driven discourse in situations approximating an "ideal speech situation" (see Mumby, 1988). Organizational communication scholars have developed these ideas to support more participatory communication and decision making in organizations and to display power-based limitations on organizational democratization (Cheney, 1995; Deetz, 1992a, 1995b; Forester, 1989, 1993; Harrison, 1993). From a participation perspective, communication difficulties arise from communication practices that preclude value debate and conflict, that substitute images and imaginary relations for self-presentation and truth claims, that arbitrarily limit access to communication channels and forums, and that then lead to decisions based on arbitrary authority relations (see Deetz, 1992a and Forester, 1989, 1993, for development).

Basically, Habermas argued that every speech act can function in communication by virtue of common presumptions made by speaker and listener. Even when these presumptions are not fulfilled in an actual situation they serve as a base of appeal as failed conversation turns to argumentation regarding the disputed validity claims. The basic presumptions and validity claims arise out of four shared domains of reality: the external world, human relations, the individual's internal world, and language. The claims raised in each are respectively: truth, correctness, sincerity, and intelligibility. Thus we can claim that each competent, communicative act represents facts, establishes legitimate social relations, discloses the speaker's point of view, and is understandable. Any claim that cannot be brought to open dispute serves as the basis for systematically distorted communication. The ideal speech situation must be recovered to avoid or overcome such distortions.

Four basic guiding conditions are necessary for free and open participation in the resolution of conflicting claims. First, the attempt to reach understanding presupposes a symmetrical distribution of the chances to choose and apply speech acts. This would specify the minimal conditions of skills and opportunities for expression including access to meaningful forums and channels of communication. Second, the understanding and representation of the external world needs to be freed from privileged preconceptions in the social development of "truth." Ideally, participants have the opportunity to express interpretations and explanations with conflicts resolved in reciprocal claims and counterclaims without privileging particular epistemologies or forms of data. The freedom from preconception implies an examination of ideologies that would privilege one form of discourse, disqualify certain possible participants, and universalize any particular sectional interest. Third, participants need to have the opportunity to establish legitimate social relations and norms for conduct and interaction. The rights and responsibilities of people are not given in advance by nature nor by a privileged, universal value structure, but are negotiated through interaction. The reification of organizational structures and their maintenance without possible dispute and the presence of managerial prerogatives are examples of potential immorality in corporate discourse. Finally, interactants need to be able to express their own authentic interests, needs, and feelings. This would require freedom from various coercive and hegemonic processes by which the individual is unable to form experience openly, to develop and sustain competing identities, and to form expressions presenting them.

In general most strategic or instrumental communicative acts have the potential of asserting the speaker's opinion over the attempt to reach a more representative consensus. In such case an apparent agreement precludes the conflict that could lead to a new position of open mutual assent. In cases where the onesidedness is apparent, usually the processes of assertion/counterassertion and questions/answers reclaim a situation approximating participation. The more serious issues in workplaces posed by modern analyses are the invisible constraints to mutual decision making in organizations. Here strategy and manipulation are disguised and control is exercised through manipulations of the natural, neutral, and self-evident. In a general way these can be described as "discursive closure" and "systematically distorted communication." Both concepts become central when we turn to look at the processes of domination in modern corporations and consider alternative communicative practices (see Deetz, 1992a, chapter 7).

The most frequent objections to Habermas, and those who have followed his work, is that he has overemphasized reason and has only a negative view of power which hampers both the conception of social change and seeing the possible positivity of power. Although Habermas has been criticized for focusing too much on consensus at the expense of conflict and dissensus, implicit in his analyses is the recovery of conflict as an essential precursor to a new consensus and the perpetual critique of each new consensus as interaction continues. What Habermas does well is give an arguable standard for normative guidance to communication as a critique of domination, even if his position is distinctly Western, male, and intellectual (see Benhabib, 1992, for a discussion of these problems and ways of recovering the critical thrust of his work). The participative conception of communication describes the possibility and conditions for mutual decision making and also provides a description of communication problems and inadequacies.

A DIALOGIC STAKEHOLDER MODEL

The development of a critical communication theory in the study of workplaces has added much to understanding organizational dysfunctions and how socially irresponsible decisions come about. Less has been done proactively in providing new workplace models to enhance their economic and social decisions. The applications become far clearer and more likely by moving from an owner/manager to stakeholder model of organizations. When critical theory concepts have been applied to organizations that are still conceptualized using an owner/manager model, the concepts are usually co-opted to less than critical goals.

Freeman has provided the most widely discussed stakeholder theory or "constituency theory" (Carroll, 1989; Freeman, 1984; Freeman & Gilbert, 1988). This theory suggests that corporations are, or should be, stewards or servants to the larger society. For Freeman (1984), the larger community to which the organization is wed is defined in terms of two levels of stakeholders: those identifiable groups or individuals on which the organization relies for survival such as stockholders, employees, and customers, and those more generally classed groups or individuals who can affect or are affected by organizational policies and work practices. It is out of this web or network of relationships that the corporation establishes with the larger community that R. E. Freeman (1991) suggested these diverse groups have a "stake" in the corporation and ethical conduct is therefore "obligatory and expected for maintenance of the relationships between the organizations and its constituents" (p. 94).

This ethical conduct and maintenance of the organizations' relationships with the community, Freeman suggested, are accomplished through conversation. In this way of approaching organizational research, the organization is conceptualized as part of the community, not separate from it. Thus, when making organizational decisions, Freeman suggested that the values and ethical standards of the community should be both represented and considered. Economic information regarding the state of the marketplace is not sufficient when making organizational decisions that will undoubtedly affect the community. Thus, emotions, bodily processes and pleasures, factors that are individually based, and in part communally shaped, that are often thought to be outside of the organization, privatized, and limited to rational decision making, become important concerns. As such, these factors that are marginalized in rational actor models play a more central and critical role in stakeholder-based approaches to workplace responsibility.

The modern corporation has a variety of stakeholders with competing interests within and between each of them resolved in internal decisions. Like the critical theorists, recognizing the existence of multiple stakeholders with competing legitimate interests suggests that corporate organizations are fundamentally political, rather than simply economic. These political processes are often closed, however, owing to a variety of practices that produce and privilege certain interests—principally managerial—in both public decision making and in the production of the type of person that exists in modern organizations and society.

Traditionally, stakeholders were considered external to the company and management groups attempted to strategically control them for the sake of "company" (though most often managerial) objectives (see Deetz, 1995b). The standard approach of management is based on narrow values and strategic control processes. The key element of transformation is for management to consider stakeholders as legitimate parts of the company. The management role then becomes the coordination of the various stakeholder needs and objectives. With a concept of service to all, "good" management attempts to generate creative decisions that meet what otherwise might appear to be incompatible objectives. Evidence supports this as a wise as well as appropriate change. The presence of diverse goals, rather than creating costly conflicts and impasse, creates the conditions whereby limited decisional frames are broken and the company learns. In the process the faulty bases of reoccurring conflicts are exposed and synergistic energy is created. Management groups need to make economically based decisions positively influencing profitability. However, corporations are not only economic-based institutions. And, importantly, taking seriously the multiple goals of stakeholders fosters creative decisions that can improve economic viability. If the variety of stakeholder interests were considered, alternative goals would serve as competitive measures of organization

Following stakeholder consideration as well as enlightened economic interests many companies have developed forums where stakeholders could be represented, but most of these have been contrived in ways that reduce the actual value representation—they lack an opportunity for voice. In order to realize dialogic ideals, both forums and voice must be considered in assessing representation.

INVENTING FORUMS FOR DISCUSSION

As seen, in traditional analyses social values entered into corporation decisions in four ways: through consumer value representation in purchasing choices, through governmental tax guidance and regulation, through manager's voluntary commitment to social values, and through investment choices of workers and capital holders in employment and stock purchases. As shown, each of these is a weak form of representation because of structural limitations and social changes (investors want short-term payoffs, managers have removed themselves from community). None of them foster the type of social interaction that leads to innovative solutions to conflicting stakeholder values and objectives. However, additional forums are developing. In many companies the opportunities for employee participation in decision making are much greater today. The customer focus of many companies provides contexts for direct consumer representation in ways that have been missing for some time. Many companies have partnering arrangements with suppliers and large customers. The growth of communication and information technologies allow for more frequent, sustained, and interactive contact among groups.

These activities have made companies more responsible, but each of these have been limited in important ways. For example, employee involvement plans have more often been developed to increase compliance, commitment, and loyalty than to broaden value debate and increase innovation. Most often the involvement is limited to application decisions and do not include representation in company-wide planning and social goal formation. Customer focus groups often function more to solicit information on tastes and pricing to aid sales rather than to determine what consumers really want. And rarely are social values solicited at all except again as they might affect sales. The new technologies are being developed in most cases to extend the corporate influence outward rather than to provide the public with better information on which to make their decisions or to enable the public to participate in corporate decision making. Most representation forums are used by management to suppress or diffuse conflict arising from stakeholder groups rather than foster genuine conflict and debate for the sake of company improvement. Nevertheless, with concerted effort these mechanisms can be transformed and utilized for quite different ends. A first step to increasing dialogic communication and stakeholder representation is the expansion of these means.

INCREASING VOICE

However, the current problem is not only the lack of sufficient opportunity for stakeholder representation. Often, as argued, the interaction itself is systematically distorted. This is referred to as a lack of voice (Gordon, 1988). The stakeholder can speak but, owing to contrived and flawed understandings, the representation is skewed. There are several ways this happens. In general, as shown by critical theorists, a prior social construction (a kind of image) stands in the place of real people in a real situation. Such constructions contain embedded values that are not disclosed. Because the construction is treated as the reality it is not open to negotiation, nor are alternative value premises considered. And generally attention is directed away from the embedded values to shared "neutral" ones. Most of my attention has been directed to how this happens to employees, especially in professional (knowledge-intensive) workplaces, but a similar analysis would follow for other stakeholders.

Here we can consider four type of social constructions regarding employees that can limit voice and thus can be considered to limit ethical processes. Each of these social constructions could be the result of open interaction, held temporarily and continuously revised in ongoing micronegotiations. They limit voice, however, when they become fixed and taken for granted, hence closed to negotiation. They violate Habermasian ideal in specific situated ways. When a stakeholder either wittingly or not accepts these construction we have present what is called *consent*. Consent designates those cases when a stakeholder enacts values that are not his or her own in what often appears to be a free act of self-representation. The stakeholder demonstrates complicity in his or her own disregard. In my various studies of knowledge-intensive professional service groups, consent processes were a routine and costly part of much of daily work (see Deetz, 1998). Each type of consent was common.

The first involves the construction of the actors. In general, voice is reduced through the fixing of roles and the reduction of personal complexity. For example, the division of labor has largely created separated realms of knowing and expertise. The success of "teams" indicate some of the price paid for this separation in traditional bureaucracies, but self-managed teams at best have only overcome part of the difficulty. The loss of voice is often even more subtle and pervasive. People have multiple identities and conflicting needs. An individual has many identities and conflicting aspirations arising from identities like being a parent, citizen, and softball player, as well as an employee. Corporations tend to sequester these other identities or elicit their support on behalf of managerial objectives. Thus, if considerations arise for the employee as a parent or citizen they are to be suppressed in favor of the employee identity. This suppression is not only costly to the individual, but also steals from the company the richer set of values that might guide corporate practices. A wide range of forms of thinking, emotions, moral principles, and values are thus set aside. The employee stakeholder in these cases speaks as a "partial" person reducing representation and value debate. Women especially, but also gradually more men, are beginning to gain voice and enrich decision making through challenging such limited conceptions. Such changes can be facilitated in many ways.

Second, despite the moves to decentralization and attacks on bureaucracy, most companies still have rather fixed structures, especially when it comes to major decisions. Workplaces that have shared authority have shown impressive gains even on most standard productivity measures. The ability to continuously renegotiate authority relations based on shifting needs and points of expertise is critical in changing environments. Voice is always limited if discussions happen within rules and authority relations rather than being about them. If stakeholders are to be partners in meeting the needs of all, it cannot be a partnership of unequals. Compliance, consent, and loss of voice are characteristic of all fixed social relations.

Third, voice requires that stakeholders are informed. In most cases the information available to stakeholders is manufactured by management groups and is both limited and skewed. Even if management does not intentionally distort stakeholder understandings, most options and data reported were produced from the same limited set of values and assumptions that more generally drive management decision making. If stakeholders are to overcome managerial limitations, they must challenge the values embedded in company information and knowledge. If this is understood, communication is no longer seen as the transfer of information or decision making with information (the standard views in most companies). Communication must be about the processes by which information is produced. Measurement is an increasingly dominant part of modern management with the impact of TQM and the general development of what Power (1994) called the *audit society*. The temptation is to let measurable outcomes substitute for important discussions where, for example, "quality" is reduced to "standard" rather than "good." Efficiency measurements cannot replace discussions of values regarding what is being measured and what is being efficiently produced.

Accounting theorists and groups working with social accounting principles are becoming much clearer about the values embedded in standard accounting practices. However, all information is fundamentally value-laden. The choice of linguistic distinctions producing categories of people (e.g., secretaries and administrative assistants), the euphemism for what things are called (business expenses or indirect salaries), the forms that are used for reports (including what is collected and what not, as well as the categorical divisions), and the creation of spurious casual relations are only the more obvious aspects of information creation. When people use information they consent to the values on which it is based and voice is usually lost if these are not their values. Opening information production activities to stakeholder discussion is a critical element of overcoming consent and gaining voice.

Widespread sharing of information is of little help if the activities of information construction are left closed and invisible.

Finally, voice is hampered by discussion that focuses on the means rather than the ends. Many modern organizations have developed a logic that emphasizes efficiency or effectiveness based on measurable indices. The means of goal attainment often become goals in themselves. And people often become treated as mere means of goal attainment rather than ends themselves. Unfortunately, in doing so the actual outcome goals become increasingly fixed and invisible. One becomes fixed on increasing performance measures without asking what is sought, its value, or alternative ways of accomplishment. The company operates like people who treat earning more money as an end without asking whether they are actually getting what the money is to give them or whether there are better ways of goal accomplishment that require less money. The processes of goal and indices creation in most companies is not an open process and does not represent the full set of stakeholder goals well. Further, the debate over preferred means of goal attainment reduces the possibility of finding ways that the goals of various different groups can be simultaneously attained.

Thus, voice is hampered through reduction of personal complexity, frozen social orders, contrived knowledge, reduction of value debate through "neutral" efficiency, and performativity standards (including TQM standards). Much of what is considered stable is the result of social constructions—constructions accomplished under conditions of unequal power.

In considering these processes, it is clear that organizational communication practices must change if workplace decisions are to be more responsible. At root, a dialogic view of communication must replace the expressionist/information/adversarial view that dominates contemporary society. Influence-centered, informational views of communication that focused on meaning transmission as if meanings were value neutral must be replaced with views that attend to participation process in the formation of social meanings. In developing a dialogic practice, choices within politically defined contexts with fixed decisional alternatives need to be shifted to concern with the constitution of political contexts and the alternatives. Concern with effective use of language has to be changed to questions of whose language it is, its social/historical partialities, and means of reclaiming alternative voices. Because corporate decisions are inevitably value-laden—they impact on what we will become as people and what kind of world we will live in—communication cannot be evaluated in effectiveness terms, but appeals to moral criteria granting all positions an equal right of codetermination. To achieve this, we must first focus on the rights of decision makers to know over the rights of speakers to speak. The founders of American democracy thought they had accomplished this with the freedom of speech, but they could not have anticipated the extent of the inequality of access to speaking forums and the difference in megaphone size. And, as importantly, their human rights philosophies were too primitive to understand the politics of experience and constraints on voice.

Good decision making requires that all relevant perspectives should be known by all. Unfortunately, in complex workplace environments, systems based on control do not assure all perspectives are known. Present organizational processes do not foster the development of all relevant positions. The desire for representation requires the building of processes that develop alternative perspectives, fosters their expression, and gives then an equal opportunity to influence decisions. The restrictions control systems place on representation may be direct through freedom limitation or coercion, but are often unobtrusive and subtle through consent. The process of representative decision making requires means of overcoming these many restrictions.

RECREATING CORPORATION DISCUSSION

Creating corporations that are economically and socially sound begins with a mutual commitment to the whole, to the entire set of stakeholders. The pursuit of self-interest—whether expressed in the name of profits, particular stakeholders, or one's own strategic advantage—works against any genuine attempt at communication or productive joint decision making. To the extent that managers or any stakeholder can personally internalize the needs of others, they grow, they free themselves from routines and habitual positions, and they begin to reclaim suppressed needs and conflicts. Having conflicting needs and goals is a reality of being human at the individual and organizational level. The answer to this condition is creativity in meeting all rather than in preferencing some and suppressing others. Both the research on and practice of conflict negotiation have taught the same. If we focus on the many goals rather than our preferred means of obtainment, we have creative options and conflicts are more productively solved. This commitment to everyone's goals implies a risk—one to managers and every other stakeholder. To give up habitual and preferred ways of self-interest fulfillment is a leap of faith, but one offering endless unthought potential.

A dialogic approach to organizational responsibility is a more productive direction. A dialogic response would aim to recover those things that are feared and excluded from rational actor models— emotions, the body, the feminine, and pleasure. In so doing, conflict, argument, and debate would not be avoided but embraced for it is in conflict that we can begin to see a potential ethical path that may otherwise be hidden by our everyday routines and "taken-for-granted" ways of understanding the world. This framework suggests that responsibility does not rest in agreement or consensus, but in the avoidance of the suppression of alternative conceptions and possibilities.

The stakeholder model of corporations complemented by adequate conceptions of communication and micropractices of negotiation can enable responsible daily practices (see Deetz, 1995b). Certainly similar projects are joined by many. The basic question shared by all is: How can we together create mutually satisfying worlds that are not yet known? Certainly these normative ideals confront contemporary organizations that have developed a discursive community where values are already inculcated into managerial decisions. These values— efficiency, performativity, and effectiveness—shape the organizational system and in so doing limit the thinkable agency, the ability to redefine and to solve organizational issues creatively. Perhaps the discourse of organizations is so deeply entrenched in and limited to one particular way of seeing, a way of seeing the world which is morally and ethically impoverished, that change from within this morally weak discourse is virtually impossible (Benhabib, 1990). Simply, members of organizations cannot envision ways of conceptualizing and addressing problems that are different from those of their organizational culture—a culture that we have suggested values and thus places an emphasis on economic efficiency with little regard for the impact that attaining such goals may have on the life of the community. If power is not equally distributed among various stakeholders, and the voices of these groups are not heard, will the situated responses arrived at through this discourse reflect the interests of anyone other than those currently in powerful positions (i.e., organizational decision makers)? Nevertheless, the dialogic model offers our best hope, a hope guided by a model of action. At the end there are not assurances, but we know better where to start. And it is here that I believe the work of the future should be directed.

APPENDIX A: 1996 CONFERENCE SCHEDULE, ORGANIZATIONAL COMMUNICATION AND CHANGE: CHALLENGES IN THE NEXT CENTURY

WORKSHOP SCHEDULE

February 8, 1996, Thursday

8:30 AM

- *Opening Remarks and Welcome,* Philip Salem, Southwest Texas State University

9:00 a.m.

- *Managing Change Through Communication,* Barry Spiker, Price Waterhouse

2:00 p.m.

- *The Strategic Communication of Change,* Phillip G. Clampitt and Laurey Berk of MetaComm Consulting and the University of Wisconsin at Green Bay

February 9, 1996, Friday

9:00 a.m.

- *Conflict Management*, Steven Beebe, Southwest Texas State University

2:00 p.m.

- *Some Lessons of Change: Information, Technology, Personnel*, Philip Salem, Southwest Texas State University, Robert Epstein, University of Central Oklahoma, and Larry Browning and Christopher Avery, Partnerwerks Incorporated and the University of Texas

February 10, 1996 Saturday

9:00 a.m.

- *Leading Through Collaboration*, Carl Larson, University of Denver

PANEL SCHEDULE

February 11, Sunday

1:30 p.m. Opening Remarks

- *The Changes and Challenges for Organizational Communication in the Next Century*, Philip Salem, Southwest Texas State University

2:00 p.m. Organizational Communication Domain

- *Rising Above It All: Transcendent Action and Organizational Spirituality*, Diane Witmer Penkoff, Purdue University
- *Organizational Futures, Communication and Scenario-Building*, Geoffrey Gurd, Duquesne University
- *Rethinking Traditional Characteristics of Organizational Communication Studies*, Ruth C. Smith, Purdue University
- *Lines of Flight: A Movement Away From Identification as Workplace Control. Toward a Theory of Control of the Body*, Dave Carlone, University of Colorado

- *Changes in Writing in the Workplace: A Literature Survey and a Case Study*, Egbert Woudstra and Lisette van Gemert, University of Twente
- *Shifting Metaphors of Organizational Communication: The Rise of the Discourse Perspectives*, Linda Putnam, Texas A & M University

February 12, 1996, Monday

9:00 a.m. Organizational Communication Theory
- *Are Organization and Communication Equivalent?* James Taylor, Francois Cooren, Helene Giroux, and Danmiel Robichaud, Universite de Montreal
- *A Case for a Renewal of Systems Inquiry in Organizational Communication Research*, Marshall Scott Poole, Texas A & M University
- *The Technology of Voice*, Renee Houston and Elizabeth Radtke, Florida State University
- *Communicating Flexibility: A Critical Investigation of the Discourse of Organizational Change*, Lars Thoger Christensen, Odense University, Denmark
- *Powerfully Speaking: An Analysis of Managers' Talk*, Ian Connell, University of Wolverhampton, UK
- *Observations on Organizational Communication Theory*, Erik Eisenberg, University of South Florida

2:00 p.m. Organizational Communication and Social Responsibility

- *Social Responsibility and the Modern Health Care System: Promoting a Consumer Orientation to Health Care*, Gary Kreps, University of Nevada, Las Vegas.
- *Information Technologies, Gender and Power in Organizations*, Catherine Becker, Radford University, Steven Levitt, and Shane Moreman, University of Texas at San Antonio
- *Social Responsibility at Issue: Corporate Social Responsibility and Implications for Organizational Communication*, Richard Jones, University of Odense Denmark
- *Multiple Stakeholders and Social Responsibility in the International Business Context: A Critical Perspective*, Stan Deetz, Rutgers

February 13, 1996, Tuesday

8:00 a.m. Organizational Communication Research Methods

- *Neural Networks Applications in Social Science Research,* Ofer Meilich, University of Southern California
- *Widening the Lens: The Use of Historical Data in Organizational Communication* Theorizing, Katherine Miller, University of Kansas
- *Issues in Organizational Communication Research Methods,* Patricia Riley, University of Southern California

11:30 a.m. Organizational Communication Applications

- *Remaking Organizational Communication and the Future: Relevance, Engagement, and Transformation in Teaching, Research and Service,* George Cheney, University of Montana, and Morgan Wilhelmsson, Sweden
- *Challenges for the Applications of Organizational Communication,* Cal W. Downs, University of Kansas

APPENDIX B: CONFERENCE PARTICIPANTS, ORGANIZATIONAL COMMUNICATION AND CHANGE: CHALLENGES IN THE NEXT CENTURY

Allyson Adrian — Arlington, VA
Christopher Avery — Partnerwerks, Inc.
Fay Barclay — Southwest Texas State University
Kevin Barge — Baylor University
Catherine Becker — Radford, VA
Steven Beebe — Southwest Texas State University
Laurey Berk — University of Wisconsin, Green Bay
P.C. Berndt — Coca-Cola Co.
Mark Borzi — Eastern Illinois University
Jarrett Bourne — Morehead, KY
Shari Bracy — Electronic Data Systems Corporation
Ann Bridgeman — Southwest Texas State University
Harold L. Bronson — University of Kentucky
Larry Browning — University of Texas, Austin
Neil Carey — The Manchester Metropolitan University

David Carlone — Boulder, CO
Lars T. Christensen — University of Odense
Thora Christiansen — Los Angeles, CA
Phillip Clampitt — University of Wisconsin, Green Bay
Stephen L. Coffman — Montana State University, Billings
Dr. Ian Connell — University of Wolverhampton
Steven R. Corman — Chandler, AZ

E. Diane Cox	Central Missouri State University
Kim Daniska	Southwest Texas State University
Stanley Deetz	Rutgers University
Janis Doerr	Colorado Springs Utilities
Cal Downs	University of Kansas
Victor Dukay	The Lundy Foundation
Deborah Dunn	Los Angeles, CA
Eric Eisenberg	University of South Florida
Frank Flauto	Southwest Texas State University
Cathy Fleuriet	Southwest Texas State University
K. Sue Foley	Franklin University
Janet Fulk	University of Southern California
Lisette van Gemert	University of Twente
Hollis Glaser	University of Nebraska, Omaha
Geoffrey Gurd	Duquesne University
Heather Harward	Southwest Texas State University
Barbara Hatch	First USA
Robert Heiling	Coca-Cola Co.
David Hess	Southwest Texas State University
Renée Houston	Florida State University
Anita C. James	Ohio University
Richard Jones	University of Odense
Maureen Keeley	Southwest Texas State University
Kathryn G. Kelley	Winona State University
Joann Keyton	University of Memphis
Bridget Kilroy	Pittsburgh, PA
David Koempel	Austin, TX
Gary Kreps	University of Nevada, Las Vegas
Tim Kuhn	Tempe, AZ
Carl Larson	University of Denver
Todd Leach	Austin, TX
Brandon Lee	Southwest Texas State University
Steven Levitt	University of Texas, San Antonio
Laurie K. Lewis	Pennsylvania State University
Andrew Lobo	Coca-Cola Co.
Victoria Locke	Southwest Texas State University
Laura Marselli	Austin, TX
James C. McCroskey	West Virginia University
John McGrath	Trinity University
JoAnn McKenzie	Austin, TX
Ofer Meilich	University of Southern California
Christina Michura	Southwest Texas State University
Barbara Miller	Austin, TX

Katherine Miller	University of Kansas
C.J. Mills	Southwest Texas State University
Bonnie Moeder	Colorado Springs Utilities
Peter Monge	University of Southern California
Shane Moreman	San Antonio, TX
Lexa Murphy	University of South Florida
Diane Penkoff	West Lafayette, IN
Patricia Phillips	Southwest Texas State University
Darrell Piersol	LBJ School of Public Affairs
Scott Poole	Texas A&M University
Sandra Pride	Tuscaloosa, AL
Linda Putnam	Texas A&M University
Elizabeth Radtke	Florida State University
Virginia P. Richmond	West Virginia University
Patricia Riley	University of Southern California
Craig Scott	University of Texas, Austin
Pam Shockley-Zalabak	Colorado Springs, CO
Ruth Smith	Purdue University
Barry Spiker	Santa Fe, NM
James Taylor	St. Petersburg, FL
Erik Timmerman	University of Texas, Austin
Leslie Tod	The Manchester Metropolitan University
William R. Todd-Mancillas	Chico, CA
Dwayne D. Van Rheenen	Pepperdine University
Juanie N. Walker	Pepperdine University
Richard Webb	University of Texas, Austin
Ben Wehman	Century Communications of San Marcos
Morgan Wilhelmsson	Jonkoping University
Lee Williams	Southwest Texas State University
Pat Witherspoon	University of Texas, Austin
Russ Wittrup	Southwest Texas State University
Egbert Woudstra	University of Twente

ABOUT THE AUTHORS

Linda Andrews, Alexandra Murphy, and Linda Timmerman are doctoral students studying organizational communication at the University of South Florida. Linda Andrews is interested in facilitating dialogue in organizational change efforts. Alexandra Murphy's research focuses on how organizational change impacts power and identity. Linda Timmerman's current work examines the complex intersection between organizational and personal life.

Carolyn Baldwin Leveque (MA, Purdue University) is a doctoral candidate at the University of Minnesota and is currently an assistant lecturer in the Department of Speech Communication at Texas A & M University, where she teaches courses in small group communication. Her research interests include computer-supported collaborative group processes, information technologies in the workplace, and the role of emergent networks in organizations.

Catherine B. Becker (PhD, State University of New York at Buffalo) is an Assistant Professor of Speech Communication at Radford University in Virginia. Her research focuses on the relationship between communication and culture. She has articles published in the areas of organizational communication, intercultural communication, and ethics.

Frank E. X. Dance (PhD, Northwestern University) is the John Evans Professor of Human Communication Studies at the University of Denver. Past editor of the *Journal of Communication* and of *Communication Education*. Professor Dance is a Fellow of the International Communication Association (ICA) and past president of both the ICA and of the Speech Communication Association. Frank was active in applied and organizational communication from their disciplinary beginnings and has served as a consultant for organizations such as IBM, the Peace Corps, NASA, Tandy Corporation, and the Executive Development Program conducted by the office of the Governor of Texas.

Stan Deetz (PhD, Ohio University) is Professor of Communication at the University of Colorado at Boulder. In 1996 he was affiliated with Rutgers University. He teaches courses in organizational theory, organizational communication, and communication theory. He is the author of *Transforming Communication, Transforming Business* (1995) and *Democracy in the Age of Colonization* (1992), as well as the editor or coeditor of eight other books.

Cal Downs (PhD, Michigan State University) is Professor of Organizational Communication at the University of Kansas and the President of Communication Management, Inc. He has taught at the University of Maryland and Northwestern, and had been guest professor at Cornell, University of Technology-Sydney, and Victoria University. He is the author of many articles and books including *The Organizational Communicator, Professional Interviewing,* and *Communication Audits.* He has been an organizational communication consultant for over 30 years.

Eric M. Eisenberg (PhD, Michigan State University) is Professor and Chair of Communication at the University of South Florida. His areas of specialty are organizational and interorganizational communication, focused primarily on the role of communication in transforming businesses and communities. Dr. Eisenberg is an internationally recognized scholar and teacher, and he is the author of over 50 journal articles and book chapters. His book, *Organizational Communication: Balancing Creativity and Constraint* (with H. L. Goodall), won the 1993 "Texty" award for the best textbook. He received the prestigious Burlington Resources Foundation Award for Excellence in Teaching in 1993.

Lisette van Gemert (PhD, University of Groningen) is working at the University of Twente in the Communication Studies Department. Her research is about the role and development of written documents in organizations. Together with Egbert Woudstra she has published articles about communication models, communication policy plans, a method for solving communication problems in organizations, mission statements and the writing of ISO-9000 procedures. In the near future she will do research on communication about the implementation of the Dutch Health and Safety Act in organizations.

Gerald Goldhaber (PhD, Purdue University) teaches organizational communication at State University of New York in Buffalo, and has been an organizational communication consultant for over 20 years. He was one of the initial contributors to and eventually the Director of the International Communication Association's Organizational Communication Audit Project over most of the project's 9-year existence. He has authored or coauthored several books, including *Auditing Organizational Communication Systems: The ICA Communication Audit, Transactional Analysis,* and *Information Strategies: New Pathways to Management Productivity,* and he was the coeditor of *Handbook of Organizational Communication.* His undergraduate textbook—*Organizational Communication,* published by Brown and Benchmark—is now in its sixth edition

Bonnie Johnson (PhD, State University of New York) is the Chair of Consumer Research, Interval Research Corporation, a Palo Alto, CA organization founded by Paul Allen and David Liddle to create new technologies and companies. Prior to joining Interval, she managed advanced technology groups at Intel, Aetna Life & Casualty, Focus Systems, and Humanware. Her Aetna group was the subject of a Harvard Business Case, and in a project funded by the National Science Foundation, she led a 2-year investigation of 200 organizations to identify the management practices that distinguished innovative users of office technology. She is the author of several books and articles on business, organization, and innovation including *Managing Organizational Innovation, The Evolution from Word Processing to Office Information Systems* (with Ronald E. Rice). Further explication of the material in this article is presented in her book, *Communication: The Process of Organizing,* published by American Press.

Gary Kreps (PhD, University of Southern California) is Professor and Dean of the School of Communication at Hofstra University. In 1996, he was the Executive Director of the Greenspun School of Communication at the University of Nevada, Las Vegas. Prior to that, he served as a faculty member at Northern Illinois University, Rutgers University, Indiana University at Indianapolis (IUPUI), and Purdue University Calumet. He has expertise in organizational communication, intervention and learning, health communication, health promotion, interpersonal/group interaction, multicultural relations, communication theory, leadership and empowerment, conflict management, and research methods. He is the Editor of two Hampton Press book series titled "Communication and Social Organization" and "Health Communication," was the Founding Editor of the SCA "Applied Communication Publication" series, and edited special issues of the *American Behavioral Scientist* and the *Journal of Health Psychology*. He is the author of *Organizational Communication: Theory and Practice*, published by Longman.

Steven R. Levitt (PhD, Ohio State University) is an Assistant Professor of Communication at the University of Texas at San Antonio. His research interests include uses and effects of information technology, human factors that affect the success of organizational innovation, technology implementation processes, and strategic work group design.

Ofer Meilich is a doctoral candidate at the Department of Management and Organization, School of Business Administration, University of Southern California. Within the broad fields of organization theory and business strategy, his areas of specialization are technological innovation in organizations, management of intangibles, and knowledge work. Current research spans the topics of strategic core competencies of firms, software management, electronic journalism, and artificial intelligence as a research tool. He has international management experience in the aerospace industry.

Katherine Miller (PhD, University of Southern California) is Associate Professor of Communication Studies at the University of Kansas. Her research on stress and burnout in human service organizations has been published in national and international journals. Her current work focuses on the communicative development and maintenance of occupational identity. She is the author of *Organizational Communication: Approaches and Processes*, published by Wadsworth.

Marshall Scott Poole (PhD, University of Wisconsin) is a Professor of Speech Communication at Texas A & M University. His research interests include group and organizational communication, information technology, conflict management, organizational innovation, and process research methods. He has published more than 70 articles and chapters, and his coauthored or edited books include *Communication and Group Decision-Making* (now in its second edition), *Working Through Conflict*, and *Research on the Management of*

Innovation. Dr. Poole is one of the principle developers of the computerized meeting support system, *Software Aided Meeting Management* (SAMM) and is currently working on a Windows-based group support environment. He has consulted for 20 years on organizational communication, teamwork, conflict management, innovation, and computerized communication technologies.

Linda Putnam (Ph. D., University of Minnesota) is Professor and Head of the Department of Speech Communication at Texas A & M University. Her current research interests include negotiation and organizational conflict and language analysis in organizations. She has published over 70 articles and book chapters in management and communication journals. She is the co-editor of *The New Handbook of Organizational Communication* (in press), *Communication and Negotiation* (1992), *The Handbook of Organizational Communication* (1987), and *Communication and Organization: An interpretive Approach* (1983). She is the 1993 recipient of the Charles H. Woolbert Research Award for a seminal article in the communication field and is a Fellow of the International Communication Association.

Patricia Riley is an Associate Professor in the Annenberg School for Communication at the University of Southern California. She has published numerous articles and book chapters and is presently working on a book on organizational change with Warren Bennis for Jossey-Bass. Her areas of interest include organizational communication and culture, information technology and organizational change, the role of voice in organizations and societies, organizational learning and processes such as reengineering, and field research methodologies.

Philip Salem (PhD, University of Denver) is Professor of Speech Communication at Southwest Texas State University. He areas of specialty include communication theory, organizational comrnunication, and interpersonal communication. He and Robert Gratz have received awards for their work on communication and technology, and they are known for their work in educational administration, including *Organizational Communication in Higher Education*, published by AAHE. He directed a project funded by the Department of Education to develop a theory of organizational factors influencing the incorporation of new units into an organization. He was the third person to receive the Outstanding Member award from the Organizational Communication Division of the International Communication Association.

Egbert Woudstra (PhD, University of Amsterdam) is the Dean of the Communication Studies programme at the University of Twente in the Netherlands. His research concerns the role and development of written documents in organizations. Together with Lisette van Gemert he has published articles about communication models, a method for solving communication problems in organizations, communication policy plans, mission statements, and the writing of ISO-9000 procedures. With other colleagues he has published a book about communication skills and was editor of a book on science communication and a book on functional communication.

REFERENCES

Abrams, P. (1980). History, sociology, historical sociology. *Past and Present, 87*, 3–16.

Ackoff, R. L., & Emery F. E. (1972). *On purposeful systems.* Chicago: Aldine Atherton.

Aikin, M., & Martin, J. (1994). Enhancing business communication with group decision support systems. *The Bulletin, 62*(3), 24-26.

Albert, S., & Whetten, D. A. (1985). Organizational identity. In L. L. Cummings & B. M. Staw (Eds.), *Research in organizational behavior* (Vol. 7, pp. 263-295). Greenwich, CT: JAI Press.

Albrecht, T. L., & Hall, B. (1991). Facilitating talk about new ideas: The role of personal relationships in organizational innovation. *Communication Monographs, 58*, 273–288.

Alderfer, C. P. (1977). Improving organizational communication through long term intergroup intervention. *Journal of Applied Behavioral Science, 13*, 193–210.

Alinsky, S. (1971). *Rules for radicals: A practical primer for realistic radicals.* New York: Vintage.

Allen, T. J., & Fustfeld, A. R. (1975). Research laboratory architecture and the structuring of communication. *R & D Management, 5*, 153–164.

Alvesson, M. (1987) *Organizational theory and technologic consciousness: Rationality, ideology, and quality of work.* New York: de Gruyter

Alvesson, M. (1990). Organization: From substance to image? *Organization Studies, 11*(3), 373–394.

Alvesson, M. (1993a). Cultural-ideological modes of management control: A theory and a case study of a professional service company. In S. A. Deetz (Ed.), *Communication yearbook 16* (pp. 3-42). Newbury Park, CA: Sage.

Alvesson, M. (1993b). *Cultural perspectives on organizations.* Cambridge, England: Cambridge University Press.

Alvesson, M., & Deetz, S. (in press). Critical theory and postmodernism. In S. Clegg, C. Harding, & W. Nord (Eds.), *The handbook of management studies*. London: Sage.

Alvesson, M., & Willmott, H. (Eds.). (1992). *Critical management studies*. London: Sage.

Alvesson, M., & Willmott, H. (1995). *Making sense of management. A critical analysis*. London: Sage.

Ammer, C. (1989). *The new A-to-Z of women's health*. New York: Facts on File.

Anderson, P. V. (1985). What survey research tell us about writing at work. In L. Odell & D. Goswami (Eds.), *Writing in nonacademic settings* (pp. 3–83). New York: Guilford

Apel, K.-O. (1979). *Toward a transformation of philosophy* (G. Adey & D. Frisby, Trans.). London: Routledge & Kegan Paul.

Argyris, C. (1971). *Management and organizational development*. New York: McGraw-Hill.

Argyris, C. (1988). Crafting a theory of practice: The case of organizational paradoxes. In R. E. Quinn & K. S. Cameron (Eds.), *Paradox and transformation: Toward a theory of change in organization and management* (pp. 255–278). Cambridge, MA.: Ballinger.

Argyris, C. (1993). *On organizational learning*. Cambridge, MA: Blackwell.

Arnold, C. C. (1974). *Criticism of oral rhetoric*. Columbus, OH: Merrill.

Arnold, C. C. (1980). Oral rhetoic, rhetoric, and literature. In. E. E. White (Ed.), *Rhetoric in transition* (pp. 157-173). University Park: Penn State University Press.

Arnold, E., Birke, L., & Faulkner, W. (1982). Women and microelectronics: The case of word processors. In J. Rothschild (Ed.), *Women, technology and innovations* (pp. 321–340). London: Pluto Press.

Arntson, P. (1989). Improving citizens' health competencies. *Health Communication, 1,* 29–34.

Autry, J. A. (1991). *Love and profit: The art of caring leadership*. New York: William Morrow.

Avery, C., & Jablin, F. M. (1988). Retirement preparation programs and organizational communication. *Communication Education, 37,* 68–88.

Avolio, B. J., & Bass, B. M. (1988). Transformational leadership, charisma, and beyond. In J. G. Hunt, B. R. Baliga, H. P. Dachter, & C. A. Schriesheim (Eds.), *Emerging leadership vistas* (pp. 29-49). Boston: Lexington

Avolio, B. J., Waldman, D. A., & Einstein, W. O. (1988). Transformational leadership in a management game simulation. *Group and Organization Studies, 13,* 59–80.

Axley, S. (1984). Managerial and organizational communication in terms of the conduit metaphor. *Academy of Management Review, 9,* 428–437.

Bacon, T. R. (1990). Collaboration in a pressure cooker. *The Bulletin, 53*(2), 4–8.

Baer, H. A. (1981). The organizational rejuvenation of osteopathy: A reflection of the decline of professional dominance in medicine. *Social Science and Medicine, 15a,* 701–711.

Bailey, F. G. (1991). Why is information asymmetrical? Symbolic behavior in formal organizations. *Rationality and Society, 3*(4), 475–495.

Bailey, K. D. (1982). *Methods of social research* (2nd ed.). New York: The Free Press.

Bakhtin, M. (1981) *The dialogic imagination* (C. Emerson & M. Holquist, Trans.). Austin: University of Texas Press.

Banks, S. P., & Riley, P. (1993). Structuration theory as an ontology for communication research. In S. Deetz (Ed.), *Communication yearbook 16* (pp. 167–196). Newbury Park, CA: Sage.

Banner, D. K., & Gagne, T. E. (1995). *Designing effective organizations: Traditional and transformational views.* Thousand Oaks, CA: Sage.

Bantz, C. R. (1989). Organizing and the social psychology of organizing. *Communication Studies, 40*(4), 231–240.

Bantz, C. R. (1993). *Understanding organizations: Interpreting organizational communication cultures.* Columbia: University of South Carolina Press.

Baran, B. (1985). Office automation and women's work: The technological transformation of the insurance industry. In M. Castells (Ed.), *High technology, space, and society* (pp. 143–171). Beverly Hills, CA: Sage.

Barker, J. (1993). Tightening the iron cage: Concertive control in self-managing teams. *Administrative Science Quarterly, 38,* 408–437.

Barker, J., & Cheney, G. (1994). The concept and the practice of discipline in contemporary organizational life. *Communication Monographs, 61,* 19–43.

Barker, J., & Downing, H. (1985). Word processing and the transformation of patriarchal relations of control in the office. In D. MacKenzie & J. Wajcman (Eds.), *The social shaping of technology* (pp. 147–164). Milton Keynes: Open University Press.

Barker, J., Melville, C., & Pacanowsky, M. (1993). Self-directed teams at XEL: Changes in communicative practices during a program of cultural transformation. *Journal of Applied Communication Research, 21,* 297–312.

Barley, S., & Kunda, G. (1992). Design and devotion: Surges of rational and normative ideologies of control in managerial discourse. *Administrative Science Quarterly, 37,* 363–399.

Barnard, C. (1938). *The functions of the executive.* Cambridge, MA: Harvard University Press.

Barnet, R., & Cavanaugh, J. (1993). *Global dreams*. New York: Simon & Schuster.

Barnett, G., & Woelfel, J. (Eds.). (1987). *Readings in the Galileo system*. Dubuque, IA: Kendall/Hunt.

Barthes, R. (1981). Theory of the text. In R. Young (Ed.), *Untying the text: A post-structuralist reader* (pp. 31–47). Boston: Routledge & Kegan Paul.

Bartunek, J. M., & Louis, M. R. (1988). The interplay of organizational development and organizational transformation. In W. A. Pasmore & R. W. Woodman (Eds.), *Research in organizational change and development: Vol. 2* (pp. 97–134). Greenwich, CT: JAI Press.

Bartunek, J., Bobko, P., & Venkatraman, N. (1993). Toward innovation and diversity in management research methods. *Academy of Management Journal, 36*, 1362–1373.

Barzun, J., & Graff, H. F. (1985). *The modern researcher*. New York: Harcourt Brace Jovanovich.

Bass, B. M. (1981). *Stogdill 's handbook of leadership: A survey of theory and research*. New York: The Free Press.

Bass, B. M., Waldman, S. A., Avolio, B. J., & Bebb, M. (1987). Transformational leadership and the falling dominoes effect. *Group and Organization Studies, 12,* 73–87.

Bastien, D. T., & Hostager, T. J. (1988). Jazz as a process of organizational innovation. *Communication Research, 15,* 582–602.

Bastien, D. T., & Hostager, T. J. (1992). Cooperation as communicative accomplishment: A symbolic interaction analysis of an improvised jazz concert. *Communication Studies, 43,* 92–104.

Baudrillard, J. (1983). *Simulations*. New York: Semiotext.

Bazerman, C. (1983). Scientific writing as a social act: Review of the literature of the sociology of science. In P. V. Anderson, R. J. Brockman, & C. R. MIller (Eds.), *New essays in technical and scientific communication: Theory, research and practice* (pp. 156–184). Farmingdale, NY: Baywood.

Becker, E. (1971). *The birth and death of meaning*. New York: The Free Press.

Beer, M., Eisenstat, R. A., & Spector, B. (1990). *The critical path to corporate renewal*. Cambridge, MA: Harvard Business School Press.

Bellah, R. N., Madsen, R., Sullivan, W. M., Swidler, A., & Tipton, S. M. (1992). *The good society*. New York: Vintage.

Benhabib, S. (1990). Afterward: Communicative ethics and current controversies in practical philosophy. In S. Benhabib & F. Dellmayr (Eds.), *The communicative ethics controversy* (pp. 330–370). Cambridge, MA: MIT Press.

Benhabib, S. (1992). *Situating the self: Gender, community and postmodernism in contemporary ethics.* New York: Routledge.

Bennis, W. G. (1984). Transformative power and leadership. In T. J. Sergiovanni & J. E. Corbally (Eds.), *Leadership and organizational culture* (pp. 64–71). Chicago: University of Illinois Press.

Bennis, W. G. (1993). Learning some basic truisms about leadership. In M. Ray & A. Rinzler (Eds.), *The new paradigm in business: Emerging strategies for leadership and organizational change* (pp. 72–80). New York: Putnam.

Bennis, W. G., & Nanus, B. (1985). *Leaders. Strategies for taking charge.* New York: Harper & Row.

Benokraitis, N., & Feagin, J. (1986). *Modern sexism.* New York: Harper & Row.

Benson, J. K. (1977). Organizations: A dialectical view. *Administrative Science Quarterly, 22,* 1–26.

Berg, P. (1985). Organization change as a symbolic transformation process. In P. J. Frost, L. F. Moore, M. R. Louis, C. C. Lundberg, & J. Montese (Eds.), *Organizational culture* (pp. 281–299). Newbury Park, CA: Sage.

Berger, P. L., & Luckmann, T. (1966). *The social construction of reality.* New York: Doubleday.

Bergquist, W. (1993). *The postmodern organization: Mastering the art of irreversible change.* San Francisco, CA: Jossey-Bass.

Berlo, D. (1960). *The process of communication.* New York: Holt, Rinehart & Winston.

Bertalanffy, L. von. (1956). General systems theory. *General Systems, 1,* 1–10.

Bertalanffy, L. von. (1962). General systems theory. *General Systems, 7,* 1–12.

Bertalanffy, L. von. (1968). *General systems theory: Foundations, development, applications.* New York: George Braziller.

Bing, C., & Titterington, D.M. (1994). Neural networks: A review from a statistical perspective. *Statistical Science, 9(1),* 2-54.

Birkerts, S. (1995). *The Gutenberg elegies: The fate of reading in an electronic age.* New York: Ballantine.

Blackeney, R. N. (1985). A transactional view of the role of trust in organizational communication. *Transactional Analysis Journal, 16(2),* 95–98.

Blair, C., & Kaul, M. L. (1990). Revising the history of rhetorical theory. *Western Journal of Speech Communication, 54,* 148–159.

Blanchard, K. (1995). Points of power. *Executive Excellence, 12(3),* 11–12.

Blau, P. (Ed.). (1975). *Approaches to the study of social structure.* New York: The Free Press.

Block, P. (1993). *Stewardship: Choosing service over self-interest.* San Francisco: Berrett-Koehler.

Bloom, A. D. (1987). *The closing of the American mind: How higher education has failed democracy and impoverished the souls of today's students.* New York: Simon & Schuster.

Bochner, A. P., & Ellis, C. (1992). Personal narrative as a social approach to interpersonal communication. *Communication Theory, 2,* 165–172.

Bohm, D. (1980). *Wholeness and the implicate order.* London: Ark Paperbacks.

Bohm, D., & Edwards, M. (1991). *Changing consciousness: Exploring the hidden source of the social, political, and environmental crises facing our world.* San Francisco: Harper San Francisco.

Boje, D. M. (1991). The storytelling organization: A study of story performance in an office-supply firm. *Administrative Science Quarterly, 36,* 106–126.

Boje, D. M. (1995). Stories of the storytelling organization: A postmodern analysis of Disney as "Tamara-Land." *Academy of Management Journal, 38*(4), 997–1035.

Boorstin, D. (1961) *The image: A guide to pseudo-events in America.* New York: Atheneum.

Bormann, E. G. (1972). Fantasy and rhetorical vision: The rhetorical criticism of social reality. *Quarterly Journal of Speech, 58,* 396–407.

Bormann, E. G. (1980). *Communication theory.* New York: Holt, Rinehart & Winston.

Bormann, E. G. (1982). Fantasy and rhetorical vision: Ten years later. *Quarterly Journal of Speech, 58,* 396–407.

Bormann, E. G. (1983). Symbolic convergence: Organizational communication and culture. In L. Putnam & M. Pacanowsky (Eds.), *Communication and organizations: An interpretive perspective* (pp. 99–122). Beverly Hills, CA: Sage.

Bormann, E. G., Cragan, J. F., & Shields, D. C. (1994). In defense of symbolic convergence theory: A look at the theory and its criticisms after two decades. *Communication Theory, 4,* 259-294.

Bormann, E., Howell, W., Nichols, R., & Shapiro, G. (1969). *Interpersonal communication in the modern organization.* Englewood Cliffs, NJ: Prentice-Hall.

Boston Women's Health Collective. (1992). *The new our bodies, our selves.* New York: Simon & Schuster.

Botan, C. M., & Frey, L. R. (1983). Do workers trust labor unions and their messages? *Communication Monographs, 50*(3), 233-244.

Bouldin, T., & Odell, L. (1993). Surveying the field and looking ahead: A systems theory perspective on research on writing in the workplace. In R. Spilka (Ed.), *Writing in the workplace: New research perspectives* (pp. 268-281). Carbondale: Southern Illinois University Press.

Boulding, K. (1968). General systems theory—the skeleton of science. In W. Buckley (Ed.), *Modern systems research for the behavioral scientist* (pp. 3–10). Chicago: Aldine.

Brass, D. J. (1985). Men's and women's networks: A study of interaction patterns and influence in an organization. *Academy of Management Journal, 28*(2), 327–343.

Brass, D. J., & Burkhardt, M. E. (1993). Potential power and power use: An investigation of structure and behavior. *Academy of Management Journal, 36*(3), 441–470.

Braverman, H. (1974). *Labor and monopoly capitalism.* New York: Monthy Review Press.

Broadhead, G. J., & Freed, R. C. (1986). *The variables of composition: Process, product in business setting.* Carbondale: Southern Illinois University Press.

Brockman, J. (1996). *The third culture.* New York: Simon & Schuster.

Brody, H. (1990, August/September). The neural computer. *Technology Review,* 43–49.

Bronowski, J. (1973). *The ascent of man.* Boston: Little, Brown.

Brown, C. E., Coakley, J., & Phillips, M. E. (1995, May). Neural networks: Nuts and baits. *Management Accounting,* 54–55.

Brown, M. H. (1985). "That reminds me of a story": Speech action in organizational socialization. *Western Journal of Speech Communication, 49,* 27–42.

Brown, R. H. (1977). *A poetic for sociology.* Cambridge, England: Cambridge University Press.

Browning, L. D. (1978). A grounded theory of organizational communication. *Communication Monographs, 45,* 93–109.

Brune R. L., & Weinstein, M. (1981). *Development of a checklist for evaluating emergency operating procedures used in nuclear power plants* (NUREG/CR–1970). Washington, DC: U.S. Nuclear Regulatory Commission.

Buber, M. (1985). *Between man and man* (2nd ed.). New York: Macmillan.

Buckley, W. (1967). *Sociology and modern systems theory.* Englewood Cliffs, NJ: Prentice-Hall.

Bullis, C. (1991). Communication practices as unobtrusive control: An observational study. *Communication Studies, 42,* 254–271.

Bullis, C. (1993). At least it is a start. In S. A. Deetz (Ed.), *Communication yearbook 16* (pp. 145–154). Newbury Park, CA: Sage.

Bullis, C., & Tompkins, P. (1989). The forest ranger revisited: A study of control processes and identification. *Communication Monographs, 56,* 287–306.

Burawoy, M. (1979). *Manufacturing consent.* Chicago: University of Chicago Press.

Burawoy, M. (1985). *The politics of production: Factory regimes under capitalism and socialism.* London: Verso.

Burkhardt, M. E., & Brass, D. J. (1990). Changing patterns or patterns of change: The effects of a change in technology on social network structure and power. *Administrative Science Quarterly, 35,* 104–127.

Burnett, R. (1991). Substantive conflict in a cooperative context: A way to improve the collaborative planning of workplace documents. *Technical Communication, 38,* 532–539

Burns, J. M. (1978). *Leadership.* New York: Harper & Row.

Burt, R. S. (1982). *Toward a structural theory of action: Network models of social structure, perception, and action.* New York: Academic Press.

Buzzanell, P. M. (1994). Gaining a voice: Feminist organizational theorizing. *Management Communication Quarterly, 7,* 339–383.

Cameron, D. (1994). Verbal hygiene for women: Linguistics misapplied? *Applied Linguistics, 15,* 382-398

Cameron, K., & Whetten, D. (Eds.). (1983). *Organizational effectiveness: A comparison of multiple models.* New York: Academic Press.

Campbell, D. E., & Campbell, T. A. (1988). A new look at informal communication: The role of the physical environment. *Environment and Behavior, 20*(2), 211–226.

Carley, K. M., & Kaufer, D. S. (1993). Semantic connectivity: An approach for analyzing symbols in semantic networks. *Communication Theory, 3,* 183–213.

Carroll, A. (1989). *Business and society: Ethics and stakeholder management.* Cincinnati: South-Western.

Carter, P., & Jackson, N. (1987). Management, myth, and metatheory— from scarcity to post scarcity. *International Studies of Management and Organizations, 17,* 64–89.

Cascio, W. F. (1987). *Costing human resources: The financial impact of behavior in organizations* (2nd ed.). Boston : PWS–Kent.

Caudill, M., & Butler, C. (1992). *Understanding neural networks: Computer explorations.* Cambridge, MA: Bradford/MIT Press.

Checkland, P. (1981). *Systems thinking, systems practice.* New York: Wiley.

Chen, M. (1987). Gender differences in adolescents' use of and attitudes toward computers. In S. Deetz (Ed.), *Communication yearbook 10* (pp. 200-216). Newbury Park, CA: Sage.

Cheney, G. (1983). The rhetoric of identification and the study of organizational communication, *Quarterly Journal of Speech, 69,* 143–158.

Cheney, G. (1991). *Rhetoric in an organizational society: Managing multiple identities.* Columbia: University of South Carolina Press.

Cheney, G. (1995). Democracy in the workplace: Theory and practice from the perspective of communication. *Journal of Applied Communication Research, 23,* 167–200.

Cheney, G., & Christensen, L. T. (forthcoming). Identity at issue: Linkages between "internal" and "external" organizational communication. In F. M. Jablin & L. L. Putnam (Eds.), *The new handbook of organizational communication*. Newbury Park, CA: Sage.

Cheney, G., & Tompkins, P. K. (1987). Coming to terms with organizational identification and commitment. *Central States Speech Journal, 38*, 1–15.

Cheney, G., & Tompkins, P. K. (1988). On the facts of the text as the basis of human communication research. In J. A. Anderson (Ed.), *Communication yearbook 11* (pp. 455–481). Newbury Park, CA: Sage.

Cheney, G., & Vibbert, S. L. (1987). Corporate discourse: Public relations and issue management. In F. M. Jablin, L. L. Putnam, K. H. Roberts, & L. W. Porter (Eds.), *Handbook of organizational communication: An interdisciplinary perspective* (pp. 165–194). Newbury Park, CA: Sage.

Cheney, G., & Wilhelmsson, M. (1996, February). *Remaking organizational communication and the future: Relevance, engagement and transformation in teaching, research, and service.* Paper presented to the ICA/SCA/SWTSU Organizational Communication and Change Conference, Austin, TX.

Cheng, B., & Titterington, D. M. (1994). Neural networks: A review from a statistical perspective. *Statistical Science, 9*(1), 2-54.

Chesler, P. (1972). *Women and madness.* New York: Avon.

Chilton, K., & Weidenbaum, M. (1994). *A new social contract for the American workplace: From paternalism to partnering* (Center for the Study of American Business, Policy Study 123). St. Louis: Washington University.

Chithelen, L. (1989, June). New technology learns Wall Street's mindset. *Wall Street Computer Review*, 19–20, 93–94.

Chomsky, N. (1966). *Cartesian linguistics.* New York: Harper & Row.

Christian, J. C., & Nykodym, N. (1986). TA: A training and development tool—the consultant's perspective. *Organizational Development Journal, 4*, 85–86.

Chua, E. G., & Gudykunst, W. B. (1987). Conflict resolution styles in low and high context cultures. *Communication Research Reports, 4*, 32–37.

Clair, R. (1993a). The bureaucratization, commodification, and privatization of sexual harassment through institutional discourse. *Management Communication Quarterly, 7*, 123–157.

Clair, R. (1993b). The use of framing devices to sequester organizational narratives: Hegemony and harassment. *Communication Monographs, 60*, 113-136.

Clair, R. A. (1994). Resistance and expression as a self contained opposite: An organizational communication analysis of one man's story of sexual harassment. *Western Journal of Communication, 58*, 236–262.

Clegg, S., & Dunkerly, D. (1980). *Organization, class and control.* London: Routledge & Kegan Paul.

Clement, A. (1994). Computing at work: Empowering action by "low-level users." *Communications of the ACM, 37*(1), 53–63.

Cockburn, C. (1981). The material of male power. *Feminist Review, 9,* 41–58.

Coffman, S. L., & Eblen, A. L. (1987). Metaphor use and perceived managerial effectiveness. *Journal of Applied Communication Research, 1–2,* 53–66.

Collins, J. C., & Porras, J. I. (1993). Purpose, mission, and vision. In M. Ray & A. Rinzler (Eds.), *The new paradigm in business: Emerging strategies for leadership and organizational change* (pp. 82–89). New York: Putnam.

Collins, J. M., & Clark, M. R. (1993). An application of the theory of neural computation to the prediction of workplace behavior: An illustration and assessment of network analysis. *Personnel Psychology 46,* 503–524.

Collins-Jarvis, L. (1993). Gender representation in an electronic city hall: Female adoption of Santa Monica's PEN system. *Journal of Broadcasting and Electronic Media, 37,* 49–66.

Conger, J. A., & Kanungo, R. N. (Eds.). (1987). *Charismatic leadership: The elusive factor in organizational effectiveness.* San Francisco: Jossey-Bass.

Conrad, C. (1983). Organizational power: Faces and symbolic forms. In L. L. Putnam & M. E. Pacanowsky (Eds.), *Communication and organizations: An interpretive approach* (pp. 173–194). Beverly Hills, CA: Sage.

Conrad, C. (1993). Rhetorical/communication theory as an ontology for structuration research. In S. Deetz (Ed.), *Communication yearbook 16* (pp. 197–208). Newbury Park, CA: Sage.

Conrad, C., & Witte, K. (1994). Is emotional expression repression oppression? Myths of organizational affective regulation. In S. A. Deetz (Ed.), *Communication yearbook 17* (pp. 417–428). Thousand Oaks, CA: Sage.

Contractor, N. S., & Baldwin, C. L. (1992, May). *Adoption of communication technologies in organizations: A dynamic formulation of the structural theory of action.* Paper presented at the annual convention of the International Communication Association, Miami, FL.

Contracter, N. S., & Eisenberg, E. (1990). Communication networks and new media in organizations. In J. Fulk & C. Steinfield (Eds.), *Organizations and communication technology* (pp. 143–172). Newbury Park, CA: Sage.

Corea, G. (1977). *The hidden malpractice: How American medicine treats women as patients and professionals.* New York: William Morrow.

Corman, S. R., & Scott, C. R. (1994). A synchronous digital signal processing method for detecting face-to-face organizational communication behavior. *Social Networks, 16,* 163–179.

Courtright, J. A., Fairhurst, G. T., & Rogers, E. L. (1989). Interaction patterns in organic and mechanistic systems. *Academy of Management Journal, 32,* 773–802.

Couture, B., & Rymer, J. (1989). Interactive writing on the job: Definitions and implications of "collaboration." In M. Kogen (Ed.), *Writing in the business professions* (pp. 73-93). Urbana, IL: NCTE & ABC.

Couture, B., & Rymer, J. (1991). Discourse interaction between writer and supervisor: A primary collaboration in workplace writing. In M. M. Lay & W. M. Karis (Eds.), *Collaborative writing in industry: Investigations in theory and practice* (pp. 87–108). Amityville, NY: Baywood.

Couture, B., & Rymer, J. (1993). Situational exigence: Composing processes on the job by writer's role and task value. In R. Spilka (Ed.), *Writing in the workplace: New research perspectives* (pp. 4-20). Carbondale: Southern Illinois University Press.

Covello, V. T. (1989). Informing people about risks from chemicals, radiation, and other toxic substances: A review of obstacles to public understanding and effective risk communication. In W. Leiss (Ed.), *Prospects and problems in risk communication* (pp. 1–25). Waterloo, Ontario, Canada: University of Waterloo.

Covey, S. R. (1989). *The 7 habits of highly effective people: Restoring the character ethic.* New York: Simon & Schuster.

Cray, D., & Hazen, M. D. (1995, November). *The message is the medium: Recovering the center of human communication studies.* Paper presented to the Speech Communication Association convention meeting, San Antonio, TX.

Cross, G. A. (1993). The interrelation of genre, context, and process in the collaborative writing of two corporate documents. In R. Spilka (Ed.), *Writing in the workplace: New research perspectives* (pp. 141–157). Carbondale: Southern Illinois University Press.

Crowston, K. (1994). Evolving novel organizational forms. In K. M. Carley & M. J. Prietula (Eds.), *Computational organizational theory* (pp. 19–38). Hillsdale, NJ: Erlbaum.

Cussella, L. P. (1982). The effects of source expertise and feedback valence on intrinsic motivation. *Human Communication Research, 9,* 17-32.

Cybenko, G. (1989). Approximation by superimpositions of a sigmoidal function. *Mathematics of Control. Signal and Systems, 2*(4), 303–314.

Daft, R. L., Bettenhausen, K. R., & Tyler, B. R. (1993). Implications of top managers' communication choices for strategic change. In G. P.

Huber & W. H. Glick (Eds.), *Organizational change and redesign: Ideas and insights for improving performance* (pp. 112–146). New York: Oxford University Press.

Daft, R. L., & Lengel, R. H. (1986). Organizational information requirements, media richness and structural design. *Management Science, 32,* 554–571.

Daft, R. L., Lengel, R. H., & Trevino, L. K. (1987). Message equivocality, media selection, and manager performance: Implications for information systems. *MIS Quarterly, 11,* 355–366.

Dahrendorf, R. (1959). *Class and class conflict in industrial society.* Stanford, CA: Stanford University Press.

Dan, A. J. (Ed.). (1994). *Reframing women's health.* Thousand Oaks, CA: Sage.

Dance, F. E. X. (1975). Speech communication: The sign of mankind. In *The great ideas today: 1975* (pp. 40–57). New York: Encyclopedia Britannica.

Dance, F. E. X., & Larson, C. E. (1972). *Speech communication: Concepts and behavior.* New York: Holt, Rinehart & Winston.

Dance, F. E. X., & Larson, C. E., (1976). *The functions of human communication: A theoretical approach.* New York: Holt, Rinehart and Winston.

Daniels, T. D., & Spiker, B. K. (1994). *Perspectives on organizational communication* (3rd ed.). Madison, WI: Brown and Benchmark.

Danon, Y. (1995). *WinNN* (Version 0.97) [Computer software]. Available: http://www.winsite.com/info/pc/win3/programr/winnn97.zip/

Davies, K. (1990). *Women and time. Weaving the strands of everyday life.* Aldershot: Avebury.

Davis, D. (1995). *The changing nature of work.* San Francisco: Jossey-Bass.

Davis, K. (1972). *Human behavior at work.* New York: McGraw-Hill.

Debs, M. B. (1985). *Collaboration and collaborative writing: A study of technical writing in the computer industry.* Unpublished doctoral dissertation, Renssalaer Polytechnic Institute, Troy NY.

Deetz, S. A. (1985). Critical-cultural research. New sensibilities and old realities. *Journal of Management, 11*(2), 121–136.

Deetz, S. A. (1990). Reclaiming the subject matter as a moral foundation for interpersonal interaction. *Communication Quarterly, 38,* 226–243.

Deetz, S. A. (1992a). *Democracy in an age of corporate colonization.* Albany: State University of New York Press.

Deetz, S. A. (1992b). Disciplinary power in the modern corporation. In M. Alvesson & H. Wilmott (Eds.), *Critical management studies* (pp. 21–45). Newbury Park, CA: Sage.

Deetz, S. A. (1995a). Character, corporate responsibility and the dialogic in the postmodern context. *Organization: The Interdisciplinary Journal of Organization, Theory, and Society, 3,* 217–225.

Deetz, S. A. (1995b). *Transforming communication, transforming business: Building responsive and responsible workplaces.* Cresskill, NJ: Hampton Press.

Deetz, S. A. (1995c). Transforming communication, transforming business: Stimulating value negotiation for more responsive and responsible workplaces. *International Journal of Value-Based Management, 8,* 255–78.

Deetz, S. A. (forthcoming). Conceptual foundations for organizational communication studies. In F. M. Jablin & L. L. Putnam (Eds.), *The new handbook of organizational communication.* Thousand Oaks, CA: Sage.

Deetz, S. A. (1996). Describing differences in approaches to organizational science: Rethinking Burrell and Morgan and their legacy. *Organization Science, 7,* 191-207.

Deetz, S. A. (1998). Discursive formations, strategized subordination, and self-surveillance: An empirical case. In A. McKinlay & K. Starkey (Eds.), *Foucault, management and organization theory* (pp. 151-172). London: Sage.

Deetz, S. A., Cohen, D., & Edley, P. (1997). Ethics and the perceptions and roles of organizing and organizations in international communication. In F. Casmir (Ed.), *Ethics in international and intercultural communication* (pp. 183-226). Mahwah, NJ: Lawrence Erlbaum Associates.

Deetz, S. A., & Kersten, A. (1983). Critical models of interpretive research. In L. L. Putnam & M. E. Pacanowsky (Eds.), *Communication and organizations: An interpretive approach* (pp. 147–171). Beverly Hills, CA: Sage.

Deetz, S. A., & Mumby, D. K. (1990). Power, discourse, and the workplace: Reclaiming the critical tradition. In J. A. Anderson (Ed.), *Communication yearbook 13* (pp. 18–47). Newbury Park, CA: Sage.

Deluga, R. J. (1988). Relationship of transformational and transactional leadership with employee influencing strategies. *Group and Organization Studies, 13,* 456–467.

Department of Trade and Industry. (1995). *Competitiveness: Forging ahead* (White paper). London: Her Majesty's Stationary Office.

Dervin, B. (1989). Users as research inventions: How research categories perpetuate inequities. *Journal of Communication, 39,* 216–232.

DeSanctis, G., & Poole, M. S. (1994). Capturing the complexity in advanced technology use: Adaptive structuration theory. *Organizational Science, 5,* 121–147.

Diesing, P. (1991). *How does social science work? Reflections on practice.* Pittsburgh: University of Pittsburgh Press.

Diethrich, E. B., & Cohan, C. (1992). *Women and heart disease.* New York: Ballantine.

Dobos, J. (1992). Gratifications models of satisfaction and choice of communication channels in organizations. *Communication Research, 19*, 29–51.

Doerfel, M. L., & Barnett, G. (1996). The use of CATPAC for textual analysis. *Cultural Anthropology Methods, 8*, 4-7.

Doheny-Farina, S. (1985). Writing in an emerging organization. *Written Communication, 3*, 158–185.

Doheny-Farina, S., & Odell, L. (1985). Ethnographic research on writing: Assumptions and methodology. In L. Odell & D. Goswami (Eds.), *Writing in nonacademic settings* (pp. 503–535). New York: Guilford.

Donnellon, A., Gray, B., & Bougon, M. (1986). Communication, meaning, and organized action. *Administrative Science Quarterly, 31*, 43–55.

Downs, A. (1967). *Inside bureaucracy.* Boston: Little, Brown.

Downs, C. W. (1989, July). *Issues in team building.* Paper presented to the Australian Communication Association meeting, Melbourne, Australia.

Downs, C. W., Adrian, A. & Ticehurst, B. G. (1995, June). *A cross cultural comparison of the relationships among communication satisfaction and organizational commitment.* Paper presented to the Pan Pacific Communication Conference, Tokyo, Japan.

Downs, C. W., & Larimer, M. (1974, May). *The status of organizational communication in speech departments.* Paper presented to the International Communication Association, New Orleans, LA.

Druker, P. F. (1973). *Management: Tasks and responsibilities.* London: Heinemann.

Dubin, R. (1978). *Theory building* (2nd ed.). New York: The Free Press.

Duncan, H. D. (1968). *Symbols in society.* New York: Oxford University Press.

Dutton, W. H., Rogers, E. M., & Jun, S. H. (1987). Diffusion and social impacts of personal computers. *Communication Research, 14*, 219-250.

Eagleton, T. (1991). *Ideology: An introduction.* London: Verso.

Easton, A. C., Eickelmann, N. S., & Flatley M. E. (1994). Effects of an electronic meeting system group writing tool on the quality of written documents. *Journal of Business Communication, 31*(1), 27–40.

Ede, L., & Lunsford, A. A. (1990). *Singular texts/plural authors: Perspectives on collaborative writing.* Carbondale: Southern Illinois University Press.

Edwards, R. (1979). *Contested terrain: The transformation of the workplace in the twentieth century.* New York: Basic Books.

Edwards, R., Watson, K. W., & Barker, L. (1988). Highly regarded doctoral programs in selected areas of communication: 1987. *Communication Education, 37*, 263–269.

Eisenberg, E. M. (1990). Jamming: Transcendence through organizing. *Communication Research, 17*, 139–164.

Eisenberg, E. M. (1994). Dialogue as democratic discourse: Affirming Harrison. In S. A. Deetz (Ed.), *Communication yearbook 17* (pp. 275–284). Thousand Oaks, CA: Sage.

Eisenberg, E. M., & Goodall, H. L. (1993). *Organizational communication: Balancing creativity and constraint.* New York: St. Martin's Press.

Eisenberg, E. M., & Goodall, H. L. (1997). *Organizational communication: Balancing creativity and constraint* (2nd ed.). New York: St. Martin's Press.

Eisenberg, E. M., & Riley, P. (1988). Organizational symbols and sensemaking. In G. Goldhaber & G. Barnett (Eds.), *Handbook of organizational communication* (pp. 131–150). Norwood, NJ: Ablex.

Eisenberg, E., & Riley, P. (in press). Organizational culture. In L. Putnam & F. Jablin (Eds.), *New handbook of organizational communication.* Newbury Park, CA: Sage.

Eisler, R. (1987). *The chalice and the blade.* San Francisco: Harper.

Elling, R. (1994). The delicate balance between text and context: A system's approach. In L. van Waes, E. Woudstra, & P. van den Hoven (Eds.), *Functional communication quality* (115-125). Amsterdam: Rodopi.

Ellis, J. (1982). *Visible fictions.* London: Routledge & Kegan Paul.

Englebretsen, G. (1995, May/June). Postmodernism and new age unreason. *Skeptical Inquirer,* pp. 52–53.

Evered, R., & Tannenbaum, R. (1992). A dialog on dialog. *Journal of Management Inquiry, 1,* 43–55.

Fahlman, S. E. (1988). Faster-learning variations on back-propagation: An empirical study. In D. Touretzky, G. Hinton, & T. Sejnowski (Eds.), *Proceedings of the 1988 Connectionist Models Summer School* (pp. 38–51). San Mateo, CA: Morgan Kaufmann.

Faigley, L., & Miller, T. (1982). What we learn from writing on the job. *College English, 44,* 557–569

Fairclough, N. (1989). *Language and power.* New York: Longman.

Fairclough, N. (1992). *Discourse and social change.* Cambridge: Polity Press.

Fairhurst, G. T. (1993). The leader–member exchange patterns of women leaders in industry: A discourse analysis. *Communication Monographs, 60,* 321–351.

Farace, R. V., Monge, P. R., & Russell, H. M. (1974). *Communicating . . . and organizing.* Unpublished manuscript.

Farkas, D. K. (1991). Collaborative writing, software development, and the universe of collaborative activity. In M. M. Lay & W. M. Karis (Eds.), *Collaborative writing in industry: Investigations in theory and practice* (pp. 13–30). Amityville, NY: Baywood.

Faulkner W., & Arnold, E. (1985). Smothered by invention: The masculinity of technology. In W. Faulkner & E. Arnold (Eds.), *Technology in women's lives: Smothered by invention* (pp. 18– 50). London: Pluto Press.

Fee, E. (Ed.). (1993). *Women and health: The politics of sex in medicine.* Farmingdale, NY: Baywood.

Fennell, D. (1988). *Investigation into the King's Cross underground fire.* London: Her Majesty's Stationary Office.

Ferguson, K. (1984). *The feminist case against bureaucracy.* Philadelphia: Temple University Press.

Ferguson, K. (1994). On bringing more theory, more voices, and more politics to the study of organizations. *Organization, 1,* 81–99.

Filby, I., & Willmott, H. (1988). Ideologies and contradictions in a public relations department: The seduction and impotence of living myth. *Organization Studies, 9*(3), 335–349.

Fine, M. (1993). New voices in organizational communication: A feminist commentary and critique. In S. P. Bowen & N. Wyatt (Eds.), *Transforming visions: Feminist critiques in communication studies* (pp. 125–166). Cresskill, NJ: Hampton Press.

Fineman, S. (1993). Organizations as emotional arenas. In S. Fineman (Ed.), *Emotion in organizations* (pp. 9–35). London: Sage.

Finet, D. (1993). The effects of boundary spanning communication on the sociopolitical delegitimization of an organization. *Management Communication Quarterly, 7*(1), 36–66.

Fisch, R., Weakland, J., & Segal, L. (1982). *The tactics of change: Doing brief therapy.* San Francisco: Jossey-Bass.

Fischer, F. (1990). *Technocracy and the politics of expertise.* Newbury Park, CA: Sage.

Fischer, F., & Sirianni, C. (Eds.). (1984). *Critical studies in organization and bureaucracy.* Philadelphia: Temple University Press.

Fisher, B. A. (1978). *Perspectives on human communication.* New York: Macmillan.

Flower, L., & Hayes, J. (1981). A cognitive process theory of writing. *College Composition and Communication, 32,* 365–387.

Ford, J. D., & Backoff, R. H. (1988). Organizational change in and out of dualities and paradox. In R. E. Quinn & K. S. Cameron (Eds.), *Paradox and transformation: Toward a theory of change in organization and management* (pp. 81–121). Cambridge, MA: Ballinger.

Forester, J. (1989). *Planning in the face of power.* Berkeley: University of California Press.

Forester, J. (1993). *Critical theory, public policy, and planning practice.* Albany: State University of New York Press.

Forman, J., & Katsky, P. (1986). The group report: A problem in small group or writing processes. *Journal of Business Communication, 23*(4), 23–35.

Forrest, S. (1991). Emergent commutation: Self-organizing, collective, and cooperative phenomena in natural and artificial computing networks. In S. Forrest (Ed.), *Emergent commutation* (pp. 1–11). Cambridge, MA: The MIT Press.

Foucault, M. (1977). *Discipline and punish: The birth of the prison* (A. Sheridan Smith, Trans.). New York: Random House.

Foucault, M. (1980). *Power/knowledge: Selected interviews and other writings, 1972–1977.* New York: Pantheon.

Francett, B. (1989, January). Neural nets arrive. *Computer Decisions,* 58–62.

Frank, A. D., & Brownwell, J. L. (1989). *Organizational communication and behavior: Communicating to improve performance.* New York: Holt, Rinehart & Winston.

Frankenberg, R. (1993). *White women, race matters: The social construction of whiteness.* Minneapolis: University of Minnesota Press.

Frederick, W. C. (1986). Toward CSR3: Why ethical analysis is indefensible and unavoidable in corporate affairs. *California Management Review, 28,* 126–155.

Freeman, J. A., & Skapura, D. M. (1991). *Neural networks: Algorithms. applications. and programming techniques.* Reading, MA: Addison-Wesley.

Freeman, R. E. (1984). *Strategic management: A stakeholder approach.* Boston, MA: Pitman.

Freeman, R. E. (Ed.). (1991). *Business ethics: The state of the art.* Oxford: Oxford University Press.

Freeman, R. E., & Gilbert, D. (1988). *Corporate strategy and the search for ethics.* Englewood Cliffs, NJ: Prentice-Hall.

Freeman, R. E., & Liedtka, J. (1991). Corporate social responsibility: A critical approach. *Business Horizons, 34,* 92–98.

Freidson, E. (1970). *Professional dominance: The social structure of medical care.* Chicago: Aldine.

Frissen, V. (1992). Trapped in electronic cages? Gender and new information technologies in the public and private domain: An overview of research. *Media Culture and Society, 14,* 31–49.

Frost, P. J., & Stablein, R. (Eds.). (1992). *Doing exemplary research.* Newbury Park, CA: Sage.

Frost, P. J., Moore, L. L., Louis, M. R., Lundberg, C. C., & Martin, J. (Eds.). (1985). *Organizational culture.* Beverly Hills, CA: Sage.

Fryer, B. (1994). Sex & the super-highway. *Working Woman, 19*(4), 51–60.

Fuchs, V. R. (1974). *Who shall live?* New York: Basic Books.

Fulk, J. (1993). Social construction of communication technology. *Academy of Management Journal, 36,* 921–950.

Fulk, J., & Boyd, B. (1991). Emerging theories of communication in organizations. *Journal of Management, 17,* 407–446.

Galbraith, J. R. (1977). *Organization design.* Reading, MA: Addison-Wesley.

Geertz, C. (1983). *Local knowledge: Further essays in interpretive anthropology.* New York: Basic Books.

Geist, P., & Hardesty, M. (1992). *Negotiating the crisis: DRGs and the transformation of hospitals.* Hillsdale, NJ: Erlbaum.

Gemert, L., van, & Woudstra, E. (1996). Writing ISO procedures: The use of sources of knowledge. In S. A. Amin & S. Fullerton (Eds.), *International business trends: Contemporary readings* (pp. 99-107). Cumberland, MD: Academy of Business Administration.

Gergen, K. (1992). Organizational theory in the postmodern era. In M. Reed & M. Hughes (Eds.), *Rethinking organization* (pp. 207–226). London: Sage.

Gevitz, N. (1982). *The D.O.'s: Osteopathic medicine in America.* Baltimore: Johns Hopkins University Press.

Giddens, A. (1979). *Central problems in social theory: Action, structure, and contradiction in social analysis.* Berkeley: University of California Press.

Giddens, A. (1984). *The constitution of society: Outline of the theory of structure.* Berkeley: University of California Press.

Giddens, A. (1987). *Social theory and modern sociology.* Stanford, CA: Stanford University Press.

Giddens, A. (1991). *Modernity and self-identity: Self and society in the late modern age.* Stanford, CA: Stanford University Press.

Gioia, D. A. (1986). Symbols, scripts, and sensemaking: Creating meaning in the organizational experience. In H. P. Sims, Jr., D. A. Gioia, & Associates (Eds.), *The thinking organization* (pp. 49–74). San Francisco: Jossey-Bass.

Glatzer, H. (1988, September). Neural computers go practical. *Software Magazine,* 26–31.

Glauser, M. J., & Axley, S. B. (1983). Consulting activities of university faculty members: Scope and depth of involvement. *Group and Organization Studies, 8,* 269–284.

Glover Campbell, P. (1991). Business communication or technical writing? *The Bulletin, LIV*(2), 6-10.

Goffman, E. (1959). *The presentation of self in everyday life.* New York: Doubleday Anchor.

Goffman, E. (1967) *Interaction ritual: Essays on face-to-face behavior.* Garden City, NY: Doubleday.

Goffman, E. (1969). *Strategic interaction.* Philadelphia: University of Pennsylvania Press.

Goldberg, A. A., & Larson, C. E. (1975). *Group communication: Discussion processes and application.* Englewood Cliffs, NJ: Prentice-Hall.

Goldhaber, G. M. (1974). *Organizational communication.* Dubuque, IA: William C. Brown.

Goldhaber, G. M. (1993). *Organizational communication* (6th ed.). Madison, WI: Brown and Benchmark.

Goodale, J. G. (1987). Employee involvement sparks diagnostic conference. *Personnel Journal, 66,* 79–87.

Goodall, H. L., Jr. (1989). *Casing a promised land: The autobiography of an organizational detective as cultural ethnographer.* Carbondale: Southern Illinois University Press.

Goodall, H. L., Jr., & Eisenberg, E. M. (1997). The dispossessed. In B. Sypher (Ed.), *More case studies in organizational communication.* New York: Guilford.

Goodman, A., Lye, K., & Gavaghan, K. (1994). *Communication futures.* London: Smythe, Dorward, & Lambert.

Gordon, W. (1988). Range of employee voice. *Employee Responsibility and Rights Journal, 1,* 283–99.

Gordon, W. I. (1994). "Wego" comes in several varieties and is not simple. In S. A. Deetz (Ed.), *Communication yearbook 17* (pp. 285–297). Thousand Oaks, CA: Sage.

Gorr, W. L. (1994). Editorial: Research prospective on neural network forecasting. *International Journal of Forecasting, 10,* 1–4.

Gorr, W. L., Nagin, D., & Szczypula, J. (1994). Comparative study of neural network and statistical model for predicting student grade point averages. *International Journal of Forecasting, 10,* 17–34.

Gorz, A. (1987). *Critique of economic reason* (G. Handyside & C. Turner, Trans.). London: Verso.

Gozdz, K. (1993). Building community as a leadership discipline. In M. Ray & A. Rinzler (Eds.), *The new paradigm in business: Emerging strategies for leadership and organizational change* (pp. 107–119). New York: Putnam.

Gramsci, A. (1971). *Selections from the prison notebooks* (Q. Hoare & G. N. Smith, Trans.). New York: International.

Granovetter, M. (1973). The strength of weak ties. *American Journal of Sociology, 78,* 1360–1380.

Gratz, R. D., & Salem, P. J. (1981). *Organizational communication and higher education.* Washington, DC: American Association for Higher Education.

Gray, B., Bougon, M., & Donnellon, A. (1985). Organizations as constructions and destructions of meaning. *Journal of Management, 11,* 83–98.

Greenbaum, H. (1971, April). *Organizational communication systems: Identification and appraisal.* Paper presented at the meeting of the International Communication Association, Phoenix, AZ.

Greenbaum, H. (1972, April). *The appraisal of organizational communication systems.* Paper presented at the meeting of the International Communication Association, Atlanta, GA.

Greenfield, S., Kaplan, S., & Ware, J. E. (1985). Expanding patient involvement in care. *Annals of Internal Medicine, 102*(4), 520-528.

Greenfield, S., Kaplan, S. H., & Ware, J. E., Jr. (1988). Patient participation in medical care: Effects on blood sugar and quality of life in diabetes. *Journal of General Internal Medicine, 3*, 448-457.

Gregory, K. L. (1983). Native-view paradigms: Multiple cultures and culture conflicts in organizations. *Administrative Science Quarterly, 28*, 359–376.

Griffin, L. M. (1952). The rhetoric of historical movements. *Quarterly Journal of Speech, 38*, 184–188.

Gronn, P. C. (1983). Talk as the work: The accomplishment of school administration. *Administrative Science Quarterly, 28*, 1–21.

Grunig, J. E. (1975). A multi-systems theory of organizational communication. *Communication Research, 2*(2), 99–136.

Grunig, J. E. (1978). Accuracy of communication from an external public to employees in a formal organization. *Human Communication Research, 5*(1), 40–53.

Grunig, J. E. (1982). The message–attitude–behavior relationship: Communication behaviors of organizations. *Communication Research, 9*(2), 163-200.

Grunig, J. E. (1984). Organizations, environments, and models of public relations. *Public Relations Research and Education, 1*, 6–29.

Grunig, J. E., & Grunig, L. A. (1992). Models of public relations and communication. In J. E. Grunig (Ed.), *Excellence in public relations and communication management* (pp. 285-325). Hillsdale, NJ: Erlbaum.

Habermas, J. (1971). *Knowledge and human interests* (J. Shapiro, Trans.). Boston: Beacon Press.

Habermas, J. (1984). *The theory of communicative action, volume 1: Reason and the rationalization of society* (T. McCarthy, Trans.). Boston: Beacon.

Habermas, J. (1987). *The theory of communicative action, volume 2: Lifeworld and system* (T. McCarthy, Trans.). Boston: Beacon.

Hackett, E. J., Mirvis, P. H., & Sales, A. L. (1991). Women's and men's expectations about the effects of new technology at work. *Group & Organizational Studies, 16*(1), 60–85.

Hackos, J. T. (1994). *Managing your documentation projects.* New York: Wiley.

Hage, G. (1980). *Theories of organizations: Form, process and transformation.* New York: Wiley.

Hall, J. (1969). *Systems maintenance: Gatekeeping and the involvement process.* Conroe, TX: Teleometrics International.

Hammer, M., & Champy, J. (1993). *Reengineering the corporation.* New York: Harper-Collins.

Handy, C. (1994). *The age of paradox.* Boston: Harvard Business School Press.

Haney, W. (1973). *Communication and organizational behavior.* Homewood, IL: Irwin.

Hanneman, R. A. (1988). *Computer assisted theory building: Modeling dynamic social systems.* Newbury Park, CA: Sage.

Hardt, H., & Brennen, B. (1993). Introduction: Communication and the question of history. *Communication Theory, 3,* 130–136.

Harris, L., & Cronen, V. E. (1979). A rules-based model for the analysis and evaluation of organizational communication. *Communication Quarterly, 27,* 12–18.

Harrison, T. M. (1994). Communication and interdependence in democratic organizations. In S. A. Deetz (Ed.), *Communication yearbook 17* (pp. 246–274). Thousand Oaks, CA: Sage.

Haslett, B. (1990). Discourse, ideology, and organizational control. In J. A. Anderson (Ed.), *Communication yearbook 13* (pp. 48–58). Newbury Park, CA: Sage.

Haslett, B. (1993). Gender, power, and communication in organizations. In B. Dervin & U. Hariharan (Eds.), *Progress in communication sciences XI* (pp. 159–177). Norwood, NJ: Ablex.

Hatch, M. J., & Ehrlich, S. B. (1993). Spontaneous humor as an indicator of paradox and ambiguity in organizations. *Organization Studies, 14,* 502-526.

Hater, J. J., & Bass, B. M. (1988). Superiors' evaluations and subordinates' perceptions of transformational and transactional leadership. *Journal of Applied Psychology, 73,* 695–702.

Haug, M., & Lavin, B. (1983). *Consumerism in medicine: Challenging physician authority.* Beverly Hills, CA: Sage.

Hecht-Nielsen, R. (1987). Kolmogorov's mapping neural networks existence theorem. *Proceedings of the Third International Joint Conference of Neural Networks, 3,* 11–13.

Heckscher, C. (1995). *White-collar blues: Management loyalties in an age of corporate restructuring.* New York: Basic Books.

Heisenberg, W. (1958). *Physics and philosophy.* New York: Harper Torch.

Henderson, H. (1993). Age of light. In M. Ray & A. Rinzler (Eds.), *The new paradigm in business: Emerging strategies for leadership and organizational change* (pp. 267–275). New York: Putnam.

Hess, J. W., Liepman, M. R., & Ruane, T. J. (1983). *Family practice and preventive medicine: Health promotion in primary care.* New York: Human Sciences Press.

Hess, R. D., & Miura, I. T. (1985). Gender differences in enrollment in computer camps and classes. *Sex Roles, 13,* 193–203.

Hessing, M. (1991). Talking shop(ping): Office conversations and women's dual labour. *Canadian Journal of Sociology, 16,* 23-50.

Hill, T., Marquez, L., O'Connor, M., & Remus, W. (1994). Artificial neural network models for forecasting and decision making. *International Journal of Forecasting, 10,* 5–15.

Hillelsohn, M. J. (1984). How to think about CBT. *Training and Development Journal, 38*(12), 42–44.

Hjelmslev, L. (1961). *Prolegomena to a theory of language* (F. J. Whitfield, Trans.). Madison: University of Wisconsin Press.

Hochschild, A. (1983). *The managed heart: Commercialization of human feeling.* Berkeley: University of California Press.

Hochschild, A. (1989). *The second shift.* New York: Avon Books.

Hofstede, G. (1980). Motivation, leadership, and organization: Do American theories apply abroad? *Organizational Dynamics, 9,* 42–63.

Honikman, K. (1987). Problems, processes, and politics: A South African research project in organizational communication. *Communication Research Reports, 4,* 71–78.

Hornik, K., Stinchcombe, M., & White, H. (1989). Multilayer feed-forward networks are universal approximators. *Neural Networks, 2,* 359–366.

House, R. J. (1977). A 1976 theory of charismatic leadership. In J. G. Hunt & L. L. Larson (Eds.), *Leadership: The cutting edge* (pp. 189–207). Carbondale: Southern Illinois University Press.

Howard, L. A., & Geist, P. (1995). Ideological processing in organizational change: The dialectic of control in a merging organization. *Communication Monographs, 62,* 110–131.

Huber, G. A. (1991). Organizational learning: The contributing processes and literatures. *Organizational Science, 2,* 88–115.

Huber, G. P., Sutcliffe, K. M., Miller, C. C., & Glick, W. H. (1995). Understanding and predicting organizational change. In G. P. Huber & W. H. Glick (Eds.), *Organizational change and redesign: Ideas and insights for improving performance* (pp. 215–265). New York: Oxford University Press.

Humpert, B. (1989, Fall). Financial applications using neural networks. *Intelligent Systems Review,* 36–45.

Huseman, R., Logue, C., & Freshley, D. (1969). *Readings in interpersonal and organizational communication.* Boston: Holbrook.

Hyde, M. J. (1990). Experts, rhetoric, and the dilemmas of medical technology: Investigating a problem of progressive ideology. In M. J. Medhurst, A. Gonzalez, & T. R. Peterson (Eds.), *Communication and the culture of technology* (pp. 115–136). Pullman: Washington State University Press.

Iannello, K. (1993). *Decisions without hierarchy: Feminist interventions in organizational theory and practice.* London: Routledge.

"In industry, failure to communicate." (1975, October 20). *Newsday,* p. 29.

Infante, D. A. (1995). Teaching students to understand and control verbal aggression. *Communication Education, 44,* 51–63.

Isaacs, W. N. (1993a). Dialogue: The power of collective thinking. *The Systems Thinker, 4,* 3.

Isaacs, W. N. (1993b) Taking flight: Dialogue, collective thinking, and organizational learning. *Organizational Dynamics, 22*(2), 24–39.

Jablin, F. (1987). Formal organization structure. In F. M. Jablin, L. L. Putnam, K. H. Roberts, & L. W. Porter (Eds.), *Handbook of organizational communication: An interdisciplinary perspective* (pp. 389–419). Beverly Hills, CA: Sage.

Jablin, F. M., Putnam, L. L., Roberts, K. H., & Porter, L. W. (Eds.). (1987). *Handbook of organizational communication: An interdisciplinary perspective.* Newbury Park, CA: Sage.

Jackell, R. (1988). *Moral mazes: The world of corporate managers.* Oxford, England: Oxford University Press.

Jansen, S. C. (1993). "The future is not what it used to be": Gender, history, and communication studies. *Communication Theory, 3,* 136–148.

Johnson, J. D. (1992a). Approaches to organizational communication structure. *Journal of Business Research, 25,* 99–113.

Johnson, J. D. (1992b). Technological and spatial factors related to organizational communication structure. *Journal of Managerial Issues, 4,* 190-209.

Johnson, M. (1987). *The body in the mind.* Chicago: University of Chicago Press.

Johnson, M. (1993). *Moral imagination: Implications of cognitive science for ethics.* Chicago: University of Chicago Press.

Jones, J. A., Kreps, G. L., & Phillips, G. M. (1995). *Communicating with your doctor: Getting the most out of health care.* Cresskill, NJ: Hampton Press.

Jones, M. O., Moore, M. D., & Snyder, R. C. (Eds.). (1988). *Inside organizations: Understanding the human dimension.* Newbury Park, CA: Sage.

Jones, W. M. (1964). *On decision-making in large organizations.* Santa Monica, CA: The Rand Corporation.

Joraanstad, P. S. (1992). *Innovational theory examined through an analysis of the term limitation movement.* Unpublished doctoral dissertation, Department of Communication, Arizona State University.

Kanter, R. M. (1983). *The change masters: Innovation and entreprenuership in the American corporation.* New York: Simon & Schuster.

Kanter, R. M., Stein, B. A., & Jick, T. D. (1992). *The challenge of organizational change: How companies experience and leaders guide it.* New York: The Free Press.

Kaplan, A. (1964). *The conduct of inquiry.* Chicago: SRA/Chandler.

Kast, F. E., & Rosenzweig, J. E. (1970). *Organization and management: A systems approach.* New York: McGraw-Hill.

Katz, D., & Kahn, R. (1966). *The social psychology of organizations.* New York: Wiley.

Katz, D., & Kahn, R. (1978). *The social psychology of organizations* (2nd ed.). New York: Wiley.

Kavanagh, J. F., & Cuttings, J. E. (Eds.). (1975). *The role of speech in language*. Cambridge, MA: The MIT Press.

Kaye, E. (1993, October). *Working Woman*, pp. 51-53.

Kelly, J. A., St. Lawrence, J. S., Smith, S., Hood, H. V., & Cook, D. J. (1987). Stigmatization of AIDS patients by physicians. *American Journal of Public Health, 77*, 789–791.

Kelly, K. (1994). *Out of control*. Reading, MA: Addison-Wesley.

Keough, C. M. (1989). A strategic content analysis of contract negotiation: Application of a structurational coding system. In B. Gronbeck (Ed.), *Spheres of argument: Proceedings of the Sixth SCA/AFA Conference on Argumentation* (pp. 569–575). Annandale, VA: Speech Communication Association.

Kerlinger, F. N. (1986). *Foundations of behavioral research* (3rd ed.). New York: Harcourt Brace Jovanovich.

Kerr, S. (1975). On the folly of rewarding A, while hoping for B. *Academy of Management Journal, 47*, 469–783.

Keyton, J. (1993). Group termination: Completing the study of group development. *Small Group Research, 24*, 84–100.

Kim, S. H. (1994). *Learning and coordination: Enhancing agent performance through distributed decision making*. Norwell, MA: Kluwer Academic Publishers.

Kim, Y. Y. (1994). Interethnic communication: The context and the behavior. In S. A. Deetz (Ed.), *Communication yearbook 17* (pp. 511–538). Thousand Oaks, CA: Sage.

Kimberly, J. R., Miles, R. H., & Associates (1980). *The organizational life cycle: Issues in the creation, transformation, and decline of organizations*. San Francisco: Jossey-Bass.

King, S., & Cushman, D. (1994). High-speed management as a theoretic principle for yielding significant organizational communication behaviors. In B. Kovacic (Ed.), *New approaches to organizational communication* (pp. 87–116). Albany: State University of New York Press.

Kinoshita, J. (1988, November). Neural networks at work. *Scientific American*, 134–135.

Kirtz, M. K., & Reep, D. C. (1990). A survey of the frequency, types, and importance of writing tasks in four career areas. *The Bulletin, 53*(4), 3–5

Kleimann, S. (1989). *Vertical collaboration and the report review process at the U. S. General Accounting Office* (UMI 3965). Unpublished doctoral dissertation, University of Maryland, College Park.

Kleimann, S. (1991). The complexity of workplace review. *Technical Communication, 38*(4), 520–526.

Kleimann, S. (1993). The reciprocal relationship of workplace culture and review. In R. Spilka (Ed.), *Writing in the workplace: New research perspectives* (56–70). Carbondale: Southern Illinois University Press.

Knapp, M. L., Hart, R. P., Frederick, G., & Shulman, G. M. (1973). The rhetoric of goodbye: Verbal and nonverbal correlations of leave-taking. *Speech Monographs, 40,* 182–198.

Knights, D. (1992). Changing spaces: The disruptive impact of a new epistemological location for the study of management. *Academy of Management Review, 17,* 514–536.

Knights, D., & Odih, P. (1995). "Its about time": The significance of gendered time for financial services consumption. *Time & Society,* 4(2), 205–231.

Knights, D., & Willmott, H. (1987). Organizational culture as management strategy. *International Studies of Management and Organization, 17,* 40–63.

Knights, D., & Willmott, H. (Eds.). (1990). *Labour process theory.* London: Macmillan.

Knoblauch, C. H. (1989). The teaching and practice of "professional writing." In M. Kogan (Ed.), *Writing in the business professions* (pp. 246–264). Urbana, IL: NCTE & ABC.

Kogen, M. (1989). (Ed.). *Writing in the business professions.* Urbana, IL: NCTE & ABC.

Koike, H., Gudykunst, W. B., Stewart, L. P., & Ting-Toomey, S. (1988). Communication openness, satisfaction, and length of employment in Japanese organizations. *Communication Research Reports, 5,* 97–102.

Kosa, J., & Zola, I. (Eds.). (1975). *Poverty and health: A sociological analysis.* Cambridge, MA: Harvard University Press.

Kosko, B. (1993). *Fuzzy thinking: The new science of fuzzy logic.* New York: Hyperion.

Kotler, P., & Roberto, E. (1989). *Social marketing: Strategies for changing public behavior.* New York: The Free Press.

Kouzes, J. M., & Posner, B. Z. (1987). *The leadership challenge: How to get extraordinary things done in organizations.* San Francisco, CA: Jossey-Bass.

Kramarae, C. (Ed.). (1988). *Technology and women's voices: Keeping in touch.* London: Routledge.

Kreps, G. L. (1986). Health communication and the elderly. *World Communication, 15,* 55–70.

Kreps, G. L. (1988a). The pervasive role of information in health and health care: Implications for health communication policy. In J. Anderson (Ed.), *Communication yearbook 11* (pp. 238–276). Newbury Park, CA: Sage.

Kreps, G. L. (1988b). Relational communication in health care. *Southern Speech Communication Journal, 53,* 344–359.

Kreps, G. L. (1989). Stories as repositories of organizational intelligence: Implications for organizational development. In J. A. Anderson (Ed.), *Communication yearbook 13* (pp. 191–202). Newbury Park, CA: Sage.

Kreps, G. L. (1990a). Communication and health education. In E. B. Ray & L. Donohew (Eds.), *Communication and health: Systems and applications* (pp. 187–203). Hillsdale, NJ: Erlbaum.

Kreps, G. L. (1990b). *Organizational communication* (2nd ed.). White Plains, NY: Longman.

Kreps, G. L. (1993). Refusing to be a victim: Rhetorical strategies for confronting cancer. In B. C. Thornton & G. L. Kreps (Eds.), *Perspectives on health communication* (pp. 42–47). Prospect Heights, IL: Waveland.

Kreps, G. L., & Kunimoto, E. (1994). *Effective communication in multicultural health care settings.* Newbury Park, CA: Sage.

Kreps, G. L., & O'Hair, D. (Eds.). (1995). *Communication and health outcomes.* Cresskill, NJ: Hampton Press.

Kreps, G. L., & Thornton, B. C. (1992). *Health communication: Theory and practice* (2nd ed.). Prospect Heights, IL: Waveland.

Kreps, G. L., Ruben, B. D., Baker, M. W., & Rosenthal, S. R. (1987, May–June). Survey of public knowledge about digestive health and diseases: Implications for health education. *Public Health Reports, 102,* 270–277.

Krippendorff, K. (1989). On the ethics of constructing communication. In B. Dervin, L. Grossberg, B. J. O'Keefe, & E. Wartella (Eds.), *Rethinking communication: Volume 1, Paradigm issues* (pp. 66–96). Newbury Park, CA: Sage.

Kuhnert, K. W., & Lewis, P. (1987). Transactional and transformational leadership: A constructive/developmental analysis. *Academy of Management Review, 12,* 648–657.

Kunda, G. (1992). *Engineering culture: Control and commitment in a high-tech corporation.* Philadelphia: Temple University Press.

Laclau, E., & Mouffe, C. (1985). *Hegemony and socialist strategy* (W. Moore & P. Cammack, Trans.). London: Verso.

Land, G., & Jarman, B. (1993). Moving beyond breakpoint. In M. Ray & A. Rinzler (Eds.), *The new paradigm in business: Emerging strategies for leadership and organizational change* (pp. 250–266). New York: Putnam.

Landers, L. (1978). *Defective medicine.* New York: Farrar, Straus & Giroux.

Laumann, E., & Knoke, D. (1987). *The organizational state: Social choice in national policy domains.* Madison: University of Wisconsin Press.

Lawson, D. P. (1996). *The organizational impact of sales force automation using Lotus Notes technology: A field study in the electronics manufacturing industry.* Unpublished doctoral dissertation, University of Kansas.

Lay, M. M., & Karis, W. M. (1991). *Collaborative writing in industry: Investigations in theory and practice.* Amityville, NY: Baywood.

Leavett, H. (1972). *Managerial psychology.* Chicago: University of Chicago Press.

Lederman, L. C., & Stewart, L. P. (1987). The Marble Company: The design and implementation of a simulation board game. *Simulations and Games, 18,* 57–81.

Lederman, L. C., & Stewart, L. P. (1991). The rules of the game. *Simulation and Games, 22,* 502–507.

Leduc, N. (1979, September). Communicating through computers. *Telecommunications Policy,* 235–244.

Lee, M., & Barnett, G. (1995, May). *A symbols and meaning approach to the organizational cultures of banks in the United States, Japan, and Taiwan.* Paper presented to the meeting of the International Communication Association, Albuquerque, NM.

Lefebvre, C., & Flora, J. (1988). Social marketing and public health intervention. *Health Education Quarterly, 15,* 299–315.

Leggiere, P. (1995, August). Agent of the third culture. *Wired,* 118–119, 172.

Lesikar, R. (1972). *Business communication.* Homewood, IL.: Irwin.

Levinson, H. (1973). Asinine attitudes toward motivation. *Harvard Business Review, 51*(1), 70-76.

Li, E. Y. (1994). Artificial neural networks and their business applications. *Information and Management, 27,* 303–313.

Lieberman, P. (1967). *Intonation, perception and language.* Cambridge, MA: The MIT Press.

Lieberman, P. (1972). *The speech of primates.* The Hague: Mouton.

Limaye, M. R. (1994). Responding to work-force diversity: Conceptualization and search for paradigms. *Journal of Business and Technical Writing, 8,* 353–372.

Lincoln, Y. S., & Guba, E. G. (1985). *Naturalistic inquiry.* Newbury Park, CA: Sage.

Lippmann, R. P. (1987, April). An introduction to computing with neural networks. *IEEE ASSP Magazine,* 4–22.

Liska, J., & Chronkite, G. (1994). On the death, dismemberment, or disestablishment of the dominant paradigms. *Western Journal of Communication, 58*(1), 58–65.

Locker, K. O. (1992). What makes a collaborative writing team successful? A case study of lawyers and social service workers in a state agency. In J. Forman (Ed.), *New visions of collaborative writing* (pp. 37–62). Portsmouth, NH: Cook.

Loseke, D. R. (1989). Creating clients: Social problems work in a shelter for battered women. *Perspectives on Social Problems, 1,* 173–193.

Lotman, J. M. (1977). Two models of communication. In D. P. Lucid (Ed.), *Soviet semiotics: An anthology* (pp. 99–101). London: John Hopkins University Press.

Lowdermilk, D. L. (1995). Reproductive surgery. In C. I. Fogel & N. F. Woods (Eds.), *Women's health care* (pp. 629–650). Thousand Oaks, CA: Sage.

Lowry, A. K. (1994). The Information Arcade at the University of Iowa. *Cause-Effect, 17*(3), 38–44.

Luhmann, N. (1990). *Essays on self-reference.* New York: Colombia University Press.

Lukács, G. (1971). *History and class consciousness* (R. Livingstone, Trans.). Cambridge, MA: The MIT Press.

Lyons, P. J. (1993). *Applying expert systems technology to business.* Belmont, CA: International Thompson Publishing.

Lyotard, J. F. (1984). *The postmodern condition: A report on knowledge* (G. Bennington & B. Massumi, Trans.). Minneapolis: University of Minnesota Press.

MacIntyre, A. (1984). *After virtue: A study in moral theory* (2nd ed.). Notre Dame, IN: University of Notre Dame Press.

Maclean, N. (1992). *Young men and fire.* Chicago: University of Chicago Press.

Mahowald, M. B. (1993). *Women and children in health care: An unequal majority.* New York: Oxford University Press.

Maibach, E. W., & Kreps, G. L. (1986, September). *Communicating with clients: Primary care physicians perspectives on cancer prevention, screening, and education.* Paper presented to the International Conference on Doctor–Patient Communication, University of Western Ontario, Canada.

Maibach, E. W., Kreps, G. L., & Bonaguro, E. W. (1993). Developing strategic communication campaigns for HIV/AIDS prevention. In S. Ratzan (Ed.), *AIDS: Effective health communication for the 90s* (pp. 15–35). Washington, DC: Taylor and Francis.

Mandel, T. (1993). Giving values a voice: Marketing in the new paradigm. In M. Ray & A. Rinzler (Eds.), *The new paradigm in business: Emerging strategies for leadership and organizational change* (pp. 164–177). New York: Putnam.

Mangham, I. (1995). The moral character of managers. *Organization: The Interdisciplinary Journal of Organization, Theory, and Society, 3,* 181–204.

Mangham, I. L., & Overington, M. A. (1987). *Organizations as theatre: A social psychology of dramatic appearances.* New York: Wiley.

March, J., & Simon, H. (1958). *Organizations.* New York: Wiley.

Maren, A. J. (1990). Introduction to neural networks. In A. J. Maren, C. T. Harston, & R. M. Pap (Eds.), *Handbook of neural computing applications* (pp. 1–11). San Diego, CA: Academic Press.

Maren, A. J., Jones, D., & Franklin, S. (1990). Configuring and optimizing the back-propagation network. In A. J. Maren, C. T. Harston, & R. M. Pap (Eds.), *Handbook of neural computing applications* (pp. 233–250). San Diego, CA: Academic Press.

Markus, M. L. (1990). Toward a "critical mass" theory of interactive media. In J. Fulk & C. W. Steinfeld (Eds.), *Organizations and communication technology* (pp. 194–218). Newbury Park, CA: Sage.

Marshall, J. (1993a). Whose agenda is it anyway: Training medical residents in patient-centered interviewing techniques. In E. Berlin Ray (Ed.), *Case studies in health communication* (pp. 15–29). Hillsdale, NJ: Erlbaum.

Marshall, J. (1993b). Viewing organizational communication from a feminist perspective: A critique and some offerings. In S. A. Deetz (Ed.), *Communication yearbook 16* (pp. 122–143). Newbury Park, CA: Sage.

Matroianni, A. C., Faden, R. R., & Federman, D. D. (Eds.). (1994). *Women and health research: Ethical and legal issues of including women in clinical studies.* Washington, DC: National Academy Press.

McCroskey, J., Larson, C. E., & Knapp, M. (1971). *An introduction to interpersonal communication.* Englewood Cliffs, NJ: Prentice-Hall.

McGee, G. W., Goodson, J. R., & Cashman, J. F. (1987). Job stress and job dissatisfaction: Influence of contextual factors. *Psychological Reports, 61,* 367–375.

McPhee, R. D. (1989). Organizational communication: A structurational exemplar. In B. Dervin, L. Grossberg, B. J. O'Keefe, & E. Wartella (Eds.), *Rethinking communication: Volume 2–paradigm exemplars* (pp. 199–211). Newbury Park, CA: Sage.

McPhee, R. D., & Poole, M. S. (1981). Mathematical models in communication research. In M. Burgoon (Ed.), *Communication yearbook 5* (pp. 159–191). New Brunswick, NJ: Transaction.

Mead, G. H. (1934). *Mind, self and society* (C. W. Morris, Ed.). Chicago: University of Chicago Press.

Mechanic, D. (1962). Sources of power for lower participants in complex organizations. *Administrative Science Quarterly, 7,* 349–364.

Meilich, O. (1995, August). *The effectiveness of publication records as screening criterion for academic tenure.* Paper presented at the Academy of Management Annual Meeting, Vancouver, Canada.

Mendelsohn, R. (1979). *Confessions of a medical heretic.* Chicago: Contemporary Books.

Mendelsohn, R. (1981). *Male practice: How doctors manipulate women.* Chicago: Contemporary Books.

Miller, J. G. (1978). *Living systems.* New York: McGraw-Hill.

Miller, K. (1995). *Organizational communication: Approaches and processes.* Belmont, CA: Wadsworth.

Miller, P., & O'Leary, T. (1987). Accounting and the construction of the governable person. *Accounting, Organizations, and Society, 12*, 235–265.

Minitab, Inc. (1995). *Minitab* (Version 10.2) [Computer software]. State College, PA: Author.

Mintzberg, H. (1971). Managerial work: Analysis from observation. *Management Science, 18*, 97–110.

Mondragon, D., Kirkmann-Liff, B., & Schneller, E. (1991). Hostility to people with AIDS: Risk perception and demographic factors. *Social Science and Medicine, 32*, 1137–1142.

Monge, P. R., Farace, R. V., Eisenberg, E. M., Miller, K. I., & White, L. L. (1984). The process of studying process in organizational communication. *Journal of Communication, 34*, 22–43.

Morgan, M., & Murray, M. (1991). Insight and collaborative writing. In M. M. Lay & W. M. Karis (Eds.), *Collaborative writing in industry: Investigations in theory and practice* (pp. 64–81). Amityville, NY: Baywood.

Morley, D. D., & Shockley-Zalabak, P. (1985). An exploratory study of the organizational communication patterns of males and females. *Communication Research Reports, 2*, 103–111.

Morris, G. H. (1988). Accounts in selection interviews. *Journal of Applied Communication Research, 15*(2), 82–98.

Morrow, P. (1981). Work related communication, environmental uncertainty, and subunit effectiveness: A second look at the information processing approach to subunit communication. *Academy of Management Journal, 24*, 851–858.

Mumby, D. K. (1987). The political function of narrative in organizations. *Communication Monographs, 54*, 113–127.

Mumby, D. K. (1988). *Communication and power in organizations: Discourse, ideology, and domination.* Norwood, NJ: Ablex.

Mumby, D. K. (1993a). Critical organizational communication studies: The next ten years. *Communication Monographs, 60*, 18–25.

Mumby, D. K. (1993b). Feminism and the critique of organizational communication studies. In S. A. Deetz (Ed.), *Communication yearbook 16* (pp. 155–166). Newbury Park, CA: Sage.

Mumby, D. K. (forthcoming). Power, politics, and organizational communication: Theoretical perspectives. In F. M. Jablin & L. L. Putnam (Eds.), *The new handbook of organizational communication.* Thousand Oaks, CA: Sage.

Mumby, D. K., & Putnam, L. L. (1992). The politics of emotion: A feminist reading of bounded rationality. *Academy of Management Review, 17*, 465–486.

Murray, E. (1972, April). *Basis for a discipline of communication epistemology in interpersonal communication.* Paper presented to the Central States Speech Association, Chicago, IL.

Nakayama, T., & Kriziek, R. (1995). Whiteness: A strategic rhetoric. *The Quarterly Journal of Speech, 81,* 291–309.

Nayaranan, V. K. (1996). *Technology and organizations.* Manuscript in preparation.

Nerone, J. (1993). Theory and history: Forum on communication, theory and history. *Communication Theory, 3,* 148–157.

Newell, G. R., & Webber, C. F. (1983). The primary care physician in cancer prevention. *Family and Community Health, 5,* 77–84.

Nicotera, A. M., & Cushman, D. P. (1992). Organizational ethics: A within organization view. *Journal of Applied Communication Research, 20,* 437–462.

Nkomo, S. (1992). The emperor has no clothes: Rewriting "Race in Organizations." *Academy of Management Review, 17,* 487–513.

O'Connor, E. S. (1995). Paradoxes of participation: A textual analysis of case studies on organizational change, *Organization Studies, 16*(5), 769–803.

O'Neill, J. (1995). *The poverty of postmodernism.* London: Routledge.

O'Neill, N., & O'Neill, G. (1972). *Open marriage: A new lifestyle for couples.* New York: Avon.

O'Reilly, B. (1989, February 27). Computers that think like people. *Fortune,* 90–93.

O'Reilly, C. A. (1980). Individuals and information overload in organizations: Is more necessarily better? *Academy of Management Journal, 23,* 684–696.

Odell, L., & Goswami D. (Eds.). (1985). *Writing in nonacademic settings.* New York: Guilford.

Orleans, C. T., George, L. K., Houpt, J. L., & Brodie, K. H. (1985). Health promotion in primary care: A survey of U.S. family practitioners. *Preventive Medicine, 14,* 636–647.

Orlikowski, W. J., & Yates, J. (1994). Genre repertoire: The structuring of communicative practices in organizations. *Administrative Science Quarterly, 39,* 541–574.

Osterberg, R. V. (1993). A new kind of company with a new kind of thinking. In M. Ray & A. Rinzler (Eds.), *The new paradigm in business: Emerging strategies for leadership and organizational change* (pp. 67–71). New York: Putnam.

Pacanowsky, M., & O'Donnell-Trujillo, N. (1982). Communication and organizational cultures. *Western Journal of Speech Communication, 46,* 115-130.

Pacanowsky, M. E., & O'Donnell-Trujillo, N. (1983). Organizational communication as cultural performance. *Communication Monographs, 50,* 126–147.

Papa, M. J. (1990). Communication network patterns and employee performance with new technology, *Communication Research, 17,* 344-368.

Papa, M. J., Auwal, M. A., & Singhal, A. (1995). Dialectic of control and emancipation in organizing for social change: A multitheoretic study of the Grameen Bank in Bangladesh. *Communication Theory, 5,* 189–223.

Paradis, J., Dobrin, D., & Miller, R. (1985). Writing at Exxon, ITD: Notes on the writing environment of an R&D organization. In L. Odell & D. Goswami (Eds.), *Writing in nonacademic settings* (pp. 281–308). New York: Guilford.

Paré, A. (1993). Discourse regulations and the production of knowledge. In R. Spilka (Ed.), *Writing in the workplace: New research perspectives* (pp. 111–123). Carbondale: Southern Illinois University Press.

Pashkow, F. J., & Libov, C. (1994). *The women's heart book.* New York: Plume.

Payer, L. (1988). *Medicine and culture.* New York: Penguin Books.

Pearce, W. B. (1989). *Communication and the human condition.* Carbondale: Southern Illinois University Press.

Peck, M. S. (1993). *A world waiting to be born: Civility rediscovered.* New York: Bantam

Pelt, W. van, & Gillam, A. (1991). Peer collaboration and the computer-assisted classroom: Bridging the gap between academia and the workplace. In M. M. Lay & W. M. Karis (Eds.), *Collaborative writing in industry: Investigations in theory and practice* (pp. 170–205). Amityville, NY: Baywood.

Pepper, G. L. (1995). *Communicating in organizations: A cultural approach.* New York: McGraw-Hill.

Pfeffer, J. (1981a). Management as symbolic action: The creation and maintenance of organizational paradigms. In L. L. Cummings & B. M. Staw (Eds.), *Research in organizational behavior* (Vol. 3, pp. 1–52). Greenwich, CT: JAI Press.

Pfeffer, J. (1981b). *Power in organizations.* Marshfield, MA: Pitman.

Phillips, G. M., & Jones, J. A. (1991). Medical compliance: Patient or physician responsibility. *American Behavioral Scientist, 34,* 756–767.

Phillips, N., & Brown, J. L. (1993). Analyzing communication in and around organizations: A critical hermeneutic approach. *Academy of Management Journal, 36,* 1547–1576.

Piazza, C. L. (1987). Identifying context variables in research on writing: A review and suggested directions. *Written Communications, 4*(2), 107–137.

Piercy, M. (1973). *To be of use.* Garden City, NY: Doubleday.

Plowman, L. (1993). Tracing the evolution of a co-authored text. *Language and Communication, 13*(3), 149–161

Pondy, L. R., Frost, P. J., Morgan, G., & Dandridge, T. C. (Eds.). (1983). *Organizational symbolism.* Greenwich, CT: JAI Press.

Pondy, L., & Mitroff, I. I. (1979). Beyond open system models of organization. In L. L. Cummings & B. M. Staw (Eds.), *Research in organizational behavior* (Vol. 1, pp. 3–39). Greenwich, CT: JAI Press.

Poole, M. S. (1997). A turn of the wheel: The case for a renewal of systems inquiry in organizational communication research. In L. Thayer & G. Barnett (Eds.), *Organization-communication: Emerging perspectives V* (pp. 47-63). Norwood, NJ: Ablex.

Poole, M. S., & DeSanctis, J. (1990). Understanding the use of group decision support systems: The theory of adaptive structuration. In J. Fulk & C. Steinfeld (Eds.), *Organizations and communication technology* (pp. 175–195). Newbury Park, CA: Sage.

Poole, M. S., Seibold, D. R., & McPhee, R. D. (1986). A structurational approach to theory-building in group decision-making research. In R. Y. Hirokawa & M. S. Poole (Eds.), *Communication and group decision-making* (pp. 237–264). Beverly Hills, CA: Sage.

Port, O. (1995, July 17). Computers that think are almost here. *Business Week, 68–71, 73.*

Posner, I. R., Baecker, R. M., & Wellner, P. (1990). *How people write together.* Unpublished manuscript, Department of Computer Science, University of Toronto.

Power, M. (1994). The audit society. In A. Hopwood & P. Miller (Eds.), *Accounting as social and institutional practice* (pp. 299–316). Cambridge, England: Cambridge University Press.

Pratt, C. B. (1994). Applying classical ethical theories to ethical decision making in public relations: Perrier's product recall. *Management Communication Quarterly, 8,* 70–94.

Prechelt, L. (1995). *Frequently asked questions (FAQ) in neural networks* (Version April 28). Available at: http://wwwipd. ira.uka.de/~prechelt/FAQ/neural-net-faq.htm I.

Putnam, L. L. (1983). The interpretive perspective: An alternative to functionalism. In L. L. Putnam & M. E. Pacanowsky (Eds.), *Communication and organizations: An interpretive approach* (pp. 31–54). Beverly Hills, CA: Sage.

Putnam, L. L. (1986). Contradictions and paradoxes in organizations. In L. Thayer (Ed.), *Organization—communication: Emerging perspectives I* (pp. 151–167). Norwood, NJ: Ablex.

Putnam, L. L. (1989). Negotiating as organizing: Two levels within the Weickian model. *Communication Studies, 40,* 249–257.

Putnam, L. L., & Cheney, G. (1983). A critical review of the research traditions in organizational communication. In M. S. Mander (Ed.), *Communication in transition* (pp. 206–224). New York: Praeger.

Putnam, L. L., & Cheney, G. (1985). Organizational communication: Historical development and future directions. In T. W. Benson (Ed.), *Speech communication in the twentieth century* (pp. 130–156). Carbondale: Southern Illinois University Press.

Putnam, L. L., & Fairhurst, G. (forthcoming). Language and discourse approaches to the study of organizational communication. In F. M. Jablin & L. L. Putnam (Eds.), *The new handbook of organizational communication.* Thousand Oaks, CA: Sage.

Putnam, L. L., & Mumby, D. K. (1993). Organizations, emotion, and the myth of rationality. In S. Fineman (Ed.), *Emotions in organizations* (pp. 36–57). London: Sage.

Putnam, L. L., & Poole, M. S. (1987). Conflict and negotiation. In F. M. Jablin, L. L. Putnam, K. H. Roberts, & L. W. Porter (Eds.), *Handbook of organizational communication: An interdisciplinary perspective* (pp. 549–599). Beverly Hills, CA: Sage.

Putnam, L. L., & Roloff, M. E. (Eds.). (1992). *Communication and negotiation.* Newbury Park, CA: Sage.

Putnam, L. L., Phillips, N., & Chapman, P. (in press). Metaphors of communication and organization. In S. Clegg, C. Hardy, & W. Nord (Eds.), *Handbook of organizational studies.* London: Sage.

Putti, J. M., Ayree, S., & Phua, J. (1990). Communication relationship satisfaction and organizational commitment. *Group and Organization Studies, 15,* 44–52.

Quesada, G., & Heller, R. (1977). Sociocultural barriers to medical care among Mexican Americans in Texas. *Medical Care, 15,* 93-101.

Quinn, D. (1992). *Ishmael.* New York: Bantam.

Quinn, R. E. (1988). *Beyond rational management: Mastering the paradoxes and competing demands of high performance.* San Francisco, CA: Jossey-Bass.

Quirke, B. (1995). *Communicating change.* London: McGraw-Hill.

Rafaeli, A., & Sutton, R. I. (1987). Expression of emotion as part of the work role. *Academy of Management Review, 12,* 23–37.

Ragan, S. L. (1983). A conversational analysis of alignment talk in job interviews. In R. Bostrum (Ed.), *Communication yearbook 7* (pp. 502–516). Beverly Hills, CA: Sage.

Rakow, L. F. (1986). Rethinking gender research in communication. *Journal of Communication, 36,* 11–26.

Rashford, N. S., & Coghlan, D. (1994). *The dynamics of organizational levels: A change framework for managers and consultants.* Reading, MA: Addison-Wesley.

Ray, M. R. (1993). What is the new paradigm in business? In M. Ray & A. Rinzler (Eds.), *The new paradigm in business: Emerging strategies for leadership and organizational change* (pp. 1–10). New York: Putnam.

Reason, J. T. (1987). Cognitive aids in process environments: Protheses or tools. *International Journal of Man-Machine Studies, 27,* 436-470.

Redding, W. C. (1967, February). *Position paper: A response to discussions at the ad hoc conference on organizational communication.* Paper presented to the Ad Hoc Conference on Organizational Communication, University of Missouri at Kansas City.

Redding, W. C. (1972). *Communication within the organization.* New York: Industrial Communication Council.

Redding, W. C., & Sanborn, G. (1964). *Business and industrial communication.* New York: Harper & Row.

Reddy, M. (1979). The conduit metaphor—A case of frame conflict in our language about language. In A. Ortony (Ed.), *Metaphor and thought* (pp. 284–324). Cambridge, England: Cambridge University Press.

Refenes, A. N. (1994). Comments on "Neural networks: Forecasting breakthrough or passing fad" by C. Chatfield. *International Journal of Forecasting, 10,* 43–46.

Reich, R. (1991, March–April). Who is them? *Harvard Business Review,* pp. 77–88.

Relman, A.A. (1982). Encouraging the practice of preventive medicine and health promotion. *Public Health Reports, 97,* 216-219.

Reynolds, P. D. (1971). *A primer in theory construction.* New York: Bobbs-Merrill.

Rice, R. E. (1993). Media appropriateness: Using social presence theory to compare traditional and new organizational media. *Human Communication Research, 19,* 451–484.

Rice, R. E., & Aydin, C. (1991). Attitudes toward new organizational technology: Network proximity as a mechanism for social information processing. *Administrative Science Quarterly, 36,* 219–244.

Rice, R. E., & Case, D. (1983). Electronic messaging systems in the university: A description of use and utility. *Journal of Communication, 33*(1), 131–152.

Riches, S. V., & Sillars, M. O. (1980). The status of movement criticism. *Western Journal of Speech Communication, 44,* 275–287.

Ricoeur, P. (1979). The model of the text: Meaningful action considered as a text. In P. Rabinow & W. M. Sullivan (Eds.), *Interpretive social science: A reader* (pp. 73-102). Berkeley: University of California Press.

Riley, P. (1983). A structurationist account of political culture. *Administrative Science Quarterly, 28,* 414–437.

Riley, P. (1991). Cornerville as narration. In P. J. Frost, L. F. Moore, M. R. Louis, C. C. Lundberg, & J. Martin (Eds.), *Reframing organizational culture* (pp. 215–223). Newbury Park, CA: Sage.

Ripley, B. D. (1993). Statistical aspects of neural networks. In J. L. Barndorff-Nielsen & W. S. Kendal (Eds.), *Networks and chaos: Statistical and probabilistic aspects* (pp. 40–123). London: Chapman & Hall.

Rogers, E. M. (1986). *Communication technology: The new media in society.* New York: The Free Press.

Rogers, E. M., & Agarwala-Rogers, R. (1976). *Communication in organizations.* New York: The Free Press.

Rorty, R. (1991). *Essays on Heidegger and others.* Cambridge: Cambridge University Press.

Rosen, M. (1985). Breakfast at Spiro's: Dramaturgy and dominance. *Journal of Management, 11*(2), 31–48.

Rothschild-Whitt, J. (1986). *The cooperative workplace: Potentials and dilemmas of organizational democracy and participation.* Cambridge, England: Cambridge University Press.

Rumelhart, D. E., Durbin, R., Golden, R., & Chauvin, Y. (1995). Backpropagation: The basic theory. In Y. Chauvin & D. E. Rumelhart (Eds.), *Backpropagation: Theory, architecture, and applications* (pp. 1–34). Hillsdale, NJ: Erlbaum.

Salancik, G. R. (1982). Commitment and control of organizational behavior and belief. In B. M. Staw & G. R. Salancik (Eds.), *New directions in organizational behavior* (pp. 1–54). Malabar, FL: Krieger.

Salancik, G. R., & Pfeffer, J. (1977). Who gets power—and how they hold on to it: A strategic contingency model of power. *Organizational Dynamics, 5*(3), 3–21.

Salchenberger, L. M., Cinar, E. M., & Lash, N. A. (1992). Neural networks: A new tool for predicting thrift failures. *Decision Sciences, 23*(4), 899–916.

Salem, P. J. (1976, February). *Organizational communication as a discipline.* Paper presented at the SCA/SWTSU Conference and Post Doctoral Program on Organizational Communication, San Marcos, Texas.

Salem, P. J. (1997). Social morphogenesis: Information and organizational change. In L. Thayer & G. Barnett (Eds.), *Organization–communication: Emerging perspectives V* (pp. 105-119). Norwood, NJ: Ablex.

Sankowsky, D. (1989). Professional norms as countertransference enactments. *Psychotherapy, 26*(3), 356–365.

Sarason, S. (1972). *The creation of settings and the new societies.* San Francisco: Jossey-Bass.

Schall, M. S. (1983). A communication-rules approach to organizational culture. *Administrative Science Quarterly, 28,* 557–581.

Schien, E. H. (1985). *Organizational culture and leadership.* San Francisco: Jossey–Bass.

Schmookler, A. (1992). *The illusion of choice: How the market economy shapes our destiny.* Albany: State University of New York Press.

Schrader, P. (Writer/Director). (1987). *Light of day* [film].

Schutte, W., & Steinberg, I. (1960). *Communication in business and industry.* New York: Holt, Rinehart & Winston.

Schutz, A. (1967). *Phenomenology of the social world.* Evanston, IL: Northwestern University.

Scott, R. (Director). (1996). *White squall*. [film].

Sellers, P. (1996, August 5). Women, sex, & power. *Fortune*, 42–56.

Seltzer, J., & Bass, B. M. (1990). Transformational leadership: Beyond initiation and consideration. *Journal of Management, 16*, 693–703.

Senge, P. (1990). *The fifth discipline: The art and practice of the learning organization*. New York: Doubleday.

Shannon, C., & Weaver, W. (1949). *The mathematical theory of communication*. Urbana: University of Illinois Press.

Sheiderman, B. (1989). Reflections on authoring, editing, and managing hyper-text. In E. Barrett (Ed.), *The society of text: Hypertext, hypermedia, and the social construction of information* (pp. 115–131). Cambridge, MA: MIT Press.

Shelby, A. N. (1993). Organizational, business, management, and corporate communication: An analysis of boundaries and relationships. *Journal of Business Communication, 30*, 241–267.

Shirk, H. N. (1991). Collaborative editing: A combination of peer and hierarchical editing techniques. In M. M. Lay & W. M. Karis (Eds.), *Collaborative writing in industry: Investigations in theory and practice* (pp. 242–261). Amityville, NY: Baywood

Shockley-Zalabak, P. (1991). *Fundamentals of organizational communication*. New York: Longman.

Sigman, S. J. (1986). Adjustment to the nursing home as a social interactional accomplishment. *Journal of Applied Communication Research, 14*, 37–58.

Simons, H. W., Mechling, E. W., & Schreier, H. N. (1984). The functions of human communication in mobilizing for action from the bottom up: The rhetoric of social movements. In C. C. Arnold & J. W. Bowers (Eds.), *Handbook of rhetorical and communication theory* (pp. 792–867). Boston: Allyn and Bacon.

Slocum, J. W., Jr., & Lei, D. (1995). Designing global strategic alliances: Integrating cultural and economic factors. In G. P. Huber & W. H. Glick (Eds.), *Organizational change and redesign: Ideas and insights for improving performance* (pp. 295–322). New York: Oxford University Press.

Smircich, L. (1983). Concepts of culture and organizational analysis. *Administrative Science Quarterly 28*, 339-358.

Smircich, L., & Stubbart, C. (1985). Strategic management in an enacted world. *Academy of Management Review, 10*, 724–736.

Smith, C. J. (1990, May/June). A neural network—Could it work for you? *Financial Executive*, 26–30.

Smith, D. C., & Nelson, S. J. (1994). Hypertext: An emerging and important medium of business and technical communication. *Journal of Business and Technical Communication, 8*(2), 231–243.

Smith, D. H., & Pettegrew, L. S. (1986). Mutual persuasion as a model for doctor–patient communication. *Theoretical Medicine, 7*, 127–139.

Smith, H., & Grenier, M. (1982). Sources of organizational power for women: Overcoming structural obstacles. *Sex Roles, 8*, 733–746.

Smith, K. K., & Berg, D. N. (1987). *Paradoxes of group life.* San Francisco: Jossey–Bass.

Smith, M. (1988, November). Neural networks: Do they compute? *Best's Review*, 70–74.

Smith, R. C. (1993, May). *Images of organizational communication: Root-metaphors of the organization–communication relation.* Paper presented at the International Communication Association Conference, Washington, DC.

Smith, R. C. (1994, November). *Images of organizational communication: Beyond an ideology of fragmentation.* Paper presented at the annual meeting of the Speech Communication Association, New Orleans, LA.

Smith, R. C. (1996, February). *Rethinking traditional characterizations of organizational communication studies.* Paper presented at the ICA/SCA/SWTSU Conference on Organizational Communication and Change, Austin, TX.

Smith, R. C., & Eisenberg, E. M. (1987). Conflict at Disneyland: A root metaphor analysis. *Communication Monographs, 54*, 367–380.

Smith, R. R., & Windes, R. R. (1975). The innovational movement: A rhetorical theory. *Quarterly Journal of Speech, 61*, 140–153.

Smith, W. J. (1987). *The doctor book: A nuts and bolts guide to patient power.* Los Angeles: Price Stern Sloan.

Snee, R. D. (1977). Validation of regression models: Methods and examples. *Technometrics, 19*, 415–428.

Sneider, I. (1986). *Patient power: How to have a say during your hospital stay.* White Hall, VA: Betterway Publications.

Snyder, R. A., & Morris, J. M. (1984). Organizational communication and performance. *Journal of Applied Psychology, 69*, 461–465.

Spilka, R. (1988). *Adapting discourse to multiple audiences: Invention strategies of seven corporate engineers.* Unpublished doctoral dissertation, Carnegie Mellon University, Pittsburgh.

Spilka, R. (1993a). Moving between oral and written discourse to fulfill rhetorical and social goals. In R. Spilka (Ed.), *Writing in the workplace: New research perspectives* (pp. 71-83). Carbondale: Southern Illinois University Press.

Spilka, R. (Ed.). (1993b). *Writing in the workplace: New research perspectives.* Carbondale: Southern Illinois University Press.

Sproule, J. M. (1989). Organization rhetoric and the public sphere. *Communication Studies, 40*, 258-265.

Sproull, L., & Kiesler, S. (1986). Reducing social context cues: Electronic mail in organizational communication. *Management Science, 32*(11), 1492–1512.

Stablein, R., & Nord, W. (1985). Practical and emancipatory interests in organizational symbolism. *Journal of Management, 11*, 13–28.

Stahl, M. J., Leap. T. L., & Wei, Z. Z. (1988). Publication in leading management journals as a measure of institutional research productivity. *Academy of Management Journal, 31*(3), 707–720.

Stata, R. (1988). The role of the chief executive in articulating the vision. *Interfaces, 18*(3), 3–9.

Steers, R. M. (1977). Antecedents and outcomes of organizational commitment. *Administrative Science Quarterly, 22*, 46–56.

Steier, F., & Smith, K. (1996). The cybernetics of cybernetics and the organization of organization. In L. Thayer (Ed.), *Organization— communication: Emerging perspectives III* (pp. 111–116). Norwood, NJ: Ablex.

Stephen, T., & Harrison, T. M. (1993). Interpersonal communication, theory, and history. *Communication Theory, 3*, 163–172.

Stohl, C. (1993). European managers' interpretations of participation: A semantic network analysis. *Human Communication Research, 20*, 97–117.

Stohl, C. (1995). *Organizational communication: Connectedness in action.* Thousand Oaks, CA: Sage.

Stone, W. S., & Allen, M. W. (1990). Assessing the impact of the new communication technologies on organizational dynamics. *Consultation: An International Journal, 9*, 229–240.

Strauss, A., & Corbin, J. (1990). *Basics of qualitative research: Grounded theory procedures and techniques.* Newbury Park, CA: Sage.

Strine, M. S. (1988). Constructing "texts" and making inferences: Some reflections on textual reality in human communication research. In J. A. Anderson (Ed.), *Communication yearbook 11* (pp. 494–500). Newbury Park, CA: Sage.

Sullivan, J. J. (1988). Three roles of language in motivation theory. *Academy of Management Review, 13*, 104–115.

Swain, A. D., & Guttmann, H. E. (1983). *Handbook of human reliability analysis with emphasis on nuclear power plant applications* (Final rep. NUREG/CR–1278). Washington, DC: US Nuclear Regulatory Commission.

Sweep, D. (1994). Rethinking constraints on public relations practice. *Public Relations Review, 20*(4), 319–331.

Tam, K. Y., & Kiang, M. Y. (1992). Managerial applications of neural networks: The case of bank failure predictions. *Management Science, 38*(7), 926–947.

Taylor, J. R. (1993). *Rethinking the theory of organizational communication: How to read an organization.* Norwood, NJ: Ablex.

Taylor, J. R. (1995). Shifting from a heteronomous to an autonomous worldview of organizational communication: Communication theory on the cusp. *Communication Theory, 5*(1), 1–35.

Taylor, J. R., Cooren, F., Girous, H., & Robichaud, D. (1996, February). *Are organization and communication equivalent?* Paper presented at the ICA/SCA/SWTSU Conference on Organizational Communication and Change, Austin, TX.

Thachankary, T. (1992). Organizations as "texts": Hermeneutics as a model for understanding organizational change. *Research in Organizational Change and Development, 6,* 197–233.

Thayer, L. (1968). *Communication and communication systems.* Homewood, IL: Irwin.

Therborn, G. (1980). *The ideology of power and the power of ideology.* London: Verso.

Thompson, J. B. (1984). *Studies in the theory of ideology.* Berkeley: University of California Press.

Thompson, J. B. (1990). *Ideology and modern culture.* Stanford, CA: Stanford University Press.

Thornton, B. C., Marinelli, R. D., & Larson, T. (1993). Ethics and women's health care. In B. C. Thornton & G. L. Kreps (Eds.), *Perspectives on health communication* (pp. 186–195). Prospect Heights, IL: Waveland.

Ticehurst, W., Downs, C. W., & Ikeda, K. (1994, June). *Communicating satisfaction in Japanese managed manufacturing organizations in Australia and Thailand.* Paper presented at the meeting of the International Communication Association convention meeting, Sydney, Australia.

Tichy, N. M., & Devanna, M. A. (1986). *The transformational leader.* New York: Wiley.

Tichy, N. M., & Ulrich, D. O. (1984). SMR Forum: The leadership challenge—a call for the transformational leader. *Sloan Management Review, 26,* 59–68.

Tompkins, P. K., & Cheney, G. (1983). Account analysis of organizations: Decision making and identification. In L. L. Putnam & M. E. Pacanowsky (Eds.), *Communication and organizations: An interpretive approach* (pp. 123–146). Beverly Hills, CA: Sage.

Tompkins, P. K., & Cheney, G. (1985). Communication and unobtrusive control in contemporary organizations. In R. D. McPhee & P. K. Tompkins (Eds.), *Organization communication: Traditional themes and new directions* (pp. 179–210). Beverly Hills, CA: Sage.

Tompkins, P. K., & Redding, W. C. (1988). Organizational communication—Past and present tenses. In G. M. Goldhaber & G. A. Barnett (Eds.), *Handbook of organizational communication* (pp. 5–33). Norwood, NJ: Ablex.

Townley, B. (1993). Foucault, power/knowledge, and its relevance for human resource management. *Academy of Management Review, 18,* 518–545.

Treadwell, D., & Applebaum, R. (1995, April). *A basic course in organizational communication: A national survey.* Paper delivered to the meeting of the Eastern Communication Association.

Treichler, P. (1987). AIDS, homophobia, and biomedical discourse: An epidemic of signification. *Cultural Studies, 1*(3), 263–305.

Trice, H. M., & Beyer, J. M. (1984). Studying organizational culture through rites and ceremonies. *Academy of Management Review, 9,* 653–669.

Trujillo, N. (1985). Organizational communication as cultural performance: Some managerial considerations. *Southern Speech Communication Journal, 50,* 201–224.

Trujillo, N. (1992). Interpreting the work and talk of baseball: Perspectives on ballpark culture. *Western Journal of Communication, 56,* 350–371.

Tucker, M., Meyer, G. D., & Westerman, J. W. (1996), Organizational communication: Development of internal strategic competitive advantage. *Journal of Business Communication, 33*(1), 51–70.

Turkle, S. (1984). *The second self: Computers and the human spirit.* New York: Simon & Schuster.

Turkle, S. (1988). Computational reticence: Why women fear the intimate machine. In C. Kramarae (Ed.), *Technology and women's voices: Keeping in touch* (pp. 41–61). New York: Routeledge.

Turner, V. (1980). Social dramas and stories about them. *Critical Inquiry, 7,* 141–168.

U.S. Department of Commerce, Bureau of the Census. (1994). *Statistical abstract of the United States* (114th ed.). Washington, DC: Author.

Vallas, S. (1993). *Power in the workplace: The politics of production at AT&T.* Albany: State University of New York Press.

Van de Ven, A. H., & Poole, M. S. (1988). Paradoxical requirements for a theory of organizational change. In R. E. Quinn & K. S. Cameron (Eds.), *Paradox and transformation: Toward a theory of change in organization and management* (pp. 19–64). Cambridge, MA: Ballinger.

Van Maanen, J. (1973). Observations on the making of policemen. *Human Organization, 32,* 407–418.

Van Zoonen, L. (1992). Feminist theory and information technology. *Media, Culture and Society, 14*(1), 9–29.

Vardaman, G., & Vardaman, P. B. (1973). *Communication in modern organizations.* New York: Wiley

Ventura, M. (1993). *Letters at 3 AM: Reports on endarkenment.* Dallas: Spring Publications.

Waldron, V. R. (1994). Once more, with feeling: Reconsidering the role of emotion in work. In S. A. Deetz (Ed.), *Communication yearbook 17* (pp. 388–416). Thousand Oaks, CA: Sage.

Waldron, V. R., & Krone, K. (1991). The experience and expression of emotion in the workplace: A study of a corrections organization. *Management Communication Quarterly, 4,* 287–309.

Wallace, A. (1961). *The psychic unity of human groups.* In B. Kaplan (Ed.), *Studying personality cross–culturally* (p. 151). Evanston, IL: Row, Peterson.

Wallis, L. (1994). Why a curriculum on women's health? In A. J. Dan (Ed.), *Reframing women's health* (pp. 13–26). Thousand Oaks, CA: Sage.

Waltzer, M. (1987). *Interpretation and social criticism.* Cambridge, MA: Harvard University Press.

Wang, S. (1995). The unpredictability of standard back propagation neural networks in classification applications. *Management Science, 41*(3), 555–559.

Watson, C. (1991). Managing with integrity: Social responsibilities of business as seen by America's CEOs. *Business Horizon, 34,* 99–109.

Watts, A. (1967). *The book: On the taboo against knowing who you really are.* New York: Vintage.

Watzlawick, P., Beavin, J. H., & Jackson, D. D. (1967). *Pragmatics of human communication: A study of interactional patterns, pathologies, and paradoxes.* New York: Norton.

Webb, E. J., Campbell, D. T., Schwartz, R. D., Sechrest, L., & Grove, J. (1981). *Nonreactive measures in the social sciences.* Boston: Houghton Mifflin.

Weber, J. R. (1991). The construction of multi-authored texts in one laboratory setting. In M. M. Lay & W. M. Karis (Eds.), *Collaborative writing in industry: Investigations in theory and practice* (pp. 49–63). Amityville, NY: Baywood.

Weber, M. (1978). *Economy and society* (G. Roth & C. Wittich, Trans.). Berkeley: University of California Press.

Wechsler, H., Levine, S., Idelson, R. K., Rohman, M., & Taylor, J. O. (1983). The physician's role in health promotion—A survey of primary care practitioners. *New England Journal of Medicine, 308*(2), 97–100.

Weick, K. E. (1969). *The social psychology of organizing.* Reading, MA: Addison-Wesley.

Weick, K. E. (1979). *The social psychology of organizing* (2nd ed.). Reading, MA: Addison-Wesley.

Weick, K. E. (1985). Cosmos vs. chaos: Sense and nonsense in electronic contexts. *Organizational Dynamics, 14,* 50–64.

Weick, K. E. (1987). Theorizing about organizational communication. In F. M. Jablin, L. L. Putnam, K. H. Roberts, & L. W. Porter (Eds.), *Handbook of organizational communication: An interdisciplinary perspective* (pp. 97-122). Newbury Park, CA: Sage.

Weick, K. E. (1990). The vulnerable system: Analysis of the Tenerife air disaster. *Journal of Management, 16,* 571–593.

Weick, K. E. (1993). The collapse of sensemaking in organizations: The Mann Gulch disaster. *Administrative Science Quarterly, 38*, 628–652.

Weick, K. E., & Browning, L. D. (1986). Argument and narration in organizational communication. *Journal of Management, 12*, 243–250.

Wendt, R. (1994). Learning to "walk the talk": A critical tale of the micropolitics at a Total Quality University. *Management Communication Quarterly, 8*, 5–45.

Wert-Gray, S., Center, C., Brashers, D. E., & Meyers, R. A. (1991). Research topics and methodological orientations in organizational communication: A decade in review. *Communication Studies, 42*, 141-154.

West, S., & Dranov, P. (1994). *The hysterectomy hoax*. New York: Doubleday.

Whalen, S. (1993). The dialectic of memory and forgetting in histories of rhetoric. *Communication Theory, 3*, 157–162.

"What are we doing on-line?" (1995). *Harpers*, p. 42.

Wheatley, M. J. (1992). *Leadership and the new science. Learning about organization from an orderly universe*. San Francisco: Berrett-Koehler.

Whicker, M. L., & Sigelman, L. (1991). *Computer simulation applications: An introduction*. Newbury Park, CA: Sage.

White, O. F., & McSwain, C. J. (1983). Transformational theory and organizational analysis. In G. Morgan (Ed.), *Beyond method: Strategies for social research* (pp. 292-305). Beverly Hills, CA: Sage.

Whorf, B. L. (1956). In J. B. Caroll (Ed.), *Language, thought and reality: Selected writings*. Cambridge: Technology Press of Massachusetts Institute of Technology.

Whyte, W. (1956). *The organization man*. New York: Doubleday.

Wiio, O. (1988). Organizational communication: Contingent views. In G. M. Goldhaber & G. A. Barnett (Eds.), *Handbook of organizational communication* (pp. 95–100). Norwood, NJ: Ablex.

Wilson, D. P. (1992). Diagonal communication links within organizations. *Journal of Business Communication, 29*(2), 129–143.

Wilson, L. (1995, December). Balance of power. *Computerworld, 29*, 119.

Winsor D. A. (1989). An engineer's writing and the corporate construction of knowledge. *Written Communication, 6*(3), 270–285

Wiseman, R., & Shuter, R. (Eds.). (1994). *Communicating in multinational organizations*. Thousand Oaks, CA: Sage.

Witkin, B. R., & Stephens, K. (1972, November). *A fault tree approach to analysis of organizational communication systems*. Paper presented to the Western Speech Communication Association, Honolulu, HI.

Woelfel, J. (1992). CATPAC users manual. In J. Woelfel (Ed.), *Principles of communication: Readings in communication science* (Appendix, pp. 1–8). Buffalo: Department of Communication, State University of New York at Buffalo.

Woelfel, J., & Fink, E. (1980). *The measurement of communication processes: Galileo theory and method*. New York: Academic Press.

Wright, D., & Sherman, S. (1970). *A survey of organizational communication at the graduate level in speech communication programs: Initial report.* Unpublished report.

Yammarino, F. J., & Bass, B. M. (1990). Transformational leadership and multiple levels of analysis. *Human Relations, 43,* 975–995.

Yates, J. (1989a). *Control through communication: The rise of system in American management.* Baltimore: Johns Hopkins University Press.

Yates, J. (1989b). The emergence of the memo as a managerial genre. *Management Communication Quarterly, 2,* 485–510.

Yates, J. (1993). Co-evolution of information processing technology and use: Interaction between the life insurance and tabulating industries. *Business History Review, 67,* 1–51.

Yates, J., & Orlikowski, W. J. (1992). Genres of organizational communication: A structurational approach to studying communication and media. *Academy of Management Review, 17,* 299-326.

Yin, R. K. (1994). *Case study research: Design and methods* (2nd ed.). Newbury Park, CA: Sage.

Young R. E., Berker A. L., & Pike K. L. (1970). *Rhetoric: Discovery and change.* New York: Harcourt.

Zahedi, F. (1991). An introduction to neural networks and a comparison with artificial intelligence and expert systems. *Interfaces, 21*(2), 25-38.

Zaleznik, A. (1977). Managers and leaders: Are they different? *Harvard Business Review, 55*(5), 67–80.

Zaleznik, A. (1990). The leadership gap. *Academy of Management Executive, 4*(1), 7–22.

Zelko, H., & Dance, F. E. X. (1965). *Business and professional speech communication.* New York: Holt, Rinehart & Winston.

Zetterberg, H. (1965). *Theory and verification in sociology.* Totowa, NJ: Bedminster Press.

Zmroczek, C., Henwood, F., & Wyatt, S. (1987). Women and technology. In G. Ashworth & L. Bonnerjea (Eds.), *The invisible decade: Women and the UN decade 1976–1985* (pp. 121–132). London: Gower.

AUTHOR INDEX

SUBJECT INDEX